DESKTOP GUIDE

TO KEYNOTES AND CONFIRMATORY SYMPTOMS

Roger Morrison, M.D.

HAHNEMANN CLINIC PUBLISHING

This book is not intended for purposes of self-diagnosis or self-treatment. Patients should not use this book without direct supervision of healthcare by a trained medical professional.

The paper used in this book is acid free and meets the requirements of the American National Standard for Information Sciences.

9

ISBN 0-9635368-0-X

Hahnemann Clinic Publishing
13974 Glenn Pines Road
Grass Valley, CA 95945

Printed in the United States of America

Dedicated to my beloved Nancy

Foreword

The perpetual challenge of all students of homeopathy, whether beginner or experienced, is the overwhelming volume of detailed symptoms in our Materia Medicas. We constantly strive to simplify the information, to sort out the clinically useful from the non-distinguishing and general symptoms, to grasp in a single picture the essential features of the remedy. Compounding this difficulty is the fact that most of our sources belong to another era in time; the rapid changes and unique pressures of modern society have brought forth new facets of our remedies, and even well-known symptoms are expressed in a modern idiom which obscures their relationship to the material in older texts.

This task of separating the truly essential from the commonplace, and adapting the form to present day expression, has been approached by Roger Morrison with characteristic dedication. Building on his innate scholarly mastery of the classical literature sources and his advanced training in Greece with George Vithoulkas, he has passed what he has been given through the filter of his own extensive clinical experience. This work, seven years in preparation, has resulted not only in a remarkable blending of the old and the new, but has come truly close to achieving the perfect balance between too much and too little. The information is reliable and clearly presented in such a form as may be easily accessed in the midst of the demands of everyday practice. Yet the true depth and precision of this text only reveals itself after careful study and reflection in the quiet of one's own home.

This book should be a mandatory addition to the library of every homeopath, occupying a place on the desk next to the repertory.

Jonathan Shore, M.D.
Bill Gray, M.D.
January 1993

Acknowledgements

At the outset of my work on this book, I asked myself, "Does our profession really need this text?" I was convinced to proceed finally, by my own desire to have at my desk exactly the book I was contemplating writing. I knew that my need for a concise reference of confirmatory symptoms must be echoed in the community. My fifteen years of study and practice is far to few to claim mastery of homeopathic materia medica. I therefore wish to state clearly that I claim little originality or discovery of the information contained in this text. Rather I have tried to be a careful and precise collector and evaluator of this information which I am sharing.

The basis of this book comes from my time of study in Athens at the Center of Homeopathic Medicine under the supervision of George Vithoulkas. The opportunity to work closely with so many well-trained homeopaths, at a center which follows some hundred thousand patients was fertile ground for learning. This was especially true because of Mr. Vithoulkas' tireless, unselfish and careful supervision of every aspect of the center. It is impossible to imagine this splendid center without Mr. Vithoulkas' guidance. It is equally impossible to imagine the current resurgence in homeopathy without the influence of this remarkable man. Mr. Vithoulkas has contributed to homeopathy on virtually every level - materia medica, repertory and philosophy. In addition to these contributions, Mr. Vithoulkas' dynamic teaching and innovative use of computer analysis and video documentation of long-term cases has excited the growth of homeopathy throughout the world. It has been a great honor to train under Mr. Vithoulkas and to be counted among his students.

I wish to acknowledge some of the many people who assisted me in the preparation of this book. During my training in Greece I was fortunate to have an opportunity to study with many inspired homeopaths including Petros and Euthymia Garzonis, Olga Delakari, and George Papafillipou. My deepest thanks goes to Vassilis Ghegas for his unselfish assistance and guidance in my education and his devoted friendship. Another of my Greek instructors was the late and much loved Irene Bachas, whose knowledge, insight and generosity inspired all who knew her.

Many other colleagues have contributed to the knowledge contained in this book. Bill Gray, Louis Klein, Alphons Geukens, and Ananda Zaren have impressed me with the accuracy and reliability of their insight into materia medica. Jonathan Shore has been a true friend, a gifted teacher and his penetrating intellect and critical judgement has given me focus and determination for this work. Most importantly, my wife Nancy Herrick has contributed to this work enormously both in encouragement and substance. She has helped me in the collection of data, in the organization of the information and in the editing of the text. If I have failed to credit her work sufficiently in the body of the text, it is because our thoughts, our work and our lives are so intertwined as to be indistinguishable.

I wish to also thank the many people who have contributed to this book through advice and editorial assistance - George Marks, Ernest Callenbach, Judi and Steve Roubideaux, Shiraz Januwala and Greg Bedayn. Thanks also to Katherine Amber for her assistance and warm friendship.

A final thanks to some special people in my life - my best friend, Phil; my teacher, Charles; my spiritual guide, Yogi Bhajan; my three children, Lynn, Todd and Naomi; my mother, Joyce; my sisters, Janet, Ellie and Julie; and especially to my late, beloved father, Martin.

Roger Morrison
1993

Introduction

The purpose of this book is to serve as a concise guide to the main keynotes and confirmatory symptoms of each of the most commonly prescribed remedies in clinical practice. I have entitled it "Desktop Guide" because I envision its place sitting handy to the interviewer to refer to during the course of case-taking. Many, many times in my practice I have reached for just such a book as this and could not find it. I reach for this book every time I wish to confirm a remedy in a case and want to ask the specific symptoms of confirmation. While there are several excellent texts of keynotes, I found none which truly compile all the most important keynotes existing. I hope that this book will fill this void.

This text is a compilation of the most essential facts of our remedies, based upon my knowledge but most especially upon the copious notes of my studies with George Vithoulkas. Mr. Vithoulkas is now presenting us with his magnificent materia medica, and yet I believe this simple list of keynotes and confirmatory symptoms will remain a useful tool in the homeopathic armamentarium. I have not attempted to include every symptom known for our remedies - this is the province of our great encyclopedias. Nor is this a proper materia medica for I have given only a sketch of the full essences of the remedies. Rather it is meant as a text of the basic and practical information which is the "bread and potatoes" of homeopathic practice.

The intention of this book is to be as useful as possible to the practitioner in the consulting room. It is therefore arranged in more or less the traditional headings of Hahnemann from " Mind" to "Skin." I have elected to place the general symptoms immediately after the mental symptoms because of the greater importance of these symptoms in confirming the remedy. I have added sections which may not be self-explanatory: "Clinical" and "Combined Symptoms" and "Comparisons."

The "Clinical" section includes the most common conditions which are treated by the remedy, but the reader should note that pathological entities are our least specific information in the selection of the simillimum.

The section "Combined Symptoms" indicates common doublets or triplets of symptomatology which can be considered strong indications for the remedy, even when the remedy is not famous for either of the component symptoms. For example, Cobaltum is not a major remedy for lumbago, nor is it among the most important remedies for seminal discharges. However when seminal discharges and lumbago are found in the same case, then Cobaltum becomes a very likely choice for the patient.I have placed these doublets and triplets in this section.

In the section "Comparisons" I have noted only the similarities between the remedies compared. The remedies mentioned are based on my experience of the most common remedies to be confused with the remedy being discussed, and the reasons for their confusion.

The symptoms are presented in two gradations: ordinary and bold print. This is to distinguish those symptoms which are regarded as keynotes from those that are less specific confirmations. A keynote is here defined as a symptom so indicative of a particular remedy that upon hearing this symptom strongly stated by the patient, our minds must turn automatically to this remedy. We must attempt in all cases to justify our prescriptions in the broadest sense possible, and should never prescribe narrowly on only one symptom. However, the keynote is a strong piece of information and is often crucial in making the final determination of the remedy.

The keynotes listed may also be used in further justifying our prescription. When we first examine a case, we must keep our minds free of prejudice regarding remedies. However, after the symptoms are well-delineated, it is often helpful to try to confirm the remedies which are suggested by our study of the case by asking the patient about the main keynote symptoms for these remedies. In this text, the prescriber can readily find the keynotes used to confirm the prescription by scanning down the page asking the patient concerning the symptoms listed in bold type.

The ◆ has been used to indicate that the remedy discussed is the most important remedy in our materia medica for the symptom denoted. This may be true even if the symptom cannot be considered a keynote of the remedy. All abbreviations follow those used by Kent in his Repertory.

As previously stated, the symptoms listed in this text come largely from my studies with George Vithoulkas. In addition I have utilized a wide variety of reliable sources as a basis for information. There are some symptoms included in this text which I have not personally confirmed but which come to us directly from highly reliable sources such as Kent or Nash or Lippe. In these instances I have included the symptoms and referenced the author or used a qualifying phrase such as "Many authors mention the symptom ...." Otherwise, I have not listed symptoms in this book simply because they were written in another text. Rather I have included almost exclusively symptoms, which I have confirmed in my own cases or cases that I have had an opportunity to examine. Also I have not included remedies of which I have only very limited experience or only theoretical knowledge. Therefore, this text is necessarily incomplete (no prescriber can claim to have seen all possible presentations of our remedies) and I welcome each prescriber to make his own additions in the margins. Despite this caveat, I have invested some seven years in preparing this text and to the best of my ability, all of the best-documented keynotes and characteristics are included. I look forward to all comments and additions from my readers.

Guide to Symbols in Text

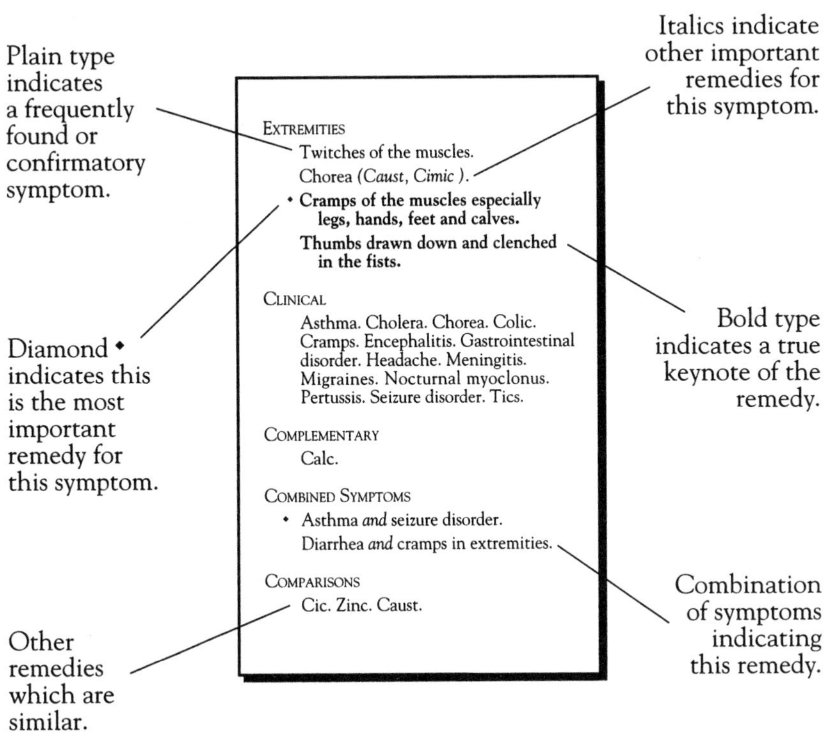

TABLE OF CONTENTS

DESKTOP GUIDE

TO KEYNOTES AND CONFIRMATORY SYMPTOMS

ABIES CANADENSIS

Abies Canadensis has one very useful keynote: the **sensation of a cold wet cloth on the back** *(Tub, Puls)*.

ABIES NIGRA

Abies Nigra is primarily a remedy for gastric conditions: peptic ulcers, gastritis, hiatus hernia, etc. The main keynote is the horrible sensation of a lump in the top of the stomach. The patient may feel as if there were a stone in his epigastrium or as if he had swallowed an egg.

GASTROINTESTINAL

- **Sensation of a lump in the epigastrium. May be described "as if one had swallowed an egg or a rock."**

Stomach pain after eating.

Gastric problems in elderly patients.

CHEST

Cardiac problems, especially in elderly patients.

CLINICAL

Cardiac disease. Gastritis. Hiatus hernia. Peptic ulcer.

COMPARISONS

Nux-V.

ABROTANUM

Abrotanum is a remedy affecting glands, joints, and mucous membranes. The main indication for Abrotanum is "metastasis." But here "metastasis" is not meant to imply metastatic cancer, but rather the idea that there is change of location or form of pathology. For example, we think of Abrotanum when mumps moves from the parotid glands to the testes, or if arthritis or diarrhea is suppressed and results in a heart condition. In complaints which change form or location or are rapidly suppressed producing entirely new symptoms we think of Abrotanum.

GENERALS

- ◆ **Metastasis; change in form or location of pathology.**
- **Marasmus; in children and infants.** The lower limbs emaciate before the rest of the body.
- Newborns fail to gain weight; wrinkled or Hippocratic face *(Aeth).*
- Emaciation despite a ravenous appetite.
- General amelioration during diarrhea *(Nat-S, Zinc).*
- General aggravation after influenza *(Gels, Scut, Nat-Sal, Influenz)*
- Aggravation from cold and cold wet weather.
- Enlarged or inflamed lymph glands.

GASTROINTESTINAL

- ◆ **Discharge from the umbilicus** especially in newborns; any eruption around the umbilicus in newborns who are eating poorly or failing to gain weight.
- Any pathology or eruption of the umbilicus.
- Diarrhea which relieves the organism (and may if suppressed result in rheumatic or other conditions).
- Hemorrhoids. Suppressed hemorrhoids.
- Rectal hemorrhage from suppressed menses.

CHEST

- Respiratory infections from suppression of eruptions.
- Cardiac disease after suppression of rheumatism or other conditions.
- Hoarseness.

EXTREMITIES

- Rheumatism. Gout. Arthritic nodosities.
- Rheumatic pains worse cold, damp weather, worse night.
- Rheumatism alternates with diarrhea or after suppressed diarrhea.
- Wasting of the lower extremities more than or earlier than the rest of the body *(opposite Nat-M, Lyc).*

CLINICAL

Arthritis. Bronchitis. Diarrhea. Failure to thrive. Gout. Hemorrhoids. Marasmus. Mumps. Respiratory infection. Rheumatic heart disease. Umbilicus, infection.

COMBINED SYMPTOMS

- Failure to thrive or emaciation *with* umbilical eruptions or discharge.

COMPARISONS

Aeth. Puls. Kali-Bi. Mag-C. Sil.

ACONITUM NAPELLUS

Although Aconite has been used in the past primarily for acute conditions arising from shock and exposure, Vithoulkas has pioneered its use in more chronic psychological conditions such as deep phobic states, panic disorder and anxiety neurosis. The complaints (the anxiety states or the acute conditions) of Aconite come suddenly and with great intensity. In both the acute conditions and the chronic psychological disorders, there is most often great anxiety and an overwhelming terror of death. In many cases this fear extends to a presentiment or a certainty that death is imminent. The patient may predict the exact age or date of his death.

In the acute conditions, we find rapidly developing inflammations of almost any organ system. These inflammations follow quickly, often only minutes or hours after exposure to wind, fright or shock. In severe acute inflammatory conditions the fear may be intense, however in more minor conditions the fear may be entirely absent. The acute illness can be tremendously violent or life-threatening. The infection and inflammation in Aconite rarely extends to the purulent stage of the illness.

Anytime that a violent or frightening event occurs (such as an earthquake or a car accident) we often must give Aconite first, even if we will need other specific acute remedies later. Aconite can release a shock or fright that has been held in the body or mind for a lifetime.

Aconite must usually be given in high potency, such as 50M or CM, because the symptoms are very intense and must be matched by the potency. This rule does not hold for more minor acute disorders.

MENTALS

Tremendous fear of death.

◆ **Feels death is imminent. Predicts or has a fixed idea of some specific time when death will come.**

◆**"Presentiment of death."** *(Arg-N, Agn)*.

Fears: ◆ **Claustrophobia.** ◆ **Fear of being in a crowd or a crowded room.** ◆ **Earthquakes.** Agoraphobia. Airplanes. Bad news. Ghosts. Heart disease.

Panic disorder with recurring episodes of tremendous fear of death, convinced that death is upon him, face full of terror, strong or even violent palpitations, marked flushing, and shortness of breath.

◆ **Anxiety states following a strong fright** such as a car accident or earthquake, etc.

Restlessness.

Panic symptoms come in evening and also just after falling asleep. Wakes 1 to 2 hours after sleep with fright, beginning after a shock.

Fear during labor, fears she will die.

Anxiety for others.

Desires company.

Frantic with pains; feels urgent need of relief.

GENERALS

Robust, plethoric and vital people.

◆ **Complaints begin after a fright or sudden, shocking events.**

◆ **Shock and fear immediately after injury, exposure or accidents.**

Symptoms come on suddenly *(Bell)*.

General aggravation after exposure to wind, especially cold, dry wind.

General aggravation from heat once the complaint is established (even the mental symptoms).

Intense pains which may cause the patient to cry out.

Restlessness. Unable to remain still.

HEAD

Vertigo, especially after a fright or shock.

Vertigo or faintness on rising or standing.

Severe headache during the fever, from exposure, when coryza is suppressed.

Colds or influenzas, come suddenly from exposure, with high fever and great heat or burning in the nostrils.

Eye

Conjunctivitis after exposure, inflamed with copious, thin discharge.

Photophobia.

Acute remedy for wounds and foreign bodies to the eyes.

Sudden blindness after fright or shock.

Ear

Otitis media which comes on suddenly (often from exposure) with intense pain and high fever *(Bell)*.

Ears bright red.

Face

One cheek red, the other cheek pale *(Cham)*.

Flushes of heat in the face.

Perspiration of face only where in contact with the pillow.

Facial neuralgia, often unbearably painful, worse exposure to wind.

One-sided facial numbness.

Facial paralysis after exposure.

Flushed, plethoric face; congestion in face.

Oropharynx

Bitter taste in the mouth, only water tastes normal.

Numbness of mouth and tongue.

Dryness, especially in the center of the tongue.

Toothache from exposure to cold.

Pharyngitis or tonsillitis, very red, burning, often from exposure.

Gastrointestinal

Great thirst, usually for cold drinks.

Desires: Fish.

Aversion: Artichokes.

Gastritis from drinking cold drinks when over-heated.

Pain about the umbilicus, especially during stool, may radiate to the chest.

Acute hepatitis.

Urogenital

- **Urine retention in infants or mothers right after delivery.**
- **Especially useful for women during labor, they feel absolutely certain they are about to die.**

Orchitis.

Uterine hemorrhage.

CHEST

- **Main remedy for early stages of croup.**

Pneumonia with sudden onset, great restlessness, fear and dyspnea, worse lying on the left side. There is often hemoptysis with "cherry red" sputum.

Angina or acute myocardial infarction with numbness into the left arm *(Cact, Rhus-T, etc.)*.

Palpitation. Tachycardia.

Palpitation and pulsations after a fright.

Heat in the chest, or a "boiling" sensation.

EXTREMITIES

Sudden inflammatory arthritis, especially after exposure.

Numbness or weakness in left arm with heart disease.

Numb and paralyzed sensations.

ACUTES

During the early phase of respiratory infections, influenza, pneumonia, tonsillitis, otitis, urinary infections, hepatitis, conjunctivitis, acute arthritis, etc.

Exanthems (Measles, Roseola, etc.).

Complaints begin suddenly and intensely and often with great pain.

Sudden, marked heat and fever alternates with chills, heat and flushing to face, pupils constricted, restlessness, thirst for cold drinks, cold extremities, and often great anxiety and fear of death.

Myocardial infarction with severe chest pain, radiating pain and numbness into left arm, horrible fear of death *(Cact, Arn)*.

Bell's palsy.

Cerebral accidents.

Trauma and its after-effects.

CLINICAL

Amaurosis. Angina Pectoris. Anxiety disorders. Arrhythmia. Bell's palsy. Cerebral accidents. Colds. Conjunctivitis. Croup. Cystitis. Gastritis. Headache. Hepatitis. Influenza. Injury and trauma. Labor. Myocardial infarction. Neuralgia, facial neuralgia. Orchitis. Otitis media. Panic disorders. Pharyngitis. Photophobia. Pneumonia. Rheumatic complaints. Shock. Tonsillitis. Toothache. Upper respiratory infection. Urinary retention. Uterine hemorrhage. Vertigo.

COMPLEMENTARY

Sulph. Arn. Coff.

Comparisons

Bell - Sudden, violent acutes, high fever, throbbing, flushed face, in robust and plethoric patients. However, Belladonna is thirstless, more predominantly right-sided and lacks the anxiety and restlessness. In Belladonna the pupils are more often dilated.

Phos - Great fear of death, desire for company, panic attacks which may be worse at twilight, anxiety for others, thirst, pneumonia symptoms similar, desire for fish.

Stram - Anxiety disorders after a shock or fright, fear of death, claustrophobia, fear of dark, wake from sleep with fright.

Op - Complaints after fright, fever, flushed face, delirium, cerebral vascular accidents.

Sulph. Rhus-T. Ferr-P. Ars. Bry.

ACTEA RACEMOSA

(see Cimicifuga)

ACTEA SPICATA

Actea Spicata is a remedy to remember in cases of rheumatism of the small joints of the hands and wrists *(Caul, Caust)*.

Extremities

Pain in the small joints of wrists, hands, fingers, ankles and feet.

Pains and swelling of joints worse from slight exertion or fatigue.

Pains worse from touch.

Comparisons

Caust. Caul. Guai.

AESCULUS

Aesculus has been used primarily in the treatment of hemorrhoids and in generalized venous congestion. It is also of great importance in arthritis of the spine and pelvic girdle, and in sciatica.

Generals

Venous dilation, distension or varices not only of the rectum but also throat, esophagus, eyes, etc.

Rectum

Hemorrhoids, congested and purple.

- **Pain often described "as if the rectum were full of sticks"** *(Coll)*.
- **Pain radiates to the small of the back and hips, especially to the sacroiliac region.**

Sharp pains shooting upward from rectum into back.

Hemorrhoids associated with back pain.

Pain in the rectum that lasts for hours after stool *(Rat, Peon)*.

Pains worse while standing, worse wiping after stool.

Hemorrhoids during pregnancy.

Constipation. Hard stool.

Back

- **Arthritis and pains in the sacrum or sacroiliac joints.** Pain in the small of the back.

Back pain worse from stooping or rising from stooping or rising from a seat.

Sciatica.

Ankylosing spondylitis. Spine rigid and frozen.

Clinical

Ankylosing spondylitis. Arthritis. Back pain. Constipation. Hemorrhoids. Sciatica. Venous congestion and varices.

Combined Symptom

- **Back pain or sciatica *and* hemorrhoids.**

Comparisons

Coll. Rat. Paeon. Aloe. Nux-V. Sulph. Ham.

AETHUSA

Aethusa has been found to be useful in severe acute disorders with marked prostration and even stupor. The main focus of this remedy is on the gastrointestinal tract. Vithoulkas characterized the Aethusa patient as reserved and self-contained but with strong inward emotions.

Mentals

Reserved people with inwardly strong emotions; loners.

- **Devotes entire life to animals, and becomes intensely attached to his pets. Collects pets in great numbers.**

Fear of going to sleep "lest he never wake up." Fear of surgery.

Talks to himself out loud.

Generals

Severe acutes with vomiting and diarrhea and extreme prostration, especially in newborns.

Trouble sleeping; wakes frequently with dyspnea and must open the window *(Lach, Acon, Grind)*.

Head

"Hippocratic" face, even in infants. Wrinkled, old-looking face.

Eruptions on tip of the nose *(Caust)*. Herpetic lesions on face.

Otorrhea.

Gastrointestinal

Intolerance to milk. The baby vomits large curds of milk; diarrhea from milk *(Nat-C, Lac-D, Sil)*.

Severe vomiting and diarrhea with dehydration.

Thirstless.

Skin

Tendency to eruptions, rashes and herpes.

Clinical

Bronchitis. Diarrhea. Eczema. Gastritis. Gastroenteritis. Herpes. Lactose intolerance. Otorrhea.

Complementary

Calc.

Comparisons

Nat-C. Nat-M. Ars. Mag-C.

AGARICUS

Agaricus is mainly a neurological remedy with twitching, spasms, and even convulsions. It may be indicated in multiple sclerosis, neuromyopathies, epilepsy, chorea, and many more minor neurological disorders such as Bell's palsy. In most of the conditions there is a marked tendency toward twitching. It is also a very useful remedy in low back pain, sciatica and allergic disorders.

The mental state of Agaricus is characterized by both anxiety and excitement. The patient may be dependent and fearful. He often has morbid thoughts about life and health which contributes to the intense fear of cancer often found in this remedy. Conversely a state of fearlessness has been confirmed. Also there can be great excitement which is sometimes exaggerated in the night ("poetical at night") and even ecstatic states. Many forms of delusions have been recorded in Agaricus.

MENTALS

- **Extreme fear of cancer.**

Anxiety about health; insignificant health problems are exaggerated, causing great fear and despair.

Excited and ecstatic states. Senses almost supernaturally acute.

"Poetic at night".

Dependency and frequent calls to the physician.

Alternating mental and physical symptoms.

Many bizarre forms of delusions have been cured with this remedy.

GENERALS

- **Twitching or spasms of almost any muscle groups.**

Generally worse before a thunderstorm.

General aggravation from coition.

Symptoms may occur diagonally, for example the right knee and the left shoulder affected.

Pain out of proportion to the pathology; unexplained by objective measurements or tests.

Generalized or localized muscular tension.

NEUROLOGICAL

Clumsiness or awkwardness in the extremities. Ataxia.

Chorea, worse from coition, better from sleep.

Convulsions, spasms and fainting after coition.

Neuralgia. Sciatica.

Neurological degenerative disorders.

Facial tics. Bell's palsy.

HEAD

Spasms and twitching of the eyelids or face.

Twitching of the face or eyelids, worse before a storm.

Hay fever, especially when associated with itching in the ears and the upper palate.

Grimacing of the mouth, especially on beginning to speak.

Ears bright red and often severe itching.

Cold spots on head.

GENITALIA

Urethritis.

Increased sexual desire or masturbation in the morning on waking.

BACK

Severe low back pain and sciatica.

◆ **Back pain which is markedly aggravated by sitting** and better from lying *(Am-M, Arg-M)*.

Electric sensations in the back.

EXTREMITIES

Awkwardness in arms and legs.

Twitching, fasciculations, and tremor of all muscles.

Muscular tension and muscle spasms.

Chilblains or cold spots, especially of the feet.

Sensation of cold or hot needles.

CLINICAL

Allergy. Anxiety. Bell's palsy. Chilblain. Chorea. Delirium. Depression. Fasciculation. Low back pain. Multiple sclerosis. Neuralgia. Neuromyopathy. Paresthesia. Phobic disorder. Sciatica. Seizure disorders. Tremor. Twitching.

COMPARISONS

Nit-Ac - Extreme fear about health, calls the physician frequently, disbelieves any proof of health.

Arg-N - Anxiety about health, dependency, neurological symptoms, ataxia, twitches.

Zinc. Rhus-T. Ars. Cupr.

AGNUS CASTUS

Agnus Castus is primarily useful in collapse or broken-down states which occur after abuse of alcohol, drugs, and over-indulgence in sex. The patient becomes aware that his health has been ruined by these excesses and this produces a great anxiety and depression. The collapse entails both a mental breakdown as well as a sexual breakdown and dysfunction. Our texts describe a situation where an overly experienced husband finds himself impotent with his new young wife.

Mentals

Great anxiety and despair about health.

Despondent and anxious, mainly about his health or impotence.

Presentiment of death; predicts the date or feels it is imminent.

Fear of death.

Dullness of mind and weak memory. Apathetic.

Chest

Absence or disappearance of milk in women after delivery, especially with the above mental symptoms.

Genitalia

◆ **Coldness of the genitals.**

Impotence often despite strong sexual arousal and fantasies *(Calad, Sel).*

Impotence, unable to maintain the erection during intercourse.

Impotence after repeated gonorrhea.

Impotence with chronic urethral discharge.

Loss of sexual appetite in people of previously excessive sexual activity.

Premature ejaculation.

Leukorrhea.

Clinical

Agalactorrhea. Anxiety. Depression. Impotence. Leukorrhea. Premature ejaculation. Sexual dysfunction - loss of libido. Urethritis.

Comparisons

Calad - Impotence often with sexual arousal, coldness of genitalia, completely flaccid penis.

Sel. Pic-Ac. Lyc. Fl-Ac. Onos.

ALLIUM CEPA

Allium Cepa is primarily a remedy for coryza, either from allergic or infectious origin. It should be mentioned that injudicious use of this remedy in common colds may in some instances suppress this minor annoyance only to precipitate acute asthmatic attacks or severe throat infections. This remedy may cure up to one third of all acute allergic rhinitis cases (hay fever), at least for that season. Permanent cure requires a deeper acting remedy once the acute symptoms have been relieved. (Note: Allium Cepa coryza often has less than the expected excoriation.)

GENERALS

General aggravation from warm rooms.

General amelioration in open air.

HEAD

- **Headache during coryza; worse in warm rooms, better in open air.**
- **Headache aggravated on closing the eyes.**

Thread-like neuralgic pains.

EYE

- **Profuse lacrimation which is usually bland, while nasal discharge is acrid and excoriating** *(opposite Euphr)*.

NOSE

Coryza with acrid nasal discharge which may even excoriate the nose or upper lip.

- **Profuse watery discharge, "like a faucet."** The patient stuffs tissue inside to stop the flow.
- **Hay fever**, worse from flowers, worse in warm rooms, worse on the left side, worse late afternoon or evening, better open air.

Nasal polyps.

THROAT

Severe pain with constant disposition to swallow after suppression of coryza with Allium Cepa is antidoted by Mercurius Corosivus.

Hoarseness, raw throat.

Severe tearing pain in the larynx during cough.

GASTROINTESTINAL

Desires: Onions.

Aversion: Cucumbers.

Chest:

Severe bronchitis or asthmatic attacks which result from the suppression of coryza with Allium Cepa often respond to Phosphorus.

Colds progress rapidly to the larynx and chest.

EXTREMITIES

Neuralgia or phantom limb pains which follow amputation (*Hyper*, *Am-M*, *Staph*).

CLINICAL

Allergy. Colds. Conjunctivitis. Cough. Headache. Nasal polyps. Neuralgia. Otitis media. Pertussis. Upper respiratory infections.

COMPLEMENTARY

Puls. Phos. Thuj.

COMPARISONS

Sabad. Euphr. Wyeth. Arund. Sin-n.

ALOE

The main sphere of action of Aloe is in intestinal disorders (in cases of gastroenteritis, colitis, etc.) and rectal disorders. Aloe also affects the smooth muscles of the veins, causing passive venous congestions in many locations.

GENERALS

Warm and aggravated by heat.

General amelioration by cold and especially cold applications.

HEAD

Headache, ameliorated by cold applications.

Severe congestive headaches, worse in the heat.

Headaches alternate with low back pain, hemorrhoids or diarrhea.

ABDOMEN

Congestion and heat in the liver.

Pains in the abdomen before stool, or driving the patient to stool.

Rumbling and distension in abdomen.

RECTUM

Diarrhea, sudden urging for stool, especially in the morning which drives him from bed *(Sulph)*.

Urgent stool at 5 AM *(Sulph)*.

Involuntary stool especially when passing flatus. Must concentrate to avoid accidents.

Diarrhea worse from eating oysters *(Lyc)*; worse from drinking beer *(Sulph, Kali-Bi)*.

Diarrhea alternates with hemorrhoids.

Mucus filled stools, or stool mixed with jelly-like lumps.

Stool mixed with gas which makes a sputtering or gurgling noise.

Involuntary or unnoticed loss of firm stool (especially where the encopresis comes from physical rather than emotional causes).

Hemorrhoids with marked congestion.

◆ **Hemorrhoids "like a bunch of grapes."**

Hemorrhoids ameliorated by cold bathing.

Flatus. Hot flatus.

BACK

Low back pain alternating with hemorrhoid or headache *(Aesc)*.

Sleep

Dreams of stool or of soiling himself.

CLINICAL

Diarrhea - infectious enteritis, colitis. Encopresis. Hemorrhoids. Headache. Hepatitis. Inflammatory bowel disease. Low back pain.

COMPLEMENTARY

Sulph. Sep. Kali-Bi.

COMPARISONS

Sulph - Diarrhea with sudden urging in the morning at 5 AM, diarrhea worse beer, sudden urging, better cold.

Podo. Nat-S. Aesc.

ALUMINA

The main focus of pathology in Alumina is in the nervous system, both central and peripheral. There is marked slowing and confusion of neural impulses. This may be reflected in simple disorders of peristalsis such as the well-known Alumina constipation where we see marked depression of the nerves innervating the rectum. In more advanced states, there are frank neurological disorders such as multiple sclerosis, myopathy, ataxia, and paralytic conditions of various origin. In other cases the pathology is expressed in the mental functioning, producing slowed thought processes, vagueness, confusion, loss of identity and severe mental impairment. In advanced cases, dementia occurs as in Alzheimer's disease or cerebrovascular diseases.

MENTALS

Mental dullness; the disorders begin with absentmindedness, memory weakness, and difficulty in concentration.

Slowness in answering questions and vague replies.

- **Cannot be hurried; hurrying causes great distress.**

Dullness of mind, worse in the morning on waking.

- **Disorientation and loss of identity: "When he speaks he is unsure if the words were spoken by himself or by another."**

Fear of knives or blood. Fear of insanity. Fear of cockroaches.

Impulse to kill himself or others with a knife, or impulses which occur on seeing a knife.

Impulses which come with weakness of mind.

Struggles to find answers to even simple questions during interview.

Despair of recovery.

GENERALS

General aggravation in the morning on waking.

Dryness of all membranes.

- **General aggravation from potatoes.**

General aggravation from heat.

Frequent colds.

HEAD

Vertigo, worse upon closing the eyes (as in disease of the posterior columns of the spinal cord).

Vertigo worse in the morning, ameliorated by breakfast.

Vertigo worse on standing, faintness on standing.

Sensation of a cobweb on the face *(Graph)*.

STOMACH

- **Aversion to or aggravation from potatoes.**

Craving for dry foods such as dry rice, all the more unusual considering the dryness of the mucous membranes.

Craving for undigestible things, such as earth or coal.

RECTUM

Severe constipation, usually without urge to stool.

- **Constipation so stubborn that the patient is impelled to assist the evacuation with his fingers.**

Constipation during pregnancy with great dryness of the rectum.

Constipation with soft stool.

Constipation of newborns.

UROGENITAL

Slowed urination, worse in the morning.
Can only pass urine during stool.

EXTREMITIES

Heaviness of limbs progressing to paralysis.

Progressive paralysis beginning in the lower extremities.

Delayed nerve transmission: if the patient is stuck with a pin, nearly a second passes before he reacts to the stimulus.

Rheumatism, worse night, better motion.

SKIN

Itching of skin without visible eruption which causes him to scratch even to the point of bleeding.

CLINICAL

Ataxia. Alzheimer's disease. Constipation. Dementia. Depression. Eczema. Fecal impaction. Multiple sclerosis. Myopathy. Paralysis. Parkinson's disease. Urinary retention. Vertigo.

COMPLEMENTARY

Bry. Ferr.

COMPARISONS

Hell - Slow speech and answering of questions, morose and depressed, poor memory.

Cocc. Graph. Nux-M. Op.

AMBRA GRISEA

Ambra Grisea has been used mainly in mental and emotional disorders. In early stage disorders it has marked introversion and shyness, followed later by silliness and marked loquacity. It has been used especially in cases of senility and mental impairment.

MENTALS

Senility and premature senility *(Alum, Bar-C, Plb, Sec)***.**

- ◆ **Asks questions but does not wait for the answer before saying something else.**

Silly loquacity.

Averse to company, especially stranger. Great shyness.

- ◆ **Intolerant of company when defecating** (can't pass stool or urine in the presence of the nurse, or if someone else is in the room or even the house or in a public restrooms).

Great sensitivity to noise and music.

Hysteria. Depression. Anxiety.

GENERALS

General aggravation from noise and music.

General aggravation from company or participating in or hearing a conversation. Excitement, agitation and inability to sleep because of conversations or develops physical conditions such as a cough.

General aggravation from lying.

HEAD

Vertigo in elderly people.

Cysts or growths under the tongue.

GASTROINTESTINAL

Constipation.

Inhibition about passing stool or even urine when others may notice.

UROGENITAL

Bleeding between the menses, worse from passing a hard stool, worse from exertion.

Itching of the genitalia.

CHEST

Cough triggered by hearing music, worse talking or reading aloud.

Dry, nervous, spasmodic cough.

Cough followed by eructation *(Sang)*.

CLINICAL

Cough. Constipation. Metrorrhagia. Pre-senile dementia. Senility.

COMPARISONS

Bar-C. Nat-M. Merc.

AMMONIUM CARBONICUM

It is easy to become disappointed with this remedy because while most remedies are under-represented in the repertory, Ammonium Carbonicum seems almost over-represented. This remedy is found listed prominently under many rubrics and many keynotes for its use are mentioned in our literature and yet it is elusive. Some years ago I came across a case of chronic fatigue syndrome which was an exact copy of a case quoted by Kent in his *Lectures on Homeopathic Materia Medica*. I have since found it a very useful remedy in cases with chronic fatigue or cardiac cases with borderline congestive failure where endurance is the main complaint of the patient. At a National Center of Homeopathy meeting in 1992, Michael Carlston of Santa Rosa, California presented several cases demonstrating a sluggish and dull-minded state, sinusitis or rhinitis and prominent blinking of the eyelids. It is indicated in cardiac and respiratory weakness, hay fever, and epistaxis.

GENERALS

Mental sluggishness. Absent-minded.
Weakness and exhaustion.
Endurance very poor for walking and especially ascending.
General aggravation during menses.
Chilly and worse from cold or cold, damp weather.
General aggravation from and aversion to bathing.
Many authors have recommended this remedy in scarlet fever.

HEAD

Epistaxis, worse washing the face *(Arn)*.
Hay fever; sneezing in the night or in the morning on waking.
Sinusitis and nasal obstruction worse during menses.
Nasal obstruction or congestion, worse night in sleep, worse menses.
Toothache.
Blinking.
Pharyngitis, ulceration of throat. Has cured cases of diphtheria.

Urogenital

Dysmenorrhea.

Scanty menses.

Chest

Tired, oppressed sensation in the chest.

Dyspnea with exertion.

Dry cough at night. Chronic rattling cough.

Persistent cough following influenza.

Pulmonary edema.

Palpitation worse from exertion.

Angina Pectoris.

Clinical

Allergy and rhinitis. Bronchitis. Chronic fatigue syndrome. Congestive heart failure. Epistaxis. Hemorrhoids. Pharyngitis. Pulmonary edema. Scarlet fever. Sinusitis. Thyroiditis.

Combined symptoms

Heart disease *with* thyroid problems *(Lycop)*.

Comparisons

Stann. Laur. Calc. Mag-C.

ANACARDIUM

Although the descriptions in our literature indicate a very disturbed psychological condition, Anacardium can be thought of in different stages of pathology. The Anacardium state often develops in individuals who are living with unbearable inner conflict. Out of this internal strife come two strong and contradictory tendencies: inferiority and cruelty. Often the patient will present with only the inferiority complex and very low self-esteem and feelings of worthlessness. It is easy, in this presentation to confuse Anacardium with the remedy Staphysagria because of the low self-esteem, internalized anger, and a type of emotional vulnerability. In other cases there is prominent hardness and anger or violence. The patient may develop great cruelty and coldheartedness. There is a dichotomy inside the patient; he is pulled in two directions at once. This schism in the personality is expressed in our literature with the description: "Delusion of an angel on one shoulder and the devil on the other."

MENTALS

Pathological inferiority and low self-esteem.

Hardness and cruelty to animals *(Med)*, **or people.**

Desire to prove himself.

- **Irresistible desire to curse, swear** *(Nit-ac, Hyos, Nux-v)*.

Severe depression, even suicidal depression.

History of abusive family, marriage or relationships.

Weakness of memory. Brain fatigue.

Fear of failure.

Fear of someone behind him *(Med)*.

Fear or delusion or dreams of being pursued.

Indecisive; conflicted feelings about many things.

Alcohol or drug abuse.

Frequently fights or history of many fist fights.

Absence of moral values.

GENERALS

- **Definite amelioration from eating.**
- **Sensation of a blunt plug stuck in a location in the body** (joints, stomach, etc.).

Sensation of a band around a single part of the body.

GASTROINTESTINAL

Ulcer and gastritis with pains better by eating.

UROGENITAL

Hyper-sexual. Sadomasochistic desires or sexual fantasies involving pain or humiliation.

SKIN

A main remedy in poison oak or poison ivy reactions with tremendous itching, often relieved by scalding water.

Eczema.

CLINICAL

Behavior disorders. Depression. Eczema. Gastritis. Headache. Inferiority complex. Manic-depression. Paranoia. Peptic ulcer. Poison oak or ivy *(Rhus poisoning)*. Schizophrenia. Suicidal states.

COMPARISONS

Staph - History of being abused, inferiority, anger issues, peptic ulcers, sexual pathology.

Nux-V. Med. Stram. Hyos.

ANAGALLIS

Anagallis is primarily a skin remedy characterized by eruptions and itching on the hands and especially the palms. It is an especially important remedy for poison oak eruptions with vesicles which burst, desquamate and then recur.

ANGUSTURA

Angustura is indicated in serious illness or where spasms and pains of bone or periosteum are prominent features. It has been recommended as a remedy for tetany and has cured cases of temporomandibular joint syndrome. This remedy is indicated especially when there is strong •**craving for coffee**.

ANTHRACINUM

Anthracinum has been used chiefly for skin conditions such as boils, ulcers, and other eruptions, especially where there is blackness or a deep blue color to the lesion and intolerable burning of the skin. Recent cases (Jeff Baker of Hawaii and others) have revealed some deeper constitutional symptoms including sexual dysfunction and loss of libido, depression, suppressed grief and headaches.

SKIN

- • **Boils, skin ulcers and eczema with tremendous burning.**
- Boils just above the scapula on the back or the back of the shoulder.
- Blue or blackened eruptions.
- Crusts and cracking of the hands or palms.

COMPARISONS

Tarent-C. Ars. Culx. Apis.

ANTIMONIUM CRUDUM

Typical adult Antimonium Crudum patients are quiet, soft, sensitive and emotional. The Antimonium Crudum child, however, is peevish and irritable and may be difficult to distinguish from Chamomilla. The differential from Chamomilla is even more difficult because both remedies have an aversion to being touched, or even looked at. In the adult, we see emotionally sensitive people who become "mellow and romantic in the moonlight." The patient is touchingly sentimental and often has a wide diversity of intellectual interests and sensitivities. Moroseness and loathing of life occurs after long illness.

The main site of action is the gastrointestinal tract - the tongue, the stomach, the rectum. Whatever happens to the person affects his digestion. Emotions are often felt in the stomach.

MENTALS

Irritable, peevish children who cannot bear to be touched or even looked at.

Sweet and sentimental patients, especially moved by the moonlight.

Sadness and loathing life.

Aversion to being touched.

GENERALS

Warm-blooded and aggravated by heat.

- **General aggravation from radiant heat, such as a stove, an open fire, a heater, etc.**

General aggravation from the sun.

Complaints may develop after cold bathing.

Loves food and eating.

General aggravation from sour wine or vinegar.

Aversion to touch *(Tarent, Cham, Kali-c)*.

Obesity.

Appearance: Soft, pleasant, rounded faces; a "grandmotherly" face. The body is soft and obese.

HEAD

Head pain from the heat of a stove or sun.

Cracks and inflammation of the corners of the mouth.

Inflamed eyelids.

Nasal obstruction, worse heat.

Cracks about the nostrils.

Aphthae in mouth.

- **Thick, white coating on tongue like fur or "like snow".**

GASTROINTESTINAL

Craving: Sour (dry) wine. Vinegar. • **Pickles**, and especially **Cucumber.**

Indigestion from dietary indiscretion. Weak digestion.

Epigastric pain from any shock or emotion.

Eructations.

Nausea, worse during headache, worse from drinking, worse from dietary indiscretions.

Diarrhea from sour food, vinegar, bread.

Alternating diarrhea and constipation.

CHEST

Cough entering a warm room.

Chronic tickling cough.

EXTREMITIES

Arthritis.

Pains in feet and on soles, worse walking.

Plantar warts. Callouses.

Nails thickened and cracked.

SKIN

• **Impetigo.**

Thick hard skin, often with cracks.

Eruptions worse radiant heat, worse bathing.

Eruptions with honey-like discharge *(Graph)*.

Chicken pox.

Warts.

CLINICAL.

Arthritis. Callosities. Chicken pox. Chronic fatigue syndrome. Cough. Depression. Diarrhea. Flushes. Gastritis. Glossitis. Headache. Menopause. Impetigo. Obesity. Peptic ulcer. Respiratory infection.

COMPARISONS

Sulph - Obesity, worse heat, indigestion, diarrhea, skin disorders.

Graph - Obesity, digestive problems, callouses, cracked skin, honey-like discharge.

Puls - Worse from heat or sun, sentimental, obese, cough, exanthems.

Carb-V. Ferr. Calc. Caps.

ANTIMONIUM TARTARICUM

Tartar emetic is thought of primarily in pulmonary conditions with great congestion and catarrh. The chest symptoms are very characteristic with a coarse, rattling noise during the respiration and a wet sounding cough. Despite the obvious mucous in the chest the expectoration is scanty. During the cough you can almost hear the movement of this thick mucous but the patient seems unable to quite get it out. You will find yourself encouraging the patient, "Come on, you can do it!" But despite the rattling and gurgling, no expectoration comes forth, and the patient seems to be suffocating. Any time suffocation and cyanosis is prominent, Antimonium Tartaricum must be considered. Clearly this is a remedy for desperately ill patients, yet ordinary bronchitis and mild respiratory illness may also need Antimonium Tartaricum.

Mentals

Irritable and peevish, especially during the acute phase of the illness.

Averse to touch.

Generals

Wasted and debilitated patients. Sepsis and shock.

Weakened state and end-stage disease with respiratory compromise and feeble pulse.

- **Overwhelming sleepiness during a cough or bronchitis**, even slipping into coma.

End-stage cases may be intensely cold with cold sweat yet worse heat and desire open air and fanning; earlier stages are warm-blooded.

Pulse weak and thready.

Children or infants with advanced respiratory or cardiac disorders.

Head

- **Cyanosis** during respiratory conditions, especially about the lips.

Hippocratic countenance; sunken features; cold sweat on forehead.

Flaring of the alae nasi.

Coated tongue.

Gastrointestinal

Nausea and vomiting with the cough.

Gastritis.

Pulsations in the abdomen.

Diarrhea during exanthems.

Was considered by our past masters an important remedy in the treatment of cholera, a disease having a current resurgence.

CHEST

- **Coarse rattling in the chest or larynx.**
- **Cough is wet and rattling but scantily productive.**
- **Coughs and bronchitis of elderly patients, especially in the winter months** *(Ammc)*.

Bronchitis of infants and elderly patients with weak chests and feeble powers of expulsion.

Difficult respiration, ameliorated by expectoration.

Marked respiratory distress; uses accessory muscles of respiration.

Respiratory difficulties of neonates *(Laur)*.

Pneumonia.

Children with rattling chests *(Kali-S)*.

Whooping cough.

Emphysema. Tuberculosis.

MUSCULOSKELETAL

Rheumatism.

Pain and heaviness in the low back and sacrum.

SLEEP

Great drowsiness, worse after coughing.

Somnolence and coma.

SKIN

Pustules.

Impetigo.

Chicken pox.

Complaints from suppressed exanthem.

CLINICAL

Bronchitis. Chicken pox. Chronic obstructive pulmonary disease. Congestive heart failure. Cyanosis. Impetigo Pertussis. Pneumonia. Respiratory infection. Sepsis.

COMPLEMENTARY

Ipec.

COMPARISONS

Laur - Weak, chilly, cyanotic, end-stages of heart disease and pulmonary conditions.

Stann. Ammc. Seneg. Hippoz. Kali-S.

APIS

Everyone knows the symptoms of a bee sting - burning, stinging, redness, and swelling. These are the main guiding symptoms of the remedy Apis, whether from infection, allergy, or inflammatory causes. Characteristically the swelling is so marked that it gives the impression of a balloon ready to burst.

The personality of Apis is characterized by a busy intensity, a vitality, and strength. It is more frequently a remedy for women. The patient is often described as "task oriented" and may reach the point of workaholism. She is generally quite healthy on the mental and emotional levels. She is a straight forward person and not at all introspective. Generally, the only symptom offered on the emotional level is irritability. An aggressiveness can come strongly forward if the patient or his family is betrayed or crossed in any way but generally not otherwise. The Apis patient can be controlling in the family and exhibits strong jealousy - like a bee protecting its hive. Mucous and serous membranes are the main locations of action of Apis similar to Bryonia.

Mentals

Active, vital and busy patients.

Irritable, especially when crossed.

Strong family orientation.

Jealousy.

Controlling, especially for family matters.

Practical and business orientation.

Presentiment of death.

Generals

General marked aggravation from heat. There can even be fainting when entering a steam bath or sauna.

Usually described in our texts as warm-blooded but many cases may be chilly though local complaints are almost always worse from heat.

◆ **General and local amelioration from cold applications.**

Stinging pains, like the bee sting it causes great swelling.

Swelling and edema; both generalized and in the local complaints.

Desires exercise and ameliorated from it.

General aggravation from suppression of sexual expression as from loss of spouse.

General aggravation at 3 PM, especially chills and fever.

Fever, quite high; alternates between dry heat and perspiration.

Anaphylaxis.

HEAD

- **Swelling around the eyes.** Sometimes too swollen to open lids.

Conjunctival swelling; with prolapse of the conjunctiva which are red, burning, and look like "raw meat", ameliorated by cold applications.

Flushes of heat. Menopausal flushes.

Herpes zoster of the face, especially the left side.

Meningitis with severe head pain, boring the head into the pillow, and "cri encephalique." The whole condition is aggravated by heat. Coma.

Head pain from behind left ear extending to the left eye or temple.

Hydrocephalus, by reputation one of the best remedies.

Head pain, worse from heat, better in open air.

Angioneurotic edema with tense swelling of the face, lips, tongue, and larynx.

Inflammation of the eyes.

Erysipelas. Poison oak.

THROAT

Pharyngitis with amelioration from cold drinks.

- **Angioneurotic edema in allergic crisis.**

Pharyngitis with bag-like swelling of the uvula.

Throat pain extending to ears.

Ulceration of the throat.

Enlarged, swollen tonsils.

CHEST

Pneumonia or pleurisy with extreme pain on inspiration; "Feels he cannot take another breath."

GASTROINTESTINAL

Thirstless.

Peritonitis.

Ascites.

Constipation during menses.

URINARY

- **Glomerulonephritis. Nephrotic syndrome, with dramatic edema of the entire body (anasarca)** and scant urine output and sediments or albuminous urine.

Cystitis with scalding pain during urination.

Retained urine, especially in newborns.

Involuntary urination from cough.

GENITALIA

Ovarian cysts especially the right side.

Severe dysmenorrhea.

Endometriosis.

Miscarriage especially in the first trimester.

Increased sexual desire but generally balanced sex life.

Complaints from suppression of sexual desires.

EXTREMITIES

Awkwardness; drops things.

Edema of extremities.

Inflamed joints, red and inflamed.

Paronychia with pains worse from heat.

SKIN

◆ **Urticaria** with burning pains.

Erysipelas with bright red discoloration and swelling.

Tense edema of the skin, so tense that "it seems the skin will rip."

Eczema with marked swelling, better from cold applications.

Herpes zoster with marked amelioration from cold applications.

ACUTES

Pharyngitis with marked redness, swelling of uvula, better from cold food or drinks.

◆ Angioneurotic edema, often with marked swelling of face, better from cold applications.

◆ Herpes zoster or Rhus poisoning of the face with markedly swollen lids which can hardly be forced open.

Acute nephritis with generalized edema, scanty urine.

Meningitis with stupor, shrieking, high fever and red face, all markedly worse from heat.

Fever with alternating sweats and dry heat.

Pleurisy or bronchitis with marked pain on inspiration.

Cystitis. Pyelonephritis. Burning dysuria, frequent urging.

Scarlet fever. Exanthems. Impetigo. Bee sting.

CLINICAL

Allergy. Angioneurotic edema. Arthritis. Asthma. Chicken pox. Connective tissue disease. Cystitis. Dysmenorrhea. Endometriosis. Erysipelas. Glomerulonephritis. Headache. Herpes. Infertility. Influenza. Meningitis. Miscarriage. Nephrotic syndrome. Ovarian cysts. Peritonitis. Pharyngitis. Pleurisy. Pneumonia. Pyelonephritis. Scarlet fever. Shingles. Urinary incontinence. Urticaria.

COMPLEMENTARY

Nat-M.

INIMICAL

Rhus-T.

COMPARISONS

Bell - Strong inflammations which are worse heat and better from cold applications, irritable, emotionally strong, thirstless, right-sided, ovarian cysts, pharyngitis, strongly painful symptoms.

Nux-V - Workaholic and competitive, desires exercise, jealous, quick-minded, cystitis, severe dysmenorrhea, endometriosis, high libido, allergic symptoms, fever and chills.

Ars. Lyc. Pall. Rhus-T.

APOCYNUM

Apocynum is one of our most important remedies in renal failure and other conditions producing edema. The patient may present with full-blown anasarca and marked ascites and pleural effusion. Some authors have dubbed Apocynum as a "chilly Apis." There is also a prominent action on the stomach producing nausea and vomiting.

GENERALS

Edema and anasarca.

Fluids are retained - urine suppressed, etc.

Perspiration supressed or minimized.

Chilly and worse from cold.

GASTROINTESTINAL

Gastritis with paralysis of the stomach.

"Hanging down" sensation of stomach.

- **Thirsty but vomits liquids immediately. Even a few drops can cause great cramping of the stomach and vomiting** *(Phos, Bism, Bry)*.
- **Chronic diarrhea with anasarca.**

Nausea and vomiting during menses.

Ascites.

UROGENITAL

Renal failure with edema of ankles, scrotum, ascites, pleural effusion.

"Chronically chilly Apis," with suppression of urine, edema, anasarca, no perspiration.

Swelling and edema of genitalia may be extreme.

CHEST

Marked dyspnea and rattling respiration.

Pleural effusion.

CLINICAL

Ascites. Diarrhea. Gastritis. Pleural effusion. Renal disease - nephritis, nephrotic syndrome.

COMPARISONS

Apis - Nephritis, retained urine, anasarca.

Ars. Phos.

ARGENTUM METALLICUM

Argentum Metallicum has its most prominent action on connective tissue and on the gonads. There is great similarity with Argentum Nitricum both in local symptoms and in personality, though Argentum Metallicum is somewhat less open, impulsive and fearful. Two of the great characteristics of Argentum Metallicum are the sudden onset of symptoms and the marked electric sensations.

GENERALS

Pains and symptoms appear suddenly.

◆ **Electric shock sensations, especially in sleep or on going to sleep.**

Aggravation at noon.

HEAD

Vertigo, often with sudden onset.

Periodic vertigo.

Neuralgic head pain.

Throat:

Hoarseness from over-exertion of the voice.

Mucous or inflammation of pharynx and larynx.

CHEST

Cough, worse from laughing.

Palpitations, worse sudden exertion, ameliorated by sighing.

Sudden attacks of palpitations.

UROGENITAL

Testicle pain or inflammation especially the right side, worse from pressure of clothing, worse walking.

Ovarian pain, said to be mainly of the left side by some authors.

Uterine prolapse.

EXTREMITIES

Inflammation or swelling of cartilage, often generalized.

Back pain, often worse sitting.

Neuralgic or electric pains, especially of the lower extremities.

Contractures of tendons.

Weakness or heaviness of limbs.

CLINICAL

Arthritis. Connective tissue disease. Cough. Laryngitis. Neuralgia. Orchitis. Ovarian tumor. Palpitation. Paroxysmal atrial tachycardia. Testicular tumor. Vertigo.

COMPARISONS

Arg-N. Agar. Spig. Zinc.

ARGENTUM NITRICUM

The main focus of pathology of Argentum Nitricum is on the nervous system. This focus is reflected in both physical pathology and in the characteristic personality and mental aberrations. Broadly speaking, the capacity to control neural, mental or emotional impulse is markedly lacking in this remedy.

The Argentum Nitricum type is extroverted and cheerful. The patient is often pathologically open. He is often unable to control his mental processes, his emotions or his actions. This weakness of mental control leads to the very characteristic impulsiveness, suggestibility, and fearfulness found in Argentum Nitricum. The patient is highly emotional and weeps easily, laughs easily, loses his temper and forgives abundantly. There is an element of childishness or naivete. Often the emotionality leads the prescriber to think of Pulsatilla. On the other hand, the fears, openness and suggestibility may also lead to confusion with Phosphorous. When the differential is between Phosphorous and Pulsatilla, Argentum Nitricum should be considered.

The impulses of Argentum Nitricum often seem almost silly. The patient may become almost hypnotized by his own thoughts. Deeper mental states of compulsiveness, superstitious thinking, and phobic disorders are also common.

On the physical plane we find that the gastrointestinal and neurological systems are the most affected. Even deep neurological disorders such as multiple sclerosis, epilepsy and many forms of ataxia may be treated by this remedy.

MENTALS

- **Impulses**, ranging from simple impetuosity to actual, disturbing or compulsive thoughts.

Impulses: •To jump from a height. To throw something at his boss. To put a screwdriver into an electric socket. Unexplainable, foolish impulses. Frightening impulses - i.e. to hurt his child.

Suggestibility.

Sympathetic.

Fears: **Claustrophobia. •Heights.** Fears even looking up at a tall building, that they may fall on him. **•Bridges**. Diseases such as cancer, heart disease, etc. Hospitals. Fear that he may attempt to hurt someone. Accidents. Fainting. Driving. Elevators. Theaters. Airplanes. Agoraphobia. **•Fear to be late.**

Anxiety for health.

Anxiety while anticipating an engagement or test.

Anxiety when alone; ameliorated in company.

Impulsive irritability which he excessively regrets.

Impulsive weeping. Remorseful weeping.

Hurried; impulsively walks faster and faster with anxiety finally becoming aware that he is running for no reason.

Superstitious or fixed ideas. Compulsive thoughts or behavior.

Weakness of memory. Mental deterioration. Dementia.

Tries to avoid any ordeal.

Anxiety in the morning on waking; feels he cannot face the day.

Morose and despairing.

Predicts the hour of his death.

GENERALS

Warm-blooded; one of the hottest remedies.

General and local aggravation from heat, sometimes chilly.

General and local amelioration from cold and from cold applications.

Periodic, severe weakness; especially during menses but may occur at any time.

- **General aggravation from eating sweets.**

Tendency for papilloma or wart formation.

NEUROLOGICAL

Staggering gait; ataxia and heaviness of legs.

Convulsions. Seizure disorders.

Twitches and tremor.

Anesthesia. Paresthesia.

Paresis.

Hemiplegia. Cerebral accidents.

Multiple sclerosis.

Cerebellar ataxia, must sit to put on pants.

HEAD

Vertigo.

Vertigo with faintness.

Headache which gradually increases and suddenly disappears.

Headache, better by binding the head.

Congestive headache.

Bright red spot on the sclera, "looks like raw meat."

Conjunctival irritation, ameliorated by cold applications.

THROAT

Splinter-like pain in the throat.

- **Hoarseness** especially in professional singers, speakers.

Complete loss of voice.

Papilloma or warts of the throat or larynx.

Ulceration in throat. Tonsillitis.

CHEST

- **Violent palpitations with the sensation that the heart will jump out of place.**

Palpitations, worse lying on the right side.

Angina pectoris.

STOMACH

- **Eructations, frequent and loud enough to earn a "reputation" with friends and family.**

Eructations, loud.

Eructations after eating sweets.

Distension, may or may not be ameliorated by eructations.

Pains, worse while lying on the right side.

Desires: **Sweets (even sugar). Salt.** Ice Cream. Cheese. Fat.

Aversion: Fat. Pork.

Marked flatus, sometimes passed with gusto and relief.

Forceful vomiting in morning with anxiety about the coming day.

ABDOMEN

Rumbling and flatulence.

Colitis.

Flatulence, worse from sugar, worse in the morning, often does not relieve the distension.

Diarrhea, worse drinking water, worse from sweets.

Diarrhea before a panic attack.

Diarrhea from anticipation.

GENITALIA

- **Impotence, worse when thinking of the problem.**

Generally sex-drive is rather strong.

Orchitis. Ovarian pains, especially right-side.

Metrorrhagia, worse after coition.

EXTREMITIES

Ataxia. Awkwardness.

Weakness and heaviness of the lower extremities.

Coldness of forearms, especially during menses.

Painless paralysis, especially of the lower extremities.

CLINICAL

Angina Pectoris. Anxiety. Arrhythmia. Ataxia. Cerebral accidents. Chronic fatigue syndrome. Colitis. Compulsive disorders. Conjunctivitis. Connective tissue disease. Depression. Gastritis. Headache. Hepatitis. Hypertension. Impotence. Irritable bowel syndrome. Laryngeal polyp. Laryngitis. Multiple sclerosis. Orchitis. Parkinson's disease. Pharyngitis. Phobic disorder. Reflux esophagitis. Seizure disorders. Tremor. Ulceration in throat. Vertigo.

COMPLEMENTARY

Lyc. Phos. (Clear Arg-N cases rarely need other remedies.)

COMBINED SYMPTOMS

- **Intense craving for both salty *and* sweets.**

COMPARISONS

Phos - Open and suggestible, many fears, vertigo, craving salt and ice cream, neurological problems, palpitations, hoarseness, numbness.

Puls - Aggravated by heat, ameliorated cold and open air, emotional and sentimental, craves sweets and ice cream, congestive headache.

Sulph - Warm-blooded, craves sweets and ice cream, digestive problems, extroverted, fear of heights.

Carb-V. Chin. Agar. Apis. Iod. Zinc. Lyc. Lac-C.

ARNICA

Arnica is often thought of in trauma and it is frequently given for any type of injury without rationale. Arnica accomplishes miracles in both acute and chronic conditions but only where indicated.

In injuries Arnica is most useful when there has been extravasation of blood. Therefore it is especially useful in contusions, sprains, or after surgical trauma when there is bruising. (An interesting experiment reported in the 1983 LIGA meeting showed Arnica markedly improved reabsorption of blood following rhinoplasty where there is often much bleeding into the soft tissue.) The pains after trauma which respond best to Arnica are of a sore or bruised quality. Perhaps the most striking use of Arnica for injuries, however, is in serious chronic conditions which originated after trauma. It can perform miracles in cases of posttraumatic arthritis, neurological damage, or even depressions. Concussion will often respond to Arnica. In the concussion the patient may slip in and out of coma, answers questions in a fog, believes there is nothing wrong and wants to be left alone. Though confused, he is less sleepy or obtunded than Opium.

In chronic cases, Arnica is mainly used in cases of arthritis and gout, heart disorders, and skin eruptions. It is also a useful remedy in labor where it promotes delivery, relieves the pains and helps to control hemorrhage.

MENTALS

Fear of heart disease, especially at night. Cardiac panic.

In serious cases when the patient is mentally obtunded or delirious, he feels or has a fixed idea that he is quite well; that he does not need a doctor. "Sends the doctor away."

Irritable and averse to company, especially with the pains.

Answers questions correctly then falls asleep as in concussion or a delirium *(Bapt)*.

Dreams of animals.

Morose, taciturn.

Stupor after head injury.

GENERALS

- ◆ **Injury with extravasation of blood; contusion, sprain, etc.**
- ◆ **Long-term consequences of trauma.**

Extremely useful in postoperative patients both for pain and to promote more rapid healing.

General aggravation from exertion.

- ◆ **Bruised sensation.** May feel, "as if beaten."

Everything feels too hard *(Bapt, Pyrog, Rhus-t)*, **even the pillow or the bed.**

Restless in bed, because he can't find a comfortable position.

General aggravation from a jar, thus afraid of being approached for fear of being touched or jarred.

General aggravation from damp, or cold and damp.

Hot head, cold body especially in fevers *(Bell)*.

Heat of upper body with coldness in the lower half.

Recurring fever. Malaria. Typhoid fever.

Putrid, "rotten egg" odors.

HEAD

- ◆ **Concussion.**

Blunt trauma or foreign body to the eye or orbit.

Dental extractions and other procedures, either for pain or bleeding.

Aids postoperative recovery from surgery or plastic surgery.

- ◆ **Epistaxis while washing face**, while coughing, or from trauma.

Hot head with cold body *(Ars)*.

Loss of sight or hearing after head injury.

Offensive breath.

Meningitis.

Stroke with red plethoric face *(Sulph, Op, Lach)*.

CHEST

- **Cough from weeping.**

Whooping cough, with soreness and epistaxis.

Angina Pectoris. Degenerative heart disease.

Costochondritis.

Pneumonia.

Hemoptysis.

GASTROINTESTINAL

Dysentery.

Gastritis.

Eructations or gas with "rotten egg" smell.

UROGENITAL

Excellent remedy in labor; often helps the sore bruised sensation of the uterus, and speeds dilation of the cervix. Also relieves the soreness which results from delivery.

Urinary retention.

MUSCULOSKELETAL

Spinal contusions.

Sprains or strains of the back with marked soreness.

Arthritis with sore, stiff joints, worse from cold and damp.

- **Acute sprains** *(Bry, Rhus-T, Ruta)*. Fractures *(Bry, Symph)*
- **Bruises** *(Bell-P)*, followed by Sul-Ac.
- **Myalgias, especially after over-exertion.**

Soreness and bruised feeling in part lain upon, whichever side. Patient must move and thus appears restless.

Joint pains, worse from a jar.

Gout.

Paralysis after trauma or stroke.

SKIN

- **Symmetrical eruptions.**

Eruptions which occur after trauma.

Eczema. Psoriasis. Boils. Purpura.

CLINICAL

Abscess. Angina. Arthritis. Cerebral accidents. Concussion. Contusions. Costochondritis. Dental procedure. Eczema. Extravasation. Gastritis. Gout. Head injury. Influenza. Injury and trauma. Labor. Malaria. Meningitis. Pertussis. Pneumonia. Post-surgical. Psoriasis. Purpura. Rheumatism. Sepsis. Sprains.

COMPLEMENTARY

Rhus-T. Acon. Sul-Ac.

COMPARISONS

Bell-P - Contusion with extravasation, sore, bruised sensation.
Bapt - Putrid, sore, bed feels hard, answers then falls back asleep.
Rhus-T. Calc. Ran-B. Ruta. Bry. Sulph. Sul-Ac. Pyrog. Op.

ARSENICUM ALBUM

One of the largest polycrests, Arsenicum can be used in disorders of virtually every organ system as well as in many serious mental and emotional conditions. Vithoulkas uses the term,"insecurity" to describe the essence of this remedy, by which he means that the patient has an often overwhelming sense of vulnerability in the world and fear for his well-being and material security. Starting from this terrible feeling of insecurity, most of the mental symptoms can be readily understood.

Anxiety. In the early phases, the most marked emotional symptoms are irritability, criticism and discontent. The patient is proper and conservative, often involved in a large, secure church community. As the insecurity becomes more extensive, the patient develops anxiety and frightening panic attacks with trembling and restlessness and great desire for company and reassurance. The patient's anxiety is most often focused on health issues. He fears death to his very core. Arsenicum can cure deep phobic disorders, such as advanced cases of agoraphobia.

Dependency. Arsenicum needs a strong support network. The patient cultivates strong, protective friends. He is dependent on his family and therefore very anxious about their well-being. Arsenicum patients are also very dependent upon their physicians and account for a large percentage of the anxious phone calls a homeopath receives.

Avarice. The patient develops avarice and fear of poverty. He feels that financial security could ward off health risks and almost death itself. He saves anything which may have a conceivable use - paper bags, rubber bands, etc. - all carefully stored and labeled - against future need.

Compulsiveness. Arsenicum is our most fastidious remedy. The patient may literally sweep the floor behind a guest as he enters the house, reflecting the desire to control the environment. He needs control at all times in order to feel more secure. He is an obsessive planner. Arsenicum can be compulsive and even ritualistic.

Despair. Finally the patient develops a despair of recovery with marked depression and even severe suicidal states. He feels unable to struggle with the anxiety and fear any longer.

Children. The Arsenicum child tends to be proper and very concerned about the opinion of others. He is often anxious and overly responsible. The great insecurity causes anxiety and caution in any dangerous situation - even driving in a car. The child pays abnormal attention to his parent's responsibilities, for example he double checks the mother about directions to their destination. He also has great concern for the parent's health. He fears that if something happens to his parent, his own security will be threatened. The child's anxiety prompts truly compulsive school work which may even extend to obsessive behavior.

Physical. The special focus of pathology in Arsenicum is in the gastro-intestinal tract including the liver, stomach and intestines. This remedy also has significant effect on the respiratory tract, mucous membranes, the heart, and in the treatment of malignancy.

Mentals

Anxious, proper, tense and worried patients.

- **Tremendous anxiety, often with great restlessness.**
- **Panic attack, especially after midnight, or from 12 to 2 AM.**
- **Anxiety about health.**
- **Great restlessness, pacing or fidgetiness.**
- **Constantly calls the doctor and is reassured only with difficulty.**

Despair of recovery.

Fear of death.

Fear of disease: Cancer. Heart disease. Multiple sclerosis. Germs.

Fears: Robbers. Poverty. Evil. Vomiting. Insanity. Agoraphobia.

Fear when alone, desire for company.

Anxiety for the well-being of family members or close friends who provide the security base.

Selfishness. Extreme stinginess. Saves everything.

- **Fastidious.**

Perfectionist.

Compulsive disorders.

- **Desire to remain in control at all times. Careful planning.**

Depression, even to the point of suicide.

Suicidal impulse, often has the fantasy of hurting himself with a knife (to slash himself). Fear of committing suicide.

Impulse to kill. Fear of killing someone.

Compulsive hand-washing. Ritualistic behavior.

- Anorexia Nervosa.

GENERALS

Chilly and generally aggravated by cold.

Desires heat; can hardly ever be too warm. During acute illness the face is hot and the patient desires open air despite coldness of the body and a desire for warm covering.

General and local amelioration by heat.

Restless. Goes from room to room, bed to chair to sofa.

Periodicity, daily recurrence, 14 day cycles, or any periodic complaint or rhythm.

◆ **General aggravation at midnight or from 12 AM to 1 or 2 AM.**

◆ **Pains are usually burning in nature (and yet better from heat).**

Offensiveness; putrid discharges.

Prostration and exhaustion which may alternate with restlessness.

Acrid, excoriating discharges.

Generally right-sided complaints.

Tendency to malignancy.

General aggravation at the sea.

Hemorrhagic tendency.

Chronic Arsenicum patients rarely develop a significant fever during an acute illness.

Considered mainly anti-syphilitic though it covers all miasms.

HEAD

During acute ailments, the head complaints are ameliorated by cold, (for example, headache during influenza, etc.) and the head feels hot but the body remains chilly *(Bell, Arn)*.

In chronic conditions of the head the pains are often burning and ameliorated by heat.

Swelling about the eyes, and often below the lower lids.

Headaches, often periodically with daily, weekly, or bimonthly cycles.

Restless tossing of the head from side to side.

Iritis, with severe photophobia.

Conjunctivitis.

Corneal ulceration.

Burning eyes and acrid lacrimation. Burning lid margins.

NOSE

◆ **Right-sided coryza.**

Hay fever.

Watery acrid nasal discharge, which drips forward but leaves the nose completely obstructed.

OROPHARYNX

Tongue discolored white.

Aphthae, often burning.

Pharyngitis, often burning pains which are better warm drinks.

Ulceration of the throat extending to whole gastrointestinal tract, with marked burning.

Ulceration of throat may be deep and rapidly spreading. The pain is burning and prevents eating.

STOMACH

Gastritis. Peptic ulcers. Gastric malignancy.

Peptic ulcers and gastritis with extreme burning.

Burning in the esophagus or stomach, with desire to sip on water (but liquids are poorly tolerated and often immediately vomited).

- **Stomach pains ameliorated by drinking milk.**

Stomach pains may be ameliorated by warm drinks and aggravated from cold drinks or food.

Stomach pain 2 AM *(Med, Lyc, Kali-C)*.

Vomiting of cold food or ice cream (mainly when there is organic pathology in the stomach).

Vomiting and deathly nausea.

- Food poisoning.

Hematemesis.

Thirstless, especially in chronic patients.

Craving cold drinks.

Craving warm liquids, especially in the early stages of acutes.

- **Thirsty for small sips frequently.**

Anorexia.

Desires: **Fat**, even lard or olive oil. **Sour**, especially **lemon**. Bread. **Alcohol**, especially wine and whiskey. Warm food.

Aversion: Farinaceous. Beans and peas.

ABDOMEN

Diarrhea often with acrid, offensive, watery stools.

Diarrhea, worse from anxiety, worse from cold drinks, worse from ice cream, worse from fruit.

Colitis of any variety.

Corrosive or mucus filled or bloody stool.

Hepatitis and end-stage liver disease or cirrhosis.

Burning hemorrhoids, relieved by heat.

Ascites.

Colic

UROGENITAL

Malignancy of testes, ovaries, uterus, breasts.

Herpes.

Right ovarian pains.

Acrid and offensive leukorrhea.

Nephritis. Renal failure. Anasarca.

Paralysis of the bladder in elderly people.

Urinary incontinence.

CHEST

Asthma, worse at 12 AM to 2 AM.

Asthma, better by sitting upright.

Dyspnea, worse lying, better sitting upright or bent forward.

Sensation as if the lungs were full of smoke or dust.

Angina pectoris.

Cardiac inflammation from suppressed eruption.

Atrial fibrillation.

Congestive heart failure with irregular rhythm, cyanosis, dyspnea ameliorated from sitting, restlessness, anxiousness, weakness and great coldness.

Cough worse cold or open air, worse drinking, especially cold drinks, worse at 1 or 2 AM.

Bronchitis. Pneumonia. Pleurisy. Pleural effusion. Emphysema.

Malignancy of the breast.

EXTREMITIES

Coldness of the extremities. Raynaud's syndrome.

Tremor, especially with anxiety.

Ulceration, of the legs, feet, and fingertips; burning ulcers.

Black discoloration of the nails.

Gangrene.

SLEEP

Insomnia, especially wakes from midnight to 1 AM.

Anxious dreams or says he feels anxious even in his sleep.

Restless sleep.

SKIN

Eczema with dry skin and intense burning and itching.

Psoriasis.

Ulcerations of skin.

Intense itching of skin without eruption *(Alum, Mez, Sulph)*.

Itching worse by scratching.

ACUTE DISORDERS

Fever from 12 to 2 or 3 AM or 12 to 2 or 3 PM.

- **Acutes with great restlessness, anxiety, chilliness and thirst for small quantities often.**

Fever and delirium. Delirium tremens.

Burning pharyngitis, ameliorated by warm drinks.

Acute gastroenteritis with vomiting and diarrhea, sometimes simultaneously *(Verat)*.

Influenza with the typical acute picture.

Acute asthmatic crisis with anxiety, restlessness and thirst.

CLINICAL

Allergy. Anemia. Angina. Anorexia nervosa. Anxiety. Aphthae. Arrhythmia. Ascites. Asthma. Bronchitis. Chronic obstructive pulmonary disease. Cirrhosis. Colds. Colitis. Compulsive disorder. Congestive heart failure. Cough. Cystitis. Depression. Eczema. Environmental Illness. Esophagitis. Fever. Food poisoning. Gangrene. Gastritis. Gastroenteritis. Glossitis. Headache. Hemorrhoid. Hepatitis. Herpes. Hodgkin's disease. Inflammatory bowel disease. Influenza. Insomnia. Iritis. Keratitis. Leukemia. Lymphoma. Malaria. Malignancy. Nephritis. Ovarian cysts. Panic. Peptic ulcer. Pharyngitis. Phobic disorder. Pleurisy. Pneumonia. Psoriasis. Raynaud's syndrome. Sepsis. Shingles. Skin ulcers. Systemic Lupus. Upper respiratory infection. Urinary retention. Vaginitis.

COMPLEMENTARY

Sulph. Phos. Nat-S. Thuj. Carb-V.

COMPARISONS

Phos - Anxiety about health and death, anxiety for others, desires company, chilly, thirsty, gastric or respiratory illness, hemorrhage, craves fat, alcohol, and milk.

Hep - Chilly and better by heat, anxious, critical, pharyngitis, craves fat and sour, cough.

Acon - Anxiety, restlessness, fear of death, fever with flushed face, thirsty for cold drinks.

Nux-V - Chilly, perfectionist, fastidious, gastrointestinal complaints, craves fat, Raynaud's syndrome.

Rhus-T - Restless, chilly, thirst for sips, eczema, angina pectoris, desire for milk.

Nit-Ac - Anxiety health, death, disease, irritable, chilly, gastrointestinal complaints, craves fat, ulcerations.

Bism. Lyc. Verat. Kali-Ar. Chin. Cann-I. Agar. Graph.

ARSENICUM IODATUM

Arsenicum Iodatum takes on the symptoms of both of its constituents. Since both Iodum and Arsenicum are restless remedies it is not very surprising that Arsenicum Iodatum has been used frequently in hyperactive children. These children can literally tear apart the doctor's office, not out of maliciousness but from restlessness. Kent reported a case of mental retardation and sinusitis cured with this remedy.

In physical complaints this remedy has a great effect in allergic conditions and respiratory disorders.

MENTALS

Tremendous restlessness.

Anxiety.

Hyperactive children, though not aggressive.

GENERALS

Warm-blooded; may be considered in cases which fit Arsenicum but are warm-blooded.

Malignancy.

HEAD

Hay fever, with acrid watery discharge.

Thick, yellow, honey-like nasal discharge was one of Kent's confirmed indications.

CHEST

Asthma.

Pneumonia.

SKIN

Psoriasis.

Eczema.

CLINICAL

Allergy. Asthma. Eczema. Hyperactivity. Malignancy. Pneumonia. Psoriasis.

COMPARISONS

Ars. Sulph. Kali-I. Iod. Lach.

Some of the most common remedies for hyperactivity in children include Tub, Verat, Sulph, Hyos, Med, Nux-V, Stram, Ars-I. Lyc. Tarent. Anac. Rhus-T.

ARTEMISIA VULGARIS

Artemisia is a convulsive remedy, especially useful in seizure disorders of children or at puberty. Both grand mal and petit mal episodes have been cured with this remedy.

Neurological

Typical "absence" episodes.

Tonic-clonic (Grand mal) convulsions with biting of the tongue and grinding the teeth.

Convulsions worse on becoming cool after exertion, worse from photic stimulation.

Chorea.

Comparisons

Cic. Cupr. Caust. Oenan.

ARUM TRIPHYLLUM

Arum Triphyllum is mainly a remedy for allergic disorders affecting the skin and mucous membranes.

Head

Great redness and irritation around the mouth and the lower half of the face. May be worse on left side, and include the left nostril and left orbit and jaw.

Cracking of the lips with a red irritated look.

Cracks at corners of mouth.

Chapped, raw lips.

- **Constantly biting lips or picking them with the fingers, may cause himself to bleed.**

Pathological boring in the nose *(Cina)***.**

Marked tingling or itching of the nose and lips.

Coryza profuse and excoriating, mainly the left side.

Fissures of tongue. Stomatitis.

Twitching or quivering of the left eyelid has been mentioned as an indication by many authors.

Offensive breath.

THROAT

Hoarseness, especially from over use of voice (*Arg-M*, *Caust*, *Rhus-T*).

Chronic cases of hoarseness.

Mucus and irritation in larynx.

Sore throat with rawness and burning, worse swallowing.

Throat ulcers.

Has been recommended for diphtheria.

CLINICAL

Allergy. Chapped lips. Diphtheria. Eczema. Fissures. Laryngitis. Scarlet fever. Stomatitis.

COMBINED SYMPTOMS

- Cracks of lips *and* hoarseness.

COMPARISONS

Rhus-T - Allergy, hoarseness, chapped and cracked lips.

Cina. Nit-Ac. Sep. Arund. All-C.

ARUNDO

Arundo is another specific remedy for allergy.

NOSE

Marked itching inside the nostrils and palate.

Coryza; sneezing.

Pain at the root of the nose or between the eyes.

Bluish mucous and mucous plugs shaped like the nostrils are described in the literature .

MOUTH

- **Salivation profuse during coryza.**

COMPARISONS

All-C. Arum-T. Wyeth.

ASAFOETIDA

Asafoetida primarily affects the gastrointestinal tract, from the esophagus through the intestines. The main characteristic is the patient's disorganized and "reversed" peristalsis. Asafoetida is also generally considered a highly hysterical remedy.

MENTALS

Hysteria, especially if combined with intestinal problems.

GENERALS

Many authors have described general aggravation or hysterical symptoms from suppressed discharges.

Listed prominently for hysterical convulsions.

Mainly a syphilitic remedy.

HEAD

Iritis or ulcerative conditions of the eyes.

Numbness in the face *(Plat)* and especially around the eyes.

GASTROINTESTINAL

Globus hystericus *(Ign, Nat-m, Lach)*.

- **Sensation of a bubble or lump in the stomach rising up into the throat. "Reverse peristalsis."**

Abdomen filled with gas and greatly distended but no flatus is passed, despite much eructation.

Empty or ineffectual eructation.

Constriction of throat or chest.

Eructations offensive.

Ineffectual urging for flatus or eructation.

Constipation.

EXTREMITIES

Ulcers of the skin, deep, painful, and with blue margins.

Considered an important remedy for periosteal and bone pains and inflammation.

CLINICAL

Bone pains. Colitis. Constipation. Convulsions. Gastritis. Globus hystericus. Hysteria. Iritis. Paresthesia. Skin ulcers. Syphilis

Comparisons:

Ign. Carb-V. Colch. Chin. Arg-N.

ASARUM

Asarum is a remedy which dramatically affects the nervous system, producing one of the most over-sensitive patients found in clinical practice. The indescribable sensitivity reaches even to the point of hysteria. This is well described in the literature with the phrase: "Sensibility increased, even from mere imagination." The patient is exquisitely sensitive, especially to noise. The etiology of this extreme hypersensitivity lies in the patient's own ambitious nature which causes him to push himself until the nervous system is at the breaking point.

MENTALS

- **Tremendous sensitivity, especially to noise.**

Tremendous erethism, nerves on edge.

Hysteria; hysterical laughing or crying.

Restless wringing of the hands.

Alcoholism.

Symptoms arising from stress or excessive ambition. Hysterically over-sensitive children who have been pushed too hard to achieve.

GENERALS

- **General aggravation from loud noise.**

Chills up and down the body, worse from emotions.

Local and general amelioration from bathing or from bathing the affected part, especially in cold water.

Chilly and aggravated from cold weather.

HEAD

Vertigo, often accompanied by a floating sensation.

- **Hyper-acuity for noise, especially noises like scratching of nails on chalkboards, or of chewing.**

Impaired hearing or even deafness.

Vertigo worse from slight motion.

GASTROINTESTINAL

Craves: **Alcohol**. Nuts. Milk.

Aversion: Onions and garlic. Fish. Fat.

Diarrhea with yellow, stringy stool.

Anorexia.

Vomiting.

UROGENITAL

Intense aversion to sex, even to sexual innuendo or jokes.

EXTREMITIES

Floating sensation.

Restlessness of fingers; wrings the hands anxiously.

SLEEP

Disturbed or prevented by slight noises.

CLINICAL

Alcoholism. Anorexia. Anxiety. Chemical hypersensitivity. Delirium Tremens. Hearing impairment. Hyper-acuity to sound. Insomnia. Multiple Sclerosis. Sexual dysfunction. Vertigo.

COMPARISONS

Ther. Nat-M. Aur. Coff. Nux-V.

AURUM

Aurum is renowned for its ability to cure the deepest imaginable depressions and suicidal states. The patient may feel no connection to life, existing in a dark and isolated void. Seeing a single patient overcome a lifetime of joyless existence and bloom into happiness after Aurum pays for every hour of our years of study.

This is a remedy that often suits people who are very intense, idealistic and who want to be the best and set high goals. When these goals are frustrated in some way, the Aurum patient will go through a period of tremendous irritability, and may even have violent ideas or thoughts. It is also a remedy which can be devastated by grief and disappointed love relations. Often the patient will have deep religious convictions. Finally, despite the spiritual work, the patient goes toward deep, clinical depressions and suicide.

Many prescribers shun the use of this powerful polycrest if suicidal feelings are not present. However, many cases which require Aurum have no suicidal intent nor even conscious depression, instead the patient presents as an overly-serious and polished individual with abnormal focus on career and achievement. Such individuals are also vulnerable to addictive behaviors and drug or alcohol abuse. Nancy Herrick of the Hahnemann Clinic presented a medley of video taped cases emphasizing the desire for meditation practice and the deep spiritual longings of Aurum patients. One of her cases was deeply disturbed and actively hallucinating.

Aurum is one of our main anti-syphilitic remedies. The physical pathology often involves headache, sinusitis, and heart disease.

MENTALS

Serious, successful, intimidating patient with melancholic demeanor.

- **Severe depression. Suicidal states.**
- **Relieved by thought of suicide** - "the exquisite relief of death".
- **Suicidal impulses by jumping from a height** or driving at break-neck speeds in a car, with an impulse to turn into oncoming traffic.
- **Suicidal from the pains.**

Ailments from grief or disappointed love.

Ailments after business reversals and humiliation.

Outbursts of anger.

- **Amelioration from music** *(Tarent)*. **Deep love of music.**

Spiritual inclination and desire for prayer or meditation.

Manic-depression. Efficient, vitalized states in mania.

Anorexia nervosa.

Egotism. Haughty and arrogant.

Fears: **Failure.** Heights. Heart disease.

Alcoholism or drug abuse (especially LSD or MDMA).

Visual hallucinations.

GENERALS

Considered mainly a syphilitic remedy.

- **General amelioration in the evening** *(Med)*.

Pains worse at night (headache, heart, bone pains, etc.).

Craving for and amelioration from open air.

HEAD

- **Boring headaches at inner angle of the right eye,** especially at the right root of the nose.
- **Pain so bad the patient hints at the possibility of suicide.**

Nasal obstruction and severe sinusitis.

Nasal malignancy. Carcinoma of the tongue or throat.

GASTROINTESTINAL

Desires: Alcohol. Milk. Bread. Sweets. Delicacies such as pastries.

Aversion: Meat.

GENITALIA

A main remedy for problems of the testicles and epididymis.

Pain, especially in the right testicle.

Undescended testicle. Malignancy of testes.

Sex drive high.

Uterine fibroids.

CHEST

Angina, worse in the evening, worse ascending stairs.

Palpitations, worse at night, worse from emotions, worse from anxiety, worse exertion.

Sensation as if the heart or chest is encased in armor.

Rheumatic heart disease. Endocarditis. Pericarditis.

EXTREMITIES

Bone pains worse at night.

Wandering rheumatic pains.

Psoriasis.

SLEEP

• **Moaning in the sleep; crying out in sleep.**

Wakes 3 or 4 hours after falling asleep.

Severe, chronic insomnia.

Nightmares.

CLINICAL

Alcoholism. Angina. Ankylosing spondylitis. Anorexia. Anxiety. Arrhythmia. Arthritis. Bone pain. Chronic fatigue syndrome. Connective tissue disease. Depression. Drug abuse. Endocarditis. Hallucination. Headache. Hypertension. Insomnia. Manic-depression. Malignancy. Mastoiditis. Nightmares. Orchitis. Sinusitis. Suicidal states. Undescended testes. Uterine fibroid. Valvular heart disease.

COMPARISONS

Nat-S - Depression, suicidal ideas, serious businessmen, strong effects from grief and music.

Nat-M - Depression and suicidal ideas, disappointed love, love for music, palpitations, headache.

Merc. Plat. Ign. Nux-V. Psor.

AURUM MURIATICUM

We prefer Aurum Muriaticum over Aurum Metallicum in a typical Aurum patient when the main focus of the case is on the heart, especially with great difficulty from palpitations. The patient may show other similarities to Natrum Muriaticum such as herpetic lesions, etc.

HEAD

Sinusitis.
Cancer of the oropharynx.

CHEST

Palpitations, worse in bed at night, wakes the patient.
Angina pectoris.

EXTREMITIES

Cracks in fingertips.
Cracks down the center of the fingernails.

SLEEP

- **Insomnia; sleep disturbed by palpitations.**

CLINICAL

Angina. Arrhythmia. Depression. Malignancy. Uterine fibroids.

COMPARISONS

Aur. Nat-M. Lycop.

AURUM MURIATICUM NATRONATUM

Aurum Muriaticum Natronatum is preferred over Aurum Metallicum when the main pathology is fibroids or uterine troubles. The fibroids may be large and very hard and cause heavy flow and dysmenorrhea. This remedy has also cured tumors of the ovaries and testes.

BADIAGA

Badiaga is considered an important anti-syphilitic remedy. Cases in our literature confirm cures of neuralgia with sudden recurring eye pains extending to the forehead. Another keynote is cough with forceful expectoration, "Mucus flies from his mouth." Badagia has cured cases of chronic rheumatism.

BAPTISIA

The typical state of Baptisia, mainly seen in serious infections, is characterized by a "drunken" or "besotted" condition. The patient is sleepy or even stuporous. He answers questions part way and falls asleep even while talking, or falls asleep immediately after he completes a sentence. Often the patient is delirious or nearly so. Usually the remedy will appear in septic conditions or serious infectious illness, but it may be indicated in less severe infections such as influenza.

MENTALS

Great confusion. Dullness of mind. Stupor. Coma.

◆ **Falls asleep mid-sentence.**

Busy delirium. Feels he is scattered all over the bed and tries to bring all the pieces together again.

GENERALS

◆ **Rapid onset of septic state** or cases rapidly approaching sepsis.

Putrid, offensive odors: mouth, stool, perspiration.

Influenza with bruised pains, uncomfortable in any position, the bed feels too hard *(Arn, Rhus-T, Pyrog)*.

HEAD

◆ **Stupid, besotted expression to the face.**

Red, dusky congestion of the face.

Mouth is horribly offensive.

Ulceration of the tongue.

The tongue is thick and speech slurred.

Influenza with a bruised sensation, uncomfortable in any position.

Mastoiditis from influenza.

THROAT

◆ **Dusky red inflammation or ulcer of the throat which is remarkably pain free.** Has cured cases of diphtheria.

Difficult swallowing; can swallow only liquids, gags on smallest solid.

GASTROINTESTINAL

Diarrhea conditions with putrid stool.

Marked abdominal tenderness.

EXTREMITIES

Sore all over the body especially the part which is lain upon; cannot find a comfortable position; even the bed feels too hard.

CLINICAL

Diarrhea. Influenza. Mastoiditis. Pharyngitis. Sepsis. Tonsillitis.

COMPARISONS

Pyrog - Fever and sepsis, soreness of the whole body, feels the bed is too hard, offensive odors, delusion of another person in his bed.

Ail. Gels. Op. Crot-H.

BARYTA CARBONICA

In most cases, Baryta Carbonica must be prescribed on the basis of the mental deficiency or emotional immaturity of the patient. Kent points out that the term "dwarfishness" describes the Baryta Carbonica patient in the physical and mental sphere as well. Mental or physical immaturity are nearly always prominent in this remedy. We think of Baryta Carbonica as mentally handicapped and in fact mental retardation will many times improve, sometimes dramatically through this remedy. In many other cases of Baryta Carbonica, however the mental function is normal, but the emotional level is very compromised, leaving the patient insecure, irresolute, horribly anxious and with strong feelings of inferiority. The patient is most often extremely dependent on his loved-ones or physician. Many cases which need Baryta Carbonica are children or elderly patients with senility, especially when the patient exhibits childish behavior.

MENTALS

- **Delayed mental development.**
- **Childish behavior. Needs reassurance. Easily influenced.**
- **Lack of self-confidence. Sense of inferiority.**

Great passivity though at times great, ineffectual irritability.

Extreme shyness: the child hides behind the mother.

Extreme difficulty in making any decision.

Anxiety disorder: Great fear, feeling of incompetence and desire for reassurance. Begs unabashedly for reassurance.

Anxiety about health and despair of recovery.

Fears: People. Being laughed at. Doing new things. Agoraphobia.

Great difficulty in school work.

Feels security in the house; too dependent to leave house on his own.

Abnormal concern over his appearance, tries to look perfect.

School phobia.

Nervous biting of the nails.

GENERALS

- **Immaturity or atrophy of parts of the body: "dwarfish."**

Frequent colds.

Cerebral accidents.

Symptoms develop after the birth of a younger sibling.

HEAD

Premature baldness, even in very young men.

Stupid expression; mouth-breathers.

Appears younger than his age.

Paralysis of the tongue.

School headaches.

Salivation. Drooling in sleep *(Merc)*.

THROAT

- **Chronic inflammation and huge swelling of the tonsils, may nearly occlude the throat.**

Hard swelling of the cervical glands.

Difficult swallowing, often difficulty swallowing liquids or saliva.

Trismus.

GASTROINTESTINAL

Desires: Eggs. Sweets.

Aversion: Fruit.

Distended belly in emaciation *(Calc, Sil, Sanic)*.

Constipation with hard stool.

UROGENITAL

- Atrophy or smallness of genitalia, testes, ovaries, uterus.

Diminished sex-drive or aversion to sex.

Impotence.

Enuresis or regression of toilet training in times of insecurity.

Prostatic hypertrophy.

EXTREMITIES

Offensive foot perspiration.

Warts.

Biting the nails.

Hemiparesis after cerebral accidents.

SLEEP

Nightmares. Wakes with panic but cannot explain why.

CLINICAL

Adenopathy. Alopecia. Anxiety disorder. Balding. Cerebral vascular accidents. Congenital malformation. Developmental delay. Enuresis. Hodgkin's disease. Mental retardation. Nightmares. Phobic disorder. Prostatitis. Prostatic hypertrophy. Sexual dysfunction. Tonsillitis.

COMPLEMENTARY

Lyc.

COMPARISONS

Calc - Problems with metabolism, recurring illness, mental slowness, anxiety about the health or future, offensive foot-sweat, craves sweets and eggs, swelling of glands.

Lyc - Feelings of inferiority and cowardice, anxiety, fear of people, craves sweets, offensive feet, distention, impotence.

Puls - Dependent and weepy patients, passivity, easily influenced, craves eggs and sweets, recurring infections in children.

Ars. Thuj. Cic. Sil.

BARYTA MURIATICA

In chronic cases, Baryta Muriatica primarily affects the nervous system producing convulsions, cerebral accidents, mental impairment similar to Baryta Carbonica and even psychotic states. The most common clinical application is in acute or subacute pharyngitis and tonsillitis with marked tonsillar swelling.

MENTALS

Manic states, especially when sexual behavior becomes prominent.

Mental dullness. Developmental delay.

GENERALS

Reported in cures of many convulsive disorders.

Electric shock sensation, especially preceding a convulsion.

• Aneurysm is considered a prime indication.

HEAD

Enlarged and hardened parotid glands.

Nasal obstruction.

Catarrh of the eustachian tubes

THROAT

Enlarged tonsils and cervical glands, especially the right side.

- **Chronic or acute inflammation of tonsils with huge swelling.**

Throat pain, worse on the right side, better from cold drinks.

Sensation of a lump in the throat which prevents swallowing.

Enlarged submandibular glands.

CLINICAL

Adenopathy. Aneurysm. Cerebral accident. Mania. Mental retardation. Mononucleosis. Otitis media. Parotitis. Pharyngitis. Rhinitis. Seizure disorders. Sexual disorders. Tonsillitis.

COMPARISONS

Bar-C. Bufo. Sec. Arg-M. Sil.

BELLADONNA

The Belladonna constitutional type is healthy, vital, and robust. The mental state is usually quite balanced except in the violent deliriums of this remedy. Belladonna is well-known for its usefulness in acute disorders and febrile conditions, but its importance in chronic diseases is less well appreciated. In all forms of disorders, the conditions are congestive, intense and often characterized by pain and throbbing or pulsation. The chronic conditions which should cause the homeopath to consider Belladonna include intensely painful migraines, sinusitis, arthritis and also hypertension. Most authors have noted that Belladonna symptoms come suddenly but these chronic conditions may start slowly and develop further and further over the years.

Acute. The acute conditions of Belladonna start suddenly, often with high fevers and great intensity of the physical symptoms. The face is red and hot, the eyes glisten, the pupils are dilated and the feet and hands are cold. The illness comes like a storm and rarely lasts long; continued fevers will rarely respond to Belladonna. Often the inflamed area will have intense heat, almost seeming to scald the examiner's hand. Typically the patient is thirstless though he may crave lemonade. The pain is often throbbing or pulsating and the inflamed part is usually deep red in color. Also noteworthy in the acute illness is the easily developed delirium or vivid hallucination. These hallucinations may come with any fever and often without significant prostration or much impairment of energy.

MENTALS

Sudden explosive anger.

Violent delirium, mania or psychosis, especially when the physical strength is almost superhumanly increased.

- ◆ **Hallucination** of a most vivid nature, especially during fever.

Fear of dogs.

Desire to strike; to bite; to pull hair; to spit.

Bruxism.

Coma.

GENERALS

Markedly affected by change of temperature: whole syndromes can be started by being chilled, becoming overheated, washing the hair (because the head gets overheated then chilled).

Can be either warm or chilly.

- ◆ **General aggravation at 3 PM** or the complaints may start at 11 AM and then peak around 3 PM.

General aggravation due to hormonal insults or imbalances such as abortions, menopause, pregnancy (these events may even initiate a chronic condition).

- ◆ **General aggravation from being jarred.**

General aggravation from motion.

General aggravation around the menstrual period.

Pains ameliorated from pressure.

Flushes of heat, menopausal or vascular.

Right-sided complaints.

Convulsions, especially ◆febrile convulsions. Eclampsia.

Grand mal. Petit mal.

Twitches or jerking.

- ◆ **Intense heat in the affected part - feels almost as if it has scalded the examiner's hand and the sensation or memory of heat lingers in the hand.**

General aggravation from light, noise, touch.

High blood pressure: Belladonna is one of the main remedies in hypertensive crisis with flushes, excitement of the cardiac system, pounding headaches and impending stroke *(Lach)*.

VERTIGO

- ◆ **In acute and chronic vertigo, worse turning the head,worse turning over in bed, worse bending forward.**

Meniere's syndrome with ringing in the ear and vertigo making the patient unable to turn in bed.

HEAD

Migraine.

Head pains often begin in occiput and radiate to the right temple or forehead and settle about the right eye (Sang).

Headache begin 3 PM or at 11 AM and peaking 3 PM.

Head pains aggravated by •light, noise, •jar, motion, sun, menses, heat, washing the hair, stepping, touch, stooping, coughing.

Head pains ameliorated by cold applications, lying in the dark, pressure, from binding the head, by sitting by lying on abdomen.

Head pains severe, pounding or pulsating. (May also be described as "like a knife" or "as if the eyes will be pushed out of the head" or as "maddening.")

Acne, very malignant type with red lesions deep in the skin and no pus showing through.

Large cysts or abscesses under the skin of face, fiery red and painful.

Sinusitis, maxillary or frontal.

Sinus pain, maxillary or frontal, right-sided, worse touch, better by hard pressure, worse by stooping forward.

Facial convulsions, especially on the right side.

EAR

Otitis media, severe pains, usually right-sided, worse at night in bed, throbbing.

Otitis media with tympanic membrane red and bulging.

THROAT

• **Acute suppurative tonsillitis**, worse on right side.

Pain aggravated by passage of air over the inflamed part.

Averse to tight collars.

STOMACH

Craving lemon and • lemonade.

Craves: Sour food. Vegetables. Sweets.

Aversion: Vegetables. Fish. Fat. Fruit. Beans.

Thirstless.

ABDOMEN

Pain and cramping along the transverse colon. Colic.

Appendicitis.

Pains aggravated by touch; better from general, firm pressure.

Cholecystitis.

RECTUM

Constipation; dryness of the rectum in most cases.

Hemorrhoids with exquisite pain and congestion.

UROGENITAL

Severe dysmenorrhea, sometimes with "bearing down" pains.

Metrorrhagia with fluid red or dark blood but mixed with large or dark clots *(Sabin)*.

Uterine hemorrhage feels hot.

Sex drive is generally low to low-normal.

Cystitis. Pyelonephritis.

Enuresis; the children typically have such deep sleep they do not awaken to urinate.

Orchitis and epididymitis.

Right-sided ovarian pains or cysts *(Apis, Lyc, Pall, Podo)*.

CHEST

Pneumonia with typical Belladonna presentation.

Mastitis with great tenderness, heat and inflammation.

BACK

Low back pain with pains extending upwards.

Back pain, herniated discs with great aggravation from motion or jarring.

EXTREMITIES

- **Cold hands and feet but face hot.**

Arthritis with hot swollen joints, typical Belladonna modalities.

Flushes of heat to extremities.

SLEEP

Position: On the abdomen.

Dreams of falling *(Thuj)*.

CLINICAL

Acne. Appendicitis. Arthritis. Boils. Constipation. Convulsions. Cystitis. Deliriums. Enuresis. Epididymitis. Exanthems. Febrile convulsions. Hemorrhoids. Hypertension. Hypertensive crisis. Influenza. Intussusception. Lower back pain. Mania - delirium or psychosis. Mastitis. Meniere's syndrome. Menopausal flushes. Metrorrhagia. Migraines. Orchitis. Otitis Media. Ovarian cysts. Pneumonia. Pyelonephritis. Sciatica. Seizure disorders. Sinusitis. Tonsillitis. Vertigo.

ACUTES

May help to abort many convulsions if used at the first indication.

Meningitis. Encephalitis.

Otitis media, mainly right-sided, often with aggravation at night in bed, intense pains which make the child scream and become frantic, bright red tympanic membrane with marked swelling.

Iritis.

Pharyngitis and tonsillitis with deep red discoloration, markedly swollen tonsils, often distinctly right-sided, worse for swallowing.

Acute cholecystitis.

Pleurisy. Pneumonia.

Mastitis, mainly right-sided, red, painful, worse from jar.

Pyelonephritis. Cystitis.

Ovarian pains and cysts, mainly right-sided, markedly painful, worse before or during the menses, worse from jar or motion.

Sciatica and low back pain with marked aggravation from motion, from misstepping and jarring.

Acute arthritis, markedly inflamed, red, swollen joint, worse from motion or jar, ameliorated by cold applications.

Influenza. Upper respiratory infection.

Early stage of any exanthem - rubella, mumps, etc.

Scarlet fever.

Appendicitis.

COMPLEMENTARY

Calc.

COMPARISONS

Acon - Sudden, intense fever and inflammation, flushes, marked pain.

Bry - Fever, marked aggravation from motion and jar, better from pressure, appendicitis, constipation, irritability.

Apis - Heat and inflammation of the affected part, flushes of heat, better from cold applications, thirstless, right-sided complaints, ovarian cysts, irritable, healthy mentally, great vitality.

Lach - Disorders of circulation and blood pressure, worse from heat, congestive, throbbing headaches, flushes, complaints around the menses, aversion to tight collars.

Glon. Meli. Lyc. Puls. Pall.

BELLIS PERENNIS

Bellis is indicated in trauma, less often than Arnica but similar in many respects. Sprains, bruises and lacerations or incisions may require Bellis. In addition, this remedy has been used for abscess, dysmenorrhea, rheumatism. Even cases of malignancy have been reported benefitted in our literature.

GENERALS

Contusion. Sore bruised sensations. Extravasation.

- **Trauma**, surgery and contusion of the trunk of the body.
- Trauma followed by proximal lymph gland swelling and coldness of the limb.

General aggravation after getting wet or taking cold drinks when over-heated and perspiring.

Surgery - both for the pains and to speed recovery.

Abscess.

HEAD

Acne.

ABDOMEN

Soreness of abdominal wall in pregnancy.

Post-operative pain and ecchymosis.

GENITALIA

Has been used successfully in cases of marked dysmenorrhea.

CHEST

Breast cancer after injury to the breast.

EXTREMITIES

Bruises, contusion and hematoma.

Sprains with ecchymosis, stiffness and coldness.

Rheumatism in "old laborers".

Abscess.

COMPARISONS

Arn - Contusions and ecchymosis, aggravation from getting wet, soreness, aids in postsurgical recovery.

Led. Sul-Ac. Ruta.

BENZOIC ACID

Benzoic acid is a remedy mainly to be thought of in arthritic and gouty cases. The urine is often highly concentrated and offensive, discharging sediments which generally relieves and detoxifies the system. When the joint pains are suppressed allopathically, rheumatic heart disorders may occur. Alternatively, urinary tract symptoms such as kidney stones (uric acid) may develop.

GENERALS

- **General amelioration when discharging sediment in the urine and worsened when the discharge slackens.**

HEAD

Tongue spongy and ulcerated or cracked, especially when associated with gout.

GASTROINTESTINAL

Watery diarrhea, often white or clear stool or with the appearance of "soap-suds."

URINARY

Offensive odor from urine.

Urine odor very strong - •smells like horse's urine *(Nit-Ac)*.

Concentrated, brownish urine, often with sediment.

Joint pains alternate with offensive urine.

Kidney stones. Calculi in bladder.

Cases of enuresis have been reported cured in our literature.

EXTREMITIES

Heart condition alternates with or results from suppressed rheumatism.

Arthritic nodosities of fingers or wrists.

Contractures of the fingers.

Gout, especially of the knee or big toe.

CLINICAL

Arthritis. Diarrhea. Gout. Kidney stones. Rheumatic heart disease.

Combined Symptoms

Rheumatism *and* offensive urine *(Colch, Berb)*.

COMPARISONS

Colch - Gout and arthritis, urinary sediments, diarrhea.

Berb. Nit-Ac. Led.

BERBERIS

Berberis is a remedy characterized by radiating pains; in arthritis, gout, low back pain, kidney colics, etc. The pains are sharp, sudden, stitching, come in "twinges" and often radiate out from the affected part or move to a different area all together. In addition to these neuralgic type of pains, Berberis is also an important remedy in colics of all regions, as well as in rheumatic complaints. Finally, Berberis affects the entire urinary system causing colic and stones, inflammation and infection of the bladder, kidney, and testes.

GENERALS

- **Sharp, stitching or colicky pains which radiate.**

Neuralgia of any location.

GASTROINTESTINAL

Cholecystitis and gallstone colic.

Anal fistula cures have been reported with this remedy in our literature.

UROGENITAL

- **Kidney stones with sharp pains radiating outward or downward.**
- Pain from ureters extending to testes, urethra, thigh.

Pain in kidney region, worse left side, worse from a jar or stepping, worse motion, worse menses, better splinting the painful side.

Numbness or bubbling sensation in region of kidneys.

Painful urge to urinate during renal colic.

Cystitis with cutting or burning pains which extend to the urethra.

Bladder pain and urging to urinate worse from motion or walking.

Bladder pain worse after urination or when not urinating.

Pain in urethra and meatus.

Urine filled with sediment.

Pain in the spermatic cord radiating to the testes.

Pain in testes worse from motion, worse when walking.

Dyspareunia.

BACK

Low back pain and sciatica with sharp, sudden pains which radiate outward or downward into the posterior thigh.

Low back pain with marked stiffness.

Low back pain, worse while lying, worse while sitting or upon rising from a seat.

EXTREMITIES

Wandering arthritis *(Puls, Form, Kali-Bi)*.

Arthritis and gout with tearing, twinging pains that radiate.

Sudden stitches of pain.

Pains worse menses, worse motion.

Knee pain, especially the left side, worse rising from a seat.

CLINICAL

Anal fistula. Arthritis. Cholecystitis. Colic. Cystitis. Gout. Kidney stones. Low back pain. Neuralgia. Pyelonephritis. Rheumatism. Sciatica. Urinary tract infection.

COMPARISONS

Benz-Ac. Lyc. Nux-V. Colch.

BISMUTH

Bismuth is a remedy which has been used mainly in gastritis and other gastrointestinal illness. It is especially useful in acutes where there is violent abdominal pain which is accompanied by great fear and desire for company. This fear, together with the thirst for cold drinks may easily lead to confusion with Phosphorus.

MENTALS

Fear of death and to be alone.

Desires company.

Anxious restlessness.

GASTROINTESTINAL

Severe pains, cramps or burning in the stomach or abdomen.

Great thirst for cold water.

Vomiting as soon as the water reaches the stomach *(Apoc)*, or as soon as it gets warm in the stomach *(Phos)*.

Vomits liquids but food retained longer.

Profuse diarrhea.

Cures of gastric malignancy are reported in the literature.

Pain in the abdomen in small spots.

Abdominal pain alternating with headache.

CLINICAL

Colitis. Gastritis. Gastroenteritis. Gastric cancer.

COMBINED SYMPTOMS

Abdominal pain *and* fear.

Abdominal pain *and* thirst.

COMPARISONS

Phos - Anxiety and desire for company or for the hand to be held, craves cold drinks, vomits when the liquid becomes warmed.

Ars. Bry.

BLATTA ORIENTALIS

Primarily an asthma remedy, Blatta may easily be confused with Calcarea Carbonica. The patient is often obese but seems strong and robust. Despite this apparent vitality the patient suffers with dyspnea and shortness of breath from slight exertion. Usually there is great allergy or sensitivity to molds, mildew, or rotting leaves.

GENERALS

Obesity.

General aggravation from exertion and ascending.

General aggravation from moldy, damp environments.

CHEST

Asthma with great wheezing, worse from exertion, •worse molds, worse damp.

Bronchitis.

CLINICAL

Allergy. Asthma. Asthmatic bronchitis. Obesity.

COMBINED SYMPTOMS

Asthma *and* obesity.

COMPARISONS

Calc.

BORAX

Borax is the bi-borate of sodium, and therefore it exhibits many similarities to the other Natrum remedies. As expected, we see as great a sensitivity in Borax as in all of the other Natrums. Additionally we find headaches, herpetic lesions, insomnia, and many other Natrum features. Emotionally, Borax patients are somewhat more practical and less refined than Natrum Muriaticum. Most of the physical complaints center upon the mucous membranes.

Mentals

Great sensitivity to noise.

- **Easily startled;** jumps from the least unexpected sound, from a sneeze or a ringing telephone.
- **Great fear from downward motion;** the infant screams out as it is being laid down in the crib; fear on descending stairs, on an escalator, in a rocking chair, etc.

Fears: Falling. Bridges. Infection.

Shrieking especially in children: during cystitis but also from disturbing dreams.

Marked irritability.

Generals

- **General aggravation from descending or downward motion.**

General aggravation before stool and amelioration after stool.

General aggravation at 10 AM (trembling, headache, etc.).

Ulcers of skin and mucous membranes.

Borland recommends Borax for air-sickness.

Head

Headache especially at 10 AM *(Nat-M)*.

- **Aphthae:** The entire oral mucosa can be affected with sensitive, bleeding, hot aphthous ulcers. The nose may be affected as well. It is one of the main remedies for canker sores of children *(after Calc and Merc)*.

Aphthae on the tongue. Glossitis. Stomatitis.

Erysipelas during pregnancy is considered a keynote by some authors.

Herpetic lesions about the lips.

Eyelids irritated.

Inversion of lids.

Otorrhea.

GASTROINTESTINAL

Cramping and diarrhea after eating fruit.
Diarrhea, especially of children.
Greenish or slimy stool.
Aphthae extending through the whole gastrointestinal tract (*Ars*).

URINARY

Bladder pain on retaining urine.
The child screams out before urination in anticipation of the pain.

GENITALIA

Leukorrhea between menses. Vaginitis.
Membranous dysmenorrhea.
Infertility.
Herpes.

CHEST

Soreness or ulceration of nipples in nursing women.
Dry cough and stitching pains in chest.
Pleurisy.

SLEEP

Sleep disturbed, especially around 4 AM.
Sleepless from being overheated.
Nightmares; child wakes shrieking.

CLINICAL

Allergy. Aphthae. Cystitis. Diarrhea. Dysmenorrhea. Glossitis. Herpes. Infertility. Insomnia. Leukorrhea. Nightmares. Pleurisy. Premenstrual syndrome. Stomatitis. Vaginitis.

COMBINED SYMPTOMS

Sensitivity to noise *and* any herpetic or aphthous condition.

COMPARISONS

Nat-M - Aphthae, infertility, sensitive to noise, headache at 10 AM.
Nat-C. Nat-S. Merc. Apis.

BOTHROPS

Bothrops is a venom remedy whose action is similar to Lachesis and Crotalus with hemorrhage, thrombosis and tendency for stroke. It is indicated during pulmonary embolus. Especially prominent are the eye symptoms, amaurosis and retinal hemorrhage.

BOVISTA

Bovista is a remedy for menstrual disorders, though it has some important skin symptoms. Ananda Zaren of Santa Barbara noted edema and puffiness - not surprising considering that Bovista is the "Puff-ball."

MENTALS

Awkwardness with a tendency to drop things.

Stammering or mistakes in speech.

Changeable moods.

GASTROINTESTINAL

- **Diarrhea before or during menses.**

UROGENITAL

- **Menses comes or markedly increases at night** or on rising in the morning; stops entirely during the day and returns at night.

Uterine hemorrhages.

Dysmenorrhea.

Bleeding between periods.

Leukorrhea before and after the menses.

SKIN

Herpes, especially of the lower extremities.

Burning vesicular eruptions which become crusted.

CLINICAL

Allergy. Aphthae. Cystitis. Diarrhea. Infertility. Insomnia. Premenstrual syndrome. Vaginitis.

COMPARISONS

Mag-C. Apis. Bor.

BROMIUM

Bromium is of the Halogen family and thus has a strong relationship to the glands, especially the lymphatics. Also like the Iodines and other Halogens there is a strong relationship to the respiratory tract.

GENERALS

Swelling and induration of glands, with stoney hardness.
Generally aggravated by heat.
Complaints come in the summer (for example, summer colds, etc.).
General amelioration by the sea.
Primarily a left-sided remedy. Symptoms go from left to right.

HEAD

Left-sided headaches.
Chronic, obstinate coryza. Nasal obstruction worse from sneezing.
Allergy to dust.
Left parotid gland swelling and inflammation.

THROAT

Large, stoney hard glands - submaxillary, cervical, goitre.
Left-sided tonsillitis or pharyngitis, may originate in the larynx.

UROGENITAL

Hardening or even tumors of the left testicle or ovary.
Flatus from vagina.

RESPIRATORY

Hoarseness or tickling cough from being over-heated.
Inflammation, coldness, constriction of the larynx; laryngospasm.
Rawness and mucous throughout the airways.
Cough worse swallowing, worse dust or smoke, worse exertion.
Pneumonia accompanied by epistaxis.
Croup. Asthma. Bronchitis.
♦ **Asthma in sailors which is aggravated on leaving the sea.**

CLINICAL

Acne. Adenopathy. Allergy. Asthma. Croup. Diphtheria. Goitre. Headache. Indurations of glands. Laryngitis. Laryngospam. Orchitis. Ovarian cysts. Pharyngitis. Pneumonia. Rhinitis. Tonsillitis. Tumors.

COMPARISONS

Med. Con. Iod. Spong.

BRYONIA

Bryonia is one of the most frequently used remedies in acute disorders. It is less frequently needed as a constitutional remedy. Bryonia is a remedy which affects mainly serous and mucous membranes: the pleura, the synovial membranes of joints, the gastrointestinal membranes, the meninges, etc. The great keynote in Bryonia is the marked aggravation from motion. Also many of the symptoms of Bryonia are related to the intense dryness found throughout the system.

The constitutional Bryonia patient is a more basic person, not a refined or sophisticated type. The patient is often very business oriented. His deepest concerns center around survival and the need to work hard for financial security. There is often a tremendous fear of poverty. Even though doing well financially, he still worries constantly about money (Psor). However, most Bryonia patients would be unlikely to identify emotional problems in the interview or even admit to abnormal fears around finance. The patient may admit to irritability and aversion to company, however his main focus will be on his physical symptoms. The most common chronic physical complaints include headache, sciatica, arthritis, and constipation. We must prescribe mainly on the characteristics of these physical symptoms and the strong modalities generally found in these patients.

Acutes. In the acute conditions of Bryonia, the patient is characteristically irritable and wants to be left alone. He may refuse to answer questions and indicates in every way that he prefers not to talk or move. He may even turn his back on the prescriber when being questioned in his sickbed. Often the patient will have high fever which generally develops more slowly than the fever of Aconite or Belladonna and may last for several days. The illness may come on slowly over the course of several days. In the acute illness there are often intensely painful conditions. The pain is virtually always aggravated by motion, even slight motion and to a lesser extent by jarring. Therefore the patient is usually found lying perfectly still to prevent the aggravation, however in some cases the pain makes the patient feel restless even though the movement aggravates. Splinting the painful side is usually helpful and the patient tends to press or to lie on the affected side. In most cases, the patient is extremely thirsty; less often he has a dry mouth with no thirst. The thirst is for large quantities of water, usually taken at infrequent intervals. The tongue is often coated, especially in the center, either white or yellowish-brown. Bryonia is also an important remedy for injury and trauma with intensely painful sprains or fractures which are worse from the slightest movement.

MENTALS

- **Averse to being disturbed; must be left alone and quiet.**
  Irritability.
  Fear of poverty or financial ruin.
- **Preoccupied with business matters.**
  Anxiety about the future.
  Complaints from being angered.
- In delirium asks to "Go home." (believes he is not at home).
  Impossible demands. Demands something then refuses it *(Cham)*.
  Reserved.

GENERALS

- **General aggravation from any motion.**
  Dryness of all mucous membranes.
- **General aggravation at 9 PM.**
- **General amelioration lying on the painful side.**
  General amelioration from pressure.
  General aggravation from dry food, bread, flatulent foods.
  Generally worse from cold drinks and better from warm drinks.
  Generally worse cold, dry weather or cold wind.
  Generally worse from over-heating, or in warm, stuffy rooms.
  General amelioration from perspiration.
  General aggravation on rising in the morning.
  Stitching pains.
  Inflammation and effusion of serous membranes.
  Right-sided complaints (except the headaches and some pleurisies).

VERTIGO

Vertigo with the sensation "as though sinking through the bed."
Vertigo worse by slight motion, worse rising in morning.

HEAD

Left-sided headaches.
- **Headache over left eye or forehead extending to the occiput then to the whole head.**

Headache aggravated by motion, even of the eyes.
Headache worse from cough, worse in the morning, worse if constipated, worse ironing, better pressure, better eyes closed.
Epistaxis on rising in the morning or if menses suppressed.
Chewing motion of the mouth.
Tongue coated white or brownish, especially in the center.
Dry mouth, with or without thirst.
Dry, cracked lips.

GASTROINTESTINAL

Great thirst.

• **Thirst for large quantities, often or at great intervals.**

Cravings: Meat. Oysters. Warm drinks, especially warm milk. Indistinct or capricious cravings.

Often desires cold drinks, though ameliorated by warm drinks.

Desires cold drinks during the chill *(Eup-Per)*.

Stomach pain worse motion, worse after eating, worse vomiting, worse dry food and dietary indiscretions, better heat.

Heaviness and lump or stone sensation especially after eating.

Vomits after solid food, retains liquid.

Alternatively vomits immediately after drinking.

Vomits from coughing.

Appendicitis. Hepatitis. Gastritis.

Diarrhea, worse morning, worse motion, worse rising from bed.

Constipation with marked dryness of the rectum.

Stool dry and hard.

CHEST

Colds travel down to the chest.

Dry, hard, painful cough; must hold the chest.

Cough worse eating, worse motion, worse entering a warm room.

Stitches in the chest upon coughing.

Mastitis with hard, hot, painful breast, better from heat.

Pleurisy. Pneumonia. Bronchitis.

EXTREMITIES

Arthritis with pains worse from the slightest motion, worse from a jar or being bumped, worse cold, better heat.

Rheumatism and stiffness of muscles and joints. Gout.

Injury. •Fracture or sprain with pain from the slightest movement.

SLEEP

Sleeps on the left side *(Sulph, Nat-m, Calc, Mag-m, Thuj)*.

Dreams of business.

CLINICAL

Appendicitis. Arthritis. Asthma. Bronchitis. Bursitis. Constipation. Coma. Connective tissue disease. Cough. Diarrhea. Epistaxis. Exanthems. Fibrositis. Gastritis. Gout. Headache. Hepatitis. Influenza. Injury. Low back pain. Mastitis. Meningitis. Migraines. Pertussis. Pharyngitis. Pleurisy. Pneumonia. Rheumatoid arthritis. Sciatica. Tendonitis. Toothache. Vertigo.

ACUTES

Meningitis, often delirious with desire "to go home". There is a characteristic movement of the mouth, with wiggling of the jaw back and forth. Encephalitis. Coma. Influenza, with intense aching which is worse from motion, severe headache, coated tongue and great thirst.

Gastritis, worse slight movement, better lying still, marked nausea and vomiting from drinking or eating, especially from dietary indiscretions, sometimes ameliorated by warm drinks.

◆ Appendicitis, perhaps 70% of the cases require Bryonia. The patient lies on the right side, worse from any motion, worse from deep inspiration, better by cold applications.

Hepatitis with jaundice, pain in liver ameliorated by lying on the right side, great nausea.

Bronchitis. Upper respiratory infection.

Pneumonia, especially right-sided, lies very still, worse rising up from the bed, better lying on the painful side, better pressure; worse from taking a deep breath so he pants shallowly to avoid inspiring; the cough causes pain in head or in chest so the patient holds the chest when forced to cough, rusty or blood-streaked sputum.

◆ Pleurisy with pain worse movements of respiration, worse motion, better pressure, better lying on the painful side.

Mastitis.

COMPLEMENTARY

Nat-M. Rhus-T. Sulph.

COMPARISONS

Bell - Acute infections with high fever, markedly inflamed joints, pleura, etc., generally worse motion and jarring, constipation, headache (though generally right side in Bell).

Nux-V - Irritable, work oriented, constipation, headache, indigestion.

Cham - Irritable, worse from from anger, worse at 9 PM (though more often 9 AM in Cham), capricious appetite.

Stel - Rheumatism with marked stiffness, worse from slight motion.

Chel - Worse motion, right-sided, desires warm milk, pneumonia, gastritis.

Rhus-T. Psor. Calc. Spig. Sep.

BUFO

Bufo has a marked power over the nervous system in general, and is an important remedy in the treatment of convulsions and mental retardation or delayed development. Vithoulkas first described the type of coarse and retarded patients that he had seen benefited by this remedy. Working from Vithoulkas' observations, Alfons Geukens of Belgium and others of his center have expanded upon our understanding of this remedy greatly.

The typical Bufo patient is mentally slow and unrefined. Geukens has reported cases of individuals who were normal or even gifted in specific mental capacities. More typically the patient is rather basic and instinctive. He angers easily. In most cases there is also a strong focus on sexuality. The patient often has a strong desire for masturbation and a great preoccupation with pornograhic material. From our literature we find the expression, "Desires solitude to practice masturbation."

Mentals

Retardation or developmental delay.

Unrefined, coarse patients who have poor control over their instinctive behaviors.

Irritable. Restless.

Geukens has stressed a love of music and cases of "Idiot Savants."

Generals

Convulsions, worse night in sleep, bites tongue in the convulsion.

Petit mal.

Appearance: •**Gaunt face with dull, distracted or stupid expression, malformed jaw and large, sensuous lips, frequent protrusion of the tongue.**

Head

• **Protruded tongue.**

Bites the tongue in convulsion.

Greasy, oily face.

Urogenital

• **Masturbation** and preoccupation with pornographic material.

Extremities

Lymphangitis, especially of the arms.

Paronychia.

Geukens adds Bufo under the rubric, "Bites nails."

SKIN

Eczema.

CLINICAL

Developmental delay. Eczema. Lymphangitis. Mental retardation. Paronychia. Seizure disorder. Sexual pathology. Tics.

COMPARISONS

Bar-M - Convulsions, retardation, irritability and sexual excitement.

Cic - Childish behavior, convulsions, skin disease.

Sulph. Zinc. Stram. Tub.

CACTUS

Cactus is a remedy characterized by horribly painful or constricting conditions and by disturbance of blood flow. It is considered primarily a cardiac remedy, but it is also useful in neuralgias and hemorrhagic conditions. In almost all cases we will find particularly violent pains associated with the condition. The pains are often described as band-like or like a wire digging in to the affected part. It is a "mean" type of pain, often so violent it makes the patient cry out in agony.

GENERALS

- **Severe, violent constricting pains.**
- **Pain like a band or a wire.**

Pain so severe that the patient cries out.

General aggravation at 11AM or 11PM.

Periodicity.

General aggravation from lying on the left side.

Hemorrhage.

HEAD

Severe congestive headache, with red face; worse from fasting, more often on the right side.

Right facial neuralgia.

Epistaxis with congestion and constriction in the head.

Constriction and choking sensation in the throat.

CHEST

- **Severe constricting pains of chest or diaphragm.**

Hemoptysis with severe pain, constriction or oppression of the chest.

Oppression and suffocation, especially in heart disease.

Asthma.

CARDIAC

- **Pain in chest or heart, "as if grasped by an iron fist."**

Angina, cardiomyopathy, myocardial infarction, and pericarditis all characterized by severe constricting pain.

Chest pain worse lying on the left side, worse exertion.

Chest pain extending into the left arm.

Palpitations, worse exertion, worse lying on left side.

Cardiac valve disease.

UROGENITAL

Severe dysmenorrhea or metrorrhagia with clots and constricting pains as each clot is passed.

Ureteral colic and calculi with bloody or clotted urine.

EXTREMITIES

Numbness or pains extending into the left arm, hand or even fingers with heart disease *(Acon, Rhus-T).*

Swelling of the left hand in heart disease.

ACUTES

Cardiac episodes with severe, constricting pains, oppression of chest, anxiety, dyspnea or even cyanosis, and coldness of extremities.

CLINICAL

Angina. Arrhythmia. Epistaxis. Headache. Hematemesis. Hemoptysis. Hemorrhage. Myocardial infarction. Neuralgia. Ureteral colic. Uterine hemorrhage. Valvular disease.

COMBINED SYMPTOMS

Heart disease *and* hemorrhage.

COMPARISONS

Spig - Intense pains of the heart, murmurs, worse lying on the left side, worse exertion, neuralgia.

Lach - Heart disease, worse lying on the left side, hemorrhage, dysmenorrhea.

Naja. Acon. Rhus-T. Phos. Kalm. Lat-M.

CADMIUM SULFURATUM

Cadmium and its salts have been reported as curative in our literature for a wide variety of malignancies. Kent reported a case of gastric cancer with marked hematemesis who was greatly palliated with this remedy. Many cases of severe enteritis or colitis have been cured with this remedy as well. The condition is associated with prostration, burning pains, offensiveness and coldness like Arsenicum. The patient is not restless, however, and may in fact have an aversion to motion like Bryonia.

GENERALS

Prostration and chilliness during enteritis, gastritis or colitis.

HEAD

Corneal opacity has been reported cured in our literature.
Bell's palsy, worse from exposure to wind *(Acon, Caust)*.

GASTROINTESTINAL

Intense nausea. Vomits after drinking.
Gastric malignancy.
Hematemesis; coffee-ground emesis.

CLINICAL

Bell's palsy. Corneal opacity. Gastroenteritis. Malignancy.

COMPARISONS

Ars. Phos. Bism.

CALADIUM

Caladium is mainly indicated in cases of sexual dysfunction. Initially there may be excessive sexual desire then followed by a marked drop in sexual abilities. Especially we think of Caladium when there is an associated craving for tobacco or cigarettes. Caladium in low potency is often prescribed to help patients stop smoking. I have experimented with this routine use of the remedy with only very limited success.

MENTALS

Kent lists in capitals the symptom, "Fear of injury" and Vithoulkas added, "Fear to cut himself while shaving".

GENERALS

Great craving for tobacco.

Febrile illness, even delirium, markedly improved after sleep.

GENITALIA

- **Impotence with absolutely flaccid penis, often described as resembling "a wet dish rag."**

Lascivious thoughts but unable to have even the slightest erection.

Nocturnal seminal emissions with totally flaccid penis, sometimes without sexual dreams at all.

Itching of the genitalia.

Voluptuous itching of the vagina leading to masturbation, especially in children.

CLINICAL

Fever. Impotence. Nocturnal seminal emissions. Pruritus of genitalia. Tobacco addiction. Vaginitis.

COMBINED SYMPTOMS

- **Impotence *and* craving for tobacco or cigarettes.**

COMPARISONS

Agn - Impotence despite strong sexual desire, cold sensation in genitalia, despondence.

Cob. Graph. Sel. Lyc.

Other important remedies for impotence include: Staph. Nux-V. Med. Sep. Con. Nat-M. Sulph.

CALCAREA ARSENICA

This is a remedy to be thought of mainly when the case shows strong symptoms of Calcarea and of Arsenicum and some keynote of Calcarea Arsenica. There are two pathological conditions where we find specific indications for Calcarea Arsenica: the first is in epileptic conditions, and the second is in cardiac disorders, especially when associated with kidney failure or nephritis. The patient is often obese as in most other Calcarea remedies. As expected from its two constituents, the patient is generally very chilly and suffers from anxiety.

MENTALS

Fear of birds *(Calc-S, Ign)*.

Anxiety. Anxiety about health, about the future.

VERTIGO

Vertigo as if floating *(Asar, Lac-C)*.

Vertigo before epilepsy.

HEAD

Kent gives this indication: Head pain goes to the side not lain upon.

GENERALS

General aggravation from cold.

General aggravation from ascending.

Obesity.

Convulsions.

Convulsion with aura of vertigo, chest pain or pain in hands.

GASTROINTESTINAL

◆ **Craving for soup.**

Peptic ulcer disease.

Colitis.

UROGENITAL

Nephritis.

CHEST

Pain or palpitation, especially before epilepsy.

Heart disorders associated with kidney disease (anasarca, swelling of extremities or periorbital region, etc.).

Asthma.

CLINICAL

Anxiety. Asthma. Cardiac disease. Nephritis. Obesity. Peptic ulcer. Seizure disorders. Vertigo.

COMBINED SYMPTOMS

Kidney disease *and* heart disease.

Epilepsy *and* cardiac disease or arrhythmia.

COMPARISONS

Calc. Ars. Kali-Ar. Lac-C.

CALCAREA CARBONICA

Calcium is one of the most ubiquitous materials in life processes, therefore it is no wonder that Calcarea is one of our main polycrests. In fact, a very high percentage of the population may require Calcarea from birth. It is a sign of a strong vitality when we see older people who still require Calcarea as their constitutional remedy, often indicating that the defense mechanism has held the pathology on basically the same level since birth. However, Calcarea is indicated in almost every variety of disease, from common colds to all forms of catastrophic illness - cancer, heart failure, neurological diseases, mental illness. It is a frequent observation that even in advanced diseases, when Calcarea is truly the indicated remedy, the chance for a resolution of the illness is very favorable.

Work and responsibility. The typical Calcarea patient is solid, responsible and hard-working. He has a strong focus on security and practical matters. When taking on any project, he is methodical and determined. This leads to a tendency to over-work - a main pathology of the adult Calcarea patient. Eventually the patient takes on more and more responsibilities until he becomes overwhelmed. When we have cases of collapse on either the physical or the mental level from over-working, Calcarea is one of the first remedies we must consider.

Security. Another strong aspect of Calcarea is anxiety and fear. Generally these fears center around security issues such as money and health. When these basic aspects are not secure, the Calcarea patient develops a strong despair and feeling that he will never recover. Other fears of the Calcarea patient center around his ability to function and continue his responsibilities.

Overwhelm. In many cases, however, the patient will overwhelm his system with his many projects and responsibilities. His mind is tired and will not hold the many projects and details in order. This creates a tremendous anxiety and fear that he may lose his mind or his sanity. Often he will have a feeling that people can see his confusion or he exaggerates the degree of his confusion in his own mind. He may be afraid that others may notice a confusion, even when the actual mental state is normal.

Phobia. Calcarea patients can be troubled with a wide variety of fears. A very high percentage of Calcarea patients have fear of heights, even feeling afraid when seeing other people in a high spot. Calcarea patients also commonly suffer from a very strong fear of mice and rats, though this phobia is less frequently present than acrophobia.

Depression. There is also a depressed stage of Calcarea in which the patient loses interest in his work and business and is utterly unable to function. He feels an unreasoning despair. In this stage, the patient may become slovenly or unkempt like Sulphur.

Children. Calcarea children tend to be plump, tired and have weak resistance to infections. Many authors have remarked that the development can be delayed in Calcarea children, with slowness in the onset of walking or talking. It is important to remember that the absence of slowed development does not contraindicate Calcarea. The child is usually strong-willed, yet often very anxious concerning security. He has problems with anxiety and fears. The child may be very curious, asking questions often about religious or metaphysical things in order to relieve these fears about life and death. These anxieties are reflected in the characteristic nightmares which disturb the sleep. Unlike other remedies with strong anxieties, the Calcarea child faces his anxiety with a conviction that he must learn enough or prepare on his own to overcome life's uncertainties. He wishes to become independent and self-sufficient. Thus the child is nice but obstinate. Even the toddler is difficult to distract from his desires. The child is also hard working, even to the point of being compulsive. Physically, the Calcarea child tends to be solid, even plump or obese. The metabolism may be slow or defective. Often the child is clammy and has a sour odor to perspiration or stool *(Rheum, Hep)*. He will often tire easily from exertion and find it difficult to keep up with his peers. Poor stamina is often indicative of Calcarea, however robust and healthy children just as often need this remedy.

MENTALS

- ◆ **Over-worked, over-burdened, overwhelmed patients.**
- **Strong sense of duty and responsibility.**
- ◆ **Works to exhaustion then must give up his job all together.**
- **Preoccupation with metaphysical concerns, such as life after death, reincarnation, etc.**
- Fears: **Heights.** ◆ **Mice or rats. Insanity.** Insects and spiders. Dogs. Dark. Diseases. Claustrophobia. Cancer. Infections. Tuberculosis. Earthquakes. Storms. Poverty. Accidents.
- **Anxiety about health.**
- ◆ **Despair of recovery.**
- ◆ **Feels that his mind is weak or that he may go insane, and that others can perceive this confusion.**
- **Obstinate.**
- Aversion to hearing bad news, such as when hearing of crimes or accidents on the news or in the paper.
- Visions of terrible faces on closing the eyes or even as soon as he lies down at night.
- Nightmares or night terrors at any age.

GENERALS

Obesity and flabbiness. ◆Patient puts on weight quickly and easily.

Chilly and generally worse from cold. (Although until age 6 or 7 the child is usually warm.)

General aggravation from cold wet weather.

General aggravation from exertion.

Poor stamina, even in childhood.

◆ **Sensation of inner trembling.**

◆ **Allergy or aggravation from aspirin.**

◆ **General aggravation from ascending stairs or a hill.**

Generally worse from getting wet.

General aggravation from coition (causing irritability, malaise, trembling, weakness, etc.).

Perspires easily from exertion, on getting cold, at night. Patient becomes cold and clammy.

Frequent colds and flus.

General aggravation from the full moon.

Seizure disorders.

Appearance: **Plump or obese patient with round, soft face, pale complexion. The face has many fine wrinkles.**

HEAD

Vertigo, worse ascending, worse looking down from a height, worse turning the head quickly.

◆ **Perspiration on the head, especially the occiput or the back of the neck at night during sleep.**

Slow closure of fontanelles in infants.

Cold head.

Migraine headaches, worse light, worse menses, worse ascending.

Acne, often quite severe.

Recurrent otitis media.

Eruptions on or under the ears. Boils under the ears.

Tinnitus, with or without vertigo.

Chronic nasal obstruction.

Hay fever.

Nasal polyps.

Cervical adenopathy.

Delayed dentition. Teeth break easily.

Recurrent aphthous ulcers of the mouth (the main remedy for this condition in infants).

Frequent tonsillitis and pharyngitis.

Goitre and hypothyroid conditions.

GASTROINTESTINAL

Cravings: ◆**Eggs. Sweets** (especially pastries and ice cream). Salt. Olives. Indigestibles as chalk, pencils, or dirt. Cheese. Nuts and seeds. Milk.

Aversions: Fat. Meat. Coffee. Slimy. Milk.

Indigestion. Sour eructations. Heartburn.

Indigestion from milk, bread, dry food.

Constipation without an urge for stool.

Patient feels no ill effects from constipation.

Clay-like stool *(Card-M)*.

Sour diarrhea, especially in infants.

Fear felt in epigastrium.

Epileptic aura felt in epigastrium.

Emaciation with distended abdomen (marasmus).

Cholecystitis.

UROGENITAL

Uterine fibroids, sometimes with marked uterine hemorrhages.

◆ **Metrorrhagia, especially around the time of menopause.**

Menses "too early, too profuse, lasting too long."

Leukorrhea, acrid or milky, worse between menses. Vaginitis.

Premenstrual syndrome with anxiety, headache, sore breasts.

Sex desire is generally high.

Kidney stones.

Enuresis.

Prostatic hypertrophy.

CHEST

Dyspnea with exertion, especially while ascending stairs or a hill; poor stamina.

Dyspnea from lying flat or from stooping forwards, especially in heavy set people.

Galactorrhea or excessive lactation.

Breast cancer.

◆ **Breasts swollen and painful especially before menses.**

BACK

Back weakness and low back pain.

Scoliosis.

Degenerative arthritis of the spine. Cervical spondylosis.

EXTREMITIES

Arthritis either osteoarthritis or rheumatoid arthritis.

Pain worse cold, damp; worse exertion; worse hanging down.

Fibrositis.

Arthritis affecting mainly the knees.

Arthritic nodosities.

Weakness of limbs, especially weakness of legs from ascending.

Cramping of the thigh, calves, foot muscles, especially in bed at night, and also when stretching or straining.

Late learning to walk.

Sprains linger or become chronic; repeated sprains of the ankles.

Weakness of muscles.

Perspiration and odor from feet.

Bunions.

Varicosities, often painful when standing or walking.

Cold, clammy extremities: cold, clammy feet and handshake.

- **Cold feet in bed at night, must wear socks to bed.** Later the feet warm-up and become too hot requiring removal of the socks then finally uncovering of the feet.
- **Nails distorted, brittle and break or peel easily.**

SKIN

Boils or abscess formation at any location of the body.

Eczema and cracking of the skin, especially in the winter.

Warts. Psoriasis.

SLEEP

Sleeps mainly on the left side.

Sleep disturbed by nightmares.

CLINICAL

Abscess. Acne. Adenopathy. Allergy. Anxiety. Aphthae. Arthritis. Asthma. Bronchitis. Chemical sensitivity. Cholecystitis. Chronic fatigue syndrome. Claudication. Colds. Connective tissue disease. Constipation. Depression. Eczema. Goitre. Gout. Headache. Heartburn. Hypertension. Hypothyroidism. Influenza. Kidney stone. Leg cramps. Low back pain. Malignancy. Metrorrhagia. Migraine. Mononucleosis. Multiple sclerosis. Muscular dystrophy. Nasal polyps. Night sweats. Nightmares. Obesity. Osteoarthritis. Otitis media. Pharyngitis. Phobic disorder. Premenstrual syndrome. Psoriatic arthritis. Rheumatoid arthritis. Rhinitis. Sciatica. Scleroderma. Scoliosis. Seizure disorder. Sinusitis. Systemic lupus. Tonsillitis. Uterine fibroid. Varicosities. Vertigo. Warts.

COMPLEMENTARIES

Bell. Rhus-T. Nit-Ac. Calc to Lyc to Sulph to Calc.

COMPARISONS

Sil - Delayed development, slow metabolism, defective bone, teeth and nails, perspiration on head in sleep, offensive foot sweat, anxiety, obstinate children, generally worse from cold, desire eggs, abscess formation, constipation.

Kali-C - Responsible and conservative people, anxiety, chilly and worse from cold or damp, constipation, craving sweets, stout or obese, arthritis, kidney stones, generally worse from coition, anxiety felt in epigastrium.

Puls - Pleasant, plump, fears of heights and insanity, desires eggs and sweets, nightmares.

Sanic. Rhus-T. Caps. Ant-C. Graph. Phos. Other Calcareas.

CALCAREA FLUORICA

Calcarea Fluorica has many of the same features as Calcarea Carbonica, however some changes occur from the addition of the fluoride element. As with Calcarea Carbonica, Calcarea Fluorica has anxiety about the health and many similar fears. Many cases have fibrous tumors and growths. The main focus is on the bones, joints and musculoskeletal system, producing hard growths, and especially exostosis.

MENTALS

Anxiety about health.

Grief, especially from sudden, unexpected losses.

Fears: Poverty. Heights. Mice.

GENERALS

Warm-blooded, and often troubled by hot flushes.

Flushes of heat with palpitations alternating with chilliness.

Tumors and nodular growths.

◆ **Exostosis.**

HEAD

Teeth crumble and break easily.

Thyroid growths or tumors.

GASTROINTESTINAL

Cravings: Sweets. Salt. Sour, especially pickles.

Cholelithiasis.

UROGENITAL

Large and hard uterine fibroids.

Peri-menopausal metrorrhagia.

BACK

Arthritis with amelioration from heat and motion *(Rhus-T)*.

- **Curvatures of the spine, may be very severe.**
- **Stiff, painful neck and bone spurs.** Pains extend down arm.

EXTREMITIES

Joint pains ameliorated from heat and motion.

- **Arthritic nodosities very prominent.**
- **Exostosis.**

Spurring of bones throughout the body. Heel spurs.

Injuries followed by fibrous growths *(Ruta)*.

CLINICAL

Arthritis. Cataract. Cervical hyperostotic spondylosis. Cholelithiasis. Exostosis. Goitre. Low back pain. Metrorrhagia. Sciatica. Scoliosis. Sinusitis. Thyroid nodules. Uterine fibroids.

COMPARISONS

Calc. Rhus-T. Ant-C. Sulph.

CALCAREA PHOSPHORICA

The personality of Calcarea Phosphorica is characterized by a discontent which is deep-seated and often beyond the patient's understanding. He feels that something is wrong internally but can't quite put his finger on what it is that bothers him. This makes him peevish and dissatisfied. He is, on the other hand, often friendly, open, and sensitive. However, he gives the impression of constant complaining, nothing is ever right or fulfilling. Often the patient complains of both mental and physical weakness or collapse. This dissatisfaction is associated with a strong desire to travel, to change the environment in the hope of finding, somewhere, a sense of happiness.

Children. Calcarea Phosphorica infants are irritable and whiny. The child cries and requires constant attention. He wants to be carried which is reminiscent of Chamomilla but he is less aggressive than Chamomilla, Cina or Antimonium Crudum. Older Calcarea Phosphorica children are very sensitive and often overwhelmed by the stresses of school. At school age the child often presents with complaints of school phobias, school headaches or stomach pains during the daytime, often at 3 PM, at the end of the school day. A strong characteristic in Calcarea Phosphorica children is a constant complaint of boredom. This feeling may often be associated with a chronic, causeless feeling of unhappiness and a generally bad attitude.

MENTALS

- ◆ **Peevish and discontented. Complaining, never satisfied**
- **Strong desire to travel.**
- ◆ **Easily bored.**
- **Sighing.**
- Desires to be carried (Cham).
- Moaning and whining, sometimes even during sleep.
- Fear or aggravation on hearing bad news.
- Fears: Thunderstorms. Dark.
- Mental dullness or weakness.
- Complaints from grief.

GENERALS

- **Obesity; flabbiness.** Also cases of emaciation.
- **General aggravation from cold.**
- **Generally worse from drafts.**
- ◆ **General aggravation at the time the snow is melting.**
- **Delayed development, slow to walk.**
- Generally worse during pregnancy.
- Symptoms may develop after a prolonged or severe acute illness.
- Weakness and fatigue.
- Vertigo, worse from wind or drafts, worse from constipation.

HEAD

- **Headaches in school aged children.**
- Headaches felt along the suture lines.
- Headaches originating in the cervical region.
- Perspiration on head at night in bed.
- **Delayed dentition or teething problems.**
- ◆ **Delayed closure of fontanelles** - rarely seen in our culture.

GASTROINTESTINAL

Chronic stomach or abdominal pains of school children, with or without diarrhea.

Cravings: **Smoked or processed meat. Hot dogs. Bacon. Salami.** Sweets. Ice Cream. Salty.

Painful swallowing felt even in the neck, chest, and abdomen.

Hemorrhoids which protrude with stool.

Diarrhea accompanied by flatus.

GENITALIA

High sexual desire, even to the point of promiscuity.

Pain in the symphysis pubis during pregnancy.

Dysmenorrhea beginning at menarche and lasting to adulthood.

BACK

Cervical pain and stiffness.

Cervical pain, worse from a draft.

Neck or back pain, worse drafts, worse exertion, worse swallowing.

Scoliosis. Spondylosis.

EXTREMITIES

Rheumatic and arthritic conditions, worse cold and drafts.

Carpal tunnel syndrome.

Arthritic nodosities.

Leg cramps.

Delayed healing of fractures or sprains. Tendonitis.

• **Growing pains in children.**

SLEEP

Deep sleep, especially in the morning hours, and difficulty waking.

CLINICAL

Arthritis. Carpal tunnel syndrome. Chronic fatigue syndrome. Dentition. Depression. Diarrhea. Headache. Hemorrhoids. Lower back pain. Neck pain. Obesity. Otitis media. Scoliosis.

COMPLEMENTARY

Ruta.

COMPARISONS

Tub - Dissatisfied, desires travel, high sex drive, craves ice cream and smoked flavored foods, arthritic conditions.

Other Calcareas. Cimic. Ign. Sanic.

CALCAREA SILICATA

This remedy is mainly used in cases of severe acne or acne rosacea. The symptoms are an amalgam of its two parent elements, thus the patient is often chilly and constipated. The keynote symptom - speaking to the dead - while striking if found in a case, is often not present.

MENTAL

- **Talks with the dead.** Converses with, dreams of, or is generally obsessed with dead friends or relatives.

SKIN

Acne and acne rosacea.

Abscesses.

CALCAREA SULPHURICA

The main guiding symptom for Calcarea Sulphurica is a strong tendency for suppuration often with a characteristic yellowish discharge and fistula formation. The discharges last for a long time with no healing or only very slow healing. There is a strong tendency for jealousy, which can take the form of sibling rivalry or may focus on love relationships.

MENTALS

Jealousy, in adults and children.

Strong personality; argumentative and bossy.

Fear of birds.

GENERALS

Warm and worse from heat.

Fistula formation.

Mild to more severe obesity. Heavy frame.

Appearance: The face and jaw often have a very square appearance.

HEAD

Acne, often quite severe.

Otitis media with chronic otorrhea.

Abscess of external ear canal. Mastoiditis.

Chronic nasal obstruction.

Right-sided coryza.

Eruptions of the scalp.

Gastrointestinal

Cravings: ◆**Green, unripe or sour fruit.** Sweets.

Rectal abscess.

Chest

Abscess or empyema.

Croup which is worse in the morning.

Musculoskeletal

Scoliosis.

Skin

Abscess formation at any location.

◆ **Boils which open and drain a yellowish pus for days, weeks, or even months at a time.**

Cystic tumors.

Cracks of the skin, worse winter, worse washing.

◆ Hydradenitis.

Clinical

Abscesses. Acne. Allergy. Behavior disorders. Croup. Eczema. Hydradenitis. Impetigo. Mastoiditis. Otitis media. Scoliosis. Sinusitis.

Comparisons

Hep. Med. Sil. Sulph.

CALENDULA

Mainly useful for treatment of wounds, abrasions and incisions. Calendula works as an antiseptic or to prevent serious infection when used topically. In cases of existing wound infections it can work dramatically to promote healing when taken in high potency internally. Calendula is also an excellent astringent. Topically it will often control bleeding from wounds of any sort - cuts, incisions, or dental extractions. It may also sooth pains in the wounds as well. In any skin condition which requires some soothing agent, creams with Calendula will often aid patients in avoiding topical cortisone. The Calendula lotions, however, which often contain alcohol bases should not be used in eczema or other dry skin conditions because the alcohol irritates or causes excessive drying.

CAMPHORA

Camphor is considered a universal antidote to homeopathic remedies. Its allopathic use is for the topical anesthetic or cooling effect of locally applied Camphor. This cold or "wintergreen" effect is also one of the guiding symptoms of the remedy: localized cold spots *(Agar)*, or painful coldness. In fact, coldness is almost always a prominent symptom of the constitution, in acute or chronic cases.

Camphor is an important remedy in collapse, as in sunstroke, fainting, or dysentery. Camphor is especially well-suited when collapse is associated with chills. One of the main guiding symptoms is, "cold but unable to tolerate covering." Nancy Herrick of the Hahnemann Clinic presented a dramatic cure using Camphor in a severe case of chronic fatigue syndrome at the International Foundation for Homeopathy case conference in 1990. In this case the patient, who was chilly, not only desired to be uncovered but craved ice cold baths which ameliorated.

MENTALS

Fear at night, especially when alone at night.

Quarrelsome. "Rage with a mania to dispute."

Many authors have reported cures of rage and mania.

Feels unloved by family. Forsaken or isolated.

GENERALS

- **Coldness and shivering but averse to covering** *(Carb-V)*.

Collapse states with coldness and depleted vitality, "the pulse is barely perceptible."

General aggravation from suppressed perspiration and discharge.

Shock from injury, infection or exposure.

Sleep extends into a coma.

Kent states: Covers during fever; uncovers once skin becomes cold.

HEAD

Pulsating headache, especially in the occiput.

Face cold and even blue.

Cold breath.

Mouth drawn into a grinning position: Risus sardonicus.

GASTROINTESTINAL

The early spread of homeopathy was due largely to its success in the treatment of cholera epidemics. Our texts report many cures of cholera with Camphor. With the recent outbreaks of cholera in the third world we should review this literature.

UROGENITAL

Nephritis. Green urine.

Cystitis with burning dysuria.

CHEST

Pneumonia or bronchitis with collapse *(Laur, Ant-T)*.

Internal coldness.

EXTREMITIES

Arthritic pains felt as cold and painful.

Cold spots. Cold hands and feet.

Cramps in the feet, especially the dorsum of foot.

SKIN

- **Rashes from exposure to sunlight** *(Nat-M, Bell)*.

CLINICAL

Arthritis. Chronic fatigue syndrome. Dermatitis. Dysentery. Fainting. Headache. Influenza. Nephritis. Pneumonia. Sepsis. Sunstroke. Urinary tract infection.

COMPLEMENTARY

Canth.

COMPARISONS

Carb-V. Laur. Ars. Phos.

CANNABIS INDICA

The need for the remedy Cannabis Indica has definitely increased because of its popular use as a recreational drug, creating a type of miasm. In fact, several cases of children whose parents abused marijuana or hashish have been cured of deep pathologies with this remedy. The personality of Cannabis Indica can be either extremely sweet or desperate and suspicious. The sweet temperament corresponds with a type of Cannabis Indica patient who is at times ecstatic and giddy. The closed and suspicious temperament corresponds to the patient who is severely anxious - generally about the health or about "losing control," which is to say losing his sanity. In both types there is often extreme confusion or periods of confusion with distortions of time and space, disorientation, and even delusions, paranoia, or hallucinations.

This remedy must usually be chosen on the basis of the mental state because typically there are few physical symptoms. The physical pathology is mainly limited to the urogenital system which emphasizes the strong relationship of this remedy to the sycotic miasm. This relationship is further reflected in the excitation of the sexual sphere and in the great usefulness of Cannabis Indica in cases of acute urethritis.

MENTALS

Great anxiety and fearfulness; panic attacks.

- **Fear of insanity** (though usually expressed as fear of "losing control").

Disoriented, disconnected, gets lost in well-known places. Also disoriented in life - unable to find direction or stick to anything.

- **Confusion, hazy thinking, draws far-fetched connections.**
- **Theorizing:** has a million ideas and explanations, for example, how esoteric fields such as astrology and science fiction combine or about health issues. It is difficult to alter his views.

Difficult concentration.

- **Fear of antidoting his homeopathic remedy; compelled to question practitioner about every aspect of his case.**

Thoughts come too rapidly and can't be grasped.

Excited, giddy and even ecstatic states.

Laughing immoderately.

Delusions of all types. Hallucination: auditory or visual.

Clairvoyance; prophetic dreams. **Out of the body experiences.**

Behavior disorders in children - loquacious, spacey, annoying.

Distorted perception of space, distance, sizes, and time duration.

Lacks a sense of identity or connection to himself or others.

Anger and rage.

Symptoms begin when he travels or moves to a new or foreign place.

HEAD

Sensation of opening and closing of the vertex.

UROGENITAL

Excessive sexual desire.

Burning with urination.

Chronic urethritis. Prostatitis.

MUSCULOSKELETAL

- **Single limbs feel light or as if they will float which is often experienced as a fearful event.**

Back pain (or kidney pain) while laughing.

CLINICAL

Anxiety. Behavior disorder. Chronic fatigue syndrome. Delusion. Depression. Phobic disorder. Manic-depression. Prostatitis. Seizure disorders. Urethritis. Urinary tract infection.

COMPLEMENTARY

Med.

COMPARISONS

Nux-M. Phos. Cann-S. Ars. Nit-Ac. Sulph.

CANNABIS SATIVA

There is a strong resemblance between Cannabis Sativa and Cannabis Indica both in the mental state and the physical pathologies. Generally the mental confusion is less severe in Cannabis Sativa than in Cannabis Indica, and Cannabis Sativa covers a wider range of urogenital symptoms.

MENTALS

Confused and ecstatic states

Mistakes while writing.

UROGENITAL

Cystits with burning during or at the end of urination with the focus of the pain in the urethra or even more specifically at the meatus.

Spasmodic closure of the sphincter interrupting the flow of urine.

Urethral discharge, irritation and swelling. Urethral stricture.

Urge for stool during urination.

EXTREMITIES

Spasm or contraction of muscles: the legs are drawn together; torticollis with the chin drawn to the chest; etc.

CLINICAL

Cystitis. Gonorrhea. Prostatitis. Torticollis. Urethritis. Urinary tract infection.

COMPARISONS

Canth. Sars. Cann-I.

CANTHARIS

Characterized by a violent and aggressive action on the tissues, Cantharis is used mainly in disorders involving the mucous membranes, especially in the urinary tract, and to a lesser extent the gastrointestinal and respiratory systems. The symptoms often come on very rapidly as with Belladonna or Aconite but progress rapidly past the inflammatory stage into severe, destructive pathology. Burning pains are almost always present in the inflammatory conditions of Cantharis. The mental symptoms are correspondingly violent. Cantharis has cured cases of mania which resemble Stramonium.

MENTALS

Anger or great irritability.

Delirium with violence, rage and often with sexual mania is described in our literature.

Fear of mirrors or other reflecting objects *(Stram)*.

GENERALS

Burning pains in the affected area.

Tenesmus.

Cases which center in a different organ system but also include the typical urinary symptoms of the remedy.

General amelioration from cold or cold applications.

HEAD

Burning in the brain.

Many authors stress the combination of meningitis or encephalitis with the typical mental or urinary symptoms.

Irritation and pain in the eyes after a burn or chemical exposure.

Erysipelas.

THROAT

Great burning pain in mouth or pharynx *(Ars, Merc-C)*, with or without vesicles.

GASTROINTESTINAL

Diarrheal conditions with great burning and tenesmus and bloody stool *(Merc-C)*.

Burning gastritis.

Peritonitis.

UROGENITAL

- **Cystitis, urethritis, pyelonephritis with tenesmus and great dysuria.**
- **Great burning before, after, but especially during urination; "each drop passes as if scalding water."**
- **Hemorrhagic cystitis.** Large clots of blood in urine.

Involuntary urination or dribbling after urination, worse during cystitis, worse during menses.

Urethritis and purulent or bloody discharge. Balanitis.

- Priapism; erections excessive, continuous, painful.

Nocturnal erections.

Erections or sexual excitement with the urethral discharge or urinary tract hemorrhages.

Inflammation of ovaries or endometritis, worse after suppressed discharges or gonorrhea.

Burning and itching of labia, worse from urination.

Retention of placenta or uterine contents.

Promiscuity.

Excessive sexual appetite, may be so extreme that the patient feels no relief from masturbation or coition. (In the routine cystitis or urinary tract infection this is rare.)

CHEST

Thick mucous, expelled with difficulty, especially with the typical mental or urinary symptoms.

Burning in the chest.

SKIN

- **Relieves the severe pain following a burn, and helps to promote healing** *(Urt-U)*.

Vesicles with itching and great burning.

CLINICAL

Balanitis. Bronchitis. Burns. Colitis. Cystitis. Eczema. Endometritis. Gastroenteritis. Meningitis. Pharyngitis. Pleurisy. Priapism. Prostatitis. Pyelonephritis. Sexual disorders. Urethral stricture. Urethritis. Urinary tract infection.

COMPLEMENTARY

Camph.

COMPARISONS

Kreos. Cann-I. Cann-S. Sars. Merc-C. Apis. Nux-V.

CAPSICUM

Easily confused with Calcarea Carbonica due to its flabby and obese appearance, Capsicum is useful mainly in depression and conditions affecting the mucous membranes. The mental state is characterized by melancholy, nostalgia and a type of inexpressible longing for the past which is described in our texts as "home-sickness."

MENTALS

Depression and nostalgia (•homesickness) which can reach even suicidal states.
Dullness of mind, slow thinking.
Alcoholism.
Sensitive to noises during the chill.
Irritability.
Fears he will get into troubles with the police.

GENERALS

Obesity; a flabby appearance.
Chilly and aggravated from cold. Chills after drinking.
Burning and irritation of the mucous membranes.
Offensive perspiration.

HEAD

Red face with small, red, dilated blood vessels on face and nose.
Mastoiditis with burning pain.
Severe headache on coughing.
Enlarged sensation in head.
Burning sensation or ulcers in mouth and throat.
"Colds" with tremendous redness and burning of the throat.

GASTROINTESTINAL

Cravings: **Pepper**. Stimulants such as coffee, spices, alcohol.
Gastritis, enteritis and diarrheas with burning and tenesmus.
Great thirst before chill; takes cold drinks which brings on the chill.
Great thirst after stool.
Heartburn and indigestion.
Colitis. Hemorrhoids.

UROGENITAL

Bladder or urethral pain , worse coughing, worse after urination.
Chronic urethritis.

CHEST

Cough with markedly offensive odor from expelled air.

Chronic hoarseness.

MUSCULOSKELETAL

Coldness in the back.

Sciatica and low back pain.

CLINICAL

Alcoholism. Colitis. Cough. Depression. Gastritis. Headache. Hemorrhoids. Low back pain. Mastoiditis. Obesity. Urethritis.

COMPARISONS

Calc. Sulph. Graph. Ant-C. Ferr.

CARBO ANIMALIS

This remedy is thought of mainly in cases with serious pathology and malignant-seeming conditions or even frank malignancies. There is generally marked weakness and depletion of vitality. The affected organs become slowly indurated, purplish and cause great burning, especially when touched. So far, the mental state is incompletely described, though a gloomy and anxious state is discussed in some texts. The symptoms of strong "homesickness" and a tendency for sitting lost in "meditation" have been confirmed. The patient may resemble Sulphur in temperament and physical symptomatology except for being very chilly.

MENTALS

Homesickness. Thoughts of his wonderful past.

Lost in thought; meditative.

Fear of heights.

GENERALS

Cold and aggravated by cold.

• **Coldness at night in bed.**

Swollen and indurated lymph glands throughout the body.

Great weakness, •worse during the menses, worse from loss of fluids (breast-feeding, hemorrhage, etc.).

Tendency to malignancy.

HEAD

Bursting or pressing headache in the vertex.

Carcinoma of face, eye, nose, mouth, throat.

Cataracts.

Many authors give as a keynote: Hearing impaired and cannot determine direction of sounds; or noises seem to "come from another world."

GASTROINTESTINAL

Gastric irritation; ulcers and malignant ulcers (*Cadm, Ornth, etc*).

Proctitis and rectal oozing.

Desires eggs.

Pancreatitis.

Swelling and induration of inguinal glands.

CHEST

Fibrocystic breasts. Abscess, tumors or cysts, more often left-side.

Breast cancer with slowly progressing masses which burn or sting and may have offensive discharges or enlarged axillary nodes.

GENITALIA

Malignancy of testes or ovaries.

Cervical or uterine dysplasia or frank malignancy, often with mid cycle bleeding or offensive and acrid discharges.

Burning pains of the cervix, "like burning coals."

Acrid leukorrhea.

Exhausting, dark, clotted menses.

MUSCULOSKELETAL

Injuries to the coccyx with chronic burning pains, worse from touch.

"Weak ankles" has been given as an indication by many authors.

SKIN

- Copper-colored eruptions.

CLINICAL

Adenopathy. Cataract. Cervicitis. Coccydynia. Chronic fatigue syndrome. Fibrocystic breast disease. Headache. Lymphoma. Malignancy. Pancreatitis. Vaginitis.

COMPARISONS

Sulph. Con. Carb-V. Chin. Calc. Sil. Sep. Am-C.

CARBO VEGETABILIS

Carbo Vegetabilis is a remedy to be thought of in debilitated or collapsed states, mainly on the physical level but also to a lesser degree on the emotional and mental planes. Carbo Vegetabilis can revive patients even from their death-bed; it restores the vital force in a most fundamental way (Ant-T, Laur). In a similar fashion, in cases of syncope and simple fainting spells, Carbo Vegetabilis can dramatically restore the consciousness of the patient. In fact it is the first remedy to be thought of in cases of fainting in the acute phase.

On the psychological plane we often find great indifference and apathy. The personality may mimic that of Sepia with apathy punctuated by irritability and cutting, critical remarks. The patient lashes out at the family if treated with anything less than total consideration and gentleness. Also the patient desires exciting or challenging events to overcome this apathetic state. Eventually with the apathy comes great fatigue which makes the patient weak and almost unable to carry out any activity.

The pathology of Carbo Vegetabilis is almost always associated with weakness. The vital force itself seems weak and the patient is cold and sluggish. The weakness may develop slowly due to organic pathology in the liver, heart, or lungs. In other cases weakness comes as a consequence of a serious infection such as pneumonia or infectious mononucleosis. In cardiac cases producing congestive failure, Carbo Vegetabilis is one of the best remedies at our disposal. The lungs are weak and asthmatic; cardiac or emphysematous dyspnea results.

There are two very distinctive characteristics which often accompany the Carbo Vegetabilis state:

1) The first is a type of "air hunger" which makes the patient ask for fresh air or to be fanned, or in today's high-tech societies the patient simply turns on an electric fan or air conditioner. This is all the more surprising because of the marked chilliness of the patient.

2) Very often the digestion is weak causing bloating, indigestion, and tremendous flatulence and eructation. This distention and eructation can often typify even the cardiac or pulmonary cases which will benefit from Carbo Vegetabilis.

MENTALS

Great indifference and apathy.

Harsh and cutting remarks. Negative and depressed.

Great irritability, especially directed at the family.

Memory poor. Concentration difficult.

Haughtiness.

Coma.

GENERALS

Coldness; cold breath, cold sweat, cold in single parts.

- **Desire to be fanned;** the patient needs extra oxygen, open air.
- **Cold but averse to being covered** *(Camph, Sec)*.
- **General aggravation from lying flat, must sit up.**

Collapse states, advanced cardiac failure, cyanosis, moribund.

- **Fainting** from indigestion, flatus, sun-stroke, infection, etc.

Obesity.

HEAD

Headache worse from lying flat, worse pressure of hat.

Face is puffy and may be bluish or cyanotic.

Cold sweat on forehead.

Cold breath and tongue.

GASTROINTESTINAL

Tremendous bloating and indigestion.

- **Frequent eructations which ameliorate both the stomach and the patient in general.** Patients may drink carbonated beverages to induce eructations in order to feel this relief.

Flatulence, worse at night, worse when lying.

Often indifferent to food, but some cases are greedy for food.

Craving: Sweets. Salt.

Aversion or indigestion from rich foods or fat *(Puls)*.

Heartburn.

UROGENITAL

Aversion or indifference to sex.

Eruptions about the genitalia; tinea cruris.

CHEST

Dyspnea and must sit up in bed.

- **Dyspnea from flatus or over-eating, better eructation.**

Pneumonia, advanced stages. Pertussis. Asthma. Emphysema.

- Congestive heart failure with anxiety, dyspnea, cyanosis, bloated appearance, ameliorated by fanning or eructation.

EXTREMITIES

Cold legs and feet.

Weakness.

Ecchymosis.

Eczema and cracks on the hands.

CLINICAL

Asthma. Chronic fatigue syndrome. Collapse. Coma. Congestive heart failure. Eczema. Esophagitis. Fainting. Gastritis. Headache. Obesity. Peptic ulcer. Pertussis. Pneumonia. Post-surgical. Syncope.

COMPLEMENTARY

Kali-C. Phos. Ars.

COMPARISONS

Sep - Indifference, irritability, chilly, averse sex, weakness, fatigue.

Lyc. Chin. Arg-N. Calc. Camph. Carb-An. Nit-Ac.

CARBOLIC ACID

Though Carbolic acid is mainly used as a specific remedy for nausea of pregnancy, it is also a deeper acting remedy which is useful in states of serious collapse. Kent describes its use in severe anaphylactic reaction to bee-sting.

GENERALS

Putrid discharges and offensiveness.

Shock and collapse.

- Anaphylaxis, especially after bee stings.

HEAD

Frontal headache, usually dull and aching or like a band.

Swelling of face and tongue after insect sting (*Apis*).

Smell acute.

Chronic rhinitis with nasal obstruction and putrid nasal discharge.

Facial neuralgia.

Pharyngitis with red throat, offensive breath, thirst.

GASTROINTESTINAL

Nausea of pregnancy with strong frontal headache, heartburn, eructation and vomiting.

SKIN

Urticaria covering the body.

Vesicular eruptions over body, especially of the hands.

CLINICAL

Anaphylaxis. Facial neuralgia. Headache. Nausea of pregnancy. Pharyngitis. Rhinitis. Shock. Sinusitis. Urethritis. Urticaria.

COMPARISONS

Lac-Ac. Sym-R. Tab. Sep. Colch.

CARBONEUM SULPHURATUM

This remedy is indicated in toxic, confused or besotted states like Baptisia. The patient thinks and answers slowly. Unlike Baptisia this results from toxicity, chemical exposure, or "unclean blood" rather than infection or sepsis. This may be accompanied by lightning-like or "jerking" pains, sudden visual disturbance, color-blindness or skin eruption.

CARCINOSIN

Carcinosin was little used in Athens during the time of my training and even less used by American homeopaths. All of us are greatly indebted to Jonathan Shore of the Hahnemann Clinic for his efforts to bring Carcinosin into more general use. Carcinosin has proven itself a fundamental nosode with an interesting amalgam of symptoms seemingly derived from other nosodes and miasms. My experience has confirmed the general consensus that this remedy is not so useful in frank malignancy as it is in premalignant states and in those with a family history of cancer and diabetes. Carcinosin has never had a true proving and, as with all remedies based upon only clinical cases, many conjectures about the main characteristics exist. Below is given a list - perhaps incomplete - of reliably demonstrated characteristics.

The personality of this remedy is generally strong and passionate and very intense. The patient often feels a sense of being unfulfilled which drives him to work excessively, push limits, or live dangerously. There is a restlessness and a desire for travel and excitement. Despite this exuberant nature, often the Carcinosin patient has suffered from suppression and abuse during his childhood. There are strong, deep bonds with the family. This may cause the patient to become markedly rebellious in life.

Children. Carcinosin children are often sensitive and sympathetic and may be rather timid. They are open and easily wounded and can be suppressed. The children are markedly sensitive to criticism and reprimand. They dislike and are intolerant of consolation (more rarely the opposite is true). As the patient reaches adolescence and puberty, there may be strong sexual instincts and passion.

MENTALS

Passionate and longing patients who over-extend themselves on many levels.

Fastidious.

Desire for travel.

History of suppression and guilty feelings.

- **Desires dancing and music.**
- **The patient loves the excitement of thunderstorms.**

Sympathetic.

Timidity.

Obstinacy.

Fears: Health and cancer. Exams. Crowds.

Difficult concentration.

Mental retardation.

Aversion to reprimand or contradiction.

Anxiety and anticipatory worries.

GENERALS

Warm-blooded and generally worse from heat.

General amelioration at the sea (though sometimes aggravated).

- **Past history of cancer or family history of cancer or diabetes.**

To be considered when well-selected remedies fail to act or do not hold for long after acting.

General aggravation in the afternoon from 1 to 6 PM or especially at 5 to 6 PM.

General amelioration in the evening.

Periodicity.

General amelioration from short naps.

Illness develops at the time of puberty.

Frequent colds and acute illness.

- **General aggravation since mononucleosis or pertussis.**

Diabetes.

- **Appearance: Dark, earthy or dusky complexion or "Cafe au lait" hue. Many times the patient has dark moles.**

Head:

- **Bluish hue to the sclera, especially in children.**

Headache deep inside the brain.

Acne.

Twitches, tics or frequent blinking of the eyes.

Recurring sinusitis.

Lump in the throat, worse on empty swallowing, worse at night or on waking, worse heat and better from cold.

Clears throat before speaking.

GASTROINTESTINAL

Craves: **Salt. Fat.** Eggs. Fruit. Milk. Sweets. **Spicy foods. Chocolate.** Onions and garlic. Ham fat. Meat. Butter.

Aversion: Fat.

Desires cold drinks.

Desires alcoholic drinks.

Abdominal pains, worse 4 to 6 PM.

Abdominal pain, ameliorated by pressure and bending forward, better from hot drinks.

Dry, hard stool.

Burning pain in the ascending colon, "like fire."

Cases of rectal prolapse are reported cured in our literature.

Constipation and inactivity of the colon.

CHEST

Asthma and recurring bronchitis.

Cough, worse talking, laughing, yawning, worse undressing or dressing, worse cold air.

Cough from a tickle in the throat.

Oppression of the chest.

Swelling and tenderness of the breasts before menses.

UROGENITAL

Sex drive increased.

Too frequent or early masturbation.

Ovarian cysts.

Menses early.

EXTREMITIES

Weakness, numbness and aching especially in the thighs.

Twitching of muscles.

Pain in legs, ameliorated from heat and gentle exertion.

SLEEP

- **Sleeps in the knee-chest position** *(Med)* or on the right side.
  Insomnia.
  Sleeplessness in children, ameliorated from being rocked to sleep.
  Sleepless from thoughts.
  Waking early or at 4 AM.
  Greatly refreshed from short naps.

SKIN

- **Moles and nevi.**
  Itch worse from undressing.
  Acne on face, back and chest.
  Boils.
  Ecchymosis.

CLINICAL

Abscess. Acne. Allergy. Asthma. Bronchitis. Chronic fatigue syndrome. Colitis. Constipation. Cough. Developmental delay. Diabetes. Dysmenorrhea. Headaches. Immune deficiency. Insomnia. Moles. Nevi. Ovarian cysts. Premenstrual syndrome. Rectal prolapse. Respiratory illness. Sinusitis. Tics.

COMPARISONS

Med - Passionate, high sex-drive, general amelioration at the sea, general amelioration in the evening, craves sweets, fat, salt, and cold drinks, sleeps in the knee-chest position, clearing the throat, asthma and allergy.

Tub - Passionate, loves travel, well-selected remedies fail, high sex-drive, blue sclera, respiratory illness, craving ham fat, milk, and salty foods, general aggravation at the sea.

Nux-V - Passionate, highly sexed, fastidious, craves fat, spicy and alcohol, insomnia, constipation and digestive complaints, twitches.

Ars - Fear about cancer, fastidious, generally worse at the sea, craving fat and alcohol, insomnia, digestive and respiratory complaints.

Sep - Loves storms, loves dancing, general aggravation at the sea, general aggravation from 4 to 6 PM, craves vinegar, constipation with inactivity of the colon.

Phos - Sympathetic, sleep ameliorates, craves fat, chocolate, spicy, salt, cough, ovarian cysts, increased sex-drive.

Calc-P. Nat-M. Caust. Staph. Con. Sanic.

CARDUUS MARIANUS

Carduus is a remedy mainly for disease of the liver: gallbladder stones or colic, acute hepatitis, chronic liver disorders, and even cirrhosis may respond to this remedy.

GENERALS

Jaundice can be marked.

Venous stasis due to portal congestion causing varices of esophagus, lower extremities, spider angioma, etc.

GASTROINTESTINAL

- **Pain in liver most marked when lying on the left side.**

Abdominal or liver pain, worse from deep inspiration, worse from any motion.

Aching pain in the liver or gallbladder, worse motion.

Tongue coated white in the center but red at the edges and tip.

Enlarged and inflamed liver, especially the left lobe.

Ascites.

Hematemesis.

Hemorrhoids.

Clay-colored stool.

EXTREMITIES

Varicosities; varicose ulcers.

COMPARISONS

Ptel. Chel. Lyc. Chin. Mag-M.

CASTOR EQUI

A specific remedy in mastitis or inflammatory conditions of the nipples which result in deep and painful cracks and even ulceration.

COMPARISONS

Graph. Phyt. Sil. Nit-Ac.

CAULOPHYLLUM

Caulophyllum acts primarily on the uterus and to a lesser extent on the joints and muscles. It is one of our best remedies in labor and is especially useful for arrested labor.

GENERALS

Inner trembling is one of Nash's indications for this remedy.

Generally chilly and worse cold.

Hysteria, weakness, changeable moods during labor.

GENITALIA

Inertia of the uterus; metrorrhagia or excessive bleeding post-partum due to weak uterine musculature.

- **Labor delayed**; the cervix remains rigid and the contractions (which feel violent to the patient) have no coordination and may change in location. Thus the labor is ineffectual.

Afterpains.

Miscarriage in the first trimester.

Threatened abortion, may stop the abortion or promote a healthy expulsion of the embryo if miscarriage is inevitable.

Infertility.

Amenorrhea.

Violent menstrual pains with drawing in the thighs (even to the feet).

Leukorrhea.

Extremities

- **Arthritis of the fingers** or toes. Especially if the fingers are the only joints affected *(Causticum is usually more generalized)*.

Joint pains worse before menses and ameliorated after the flow.

CLINICAL

Arthritis. Dysmenorrhea. Infertility. Labor - arrested or ineffective. Leukorrhea. Metrorrhagia. Miscarriage. Vaginitis.

COMBINED SYMPTOMS

Joint pains *and* menstrual disorders or miscarriages.

COMPARISONS

Caust. Cimic. Puls. Sabin. Xanth. Vib.

CAUSTICUM

As with any polycrest, Causticum can affect all organ systems. The main areas of concentration, however, are the nervous system and the connective tissues. There is often a history of slowly progressive debility, stiffness, and - if the pathology is strong - paralysis.

The character of Causticum is serious, intense, and sensitive. The patient is often exceedingly sympathetic - crying from hearing news bulletins or from seeing unfortunate people or creatures. This sympathy may also take the form of social activism with an intolerance of injustice and a hatred of those who create injustice. The Causticum patient may be rebellious even to the point of violent political extremism.

If the pathology progresses to the mental plane, we can find great mental dullness and forgetfulness. This dullness produces in the patient a great anxiety that he will forget something. Finally a type of compulsive neurosis can occur. The patient feels absolutely compelled to check and recheck for dangerous mental lapses (i.e. he checks to see if he has turned off the stove and then has to recheck a short time later).

Children. Causticum children are sensitive and excitable. They are extremely aware of others and sympathetic for the suffering of others. The emotions are very intensely felt. A Causticum child may burst into tears from a slight provocation. There can be many fears in Causticum children, especially of the dark. Compulsive and perfectionistic behavior may also occur. The teenagers are rebellious and highly idealistic.

MENTALS

- **Sincere, very intense, idealistic patients.**
- **Great sympathy. Unable to tolerate other's suffering.**
- **Great anger over injustices** toward himself or others (example: a fellow worker's mistreatment, or the plight of Hispanics).

Incensed. Much anger or concern about the environment.

- **Rebellious. Pollitical.** Hates authority. Self-righteous.

Complaints from grief; often there is a history of many repeated griefs. Alcoholism after grief. Depression.

- **Checking and rechecking tasks compulsively.**

Stammering, especially when excited.

- **Fear that "something bad will happen."**

Fears: Dark. Dogs or other animals. Ghosts.

Overly-sensitive children; weep from trifles.

Mental dullness and forgetfulness.

Hurriedness; eats fast; rushes in tasks.

History of sexual abuse or violence in the family.

GENERALS

Chilly and worse from cold.

• **Prefer and ameliorated by cloudy, wet or rainy weather.**

General and local aggravation from drafts.

General aggravation at 4 PM.

General aggravation from suppressed eruptions (neurological, etc.).

Pains often described as a "cut" or "wound." Also may have the sensation of a "rock" internally.

Appearance: lean, dark and intense; may be very refined.

NEUROLOGICAL

Paralysis, especially of flexor muscles, especially on right side.

Slowly progressive paralysis.

Paralysis: cerebral accidents or neuro-degenerative disorders.

Chorea worse in sleep, worse on the right side.

Seizure disorder; generalized convulsions, worse in sleep, worse during menses, worse on right side of body.

Petit mal.

Twitching, jerking, tremor, convulsions after fright or grief.

Numbness of the left side of the body.

HEAD

Eruptions on face, especially the •tip of the nose *(Aeth)*.

Warts on the nose, eyelids.

Right-sided facial neuralgia, worse from wind.

Right-sided Bell's palsy, worse from cold winds *(Acon)*.

Paralysis of the tongue.

Heaviness or paralysis of eyelids.

Strabismus.

Twitches of the face.

Temporomandibular joint disease or spasms, worse on right side.

Sinusitis.

Eruptions in the occipital region.

Acne. Rosacea.

THROAT

• **Constant desire to clear the throat.** Feels there is mucous in the throat which he clears only with difficulty.

Hoarseness, worse with almost every cold, worse in the morning, worse from over-use, better from cold drinks.

Constant desire to swallow.

Paralysis of esophagus.

Torticollis.

GASTROINTESTINAL

Cravings: **Salty. Bacon and smoked meats.** Cheese. Eggs.

Aversion: **◆Sweets.**

Stomach pains, ameliorated by cold drinks *(Phos)*.

Constipation, better from standing. Stool covered with mucous.

Rectal fissure.

UROGENITAL

◆ **Incontinence of urine from cough or sneeze**, especially in older women. Stress incontinence.

Paralysis of the bladder; retention from long holding of the urine.

Frequent urging to urinate.

Enuresis (may last even into adult years).

Insensible loss of urine.

Impotence.

Aversion to coition in women.

Loss of pleasure even if orgasm occurs in men or women.

CHEST

◆ **Coughs deeper and deeper** trying to reach the mucous.

Cough, better by cold drinks, worse bending forward.

Bronchitis with hard racking cough.

Raw feeling in the chest, or "as if a rock" were inside.

Asthma arises in situations of intense or suppressed emotions.

Asthma worse from exertion.

BACK

Low back pain and sciatica.

Cervical tension. Spondylosis. Torticollis.

EXTREMITIES

Rheumatic complaints, worse cold, worse over-use and strain, worse bathing, worse dry weather.

Arthritis of the hands and fingers; ulnar deviation.

Right deltoid pain.

Gout.

Restless legs at night in bed.

Cramps of the calves and feet.

Carpal tunnel syndrome.

Slowly progressive paralysis.

Ataxia; dragging foot while walking.

Contractures of muscles and tendons. Hard, indurated tendons.

Warts on hands and especially near the ◆fingernails.

SKIN

Warts.

Herpes. Eczema. Acne. Boils.

CLINICAL

Abscess. Acne. Alcoholism. Allergy. Anxiety. Arthritis. Asthma. Ataxia. Bell's palsy. Bronchitis. Carpal tunnel syndrome. Cerebral accidents. Chorea. Compulsive disorder. Constipation. Contracture. Cough. Dysphagia. Eczema. Enuresis. Fibrositis. Gout. Herpes. Impotence. Low back pain. Multiple sclerosis. Myalgia. Neuralgia. Neuro-degenerative disorders. Parkinson's disease. Rheumatism. Sciatica. Seizure disorder. Sexual dysfunction. Sinusitis. Tendonitis. Tics. Torticollis. Tremor. Urinary incontinence. Vaginitis. Warts.

COMPLEMENTARY

Coloc. Staph.

INIMICAL

Phos.

COMPARISONS

Phos - Sympathy, fear of something bad happening, of dark, etc., chest congestions, desires cold drinks, hoarseness, rheumatism, neurological disorders.

Sep - Sexual dysfunction, urinary incontinence, chilly, anxious, weeping, thin and dark.

Calc-P - Dissatisfied, chilly and worse drafts, rheumatism and neck pain, craves smoked flavored food.

Staph. Plb. Tub. Nat-M. Nux-V.

CEANOTHUS

This is a remedy to be thought of in cases affecting the lymphatic system or blood cells including conditions such as polycythemia or leukemia, especially when there is ♦marked or huge **enlargement and tenderness of the spleen.** Eric Sommerman of Minneapolis reported (in the International Foundation for Homeopathy case conference 1992) a dramatic cure of a case of Hodgkin's disease beginning with Ceanothus.

CEDRON

When we see complaints of a periodic nature where the •**symptoms return at exactly the same hour every day**, we must strongly consider Cedron. Especially the complaints may come at 9 AM.

CLINICAL

Fever. Headache. Malaria and recurrent fever. Neuralgia.

COMPARISONS

Nat-N. Chin. Chin-S.

CHAMOMILLA

Chamomilla is characterized by an unsurpassed hypersensitivity to pain and an angry, almost accusatory response to that pain. Often the patient seems to complain of more discomfort than could possibly be felt from the existing condition. Furthermore the complaining is usually hostile and vehement. There is always irritability running through the case. Sometimes this irritability is of the nerves rather than the mind, causing an overly-strong reaction to stimuli - as if the nerve itself is on edge. Although it may be used for deep and chronic conditions, Chamomilla is most commonly used as a remedy of childhood acute disorders. Whenever a case or a syndrome is accompanied by great irritability and anger (or if the complaint is initiated by anger), we must consider Chamomilla (*Staph*, *Coloc*, *Nux-V*).

MENTALS

Anger. Great irritability.

- **Irritable infants or children,** they may even strike or kick at the parent (or doctor).
- **Must be carried**; cries angrily if put down and parents must walk up and down to quiet him.
- **Inconsolable** children and infants.
- **Aversion to being touched.** Shies angrily away from being touched.
- **Capricious; demands something then throws it away** (often at someone) no sooner than he receives it.
- **Fear of wind.**
- **Abnormally sensitive to pain.**

Weeping in the sleep.

Restlessness.

GENERALS

- **Over-sensitive to pain; pains seem unbearable.**
  Complaints after anger (fever, metrorrhagia, pains).
- **Complaints during teething**: diarrhea, fever, irritable.
- **General aggravation at 9 AM** (or 9 to 10 PM).
  Aggravation at night.
  Warm-blooded, though many local complaints better by heat.
  General aggravation from coffee.
  Spasm and even convulsive activity, especially in children.
  General aggravation from wind.
  Many authors speak of pains with numbness as a keynote *(Gnaph)*.

HEAD

- **One cheek red, one cheek pale.**
  Acute or chronic otitis media *(Puls, Merc)*.
  Ear pain worse touch, worse from wind.
  Facial neuralgia.
  Heat in face or eyes.
  Face perspiring after eating.
  Toothache: worse coffee, worse warm things, worse anger, better from cold drinks.
- **Painful or difficult dentition and teething.**

GASTROINTESTINAL

- **Diarrhea during teething.**
  Stool with "rotten egg" odor.
- **Stool like cut grass or spinach.**
  Colic.
  Abdominal pain, worse touch, worse coffee.
  Relieves the nausea and vomiting from narcotic use.
  Thirsty for cold drinks.

UROGENITAL

- Uterine hemorrhage after anger.
  Severe dysmenorrhea, pains may extend to thighs *(Vib, Xanth)*.
  Severe labor pains, markedly irritable.

CHEST

Cough, especially dry cough, worse 9 to 12 at night.
Breath-holding in angry children.
Croup. Bronchitis.
Asthma.

EXTREMITIES

Feet hot and must be put out of covers at night.

- "Arthritic pains, worse night in bed, ameliorated by walking about," is often quoted as an indication.

Osteomyelitis.

SLEEP

Restless sleep, wakes often.

Weeping in sleep.

ACUTES

- Otitis media - child wakes at night crying, inconsolable, angry and must be carried (often provoking late night calls waking the doctor), won't tolerate being touched or examined, hysterical when physician attempts to look in the ear.
- Teething - irritable infants, sore gums, often provokes diarrhea.
- Colic - child inconsolable, arches back, cries angrily.

Fever - one-sided chill, face flushed on one cheek, perspiration of covered parts and of scalp, thirsty, restlessness and irritability.

CLINICAL

Asthma. Behavior problem. Colic. Cough. Dentition. Diarrhea. Dysmenorrhea. Fever. Menopausal flushes. Metrorrhagia. Neuralgia. Osteomyelitis. Otitis Media. Premenstrual syndrome. Toothache.

COMPLEMENTARY

Calc.

INIMICAL

Sulph.

COMPARISONS

Cina - Irritable children, aversion to being touched, capricious, must be carried.

Calc-P - Irritable, complaining, inconsolable, head sweat, teething problems.

Ant-C - Irritable children, averse to touch, diarrhea, warm-blooded.

Puls. Sulph. Rheum. Hep. Nux-V. Coloc.

CHELIDONIUM

Although primarily thought of as a liver remedy, Chelidonium is useful in a wide variety of right-sided conditions. In most cases the symptoms will include or alternate with liver dysfunction or biliousness (for example, headaches or pneumonias are often accompanied by belching or indigestion).

MENTALS

Domineering people.

GENERALS

Right-sided complaints.
Generally worse at 4 AM or worse at 2 or 4 PM.
Jaundice. Neonatal jaundice.
Chilly, worse cold, worse change of weather.
General amelioration after lunch.
General aggravation from motion.

HEAD

Right-sided headache or neuralgia (especially supra-orbital).
Coldness especially of the occiput.
Facial pain radiating to teeth or eye.
◆ Facial neuralgia especially if associated with liver conditions.
Numbness of face, especially right side.
Yellow coating of tongue, often with imprints of teeth.

GASTROINTESTINAL

Right upper quadrant pain: liver or gallbladder.
Abdominal pain radiating through to back.
◆ **Abdominal pain radiating to right scapular region.**
Abdominal pain ameliorated lying left side with legs drawn up.
Abdominal pain ameliorated by eating *(Graph)*.
Abdominal pain extending across the abdomen.
Abdominal pain ameliorated by heat.
Abdominal pain better warm drinks or warm milk.
Abdominal pain ameliorated by stool.
Vomits everything except warm drinks.
Indigestion from fats.
Indigestion, nausea, eructations, flatus.
Cravings: **Cheese. Warm drinks. Milk.**
Aversions: Cheese. Spinach.

CHEST

Right-sided pneumonia with pains through to the back, desire for warm drinks, painful cough, hemoptysis.
Right-sided intercostal neuralgia, worse motion.

EXTREMITIES

Right scapular or shoulder pain (less often left-sided).

Coldness of the fingertips.

Joint pains, especially right-sided.

Stiff, painful neck, especially on the right side.

CLINICAL

Bursitis. Cholecystitis. Cholelithiasis. Gastritis. Hepatitis. Jaundice. Malignancy. Migraine. Nausea. Neuralgia. Pneumonia.

COMPLEMENTARY

Lyc.

COMPARISONS

Lyc - Right-sided complaints, liver and gallbladder disorders, pneumonia, one hand cold, eructations, headache.

Bry - Worse motion, desires warm milk, pneumonia, neuralgia.

Chin. Sang. Sulph.

CHIMAPHILA UMBELLATA

A specific remedy of urinary tract disorders, Chimaphila produces frequent urging, dysuria, and even gross hematuria in cystitis, urethritis, and most especially prostatitis. Chimaphila is nearly a specific for urinary retention in benign prostatic hypertrophy.

UROGENITAL

Retained urine; must press long before urination begins.

- **Retention of urine with enlarged prostate.**

Dysuria. Frequent urging.

Forked stream of urine *(Thuj)*. Urethral stricture.

Prostatitis. Benign prostatic hypertrophy.

- **Sensation of a ball in the perineum.**

COMPARISONS

Cop. Med. Thuj. Sulph. Con. Sep. Sel. Cann-I. Puls. Parier.

CHINA OFFICINALIS

China was the first remedy proved by Hahnemann, but Vithoulkas' observations elucidated the personality of the remedy. The China patient is introverted, intense and "touchy." The internal sensitivity is similar to Natrum Muriaticum; the tendency to take offense is more reminiscent of Nux Vomica. This combination of sensitivity, idealism and extreme touchiness makes China a useful remedy in teenagers. China has great excitability, sometimes described as "nervous erethism." This excitability is sometimes expressed by a "Walter Mitty" tendency - at night the patient lies sleepless with fantasies of heroic deeds or great plans for the future. He is embarrassed by these thoughts on waking the next day.

China has two classic characteristics: complaints which follow loss of body fluids (i.e. hemorrhage, diarrhea, discharge from boils) and periodic fevers. Today, however, we less commonly observe these features in their original forms because of the advent of intravenous therapy, antibiotics, and anti-diarrheals. Children of parents who have suffered from malarial conditions and were treated with quinine drugs, may require Cinchona. China affects mainly the intestines and liver, and less often the head and extremities, producing migraines, neuralgias and musculoskeltal problems.

MENTALS

Irritable, sensitive, "touchy."
"Walter Mitty" thoughts in the evening or at night in bed.
Fear of animals, even •domesticated animals. Dogs.
Gloomy, morose. Depressed. Mood swings.
Mistakes in speech and writing.
Sensitive to stimuli, especially noise.
Poetic. Artistic.
Touchy, moody, sarcastic, idealistic teenagers.

GENERALS

• **Fluid loss aggravates** - hemorrhage, diarrhea, nursing, pus, etc.
• **Periodicity, especially every two or seven days.**
Generally worse in foggy or cold, damp weather.
General aggravation in the autumn.
General aggravation from touch.
General and local amelioration from hard pressure.
Aversion to touch, especially light touch.
Anemia.
General aggravation from drafts.
Debility, weakness, collapse, pallor.
Night sweats.

Head

Headache ameliorated from hard pressure.

Headache which is neuralgic in quality.

Headache worse hemorrhage, worse while lying, better standing.

Headache periodically, every day, every second or seventh day.

Headache with gallbladder or liver disorders.

Tinnitus with headache.

Brain feels loose as if striking the sides of the skull.

Sensitivity of scalp, even to the touch of the hair *(Sel)*.

Facial or ciliary neuralgia.

Sensitivity to odors.

Epistaxis.

Cold sweat of face, especially about the nose and upper lip.

Bitter taste in the mouth; food or tobacco tastes bitter.

Gastrointestinal

- **Bloated, distended, flatulent but with no relief from eructation or expelling gas.**

Gallbladder disease. Galbladder colic.

Frequent rumbling, eructation, and flatus.

Diarrhea worse from fish, fruit, milk. Colitis.

Periodic diarrhea. Chronic diarrhea.

Cramping abdominal pains, better bending double, worse with chill.

Hepatitis, even cirrhosis. Hepatomegaly.

Splenomegaly.

Gastritis. Hematemesis.

Anorexia. Appetite decreased but returns after the first bite.

Great hunger at night and must get up to eat.

Digestion disordered: Fruit. Milk. Fat. Beer.

Cravings: **Sweets.** Salt. Spicy.

Aversion: Hot foods. Fruit. Fat. Butter.

Genitalia

Bloody leukorrhea.

Severe dysmenorrhea.

Metrorrhagia, dark flow. Also cases of amenorrhea.

Tremor with menses.

Chest

Asthma in the fall.

Cough worse laughing, worse lying with head low.

Pneumonia. Bronchitis.

EXTREMITIES

Skin sensitive or painful during fever.

Myalgia, arthralgia worse from touch.

Edema and pitting of the lower extremities with pallor of limb.

One hand cold, the other warm *(Chel, Lyc)*.

Sciatica.

SLEEP

- **Insomnia from excited thoughts and heroic fantasies.**

Insomnia, sleep disturbed by slight noises.

FEVER

- **Periodic fever, malaria, even family history of malaria.**

Chills, rigors alternating with heat.

Hectic fever.

CLINICAL

Anemia. Arthritis. Asthma. Cholecystitis. Chronic fatigue syndrome. Cough. Diarrhea. Fever. Gastritis. Headache. Hepatitis. Influenza. Inflammatory bowel disease. Insomnia. Malaria. Migraine. Myalgia. Neuralgia. Peptic ulcers. Sciatica. Splenomegaly. Vaginitis.

COMPLEMENTARY

Ferr.

COMPARISONS

Nux-V - Irritable, over-sensitive and offended, gastrointestinal symptoms, chilly, neuralgia, aggravated by drafts.

Nat-M - Fever, migraine, sensitive, insomnia, averse to fat.

Lyc. Ign. Ars. Chin-S. Chin-Ars. Carb-V.

CHININUM SULPHURICUM

In most respects this remedy corresponds closely to China Officinalis. There are several symptoms which lead to the preference of Chininum Sulphuricum as noted below. Additionally we may prefer Chininum Sulphuricum if the history indicates a triggering of symptoms which resemble China but which began after taking the sulphate of China either for prophylaxis or treatment of malaria, or to induce abortion.

MENTALS

Fear of evil or of misfortune.

Fear of animals.

Anxiety for others; anxiety about finances.

Similar mental symptoms to China.

GENERALS

Periodicity, symptoms at the same hour daily, especially 3 PM.

Recurrent daily fever. Strikingly high temperature. Chills, rigors.

May feel better during the recurrent fevers.

Weakness and debility, especially from fluid loss.

Fever of unknown origin.

Appearance: Thin face with dark circles about eyes. Face has the appearance of chronic suffering.

HEAD

Meniere's syndrome *(Cocc, Phos, Sil)*.

Tinnitus, worse during a chill, worse during vertigo.

Headache comes on during sleep, especially at 3 AM.

Heat in the head during the headache, better cold applications.

Head pain better from hard pressure.

Headache with digestive disturbance.

Dark circles about eyes.

GASTROINTESTINAL

Aching in the liver or spleen, worse during a chill.

MUSCULOSKELETAL

Great sensitivity of spine.

◆ Cannot lean back in the chair due to sensitivity.

Pain in the spine, worse from inspiration, worse touch.

◆ Acute arthritis, especially if associated with erythema nodosum.

SKIN

Erythema nodosum.

CLINICAL

Arthritis. Erythema Nodosum. Fever. Headache. Lumbago. Meniere's syndrome. Malaria. Migraine. Neuralgia. Recurring fever.

COMPARISONS

Cedr. Chin. Phos. Sal-Ac.

CHLORALUM

Chloralum is a remedy to be thought of when we see a combination of •**skin disorders and intense insomnia.** Generally thought of in urticarial conditions, worse from wine; burning urticaria.

CHLORUM

Chlorum is a rarely prescribed remedy which is used most often in respiratory conditions, especially laryngospasm. There is a constriction of the glottis which produces stridor and a suffocating sensation; said to be worse during expiration though also on inspiration, worse from sleep.

CICUTA

Cicuta is a remedy for the nervous system. It is indicated in cases of epilepsy and in mental retardation. The mental state is characterized by childishness and over-excitement. The convulsions of Cicuta are among the most violent found in any remedy and often accompanied by opisthotonos, or bizarre contortions. Often there is unconsciousness, sleeping, or a dull dream-like postictal state following the convulsion continuing for an inordinately long period of time - even a whole day. Sometimes there are multiple convulsions following closely one upon the other.

MENTALS

Childishness; patient feels like a child.
Retardation after head injury.
Aversion to company.
Delirium. Dementia.
Anxiety and suspicion. Anxious before the convulsion.

NEUROLOGICAL

• **Violent convulsions: •Contortions. Opisthotonos.**
Convulsions after head injuries *(Arn, Nat-S, Hyper).*
Shrieking before the convulsion.
Convulsions worse from heat, during sleep, being touched, noises.
Tetanus, eclampsia, meningitis with convulsions.
Petit mal, blank for long periods.
Sudden, strong jerks and spasms. Chorea.

HEAD

Head drawn backward; spasms of the cervical spine.

- **Frightful contortions of face during convulsions.**

Eruptions on head; pustules which burn and coalesce forming thick yellow scabs on the face or scalp.

Biting of the tongue during convulsions.

Shocks in the head.

Idiotic expression on the face.

Strabismus.

GASTROINTESTINAL

Craving inedible things - dirt or charcoal.

Shocks in the abdomen.

Vomiting during or alternating with convulsion.

MUSCULOSKELETAL

Opisthotonos. Arching of the back.

Spasms and twitches of the extremities.

Shock sensation in the limbs.

CLINICAL

Convulsion. Head injury. Mental retardation. Opisthotonos. Pustule on scalp. Seizure disorder. Strabismus. Twitches and spasms.

COMPARISONS

Art-V. Cupr. Bar-M. Bufo.

CIMICIFUGA

Actaea Racemosa - as listed in Kent's materia medica - is a remedy affecting mainly the nerves and muscles. Often the patient comes with a main complaint of pain which is not clearly diagnosable and which seems to have characteristics both of a neuralgia and of rheumatism. The location of the pain is usually in the muscles themselves - the neck, back, and uterus being very common sites. The quality of the pains is often sharp or stitching - very reminiscent of the pains of Berberis.

The Cimicifuga patient is excitable, extroverted, and forceful. Usually we find great loquacity and jumping from subject to subject. The emotions are vivid and hysterical in nature. The patient suffers with strong phobias - death, insanity, injury. Also in a later stage which usually follows a set-back of some kind, the patient may become gloomy or even suicidal.

MENTALS

Loquacity; changes from one subject to the next.

Sighing.

Great dullness or fogginess of mind during headache.

Hysteria.

Changeable mood.

Gloomy, morose. Everything seems wrong in her life.

Fears: **Insanity.** Death. Murder.

GENERALS

Chorea, worse menses, worse from pressure, worse on side being lain upon, associated with rheumatism.

General aggravation from menses.

General aggravation from cold or drafts.

General aggravation after injury to the spine.

HEAD

Severe headaches, especially in the vertex or radiating to or from the cervical region.

- **Severe headache and dullness of mind associated with extreme cervical stiffness.**

Pressing outward from the vertex, or a fullness sensation.

Headache as if the top of the head would open up or "fly off."

Headache with pain in the eyes, worse motion of the eyes.

Stitching pains in the eyes.

GASTROINTESTINAL

Sinking sensation in the epigastrium.

GENITALIA

Severe dysmenorrhea, worse as the flow increases.

Cramping, shooting pains across pelvis or into thighs during labor, after delivery; changeable pains.

Failure to progress in labor. Retained placenta.

Menses irregular and may be suppressed by emotions or stress.

Neuralgic pains in the ovaries.

BACK

Severe cervical pain, almost a neuralgia; stiffness and drawing in the neck. Neck spasms.

Fibrositis. Spasms of the paraspinal muscles.

Sciatica.

Injuries to the spine.

EXTREMITIES

Rheumatism affecting especially the muscles.

Chorea.

Stitching pains, darting about, worse cold damp weather.

Arthritic pains, worse cold.

Muscle twitches.

CLINICAL

Anxiety. Arthritis. Cervical stiffness. Chorea. Depression. Dysmenorrhea. Fibrositis. Hysteria. Labor. Migraine. Neuralgia. Phobic disorder. Rheumatism. Sciatica. Twitches.

COMBINED SYMPTOMS

- Rheumatism *and* loquacity.
- Rheumatism *and* dysmenorrhea.

Hysteria *and* back or neck spasm.

COMPARISONS

Caul. Lach. Ign. Calc-P. Phos. Arg-N. Lac-C.

CINA

Although the routine use of remedies is not recommended, it is easy to understand the enthusiasm some older homeopaths had for Cina in the treatment of worms, especially pinworms. On observing a child with pinworms one sees a great restlessness and an almost frantic state of mind, also marked irritability, and a tremendous urge for scratching and boring occur. Such are the characteristics of Cina, and thus the strong association of this remedy in the treatment of these parasites.

Cina is mainly a remedy needed during childhood. The typical child is irritable in the extreme, perhaps even more so than Chamomilla. He cannot stand to be touched or even looked at or held. He cannot be quieted and is very capricious. He may even strike or more often pinch or scratch the parents when frustrated. The anger can lead to tantrums and even to convulsions. The child may be precocious and hard; he cannot be reprimanded and will not tolerate parental authority.

Convulsions are a strong part of this remedy. The nervous system is irritated which may lead to meningitis or epilepsy. Spasms of all parts of the body occur.

MENTALS

Angry, striking, pinching children *(Cham)*.

Aversion to being touched (and yet may demand to be carried).

- **Convulsions from being scolded or disciplined.**

Shrieking.

NEUROLOGICAL

- **Convulsions associated in any way with worms.**

Convulsions or spasms from being touched, from being scolded.

HEAD

- **Pale or bluish discoloration around the mouth.**

Face pale with fine, almost translucent skin which shows the veins.

Pale face even during fever.

Hot flush and redness of face.

Sees colors before the eyes.

Many authors emphasize a tendency for yawning.

- **Irresistible urge to bore in the nose with the fingers.**

Grinds teeth in sleep.

GASTROINTESTINAL

Gurgling in the esophagus from cough or when swallowing.

Cramping and diarrhea; wants to lie in the knee-chest position or over the mother's shoulder; better pressure.

Many cravings and yet insatiable.

Averse to mother's milk.

- **Worms in the stool; pinworms. Itching rectum.**

CHEST

Gagging from the cough; violent cough with spasms of the limbs.

Pertussis.

EXTREMITIES

Spasms of the hands and feet.

Warts.

CLINICAL

Behavior disorders. Bruxism. Colic. Diarrhea. Fever. Otitis media. Pertussis. Seizure disorders. Worms, especially pinworms.

Comparisons

Cham. Arum-T. Med.

CINNABARIS

Mercury sulphide is by tradition listed under the name Cinnabaris. The majority of the symptoms of this remedy are very closely allied to Mercurius Solubulis. We especially think of Cinnabaris in cases which demonstrate the typical Mercury symptoms but in which there is a predominance of the genital or rectal lesions so typical of Cinnabaris.

HEAD

Fullness and congestion, especially in the vertex and forehead.
Pains radiating from the area of the inner canthus to the forehead.
Sinusitis of ethmoid and frontal sinuses.

GENITALIA

◆ **Rectal condylomata**. Genital condylomata.
Condyloma of the foreskin.
Balanitis. Pus under the foreskin.
Ulcers of the penis.
Swollen inguinal glands.

SKIN

Condyloma shaped like a fan; bleed easily.

CLINICAL

Balanitis. Condylomata. Phimosis. Sinusitis.

COMPARISONS

Nit-Ac. Thuj. Nat-S. Merc.

CISTUS CANADENSIS

This is a remedy primarily to be considered in cases of chronic rhinitis, sinusitis, and recurrent upper respiratory illness. Cistus is easily confused with Calcarea because the patient is often chilly, fatigued, and can be flabby in some cases.

GENERALS

Chilly, worse from cold or cold air.
Cold sensation: mouth, throat, stomach, etc.
General aggravation in the winter.

NOSE

Chronic rhinitis and sinusitis.

- **Burning or icy cold sensation in the nose and pharynx, worse inhaling, especially inhaling cold air.**

Recurring upper respiratory illness.

Thick, yellowish discharges.

Violent paroxysms of sneezing, worse inhaling cold air.

THROAT

Chronic post-nasal drip.

Burning in the throat, worse from inhaling. Tonsillitis.

Dryness of the throat, ameliorated by swallowing.

Cervical adenopathy; strings of glands in neck.

STOMACH

Craving for cheese.

EXTREMITIES

Coldness of extremities.

Chilblains; cracked and bleeding fingertips in winter.

CLINICAL

Cervical adenitis. Chilblains. Malignancy. Recurring colds. Sinusitis.

COMPARISONS

Sil. Calc. Psor. Carb-An.

CLEMATIS

The primary focus of Clematis is on the urogenital system, and to a lesser extent on the skin. Clematis is also a specific remedy for toothache.

HEAD

Toothache; worse from hot drinks, better by holding cold water in the mouth or by drawing in cold air over the tooth.

Conjunctivitis. Coryza. Sneezing.

UROLOGICAL

Cystitis; burning pain at onset of flow.

Urination incomplete or interrupted. Involuntary urination.

Genitalia

Orchitis, especially right testicle.

- **Drawing upward of the testes.**

Orchitis, especially after suppressed gonorrhea.
Stoney hard swelling of testes. Painful swelling, worse at night.
Urethritis. Urethral stricture. Prostatitis.
Swollen inguinal glands.

Skin

Burning vesicular eruptions; eczema.
Eruption worse from washing.

Clinical

Allergy. Conjunctivitis. Cystitis. Eczema. Orchitis. Toothache.

Combined Symptoms

Orchitis *and* skin symptoms.

Comparisons

Puls. Arg-M. Rhod. Rhus-T. Med. Canth.

COBALTUM

Cobaltum is to be thought of any time we see the combination of nocturnal emissions and back trouble *(Nat-P, Staph, Nit-Ac, Sel)*. The back pain and sciatica are ameliorated by lying and worse from sitting and may be accompanied by weakness or pains in the legs. It is also a remedy to be considered in the treatment of impotence.

Combined symptoms

- **Low back pain or sciatica *and* nocturnal emissions.**

COCA

Although we expect to find strong symptoms produced by the abuse of this substance, the particular mental pathology has not yet been identified. Hering and Kent have emphasized bashfulness and timidity.

Coca

Generals

- **Altitude sickness**; breathless, headache, weak in high altitudes.
  Buzzing in the ears.

Respiratory

Emphysema and dyspnea from slight exertion.
Dyspnea in elderly patients.

Genitalia

Impotence. Loss of libido.

Skin

- **Formication.** Sensation as if a grain of sand under the skin.

COCCULUS

Cocculus is a remedy affecting mainly the central nervous system and in most cases there is at least some component of vertigo. It is a remedy to be thought of in cases of progressive neurological disorders. In these serious and rather introverted people, there is often a fundamental weakness of the nervous system. This weakness is generally reflected first as an over-excitability of the nerves producing restlessness, dizziness, and agitation. Later, as the system becomes more dysfunctional, the nerve conduction becomes distorted and delayed. The patient then becomes weak and confused. In the end-stage, pinpricks may require a full second to register on the patient who is in a nearly stupefied state.

On the psychological level, we see a strong tendency to anxiety during the early stages. The teen-aged girls, often described in our texts as "romantic and sensitive" are extremely tense and often suffer with dysmenorrhea. The patient's anxiety revolves about his responsibilities and health. The patient is concerned about both his own health and that of loved ones. This anxiety, along with the weakness of the nervous system explains the most famous keynote symptom: "Aggravation from night-watching." With loss of sleep and worry about the health of a loved-one, the patient breaks down with headache, dizzy spells and weakness. Anytime intense concern for the physical or mental well-being of another person causes a sense of overwhelm and deep pathology in our patient, we must consider Cocculus. Symptoms develop from any type of stress or grief. Finally, in more broken-down cases we find a state which is similar to Helleborous or Alumina with great passivity, dullness of mind and slowed reactions.

Mentals

- **Bad effects from grief, anger or from nursing a sick loved-one.**

Exhausted and sick from anxiety over a loved-one.

Slow mental processes. Time passes quickly. Stupefaction.

Anxiety and nervousness.

Anxiety about health; asks to be tested to rule-out diseases.

Sadness and grief.

Sensitive, sympathetic and delicate. "Sensitive and romantic girls."

Generals

- **Generally worse from loss of sleep; even an hour deficit.**
- **General aggravation from "night-watching" which means from worrying and caring for others.**

Sensitivity to alcohol, causing great confusion.

Fainting, often with hysteria.

Stretching in bed at night.

Sleepless from worry; cannot relax from his worries.

Neurological

Slowed nerve conduction; has nearly a full second delay before perceiving a pin-prick *(Alum, Plb).*

Chorea, especially of the legs. Convulsions.

Paralytic stiffness of parts that have been at rest. He groans as the part is moved then can move it normally. Cannot open the eyes on waking, etc.

Progressive paralysis, as in multiple sclerosis. Ataxia.

Vertigo

- **True vertigo, the world seems to spin.**

Must lie down from the severity of the vertigo; nausea on attempting to rise.

- **Motion-sickness** (nausea, diarrhea, etc.). **Seasickness.**
- **Great vertigo on watching moving objects or when watching objects while he is riding in a car or train.**

Feels as if intoxicated or as if separated from his body.

Vertigo worse for sitting, worse from loss of sleep.

Head

Headache and migraines, worse from riding in a car, worse from loss of sleep, worse from alcohol.

Facial neuralgia.

Tongue feels thick and paralyzed.

Gastrointestinal

Great nausea, worse from motion or during vertigo.

Nausea at the mere thought or smell of food.

"Liver pain and swelling, worse from anger." is considered a keynote by many authors.

Abdominal pains as from stones rubbed together or sensation of a stone in the umbilicus has been emphasized by some authors.

Urogenital

Severe dysmenorrhea, weakness during menses.

Profuse menses, worse from standing or walking.

Uterine inflammations or growths.

Back

Weak, paralyzed feeling in low back, worse menses.

Weakness of the neck, as if he cannot hold up his head.

Trembling in the back.

Extremities

Numbness of hands or feet, or alternating between hands and feet.

Paralysis, especially or first felt in the lower extremities.

Tremor of the hands, worse eating, worse raising the hands.

Cracking of knees on motion.

Red spots on the skin with great itching, worse at night in bed.

Clinical

Anxiety. Chronic fatigue syndrome. Depression. Dysmenorrhea. Headache. Low back pain. Migraine. Motion or sea-sickness. Multiple sclerosis. Nausea. Neuro-degenerative disorders. Vertigo.

Comparisons

Alum. Con. Nat-M. Phos. Calc. Caust. Staph. Puls. Ph-Ac. Hell.

COCCUS CACTI

Almost all the symptoms which typify this remedy are referable to its effect over coughs. These paroxysmal coughs come on especially in the winter or from exposure to cold. It is one of our best pertussis remedies. Coccus Cacti is also considered a remedy in kidney colic.

Cough

Paroxysms of cough.

Cough from tickling or irritation in the larynx.

Cough worse at 6 AM, 11 or 11:30 PM.

Cough better drinking, especially cold drinks *(Caust, Cupr)*.

Cough worse from a warm room or by warm food or drinks.

Cough better cold or open air.

The cough produces copious, thick or ropey mucous *(Kali-Bi)*, often associated with retching or vomiting.

May also have tickling dry cough. Choking cough.

Whooping cough. Bronchitis. Croup.

Comparisons

Rumex. Spong. Dros. Caust. Kali-Bi.

COFFEA

The effect of the crude substance coffee - wakefulness and improved alertness- has been exploited by every college student. Many of these can also attest to the accompanying nervousness, restlessness, and over-sensitivity to stimuli which occurs when coffee is used in excess. The Coffea type is therefore highly sensitive, nervous and over-reactive. There can be a weakness of will or excessive tolerance similar to Staphysagria wherein the patient is suppressed or even abused by his family or spouse. The excitement of mind can go to extreme ecstatic states. But when the mind becomes overstimulated, then pathology develops.

The resulting pathology is generally felt in the nervous system, first with the characteristic insomnia, but also with inflammation of the nerves, neuralgia, and general weakness.

Mentals

Excitement of the mind. The perceptions are acute and the thinking rapid. This results in uncontrollable thoughts and racing mind.

Ecstatic states.

Bad effects from joy or surprise (insomnia, weakness, etc.).

Anything stimulating the nervous system can produce symptoms.

Great sensitivity to noise, taste, and other stimuli.

Great sensitivity to touch.

Ailments from grief. Sympathetic.

Mild, timid and suppressed.

Generals

General aggravation from stimulation or strong emotions.
Strong aggravation or nervousness from drinking coffee.
Often thin and sickly or pinched appearance.
Great fatigue and debility in over-sensitive patients.
Tremor.

Head

Headaches; worse music, worse noise, worse noise of footsteps.
Headache or migraine "as if a nail were driven into head."
Head or face pain, better from cold applications.
Facial neuralgia; worse from noise, worse from excitement.
Tooth pain; better from cold water being held in the mouth.
Tinnitus; buzzing sensation in the head, especially the occiput.

Chest

Emaciation of mammae.
Palpitation from excitement.

Sleep

Insomnia. Wakes from the slightest noise.
Insomnia from racing thoughts and activity of the mind.

Clinical

Chronic fatigue syndrome. Insomnia. Headache. Migraine. Neuralgia. Toothache. Tremor.

Comparisons

Staph. Nat-M. Chin. Sep. Nux-V. Kali-P. Ther.

COLCHICUM

Colchicine has been long known to medicine and is still used as one of the main remedies in gout, by both homeopaths and allopaths alike. Most of the homeopathic uses of this remedy can be traced to its relationship to gout. Thus, most of the symptoms are musculoskeletal, and secondarily renal from the effects of uric acid crystals on the urinary tract. Colchicum also has a strong effect on the digestive tract with nausea, diarrhea, gastritis, and fantastic distention of the abdomen.

GENERALS

General aggravation from cold or cold damp.

General aggravation from changes of weather and therefore worse in the spring (except for the autumn diarrheas).

- **Great sensitivity to odors causing nausea, vomiting, faintness, etc.**

HEAD

Stiffness and coating of the tongue.

GASTROINTESTINAL

Tremendous abdominal distension, trapped gas.

Diarrhea coming especially in the autumn, often clear or jelly-like, or bloody diarrhea.

Painful urging for stool.

Violent retching and vomiting.

Horrible nausea from odors, especially from eggs and fish.

Nausea of pregnancy.

URINARY

Nephritis with great edema.

Dark or even "ink-like" urine.

The urine sediment may alternate with the rheumatic complaints *(Benz-Ac)* or heart symptoms.

EXTREMITIES

Gout with great inflammation of joints; gouty pains worse from the least motion.

Arthritis with "paralytic" pains.

Acute rheumatism.

Wandering arthritis; pains often go from left to right.

Joint pains worse from slight motion *(Bry)*.

CLINICAL

Arthritis. Gastroenteritis. Gout. Nausea of pregnancy. Nephritis.

COMPARISONS

Benz-Ac - Marked gouty tendency, pains worse from motion, urinary disorder and offensive, renal calculi, problems from suppressed urine sediment, tongue painful and coated.

Bry. Berb. Lyc.

COLLINSONIA

Collinsonia is a remedy to be thought of mainly in cases of hemorrhoids and rectal pathology *(Aesc, Rat, Paeon)*.

RECTUM

Hemorrhoids. Rectal fissures.

Sensation that the rectum is full of small, sharp sticks *(Aesc)*.

Constipation and hard stool.

COMBINED SYMPTOMS

Alternation or combination of heart symptoms or palpitations *and* hemorrhoids *(Lycop)*.

COLOCYNTHIS

We must think of Colocynthis any time the case centers around colic. This colic can be of the gallbladder (gallstones), of the ureter (kidney stones), the uterus (dysmenorrhea), but is most often intestinal. Colocynthis is also useful in cases of neuralgia and sciatica. In all of these conditions we can identify certain common aspects: the pains are almost always better from pressure and often ameliorated by bending double and from heat. Usually the patient is very restless with the pain.

The Colocynthis constitutional type is proper and reserved. He has strong opinions of right and wrong. When he is contradicted he may become very upset. This is especially the case if he feels in some way slighted or humiliated. Colocynthis is one of the main remedies which has complaints after becoming angry, indignant or humiliated. The central nervous system mediates a cramp or neuralgia which is a physical metaphor of anger in the nerves.

MENTALS

◆ **Bad effect from anger, indignation, excitement.**

Impatient and easily angered.

GENERALS

Restlessness, especially during the pains.

General and local amelioration from hard pressure.

Aggravation at 6 AM or 4 to 5 PM.

General amelioration from drinking coffee *(Cham, Ign)*.

HEAD

Headache, better from hard pressure, better from coffee.

Left facial neuralgia, worse motion, worse touch, pain in paroxysms, stitching or burning pains.

GASTROINTESTINAL

Abdominal pains ameliorated by pressure, by lying face downward.

- **Abdominal pains ameliorated by bending double.**
- **Abdominal pains worse from anger, indignation, or excitement.**

Severe cutting, cramping pains in the abdomen.

Abdominal pains worse before diarrhea, worse from drinking, better from coffee.

Cramping or contraction around the umbilicus.

Diarrhea and colic, worse from eating, worse from fruit, worse from strong emotions.

Cramps radiating to pubic region.

GENITALIA

Dysmenorrhea, better heat and pressure *(Mag-P)*.

Menses suppressed after anger.

Ovarian pains.

BACK

Back pain, worse from breathing, worse from lying down.

Right-sided sciatica, or less often left-sided sciatica, better lying on the painful side, worse heat of bed.

EXTREMITIES

Cramps of the thighs and calves.

CLINICAL

Abdominal pain. Cholecystitis. Colic of newborns. Dysmenorrhea. Facial neuralgia. Gastroenteritis. Headache. Irritable bowel syndrome. Kidney stones. Neuralgia. Sciatica.

COMPLEMENTARY

Staph. Caust.

COMPARISONS

Staph. Cham. Mag-P. Nux-V.

CONIUM

Conium has deep pathology on many levels. In the nervous system we find serious degenerative disorders. In the sexual sphere we find marked dysfunction. Furthermore, Conium is one of our main remedies to combat malignancy and premalignant conditions. The complaints of Conium originate slowly and progressively. Often the patient is unable to exactly date the onset of the problem. The pathology generally results from progressive paralysis or progressive induration leading toward malignancy.

Vithoulkas has brought to light the deeper emotional essence of the remedy which has been further elaborated by Louis Klein of Vancouver, Canada. The typical patient is practical, earthy and materialistic. The mental pathology occurs from a type of slowly advancing "induration" of the mind. The patient develops an emotional flatness or hardness which eventually leads to indifference and depression. On the mental level we see fixed ideas and superstitions. Eventually we can see progressive mental deterioration, forgetfulness and senility.

MENTALS

Emotionally closed, flat, or hard people.

Mental dullness or confusion. "Brain fag."

Depression.

Anxiety, hysteria, sadness, all from suppression of the sexual instinct (after divorce or death of a spouse).

Superstition.

Senility.

GENERALS

General aggravation from suppression of sexual desires.

◆ **Tumors or induration of glands**, there may be itching in the gland.

Malignancies, or history of breast or other cancers.

◆ Perspiration on closing the eyes.

Weakness and trembling after stool.

Head:

Vertigo, worse lying, worse turning in bed.

Photophobia.

◆ **Lacrimation with photophobia.**

Boring in the nose with finger.

Cancer of the lip, especially in smokers.

Exophthalmus.

Troublesome cerumen.

NECK

Hard, swollen cervical glands.

Exophthalmic goitre.

UROGENITAL

Premature ejaculation, even during the foreplay.

Impotence.

High sexual drive.

Prostatic enlargement or cancer; weight or heaviness felt in the perineum *(Chim, Sep)*.

Prostatic discharge.

Paralysis of the bladder. Urination interrupted despite straining, then flows easily after he relaxes.

Cancer or tumors of the testes, prostate, ovaries, uterus.

Whitish, acrid or bloody leukorrhea.

CHEST

- **Cancer of the breast, hard and often with axillary lymph nodes.**
- **History of breast cancer.**

Swelling and tenderness of the breast before the menses.

Itching of the breast.

Cough, worse on first lying and compelled to sit up.

Cough from tickle or dryness in the larynx.

Extremities

Progressive weakness even to the point of paralysis *(Caust)*, generally beginning in the thighs or legs. Ataxia.

- **Difficulty rising from squatting.**

Numbness.

Clinical

Ataxia. Cervical dysplasia. Cervicitis. Cough. Dementia. Depression. Exophthalmus. Hyperthyroidism. Impotence. Lymphoma. Malignancy. Multiple sclerosis. Neuro-degenerative disorders. Premature ejaculation. Prostatitis. Senility. Sexual dysfunction. Uterine fibroids. Vaginitis. Vertigo.

Complementary

Tub.

Comparisons

Sep. Ph-Ac. Cocc. Carb-An. Caust.

CORALLIUM RUBRUM

We must think of Corallium Rubrum in colds, coughs or coryza when we have the typical food craving for sour (also craving or aversion to salt). Post-nasal mucous is often profuse. The remedy also covers pertussis and chronic low-grade coughs.

Combined Symptoms

Craving for sour *and* allergy or coryza.

CROCUS SATIVUS

Crocus is to be considered any time we find a combination of the typical mental symptoms with vascular or hemorrhage problems. The characteristic of the hemorrhage is dark, stringy clots.

Mentals

Hysteria; alternating moods.
Desires to sing, dance, jump, hug and kiss everyone.
Uncontrollable laughter.
Alternatively is irritable or even violent.

Generals

Hemorrhage with clots which may be held together in a string.

Head

Epistaxis, with clots or strings of clots.
Twitching of lids.

Gastrointestinal

Sensation of something alive or moving in the abdomen *(Thuj)*.
Sensation or delusion of being pregnant.

Genitalia

Metrorrhagia with dark, clotted, offensive blood.

Chest

Palpitations, with the sense of something jumping in the heart.

EXTREMITIES

Chorea and twitches.

Clinical

Arrhythmia. Chorea. Delusion. Epistaxis. Hemorrhage. Hysteria. Metrorrhagia. Tics. Twitches.

COMBINED SYMPTOMS

Hemorrhage *and* hysteria or twitches.

COMPARISONS

Ign. Hyos. Zinc.

CROTALUS CASCAVELLA

Many of the snake venoms have these common symptoms: cardiac symptoms, hypertension, hemorrhage which is dark and often passive, an intolerance to collars. Generally the venoms have left-sided symptoms, though both of the Crotalus remedies have also right-sided symptoms strongly. We can distinguish Crotalus Cascavella from the other venoms by some of the mental symptoms and by the skin disorders.

MENTALS

Delusions and fears of ghosts, spirits, voices.

◆ **Dreams of spiders.**

Memory weak; difficulty in following instructions

Speech difficult; tongue feels thick.

EXTREMITIES

Right-sided paralysis.

SKIN

◆ **Aggressive, burning urticaria which come in crops over a single region of the body.**

CLINICAL

Delusion. Dementia. Dysarthria. Hemorrhage. Paralysis. Urticaria.

COMPARISONS

Manc. Lach. Med. Strych.

CROTALUS HORRIDUS

Crotalus Horridus affects mainly the cardiovascular system and the blood. There is a close resemblance to Lachesis, but with more tendency for hemorrhage and sepsis. The personality of Crotalus Horridus is less intense and aggressive than Lachesis. Often the patient is melancholic and sluggish. The patient has delirium during sepsis or from cerebral accidents.

GENERALS

Wide-spread bleeding - from any orifice, even tears or sweat.

◆ **Sepsis** often with generalized hemorrhage as in disseminated intravascular coagulation.

Bleeding tendency with dark but unclotted blood.

Generally worse during sleep.

Jaundice.

Collapse states.

HEAD

◆ **Retinal hemorrhage** *(Ham, Phos, Lach, Sulph)*.

Varicosities of the face and nose.

Tongue swollen and protruding from the mouth.

Epistaxis.

THROAT

Left-sided pharyngitis, tonsillitis, peritonsillar abscess, diphtheria; the patient cannot swallow, looks nearly septic.

Intolerant to collars.

GASTROINTESTINAL

Craving: **Pork.**

Gastrointestinal bleeding.

CHEST

Angina.

Chest pain, worse while lying on the left side, worse ascending.

Hemoptysis.

EXTREMITIES

Varicosities.

SKIN

Ecchymosis. Purpura.

Erysipelas. Boils. Urticaria.

Clinical

Abscess. Angina. Delirium. Hemorrhage. Myocardial infarction. Pharyngitis. Purpura. Sepsis. Tonsillitis. Varicosities.

Comparisons

Lach - Hemorrhage with dark blood, purple or black lesions, worse tight collars, worse sleep, worse lying left side.

Bapt. Sul-Ac. Sec.

CROTON TIGLIUM

The two areas affected by Croton Tiglium are the skin and intestines.

Generals

Drawing pains as if with a string - nipples, eyes *(Par, Plb)*.

Gastrointestinal

- **Diarrhea which comes in one sudden, urgent gush.**
- **Diarrhea worse immediately after eating or drinking.**

Rumbling and gurgling of the abdomen.

Abdominal pain extending downward toward the rectum.

Abdominal pain better by warm milk *(Ars, Chel, Graph)*.

Urogenital

Vesicular eruptions.

Chest

Pain and drawing in nipples; pain extends from nipples to back.

Pain in the nipples on nursing; pain from touch of clothes.

Skin

Vesicular eruptions with unendurable itching.

Poison oak with eruptions on the genitalia and face.

Rash alternating with diarrhea.

Clinical

Colitis. Dermatitis, especially Rhus poisoning. Diarrhea. Mastitis.

Comparisons

Gamb. Ars. Rhus-T.

CUBEBA

Cubeba is primarily to be thought of in urological conditions and infections (prostatitis, cystitis, etc.). Especially we can be guided to use this remedy when the characteristic **craving for nuts** is found.

CUPRUM

Most of the symptomatology of Cuprum can be highlighted by the great tendency toward convulsion. Cuprum has cramps and spasms which occur in virtually every system: the respiratory system (asthma), the gastrointestinal system (colic and spasmodic vomiting), the musculoskeletal system (leg cramps), but most importantly in the nervous system. Cuprum is the foremost specific remedy for seizure disorders and epilepsy. Vithoulkas described the Cuprum patient as having intense emotions or impulses which are strongly suppressed. To maintain control over strong inner emotions, the patient rigidly closes down every expression. This makes the patient appear absolutely closed. The convulsion and spasms occur from the release of this rigid tension. Eventually, the patient closes so much that he becomes dull and slow, even to the point of senility.

MENTALS

Extremely closed patient.

Mental dullness and slowness.

Mania. Violent behavior.

Fear of fire.

NEUROLOGICAL

- **Convulsions or other neurological problems after suppressed eruptions** *(Cic, Zinc)*.
- **Bellowing or shrieking before the convulsion.**

Convulsion worse at night, worse pregnancy or menses, worse vexation or excited emotions, worse during sleep, worse getting wet.

Cramps and spasms of muscles.

Aura felt in solar plexus or extremities.

GENERALS

General amelioration from cold drinks.

Generally worse from suppressed eruptions.

HEAD

Facial grimaces which he tries to hide or disguise.

Convulsions of the face.

Face turns blue, cyanotic during convulsion or during asthma.

Migraine. Headache at the root of the nose.

Urge to dart the tongue out of the mouth.

Loss of vision before the convulsion.

GASTROINTESTINAL

Sudden convulsions of the stomach with vomiting.

Spasms of the abdomen and colicky pains.

Abdominal cramps worse from motion *(Bry)*.

Vomiting before convulsions.

Cuprum is considered one of the main remedies for cholera.

CHEST

Paroxysms of cough, very severe.

Cough better by cold drinks *(Caust, Coc-C)*.

- **Sudden attacks of suffocation,** worse 3 AM, worse emotions.

Whooping cough with severe paroxysms leading to cyanosis.

EXTREMITIES

- **Cramps of muscles especially legs, hands, calves.**

Muscle cramps, worse sleep, worse coition.

- **Thumbs drawn down and clenched in fists.**

Convulsions begin in the hands and spread to body.

Twitches of the muscles, worse in fingers and toes.

Chorea *(Caust, Cimic, Mygal, Rhus-T, Zinc, etc.)*.

CLINICAL

Asthma. Cholera. Chorea. Colic. Cramps. Encephalitis. Gastrointestinal disorders. Headache. Meningitis. Migraine. Nocturnal myoclonus. Pertussis. Seizure disorder. Tics. Twitches.

COMPLEMENTARY

Calc.

COMBINED SYMPTOMS

- Asthma *and* seizure disorder.

Diarrhea *and* cramps in the extremities.

COMPARISONS

Cic. Zinc. Bufo. Caust.

CURARE

This neurotoxin has been used medically to induce paralysis in patients during surgery or mechanical ventilation. Homeopathically it is therefore mainly indicated in cases of paralysis or progressive paresis such as multiple sclerosis, amyotrophic lateral sclerosis, etc. Louis Klein of Vancouver, Canada recently reported a brilliant cure of a case of myasthenia gravis with Curare.

MENTALS

Abuse issues. Self-abuse - bites or strikes himself, rips his clothes.
Aversion to company; "shuts herself away."
Irritable and aggressive.

NEUROLOGICAL

Progressive paresis, especially of extensor muscle groups.
- **Weakness of hands in piano players.**
- **Difficult swallowing - must drink in order to swallow.**

COMPARISONS

Plb. Caust. Con.

CYCLAMEN

Cyclamen is often referred to as "a chilly Pulsatilla" because of the menstrual difficulties and the strong indigestion from fats. The patient often suffers from weakness and anemia and prominent visual symptoms. We can distinguish Cyclamen from Pulsatilla because it is aggravated by open air, and tends to be thirsty as well. Furthermore the Cyclamen patient rarely has the robust, rosy look of the typical Pulsatilla patient. The Cyclamen patient is often depressed and remorseful; feels she has neglected a duty. There may be a deep, inner sense of grief. Both Cyclamen and Pulsatilla are sympathetic, moody and have a tendency for weepiness.

GENERALS

Generally worse from cold.
General aggravation from suppressed menses.
Weakness and lassitude.
General aggravation from pork and fat.

HEAD

Vertigo, worse menses, worse suppressed menses.

Headache with vertigo or flickering vision.

Migraine.

Pale face with dark circles under eyes.

Allergy.

EYES

◆ **Flickering before the eyes and visual disturbances.**

Dimness of vision. Diplopia. Strabismus.

Swelling around the eyes.

Right-sided ear pain.

GASTROINTESTINAL

Indigestion from fat and pork.

Food and saliva tastes salty.

Craving: Lemonade.

Aversions: **Meat. Fat. Pork. Butter.**

GENITALIA

Severe dysmenorrhea, labor-like pains.

Menses easily suppressed, worse getting wet, worse exertion.

Amenorrhea.

Menses too early, too profuse. Menses black and clotted.

Prostatitis, worse passing stool or urine, worse sitting or walking.

EXTREMITIES

Sore, painful heels, worse sitting, worse standing but less noticed when walking.

Aching in the ankles.

Writer's cramp felt from forearm to fingers. Contracted fingers.

CLINICAL

Allergy. Anemia. Dysmenorrhea. Gastritis. Headache. Menstrual disturbances. Migraine. Strabismus. Vaginitis. Vertigo. Visual disturbances. Writer's cramp.

COMPARISONS

Puls - Menstrual irregularities and easy suppression of menses, blonde, leukophlegmatic constitutions, aversion and aggravation from fats and pork, heel pains, prostatitis.

Chin. Sep. Nat-M.

DIGITALIS

Allopathically Digitalis is used to slow the rapidly fibrillating heart. In homeopathy this plant is often indicated in cases when the pulse rate is abnormally slow. While cardiac symptoms are foremost, this remedy is also indicated in prostatic and other urinary disorders, and in hepatitis, often associated with the characteristic slowing of the pulse.

Mentals

Fear of death from cardiac symptoms.
Fear of the heart stopping.
Remorse; guilty feelings.

Generals

- **Slowness of pulse** may accompany any other disorder.

General aggravation from coition (indigestion, angina, etc.).
Faintness and pallor.
Cyanosis.

Head

Vertigo with slow pulse.
Yellow or green halo seen around objects.

Gastrointestinal

Hepatitis with tender, hard liver.
Jaundice with pale or whitish stool.
Nausea with deathly sinking sensation in stomach.
Nausea worse from odor of food *(Colch, Cocc, Sep, Ars)*.

Urogenital

Prostate enlarged and inflamed, especially in elderly patients.
Urinary retention with enlarged prostate.
Seminal or prostatic discharge.
Constant urge for urination at night.

Cardiovascular

Slow pulse; bradycardia or tachycardia with slow conduction.
Sensation that the heart will stop beating, worse from exertion.
Angina worse from coition, worse excitement, worse exertion.
Angina extends to left arm with numbness and weakness in limb.
Congestive heart failure.
Rheumatic heart disease.

- **Palpitations after grief.**

CHEST

Hemoptysis from suppressed menses is considered a keynote.

Dyspnea or even asthma associated with heart disease.

Wakes suddenly from sleep with gasping and fear of suffocation *(Lach, Sulph, Op, Grind)*.

CLINICAL

Angina. Arrhythmia. Congestive heart failure. Hepatitis. Nausea. Prostatitis. Rheumatic heart disease.

COMBINED SYMPTOMS

Liver *and* heart problems.

COMPARISONS

Chel. Nux-V. Spong. Lach.

DIOSCOREA

Dioscorea is a remedy for gastrointestinal disorders. The guiding symptom is a tendency to stretch or bend backward to relieve the abdominal pains *(opposite Coloc)*. During the interview, the patient may sit in the chair leaning far backward to keep the abdomen from flexing.

GASTROINTESTINAL

- **Severe abdominal cramps, better by bending backwards** or by sitting upright.

Acute diarrhea, sometimes hemorrhagic.

Paroxysms of cramps, worse bending forward, better eructation.

Colicky infants who arch their backs.

Nausea at the thought of food.

MUSCULOSKELETAL

Low back pain. Sciatica, usually right-sided.

Cramps in the fingers and toes during labor.

CLINICAL

Colic. Gastroenteritis. Kidney stone. Sciatica.

COMPARISONS

Nux-V. Coloc. Bell.

DOLICHOS

Dolichos produces tremendous itching over the entire body with no visible eruption. The itch may be due to intrinsic skin conditions but in most cases results from liver disturbance and jaundice or sometimes from pregnancy or advanced malignancy. The symptoms are worse at night and often cause despair or even suicidal thoughts.

GASTROINTESTINAL

Hepatitis, with jaundice and pale or white stool.

SKIN

- ◆ **Tremendous, unbearable itching without eruption.**

Itching, worse at night, worse in pregnancy, better cold bathing.

COMPARISONS

Card-m. Chel. Sulph. Ars.

DROSERA

Drosera is predominantly a cough remedy and is especially famous for its relationship to pertussis. However we can use Drosera in any respiratory infection, and in coughs resulting from irritation in the larynx. Drosera also has cramping of muscles. It is interesting to note how often our pertussis remedies have neurological symptoms.

THROAT

Dryness and irritation of throat or larynx, provoking cough.

Constriction in throat or chest, worse talking, better walking.

COUGH

- ◆ **Violent paroxysm of coughing, sometimes so severe the patient cannot catch his breath or becomes cyanotic.**

Cough, worse after midnight.

- ◆ **Cough so severe as to produce epistaxis.**

Cough, worse eating.

Cough worse immediately upon lying at night.

Vomiting from the cough.

Painful cough; the patient must hold his chest when coughing.

Drosera has been used by many authors in cases of tuberculosis.

EXTREMITIES

- ◆ Cramping of the hand on grasping; unable to release grip.
- Twitches in the shoulder.

CLINICAL

Bronchitis. Croup. Pertussis. Tuberculosis. Writer's cramp.

COMPARISONS

Spong. Rumex. Coc-C. Cupr.

DULCAMARA

Dulcamara is a remedy which is often over-looked. The keynote aggravation from damp weather is so strong, it is understandable how often we misprescribe remedies such as Kali Carbonicum or Calcarea Carbonica when we should think of Dulcamara. Most of the complaints of Dulcamara are related to the mucous or serous membranes. It is an important remedy in allergic and herpetic conditions.

The Dulcamara patient is generally stout, rather uptight and domineering. Often much of the interview is centered around the patient's concerns and disagreements with his family. It can be very difficult to interrupt the patient in such a discussion to bring the discussion back to the patient's own health problems.

MENTALS

- Anxiety about the family.
- Domineering about and preoccupied with family matters; spends the entire interview discussing family controversies.
- Opinionated and "uptight."

GENERALS

- **General aggravation from damp or cold, damp weather.**
- ◆ **General aggravation from change of weather** especially when warm days are followed by cold evenings (in autumn).
- **General aggravation from suppressed eruptions.**
- **General aggravation from catching cold (conjunctivitis, diarrhea cystitis, low back pain, etc.).**
- General aggravation from drafts.
- Allergy to cats (*Tub, Sulph, Kali-C, Ars, Puls*).

HEAD

Headache from suppression of sinusitis or facial eruptions.
Headache, sinusitis: worse cold, damp weather, worse after chill.
Headache better during mucus discharge.
Bell's palsy with difficult speech.
Facial neuralgia from suppressed facial eruption.
Thick catarrh with yellowish mucus filling sinuses and inner ears.
Ear pain, especially left ear, worse night, worse cold, damp.
Hay fever, especially at the end of summer or in fall.
Nasal obstruction, colds or coryza from cold, damp weather.
Crusty eruptions on head or face.
Herpes about the lips.
Tinea capitis.
Warts on the face.

GASTROINTESTINAL

Diarrhea, worse cold, damp weather or worse cold foods.
Abdominal cramps.

UROGENITAL

- **Urging for urination when chilled.**

Eruptions on genitalia, especially between the scrotum and thigh.
Genital herpes.

CHEST

Cough or asthma which come on in cold, damp weather.
Bronchitis. Pneumonia.

MUSCULOSKELETAL

Rheumatism.
Low back pain, worse stooping, worse after catching a cold.
Chills beginning in the back *(Gels, Eup-Per)*.
Stiffness and joint pains, worse cold, damp, worse getting wet.
Warts of the hand.

SKIN

- **Flat, smooth warts.**

Urticaria. Tinea corporis. Tinea versicolor. Eczema. Impetigo.

CLINICAL

Allergy. Asthma. Bell's palsy. Bronchitis. Connective tissue disease. Diarrhea. Headache. Herpes. Hypertension. Lower back pain. Neuralgia. Otitis. Pneumonia. Rheumatism. Sinusitis. Tinea. Warts.

COMPLEMENTARY

Sulph. Calc.

COMPARISONS

Kali-C. Rhus-T. Calc. Sil.

ELAPS

Elaps is a snake venom and, as expected, it has many symptoms similar to Lachesis. The patient is often suspicious, intense and haughty. Hemorrhagic conditions with dark or black blood are common.

MENTALS

- **Fear of rain.** Fear of stroke. Fear of snakes.

HEAD

Offensive nasal discharge.

CHEST

Hemoptysis with black blood.

Angina pectoris.

- **Coldness in chest or stomach**, especially after cold drinks.

GASTROINTESTINAL

Cold sensation in the stomach, worse from cold drinks.

Cravings: **Ice. Oranges. •Salads.** Yogurt. Aversion: Banana.

Gastritis. Peptic ulcers. Esophageal spasms.

Abdominal pains ameliorated by lying on the abdomen.

Hematemesis, black blood.

GENITALIA

Severe dysmenorrhea, often with the typical black flow.

Premenstrual syndrome.

CLINICAL

Angina. Dysmenorrhea. Esophageal spasm. Hemorrhage. Peptic ulcer. Premenstrual syndrome. Sinusitis.

COMPARISONS

Lach.

EQUISETUM

Equisetum is a remedy for the urinary tract. It is a useful remedy in simple cystitis although less frequently indicated than Sarsaparilla, Nux Vomica, or Cantharis.

URINARY

- **More urging when the bladder is nearly empty; less urging and less dysuria when there is more urine.**

Pain or fullness in the bladder, even after voiding.

Frequent urging for large amounts of urine.

Pain at the end of urination *(Sars)*.

Enuresis.

Constant full sensation in the bladder during pregnancy, not relieved by urinating.

CLINICAL

Cystitis. Enuresis.

COMPARISONS

Sars. Canth. Nux-V.

ERIGERON

Erigeron is a remedy for hemorrhage, primarily but not exclusively of the uterus. The hemorrhage is nearly always aggravated by motion.

GENERALS

- **Hemorrhage worse from least motion** (hematemesis, hematuria, metrorrhagia). Stays in bed to avoid hemorrhage.

HEAD

Epistaxis with flushed face.

UROGENITAL

Spontaneous or threatened abortion.

Uterine bleeding worse from motion or exertion.

Menses or uterine hemorrhage, with bright red blood.

Marked irritation of the bladder and rectum.

Hemorrhage from renal calculi.

CLINICAL

Epistaxis. Hemorrhage. Miscarriage. Peptic ulcer. Renal calculi.

COMPARISONS

Ust. Mill. Sabin. Sec.

EUPATORIUM PERFOLIATUM

Eupatorium Perfoliatum is famous for its use in influenza but also covers recurrent febrile conditions and malaria. We are guided to this remedy by the tremendous bone pains which accompany the febrile conditions. The patient often complains of unbearable pains in the limbs or the back, sometimes in the muscles but most typically felt directly in the bones. The pain is often described "as if the bones are broken." This symptom guided Karl Robinson of Albuquerque, New Mexico to use Eupatorium Perfoliatum to alleviate pains in fractured bones.

GENERALS

Tremendous aching, "as if the bones are broken."

High fever preceded by chills, especially from 7 to 9 AM.

Pain worse from motion.

HEAD

Periodic headache.

Headache during or after the fever.

Head heavy, must lift it with his hands from the pillow.

GASTROINTESTINAL

Great thirst for cold drinks, especially during the chill, or even during the rigors.

Cravings: Cold foods. Ice cream.

Nausea and vomiting worse during the chills, worse from motion.

Thirst before the chill.

CHEST

Raw, painful cough.

BACK

Back pain, excruciating.

Back pain prior to or during the chill.

Chills felt first in the back.

EXTREMITIES

- **Pain "as if the bones are broken."**

Tremendous aching and stiffness in the limbs, often in the bones.

May help relieve the pain of acute fractures *(Symph, Bry, Arn)*.

ACUTES

- **Influenza** with high fever, flush, chills or even rigor with paradoxical thirst for cold drinks, scanty perspiration. The patient is restless and complains of intense aches and may describe the pains as being in the bones.

CLINICAL

Fever. Fractured bones. Influenza. Malaria. Periodic fever.

COMPARISONS

Bry. Pyrogen. Nat-M.

EUPHRASIA

One of our most important coryza and hay fever remedies is Euphrasia. We think of Euphrasia when we find a case of coryza or allergy which is centered especially in the eyes.

HEAD

- **Coryza with bland rhinorrhea and acrid, profuse lacrimation** *(opposite to All-C)*.
- **Eyes burning, irritated; photophobia; intense blinking.**

Copious, thin discharge from eyes and nose.

Pus in both inner and outer canthi.

Injury to the eye.

CHEST

- **Cough only in daytime**, better lying, better in bed at night.

Cough with great lacrimation.

Allergic asthma. Hay asthma.

CLINICAL

Allergy. Colds. Conjunctivitis. Iritis. Pertussis. Measles.

COMPARISONS

All-C. Sabad. Puls. Apis.

FERRUM

Ferrum exemplifies the occasional coincidence of homeopathic and allopathic functioning of one substance. The allopath uses iron in macro-doses to facilitate hemoglobin production by saturating the body with this basic metabolite, whereas the homeopath uses the remedy Ferrum to strengthen the organism's defenses. Many homeopathic authors have hypothesized that the allopath has good results with iron supplementation because of its homeopathic action in cases of anemia due to different causes.

The Ferrum constitution is easily confused with other polycrests such as Calcarea or Pulsatilla. The patient is often stout, plethoric, weak and most commonly suffers with circulatory dysfunctions or anemia. The patient often complains of weakness much more marked than we expect from observing him. This is because the face has a rosy, flushed look which is taken as a sign of health rather than a sign of a disturbed circulation. The patient may be irritable and over-sensitive along with this weakness. Furthermore there is often a strong preoccupation with business matters. The patient can be quite aggressive or domineering.

MENTALS

Great sensitivity to noise, especially the rustling of paper.
Irritable, worse from noise or from contradiction.
Forceful, determined, and preoccupied with business matters.
Overly sensitive.

GENERALS

- **Generally worse from exertion or from sitting still. The patient feels best when walking about slowly.**

Flushes of heat, worse from slight exertion, worse from rest.
Anemia, often after hemorrhage.
Obesity.
Profuse perspiration.
Usually chilly patient but can be worse from heat.
General aggravation after midnight.

HEAD

- **Long continued headaches**, often lasting 2 to 3 days.

Headache in one spot in the left temple. Frontal headache.
Periodic headache, especially every 14 days.
Headache, often pulsating, worse after midnight, better lying.
Epistaxis.
Red flushed face, or pale face which flushes easily.

GASTROINTESTINAL

Regurgitation or nausea and vomiting, worse after eating or even while eating, worse after midnight. Post-operative vomiting.

Ravenous appetite alternates with loss of appetite.

Abdominal pains, worse from movement.

Diarrhea, often painless, worse during or after eating.

Cravings: Sweets. Bread and butter. Tomatoes.

Aversion: Eggs. Tomatoes.

UROGENITAL

Metrorrhagia with flushes.

Uterine fibroids.

Enuresis.

CHEST

Difficult respiration, better by walking slowly.

Cough, worse motion, better slow walking.

Palpitation, worse from motion.

EXTREMITIES

Backache, ameliorated slow walking.

Arthritis, especially the upper extremities and shoulders (Ferrum Muriaticum and Ferrum Phosphoricum are especially for right shoulder pain).

Varicosities, especially worse during pregnancy.

Cramps in the feet.

Cold extremities.

CLINICAL

Anemia. Arrhythmia. Arthritis. Bursitis. Chronic fatigue syndrome. Diarrhea. Epistaxis. Gastritis. Hemorrhage. Migraine. Obesity. Sciatica. Varices. Vertigo.

COMPLEMENTARY

China.

COMPARISONS

Puls - Obese, irritable, flushing, headaches, general amelioration by gentle motion.

Sulph - Obese, often worse heat, craves sweets and averse to eggs, gastritis, diarrhea.

Nux-V - Irritable and business oriented, chilly, sensitive to noise.

Chin. Ant-C. Graph. Calc.

FERRUM IODATUM

Closely related to Ferrum Metallicum, Ferrum Iodatum is most often used as a colitis remedy and is also important in the treatment of hyperthyroidism. Ferrum Iodatum is even more similar to Pulsatilla than Ferrum Metallicum because of its aggravation from heat.

GENERALS

Obesity.
General aggravation from heat; warm-blooded.
Face flushes after drinking wine.
General aggravation from tobacco or from smoke.
Weakness, debility, perspiration.

GASTROINTESTINAL

Colitis associated with bloating, fermentation, belching.
Craving for sardines or salty fish.

EXTREMITIES

Hot feet, puts them out of covers.

CLINICAL

Colitis. Goitre. Hyperthyroidism. Graves disease. Hypertension.

COMPARISONS

Ferr. Sulph. Puls.

FERRUM PHOSPHORICUM

It is often difficult to prescribe Ferrum Phosphoricum because the type of case which requires this remedy is usually without localizing or characterizing symptoms. It is almost a diagnosis of exclusion. The typical case presents with high fever, often debilitating, and obvious inflammation of the affected part, be it throat, stomach, lungs, etc. And yet, despite the severity of the disease process, we find only general and vague symptoms which do not guide us to any particular remedy.

In constitutional cases we find both Phosphorous and Ferrum characteristics. The patient is generally thin, often with a slight flush. He is open natured, alert and has abundant ideas. Especially prominent are gastrointestinal and respiratory problems.

GENERALS

High fever- usually 102 degrees or higher.

- **Fever but no localizing or individualizing symptoms.**

Right-sided complaints (pneumonia, shoulder pain, etc.).

Anemia.

HEAD

Flushes or redness or pallor. Circumscribed red spots on cheeks.

Photophobia and headache with fever.

Epistaxis.

Tonsillitis; tonsils red and swollen.

GASTROINTESTINAL

Thirsty for cold drinks (or less often prefer warm drinks).

Vomiting after eating.

CHEST

Pneumonia, often right-sided.

Hemoptysis, bright-red blood.

Pleurisy.

CLINICAL

Anemia. Bursitis. Colds. Epistaxis. Gastritis. Hemorrhage. Influenza. Otitis media. Pharyngitis. Pleurisy. Pneumonia. Tonsillitis.

COMPARISONS

Bell. Phos.

FLUORICUM ACIDUM

The personality of Fluoric Acid has been elucidated by Vithoulkas. To briefly describe these traits, the Fluoric Acid type is generally materialistic, domineering, and preoccupied with the fulfillment of his sexual cravings. The patient seems uncaring or indifferent toward loved ones or family. Internally he feels isolated and often anxious.

Many homeopaths have speculated about the health effects of the fluoridation of our water supplies. This is an especially alarming thought because of the deep action of this remedy, affecting the metabolism, the bones and the connective tissue.

MENTALS

Domineering, materialistic with sexual preoccupation.
Lascivious thoughts. Amoral.
Hurried; rapid speech; rapid eating.
Isolated from others; indifferent to loved ones.
Vithoulkas mentions a fear of suffering.

GENERALS

Generally worse from heat; extremely warm-blooded.
General aggravation from warm drinks or application.
General aggravation in the summer.
General amelioration from cold bathing.

HEAD

Coryza. Copious, watery discharge. "Runs like a faucet".
Falling of hair; alopecia areata.
Headache, worse from not urinating and better from urination.
Headache along the suture lines.
Discolored or breaking teeth. Easy caries of teeth.
Sore throat, worse from inspiring cold air.

UROGENITAL

Excess sexual desire, promiscuity. Deviant sexual desires.
Priapism, erections frequent and excessive.
Impotence, usually after sexual excesses.
Prostatic hypertrophy and frequent or even involuntary urination.
Uterine or rectal prolapse.

EXTREMITIES

Varicose veins, often painful.
Distortion or weakness of the nails.
Feet hot and must be uncovered at night. Offensive feet.
Osteomyelitis. Caries of bones.

CLINICAL

Allergy. Bone disorders. Peptic ulcer. Sexual disorders. Varices.

COMPLEMENTARY

Silica.

COMPARISONS

Med - Warm, feet out of covers, hyper-sexual, hurried, selfish.
Sulph. Calc-F. Sul-Ac. Nit-Ac.

FORMICA RUFA

Formica Rufa covers a specific form of **migratory arthritis**. The joints become red, hot, inflamed, and exquisitely painful especially from slight movement. The pain persists in one location for about 24 to 48 hours and then resolves. When one joint returns to normal, another joint becomes inflamed as the process migrates from joint to joint. This is why the patient complains he can only find one comfortable sleeping position - but that the position changes nightly. The syndrome may be accompanied by rashes or vasculitis which resemble red ant bites.

GAMBOGIA

Gambogia is a remedy affecting mainly the gastrointestinal system. It may be used in acute gastroenteritis or in chronic conditions such as ulcerative colitis or Crohn's disease.

MENTALS

Severe depression, even suicidal thoughts.

Depression alternating with diarrheal conditions or starting from the suppression of diarrhea.

Hyper-sexuality, especially in patients with colitis *(Grat, Lyc)*.

GENERALS

Chilly, craves warm humid environment.

HEAD

Cold sensation in the teeth, or sensitivity to cold.

Aphthae and stomatitis.

GASTROINTESTINAL

Diarrhea and vomiting together *(Ars, Verat)*.

Severe diarrhea with sudden gushing of stool.

- **Diarrhea in old people.**

Severe periumbilical burning or stitching pains before diarrhea. Abdominal pains better after stool in chronic cases but in acute cases there is tenesmus and exhaustion after stool.

Yellow or greenish stool or in some cases bloody stool.

Rumbling of the abdomen before stool.

Excoriation of the anus.

EXTREMITIES

Rheumatism.

Injury to coccyx.

CLINICAL

Arthritis. Colitis of any category. Depression. Food poisoning. Gastroenteritis. Proctitis. Rheumatism. Sexual pathology.

COMPARISONS

Crot-T. Podo. Ars. Grat.

GELSEMIUM

We think of Gelsemium when the chief complaint of the patient is weakness or when the main problem is accompanied by weakness. This weakness can be seen on all levels - mental, emotional, and physical. Nearly all of the physical conditions which respond to Gelsemium can be traced to this all pervading weakness. In advanced cases the weakness extends to paresis and even paralysis. Gelsemium is a remedy we can think of in neurological cases which lead to gradual paralysis.

On the emotional level this weakness is expressed as a cowardice or an inability to face any challenge. In our texts we often see described the use of Gelsemium to counteract cowardice on the battle field; hopefully none of us will be called upon to put Gelsemium to this use ever again. However, this is a useful way to remember the remedy. Before the battle (or any major challenge), all sorts of autonomic reactions or dysfunctions occur - trembling, weakness, diarrhea, urgent urination.

In a more mundane sense, Gelsemium can be said to be the main remedy for stage fright, both acutely and as a chronic complaint. The patient has a feeling of weakness and inability which paralyzes him when he must confront any challenge. Gelsemium is unbelievably effective for relief of the severe anxiety often experienced before tests, interviews, and performances.

On the mental level we see weakness, forgetfulness, and dullness of thought. There can be an aversion to mental work, the patient feels he cannot make the slightest effort to think. The patient may show all signs of weakness and weariness - slumping in the chair, limpness of the extremities and a very characteristic drooping of the eyelids. In more serious, chronic cases the Gelsemium patient is rarely able to lead an active life or even to hold down a job.

MENTALS

Timid, quiet, reserved.

Cowardice.

• **Stage fright.** Helps acutely the terror before a performance.

• **Complaints when anticipating an event.**

Complaints come after a fright.

Complaints from hearing bad news.

Fears: In a crowd. Of falling. •That his heart would stop. Exams.

People who give up their work, unable to face it any longer.

Sadness but unable to cry. Depression.

GENERALS

General aggravation from anticipation, fright, bad news, excitement.

• **Trembling from exertion, fright or anticipation.**

Great fatigue and weakness; incapacitated by fatigue.

Generally better from urination (dullness, headache, neuralgia).

General aggravation at 10 AM.

Sticky perspiration over whole body.

Chills alternating with flushes of heat. Chills with trembling.

Complaints which linger since the time of an influenza.

Sleepy and weak during labor.

Apathy and indifference to his condition.

Appearance: Soft face with fine superficial wrinkles. Face flushed and sleepy looking. "Worn-out" expression.

HEAD

Vertigo, may start in the occiput; sensation as if falling.

• **Headache beginning in the occiput or neck and radiating to the forehead.**

• **Headache ameliorated by urination.**

Heavy head, feels as if he can hardly lift it.

Headache worse wine, worse at 10 AM, "maddening" headache.

Coryza, especially on the left side.

Facial neuralgia.

Numbness and heaviness of tongue.

EYE

• **Eyelids heavy and drooping**; can hardly keep the eyes open.

• **Diplopia,** often before or during the headache.

Ptosis.

Diplopia from weakness of the extraocular muscles.

Slow accommodation of vision.

GASTROINTESTINAL

Thirstless.

- **Diarrhea from fright, anticipation, or bad news.**

Diarrhea with frequent urination.

UROGENITAL

Menstrual or labor pains extending into the back.

CHEST

- **Feels heart will stop beating, causing him to jump-up; fears heart will stop unless he stays in motion.**

Congestive heart failure (*Am-C, Ant-T, Ars, Carb-V, Dig, Glon, Hydrc, Kali-C, Kalm, Lach, Laur, Lycop, Naja, Phos, Sulph)*

Hoarseness, loss of voice, worse from fright.

Empty feeling in the chest.

BACK

- **Chills running up and down the back.**

Aching and stiffness in neck which may extend to forehead.

EXTREMITIES

- **Trembling of extremities, especially the legs, from slight exertion.**

Chills begin in the hands or feet.

Heaviness and trembling of the extremities, especially the legs.

Paralysis of the extremities.

Writer's cramp.

SLEEP

Sleepless from anticipation or excitement.

CLINICAL

Anxiety. Chronic fatigue syndrome. Diarrhea. Diplopia. Fever. Hay fever. Headache. Influenza. Insomnia. Laryngitis. Migraine. Multiple Sclerosis. Myesthenia Gravis. Neuralgia. Paralysis. Tremor. Upper respiratory infection. Vertigo.

COMPARISONS

Stann - Weakness, trembling of extremities, empty or hollow sensation in chest.

Sil - Weakness, stage-fright, anxiety over trifles, headache from occiput to forehead.

Lyc. Mur-Ac. Ph-Ac. Sep. Laur.

GLONOINUM

Nitroglycerine (as a "side-effect" of its allopathic use) produces a pulsating, congestive headache which is the primary indication for its homeopathic use. Glonoinum has a dramatic action on the circulation, producing flushes, palpitation, hypertension, and heart disease.

MENTALS

- **Confusion as to location. "Lost in well-known places."**

Confusion on waking at night; confusion from inhaling fumes.

GENERALS

General aggravation from sun. Sunstroke.

Symptoms come and go with the sun.

HEAD

Pulsating, bursting headaches *(Bell, Lach, Meli, Puls).*

Headaches worse from the sun; headaches come and go with the sun even without direct exposure.

Headache accompanied by injection of the sclera, by flushed face, by bounding carotids.

Headaches worse from alcoholic drinks, worse motion, worse jar, worse from heat, from tight collars.

Headaches better from external pressure, better lying in the dark.

Hot flashes, menopausal flushes.

STOMACH

Craving tobacco.

CHEST

Congested sensation, pulsations with a hot sensation in the chest.

Intense pulsation of the heart with visible pulsing in the carotids.

Angina. Heart murmurs. Arrhythmia. Congestive heart failure.

CLINICAL

Arrhythmia. Dementia. Flushes. Headache. Hypertension. Menopause. Migraine. Sunstroke. Valvular disease.

COMPARISONS

Bell - Intense headache, worse sun and jarring, better dark, pulsing of carotids, flushes, hypertension.

Meli. Puls. Lach.

GNAPHALIUM

Primarily indicated in sciatica, Gnaphalium produces an alternation of numbness and pain in the affected leg. Sometimes the patient may instead complain of a "numbing" type of pain. There may be similar pain and numbness in other systems as well, such as in dysmenorrhea, neuralgia, etc.

MUSCULOSKELETAL

Sciatica, right side more affected than left.
Sciatica with pain and numbness simultaneously.

COMPARISONS

Cham. Coloc. Tell. Gins. Dios.

GRAPHITES

The typical Graphites case is a coarse, bland, laborer or "peasant" type. The patient is classically obese, thick-skinned, and slow thinking. It must be remembered that there is a spectrum within every remedy, and therefore we may prescribe Graphites in intellectuals and artists when the other parts of the case fit. Often these less typical patients will at least complain of some mental dullness, a hint of the usual foggy state of Graphites.

Most cases which require Graphites seek help for physical conditions related to skin and mucous membranes. As with most carbon remedies, the metabolism is strongly affected in Graphites, causing obesity, abnormal callous and nail formation, and growths of all sorts.

MENTALS

- **Simple, basic, earthy and unrefined patients.**
Slow thinking, irresolution, poor concentration.
- **Weeping from music** (especially in dull, heavy-set people).
Anxiety and dullness in the morning on waking.
Restless, agitated anxiety.
Restlessness and anxiety at night.
Depression and causeless weeping.
Irritability.
Memory weak for recent events.

Graphites

Generals

More often chilly than warm-blooded. May have flushes of heat.

Obesity.

Generally worse in morning on waking (sad, anxious, dull).

General aggravation from suppressed discharges.

Fissures, especially where skin and mucus membranes meet.

Sudden episodes of weakness, in robust looking people.

Generally has left-sided complaints.

General aggravation from the heat of the bed.

Vertigo, worse in morning, worse rising, worse stooping.

Head

- **Headache with numb or empty sensation** *(Cocc, Plat)*.

Empty feeling in the head. Intoxicated feeling in the head.

Left-sided headache.

Hair loss at the temples. Alopecia.

Severe acne.

Eruptions on the scalp, especially the occiput.

Psoriasis of the scalp.

- **Cracks behind the ears, eruptions behind the ears.**
- **Cobweb sensation on face** *(Alum)*.

Eyes

Photophobia.

Acute or chronic conjunctivitis.

Keratitis. Blepharitis.

Redness at the margins of the eyelids. Eyelids agglutinated.

Cracks of eyelids and canthi. Styes.

Ears

- **Eruptions or cracks behind ears** *(Calc, Sil, Lyc, Petr, Sulph)*.
- **Chronic discharges from the ears**, especially left ear; general aggravation from suppression of otorrhea.
- **Otitis externa. Otitis media.**
- **Hearing loss, better from background noise such as when riding a train.**

Tinnitus especially the left ear, worse at night.

Thick ear discharges.

Nose

Allergic rhinitis, polyps.

Recurring colds.

Cracks at nasolabial folds.

MOUTH

Cracks of the lips and corners of the mouth.

Fever blisters.

Halitosis, breath with odor of urine.

THROAT

Goitre; exophthalmus.

GASTROINTESTINAL

Desires: **Chicken**. Beer. Sweets. Bland food.

Aversion: **Sweets**. Salt. Meat. Fish. Soup.

Gastritis or ulcers with pains better by eating or better from drinking milk *(Ars)*, or from warm drinks.

Thirsty cold drinks.

Sensation of trapped gas.

Constipation with large hard stool; stool stays in rectum with no urge to expel it.

Rectal itching. Hemorrhoids.

UROGENITAL

Eruptions of genitalia; eruptions on upper, inner thigh.

Herpes.

Excessive sexual drive (early development of sexual instinct).

Decreased sexual desire or performance. Aversion to sex develops in later stages.

◆ **Loses the erection during intercourse.**

Ovarian tumors, uterine malignancy, cervical condyloma.

Amenorrhea.

CHEST

Eruptions in axilla, under breasts.

Cracks of the nipples.

Asthma from suppressed eruptions.

Breast malignancy.

MUSCULOSKELETAL

Thickened nails, very hard. Deformed nails.

◆ **Callosities** of elbows, knees, hands.

Arthritis.

Toes swell during the menstrual period.

Feet hot, offensive, and puts them out of covers.

Cold extremities.

Numbness of forearms.

SKIN

- **Thick skin, often with cracks.**

  Skin unhealthy - easy infections, abscesses, slow to heal.

  Eczema. Psoriasis. Scales. Tinea. Urticaria. Herpes.

  Eruptions itch, worse from heat of the bed, scratches to the point of bleeding.

- **Eruptions ooze a thick, yellow or "honey-like" fluid which dries into golden crystals on the skin.**

  Keloids. Poison oak. Erysipelas.

CLINICAL

Abscess. Acne. Alopecia. Arthritis. Asthma. Blepharitis. Conjunctivitis. Connective tissue disease. Constipation. Dementia. Eczema. Fissures. Flushes. Gastritis. Goitre. Headache. Hearing loss. Hemorrhoids. Herpes. Impetigo. Keloids. Keratitis. Malignancy. Obesity. Otitis externa. Otitis media. Peptic ulcer. Photophobia. Psoriasis. Sexual dysfunction. Styes. Vaginitis. Vertigo.

COMBINED SYMPTOMS

- **Aversion to meat, salt and sweets as a combination.**

COMPARISONS

Sulph - Obese, skin troubles - itching worse heat, oozing, etc. gastritis, thirst for cold, hot feet, offensive odors.

Calc - Obese, bland personality, constipation, dry, cracked skin, polyps, chronic discharges and infections.

Ant-C - Obese, thick or cracked skin with thick or honey-like discharge, cracked lips, peptic ulcer, gastritis.

Puls - Obese, bland, weepy, flushes, conjunctivitis, otitis media.

Ferr. Phos. Med. Caps.

GRATIOLA

When we see the combination of sexual excesses and gastro-intestinal problems we think of Gratiola *(Lyc, Nux-V, Gamb)*. This is primarily a woman's remedy and may be confused with Platinum due to the haughty character and sexual over-stimulation.

MENTALS

Arrogant, haughty women *(Plat, Lach, Sulph, Nux-V)*.

Promiscuity.

Sensation that the head or body is small *(opposite Platina)*.

GENERALS

Left-sided symptoms.

Many authors list the symptom, "Vertigo while eating."

GASTROINTESTINAL

Alternation of constipation and diarrhea.

Watery diarrhea.

Gastritis.

Cold sensation in the abdomen.

UROGENITAL

Nymphomania.

Left-sided renal colic.

Left-sided ovarian tumor or ovarian pains.

Masturbation in young girls.

CLINICAL

Gastritis. Irritable bowel syndrome. Ovarian tumor. Peptic ulcer. Renal colic. Sexual disorders. Vertigo.

COMBINED SYMPTOMS

Sexual pathology *and* **gastrointestinal disorders.**

COMPARISONS

Lyc - Promiscuity, digestive complaints, haughtiness, renal colic.

Plat. Nux-V. Gamb.

GRINDELIA

Grindelia is a remedy to consider in more advanced cardiac or respiratory illness when the patient has the characteristic **sleep apnea**. He starts up from sleep with a sensation of suffocation or with actual apnea *(Lach, Dig, Samb, Spong, Sulph, Op)*.

GUAIACUM

Guaiacum is an arthritic remedy with the keynote characteristic of amelioration from cold applications *(Led, Lac-C, Puls, Rad, Sulph)*. Many body workers and physicians in general recommend the use of ice or cold applications in arthritic conditions so our patients may come in telling us of amelioration from cold. It is true that enough ice can numb almost any pain. We should mainly take notice of this symptom when our patient has instinctively, on his own accord, used cold for his pains.

HEAD

Facial neuralgia.

Swollen sensation of eye.

GASTROINTESTINAL

• **Craves apples.**

Diarrhea.

CHEST

Guaiacum has been recommended by many authors for pleuritic pains of tubercular origin.

MUSCULOSKELETAL

Arthritic pains ameliorated by cold applications, worse from heat, worse from motion.

Left wrist pain or carpal tunnel syndrome.

Acute rheumatism. The joint feels hot or even burning, worse from slight motion.

Pains of the dorsal region of the back.

Sciatica, worse heat.

Joint pains, and acute inflammations better from cold.

Contractures, especially of the hamstrings *(Cimx)*.

Gout.

CLINICAL

Arthritis. Carpal tunnel syndrome. Gout. Headache. Neuralgia. Pleuritis. Sciatica.

COMPARISONS

Led. Puls. Sulph. Viol-O.

HAMAMELIS

When the main pathology of a case centers on the circulation with extraordinary weakness of veins we think immediately of Hamamelis. The veins dilate, are fragile, allowing easy phlebitis or hemorrhage.

GENERALS

- **Weak veins: Varicosities and passive hemorrhage.**

Sore, bruised sensation; injuries with bruising or hemorrhage.

Hemorrhage during menses or from suppressed menses.

HEAD

- **Epistaxis combined with varicosities or hemorrhoids.**

Epistaxis, worse during menses ("vicarious" bleeding).

Contusions about the eye, "black ey.e" Hemorrhage in the eye.

Esophageal varices.

GASTROINTESTINAL

Bleeding hemorrhoids.

Bloody stool.

Cases of hematemesis are reported cured in our literature.

GENITALIA

- **Varicocele.**
- Varicosities of the vulva.

Orchitis.

EXTREMITIES

- **Varicose veins, large and sore and easily irritated and stinging; easily begin to bleed.**

Varicosities, worse during pregnancy, worse menses.

Thrombophlebitis. Varicose ulcers.

Bruising and ecchymosis. Purpura.

CLINICAL

Ecchymosis. Epistaxis. Hemorrhoids. Injury. Phlebitis with or without thrombosis. Varicocele. Varicosities.

COMBINED SYMPTOMS

- **Epistaxis *and* hemorrhoids or varicosities.**

COMPARISONS

Puls. Fl-Ac. Arn. Aesc.

HEKLA LAVA

Hekla is a remedy useful in abscess or exostosis of the jaw, especially of dental origin. The abscess often presents as an impressive swelling which is extremely hard. Exostosis of any region of the body may require Hekla Lava.

COMPARISONS

Sil. Calc. Calc-F.

HELLEBORUS

Helleborous produces stupefaction in all of its complaints, whether a migraine which produces a temporary dullness of mind or in organic brain conditions. The stupefaction as Hahnemann described it is a state "where with sight unimpaired, nothing is seen very clearly; with hearing perfectly sound nothing is heard distinctly." The patient seems cut off from the world and from his own thoughts and perceptions. He answers slowly and with great difficulty. Memory and concentration are almost paralyzed. At times he feels almost no emotion; indifferent to the surroundings. At other times this state may be terrifying and the patient feels as if something indescribable and catastrophic is happening to him. Also there may be great remorse and guilty feelings.

MENTALS

- **Stupefaction and mental dullness.**
- **Mind slow, answers slowly and with great effort.**
- **Memory weak**, can hardly remember what was said to him.
- **Mind is completely blank** with almost no thoughts passing.

Concentration difficult.

Mental dullness with headache.

Guilty feelings and remorse. Even suicidal feelings because of his poor performance.

Depression.

Apathy and indifference.

Anguished state; cannot comprehend what is happening; begs for help. Wild, whirling sensation in the brain.

- Must concentrate continuously on his activity or "his hands forget what they were doing."

GENERALS

General aggravation from 4 to 8 PM *(Lyc, Alum)*.

Chilly.

Delirium in encephalitis or meningitis.

HEAD

Headache with stupefaction.

Occipital headache, ameliorated on closing the eyes.

Rolling of the head, especially in meningitis.

Fearful, pleading or questioning look in the eyes.

Staring, vacant look.

Shakes his head to dispel the wild sensation inside.

Strokes and rubs the forehead when attempting to concentrate.

Meningitis, coma and chewing motion of mouth.

Head injury with mental dullness and confusion. Concussion.

• **Brow furrowed** during meningitis or encephalitis.

Wrinkled forehead, especially when trying to think.

GASTROINTESTINAL

Colitis with mucous and copious, watery stools.

Ulcerative colitis.

Thirstless.

Aversion: •Apples. Vegetables.

EXTREMITIES

• **Awkwardness, especially if he takes his mind from what he is doing even to speak.**

Involuntary movements; hemiballism.

CLINICAL

Alzheimer's disease. Ataxia. Coma. Dementia. Depression. Encephalitis. Head injury. Headache. Leukemia. Malignancy. Meningitis. Migraine. Ulcerative colitis.

COMPARISONS

Alum - Mental dullness, difficult memory and concentration, answers slowly, general aggravation at 4 PM.

Ph-Ac - Mental weakness, indifference and apathy, answers questions slowly.

Cocc - Mental dullness and stupefaction, slow in speech, poor co-ordination.

Op. Bry. Merc. Phos.

HELONIAS

Helonias is an hysterical remedy with a focus on the female hormonal and genital system. The famous keynote symptom is a great "consciousness of the uterus," however this symptom is not required in order to use the remedy.

MENTALS

- **Consciousness of the womb.**

Problems worse from thinking about them *(Ox-Ac)* and better when the mind is occupied.

Hysteria; depression; irritability.

GENERALS

Diabetes. Cases of both diabetes mellitus and diabetes insipidus have been reported cured in our literature.

Great fatigue.

GENITALIA

Uterine prolapse, worse after pregnancy. Holds the belly.

- **Feels the uterus at all times, feels it move and shift with her movements.**

Uterine fibroids.

Soreness or heaviness in the pelvis.

Leukorrhea. Vaginitis.

Metrorrhagia.

Threatened or incomplete abortion.

Soreness of breasts especially the nipples.

MUSCULOSKELETAL

Back pain and heaviness.

CLINICAL

Back pain. Diabetes insipidus. Diabetes mellitus. Dysmenorrhea. Leukorrhea. Metrorrhagia. Miscarriage. Uterine fibroids or prolapse.

COMBINED SYMPTOMS

Fatigue or hysteria *combined with* prolapse or other uterine complaints.

COMPARISONS

Sep. Puls. Murx. Phos.

HEPAR

The Hepar personality is characterized by a sense of vulnerability on all levels - mental, emotional, and physical. Hepar is exquisitely sensitive to all types of pain and often seems to complain greatly out of proportion to his illness or injury. The patient often seems to have no barriers to outside forces. The desire for protection which the Hepar patient feels may lead him to limit his activity - even to the point of agoraphobia. The patient may go to great lengths to ensure his security such as marrying into a wealthy family rather than waiting for someone he loves. In fact, even the pain of others may affect the patient strongly; even hearing of an accident may send shivers through the body, or even vomiting. When the patient feels that his security is threatened he may react with anger or even rages. He has strong, violent impulses, but also suicidal impulses. Hepar children may also be irritable and abusive.

Physically the Hepar constitution is also vulnerable. Infection comes easily into the patient both systemically - in all forms of fever or even sepsis, and locally - with abscess formation and suppuration. Furthermore the patient is vulnerable to any external force - weather, noise, light, chemicals and especially cold. These external events seem to penetrate the patient more easily than any other remedy type.

MENTALS

Oversensitivity to all external stimuli, especially pain.
Agoraphobia.
Anxiety and hypochondria.
Irritable and angry outbursts. Critical. Impatient. Hurried.
Discouraged or even suicidal over his suffering.
Violent impulses. Impulse to stab or kill.
Fire - fears, dreams, impulses toward pyromania.
Fears: Hearing of violent accidents or movies. Injury. Dentist.

GENERALS

Chilly and aggravated from cold. One of the coldest remedies.
- **Intolerant of becoming cold, even one part of the body.**
- **Generally worse uncovering a hand or foot**, or touching a cold object such as a bottle from the refrigerator.

Intolerant to drafts, and especially to cold dry winds.
Offensive odors from discharges, perspiration, etc. - especially sour odors or old cheese odors.
Swelling and induration of glands (cervical, inguinal, etc.).
Stitching or splinter-like pains (*Nit-Ac, Arg-N, Sil*).
Intense sensitivity to pain - complains intensely.

HEAD

Head sensitive to uncovering (ear pain, headache, etc.).

Severely painful otitis media, child wakes at night shrieking and cannot be comforted *(Cham, Bell, Lach)*.

◆ **Ears exquisitely sensitive to wind or open air.**

Otorrhea.

Iritis. Corneal ulcers.

Conjunctivitis.

Eruptions about eyelids. Blepharitis.

Sinusitis with thick discharge and post-nasal discharge.

Severe acne and rosacea.

Dental abscesses. Toothache.

THROAT

◆ **Pharyngitis with the characteristic stitching or splinter-like pains in the throat.**

Tonsils swollen and suppurative.

GASTROINTESTINAL

Desires: **Fat. Sour especially vinegar.** Pickles. Spicy. Pungent.

Sour smelling stool.

Constipation with soft stool.

Rectal abscess.

UROGENITAL

Weak bladder with dribbling and retarded urine.

Urethral stricture.

Recurring cystitis or pyelonephritis.

Prostatitis.

Balanitis.

CHEST

Croup, worse from exposure, worse at night.

Laryngitis. Laryngeal polyps or warts.

Bronchitis. Pleurisy. Pneumonia.

Asthma.

Lung abscess.

Mastitis. Breast abscess.

Boils in axilla.

EXTREMITIES

◆ **Paronychia.**

Cold extremities. Raynaud's syndrome.

Skin

Abscess, exquisitely painful. Skin heals slowly, suppurates easily.

Cracking skin and eczema. Skin ulcers. Impetigo. Warts.

Clinical

Abscess. Acne. Adenopathy. Agoraphobia. Allergy. Anxiety. Asthma. Balanitis. Behavior disorder. Blepharitis. Bronchitis. Constipation. Croup. Depression. Eczema. Iritis. Laryngitis. Mastitis. Otitis media. Paronychia. Pharyngitis. Pleurisy. Pneumonia. Prostatitis. Rectal abscess. Sinusitis. Tonsillitis. Urethral stricture. Urethritis. Warts.

Comparisons

Sil - Chilly, worse uncovering, abscesses and suppuration, splinter-like pains, otitis media, tonsillitis, felons, adenopathy, cold, clammy feet, offensive perspiration.

Ars - Agoraphobia, irritability, anxiety, chilly and worse cold, craves fat and sour, offensive odors.

Calc. Sulph. Psor. Graph. Nit-Ac. Nux-V. Mez. Merc. Rheum.

HYDRASTIS

Easily confused with Kali Bichromicum, Hydrastis is a remedy for infections with thick and ropey discharges especially in the upper respiratory tract. All of the mucous membranes can be affected in this remedy. That Hydrastis is a deeper-acting remedy than is generally credited can be appreciated when considering the large numbers of cases of malignancy which have been reported cured with this remedy in our literature (breast, gastric, etc.).

Head

Thick, ropey discharges from the sinuses.

Marked post-nasal mucus.

Chronic otorrhea.

Tongue swollen, coated, indented by teeth. Slimy, coated teeth.

Aphthae.

Gastrointestinal

Gastric ulceration - benign or malignant.

Thick, stringy vomitus.

Constipation.

Urogenital

Urethritis. Cervicitis.

Chronic stringy, yellow leukorrhea.

Chest

Bronchitis with thick expectoration.

Clinical

Bronchitis. Constipation. Gastric ulcers. Leukorrhea. Malignancy. Otitis media. Sinusitis. Vaginitis.

Comparisons

Kali-Bi. Kali-S. Merc.

HYDROPHOBINUM

Vithoulkas' dramatic Hydrophobinum case of an agoraphobic patient first demonstrated the deeply phobic nature of this remedy. In most cases the patient will give a history of anti-rabies immunization although at times merely the report of a serious animal bite or the immunization of a parent will suffice if the symptomatology is clear. G. Mortelmans of Belgium reported (and I confirmed in another case) two cases of phobia, especially to dogs, which developed after a car accident. Richard Pitcairn of Portland is a veterinarian who noted Lachesis to be almost specific in the treatment of rabies vaccine reactions in animals and thus pointed to its relation to the Lyssin miasm. Louis Klein of Vancouver has related Hydrophobinum to compulsive disorders, family abuse issues and strong feelings of isolation and torment or ridicule.

Mentals

Fears: Suffocation and choking. Driving. Injury. Claustrophobia. Fears water or running water. Airplanes. Fear of insanity. Fear alone. Fear something bad will happen. Agoraphobia.

Heightened awareness and hyper-activity of the mind followed eventually by dullness of comprehension and depression.

Violent rage. Irritable and critical. Anger followed by remorse.

Impulse to stab himself.

Desires to bite when angry. Growls.

Compulsive disorders. Ritualistic.

Feelings of isolation and of being ridiculed or tormented.

History of physical or sexual abuse.

GENERALS

- **History of rabies vaccine in patient or family.**

History of a animal bite, especially from immunized animals.

General aggravation from glistening objects.

- **General aggravation from hearing or seeing running water** (fear, irritability, urge for urine, etc.).

Convulsions, worse from light, from liquids, from trying to swallow, from running water.

Aggravated by the sun.

Hypersensitive to all stimulation - odors, light, noise.

Sensitive to wind or being fanned.

HEAD

Headache on hearing running water.

Photophobia; sensitive to glistening objects.

Excessive saliva with frequent need to spit it out.

Choking sensation on swallowing pills, or even water.

GASTROINTESTINAL

Craves: **Chocolate.** Tobacco. "Strange things" while pregnant.

Aversion: **Water.**

- **Urging for stool on hearing running water.**

Diarrhea.

UROGENITAL

- **Urge for urination, or involuntary urination on hearing the sound of running water.**

Urinary tract infections.

Excessive sexual energy.

Dyspareunia. Vaginitis.

MUSCULOSKELETAL

Opisthotonos.

Right hip pain.

Keloids. Wounds close too quickly.

CLINICAL

Agoraphobia. Arthritis. Diarrhea. Dyspareunia. Headache. Phobic disorders. Seizure. Urinary tract infection. Vaginitis.

COMPARISONS

Ars - Phobias and agoraphobia, impulse to stab or cut himself.

Merc. Hep. Phos. Stram.

HYOSCYAMUS

The mental picture of Hyoscyamus is so striking that it is difficult to prescribe this remedy without some element of this picture being present. However, all remedies have stages of pathology and thus we will not always see the flamboyant stage of exhibitionism or mania. In the typical case, there is over-excitement, loquacity, and abnormally extroverted behavior. In early stages the patient is happy and joking, often mischievously playing pranks or jesting. Annoying, silly behavior and silly laughter are common. Though Hyoscyamus is the most "passive" of the mania remedies, the patient can be malicious and calculating. This remedy can have the same violence and aggression as Stramonium, but typical cases are more mild; thoughts and speech are more violent than actions. Likewise, Hyoscyamus which is a hyper-sexual remedy, enjoys thoughts or conversation around sexual matters nearly as much as sex itself.

There is a strikingly absent moral or inhibitory ethic in many cases, which is described as "shamelessness" in our texts. We find this shameless behavior in all ages, often taking the form of desire to expose the body and sex organs. This exhibitionism is often accompanied by strong sexual arousal and even public masturbation. There is often an enjoyment of the shocked response by witnesses. This desire to provoke or shock people may even outweigh the actual sexual arousal.

We also see shameless language, cursing or telling ribald jokes in inappropriate circumstances. During sexual arousal the patient may have the desire to curse. The shamelessness can also be seen in the frankness and lack of embarrassment with which the patient relates his symptoms during the interview. Conversely we find a soft type of patient who is very passive, feels unnecessarily shameful, and is depressed and hurt by disappointments. Hyoscyamus is a remedy to remember in cases of depression or mania after romantic relationships are broken.

In highly sexual remedies we expect an element of jealousy. Hyoscyamus can be as jealous as Lachesis, both towards his lover or towards a rival sibling. Hyoscyamus also has suspicious thoughts about others' intentions - fear of being harmed or poisoned. Other main fears of Hyoscyamus include dogs, animals and water. The suspicion in Hyoscyamus may evolve to true paranoia and delusions. Hyoscyamus is a remedy for even advanced psychosis. In the full-blown Hyoscyamus case the patient presents a wild picture with restlessness, dancing and gesticulation, and sexual mania. The dancing is generally sinuous and may resemble a type of chorea. The patient speaks rapidly and changes the subject frequently, laughs immoderately, rolls on the ground, exposes himself and so forth.

Children. Hyoscyamus is one of our most important remedies in behavior disorders of children, and there is a wide range of behavior problems. The child may simply have poor control over his impulses - talking, joking, throwing tantrums at the most inappropriate times. There are often tremendous difficulties with other siblings; jealousy, provoking of fights and abuse. The Hyoscyamus child should be watched carefully to avoid violence toward younger siblings which can come in a coldly malicious, detached, and dangerous form. In most, but not all cases, there is precocious sexual behavior: masturbation, secretive sexual play with other children, exhibitionism. Sexual innuendo is constantly brought into the conversation. Cursing is a strong characteristic, often used especially for shock value by these provocative children.

MENTALS

Loquacity.

Jealousy. Suspicion.

Ailments from disappointed love.

Mania, with rage and increased strength, with dancing, with wild talking and laughing.

Cursing. Lewd talk. Ribald jokes.

- **Exhibitionism. Wants to be naked. Touches genitals.**
- **Silly, annoying behavior**, especially in children.

Jesting. Practical jokes. Antics.

Desire to kill (without acting on the desire).

Coldly malicious impulses.

Gestures, chorea-like; dancing; restless fingers; picks at bedclothes.

Fears: Poison. Dogs. Water. Rats. Being alone.

Depression and shameful feelings.

GENERALS

Convulsions, worse fright, worse menses, worse sleep.

Shrieks during epilepsy.

- Psychomotor seizures. Petit mal.

Coma, stupor, delirium from cerebral accident, alcohol or fever.

Restlessness.

HEAD

Vertigo or tinnitus before convulsions.

Grinding of teeth and froth at mouth during the convulsion.

Bruxism.

Spasms and twitches and squinting of the eyelids.

Strabismus.

THROAT

Dysphagia, choking on swallowing even liquids.

GASTROINTESTINAL

Involuntary stool from excitement.

Fecal impactions of elderly people.

UROGENITAL

- **Desire to masturbate in public; handles the sexual organs publicly.**

Masturbation in young children.

Promiscuity. Hyper-sexuality.

Lewd speech during sex.

Involuntary urine; incontinence during convulsion.

CHEST

Tickling cough, worse lying at night.

EXTREMITIES

Gestures which are often rhythmic and bizarre.

Picking at things with the fingers.

Twitching and jerking of extremities, especially hands and feet.

Paralysis, hemiparesis.

Convulsions.

SLEEP

Sleeplessness from mental agitation.

Nightmares.

Bruxism.

CLINICAL

Behavior disorder. Cerebral accident. Cough. Delirium. Encephalitis. Encopresis. Enuresis. Fecal impaction. Fever. Hyperactivity. Manic-depression. Meningitis. Paranoia. Schizophrenia. Seizure disorder. Sepsis. Sexual disorder. Strabismus.

COMPARISONS

Stram - Behavior disorders and mania, violence, fear of water, hyper-sexual, convulsions, strabismus, loquacity, jealousy, twitches and tics.

Lach - Loquacity, jealousy, fear of poisoning, violent temper, hyper-sexual, difficulty swallowing, cerebral accidents.

Verat. Tarent. Bell. Anac. Arg-N.

HYPERICUM

Hypericum is an injury remedy, especially for injuries to the nerves and spine. The hallmark of Hypericum is the sharp and shooting quality of the pains. This remedy may help to prevent tetanus.

GENERALS

- **Injuries: Contusions, lacerations, punctures to parts rich in nerves:** tips of fingers, tongue, teeth, eyes, genitalia.

  Pain after dental procedures.

  Injury to larger nerves - i.e. median nerve tears or laceration.

  Convulsions due to trauma of the head or spine. Concussion.

BACK

- **Injuries of spine (fractures, sprains) with sharp shooting pains, worse raising arms,** movement, worse urination.
- **Injuries to the coccyx** due to falls, blows, labor and delivery.

EXTREMITIES

  Phantom limb pain. Painful scars.

- Puncture wounds, lacerations or crushing injuries to fingertips.

COMPARISONS:

  Led. Arn. Nat-S. Ruta. Rhus-T.

IGNATIA

Each of the famous "grief remedies" - Ignatia, Natrum Muriaticum, and Phosphoric Acid - has its own characteristics. We think of Ignatia when we see an element of spasticity and hysteria in the grief state. It is primarily, although far from exclusively, a remedy for women. While there are many true constitutional Ignatia cases, the majority of cases where Ignatia is indicated have this state imprinted on top of another remedy due to a specific grief or set of griefs. This fact has led many authors to state that Ignatia is a short-acting or superficial remedy. It is certainly the case that when grief has caused pathological changes in the tissue rather than functional disorders we prefer remedies like Natrum Muriaticum or Aurum. However as noted below, Ignatia covers many particular physical disorders, some of which are serious indeed, especially in the neurological sphere.

The Ignatia type is romantic and idealistic in all her dealings with the world. These characteristics together with the usual emotional over-sensitivity of the patient makes her almost a set-up for disappointments. The disappointments often lead the patient to become bitter and even hardened. The Ignatia patient has easily hurt feelings. And yet it is often difficult or even impossible for the patient to release the emotions. Instead they remain cramped inside. Often this cramping of emotions leads to defensiveness and may cause the patient to act in a rude, suspicious or challenging manner toward the prescriber.

As previously stated we often find a need for Ignatia following an acute grief. The full depth of sorrow and grief which we find locked in the heart of an Ignatia patient can be enormous, unendurable. Of course sorrow is not a pathology in and of itself. We use Ignatia only when the grief is "stuck" or lasts excessively or produces symptoms.

MENTALS

- ◆ **Ailments after grief** (headache, amenorrhea, chorea, etc.).
- ◆ **Ailments after romantic disappointments.**
- ◆ **Easily hurt feelings; easily offended.**
- ◆ **Sighing**, especially common in older patients, often loud sighs.
- **Desire to avoid crying giving way to sobbing.**
- **Aversion to consolation.**
- **Stormy relationships filled with recrimination. Jealousy.**
- **Alternating moods** - laughing to weeping (*Puls, Merc, Croc*).
- ◆ **Hysteria or hysterical symptoms** such as numbness, paresthesia, paralysis, etc.
- ◆ **Fear of birds** or chickens. Claustrophobia.
- **Desire for and amelioration from traveling.**
- **Great defensiveness and touchiness.**
- **Rude or suspicious and doubting patients.**

GENERALS

- **General and local complaints better when traveling.**
- **General aggravation from eating sweets** (*Arg-N*).
- Paradoxical symptoms - inflamed joints which are better when pressed, sore throat better when swallowing, etc.
- Aversion to tobacco smoke or smokey rooms.
- Amelioration in the rain.

NEUROLOGICAL

- Tics, twitches, spasms especially coming after grief.
- Convulsions. Petit mal. Encephalitis. Chorea.
- Hysterical paralysis or anesthesia.

HEAD

- **Perspiration only on the face**; perspires first on face or lip.
  Headaches after a grief.
  Headache with pain like a nail driven into head.
  Alopecia, especially after grief *(Ph-Ac)*.
  Hirsutism.
  Tendency to bite tongue or inner cheeks when speaking or chewing.
- **Lump in the throat.**

GASTROINTESTINAL

Cravings: **Cheese.** Fruit.
Aversion: **•Fruit.**
Bulimia.
Hiccoughing paroxysms.
Rectal spasms, fissure, hemorrhoids, prolapse.
Sensation of poker or a knife in rectum.

CHEST

- **Irresistible paroxysm of cough without signs of illness.**
- **Sighing.** Yawning.
  Constriction or sensation of weight in the chest with dyspnea.
  Palpitation from grief *(Dig)*.

MUSCULOSKELETAL

Back spasms, especially after a grief.
Arthritis.
Cramps or drawing pains.

SLEEP

Insomnia or more commonly, excessive sleepiness after grief.
Dreams of water or waves breaking over her.

CLINICAL

Arthritis. Arrhythmia. Asthma. Bulimia. Chorea. Chronic fatigue syndrome. Cough. Depression. Encephalitis. Environmental illness. Globus hystericus. Headache. Hirsuitism. Hysteria or conversion reactions. Low back pain. Migraine. Obesity. Rectal cramp. Rectal fissure. Rectal prolapse. Spasm. Tics.

COMPLEMENTARY

Nat-M. Sulph. Calc. Sep. Apis.

INIMICAL

Nux V.

COMPARISONS

Nux-V - Spasms, cramps and tics, sensitive to criticism, jealousy, rectal pathology, constipation.

Nat-M - Complaints from grief and disappointed love, hysteria, aversion to consolation, globus hystericus, sighing, back pains.

Chin. Caust. Calc-P. Strych. Plat. Sep.

IODUM

The relationship between Iodine and the thyroid gland is well known, therefore it should be no surprise that Iodum reproduces a state similar to clinical hyperthyroidism. The metabolism is accelerated to a remarkable degree producing restlessness, emaciation with great hunger, and tremendous heat. The patient suffers from an anxious restlessness which he cannot easily contain. Deeper states of pathology with impulses and compulsive neurosis also occur.

MENTALS

Hurried, nervous and restless patients.

Violent impulses if forced to be inactive. Great irritability.

Compulsive neurosis. Checks things repeatedly. Ritualistic.

Patients come with many or scattered lists.

Anxiety, better from exertion, better by eating.

Nervous agitation.

Generals

General amelioration by moving or exerting.

• **Generally worse from fasting and better from eating.**

Great heat, one of the warmest patients in the materia medica (though may have cold extremities).

Generally worse heat and better cold or cold bathing.

General aggravation if impulse for activity is restrained.

• **Emaciation despite a voracious appetite.**

Enlargement of glands, liver or spleen, in emaciated patients.

Pulsations felt through whole body even to the fingertips or toes.

Weakness from ascending.

General amelioration in open air.

HEAD

Exophthalmus in hyperthyroid patients.

Allergy, hay fever, acrid nasal discharge.

Goitre, large and in some cases painful.

Twitching of the eyelids, especially the lower lids.

Headache from fasting.

Dry nasal obstruction; loss of smell.

Appearance: Dark complexion and hair.

GASTROINTESTINAL

Ravenous appetite, insatiable.

◆ **Emaciation despite eating voraciously.**

Jaundice with enlarged liver and spleen.

Chronic diarrhea in emaciated children.

UROGENITAL

Atrophy of the sexual organs - testes, ovaries, breasts, nipples which may follow an initial enlargement.

Acrid leukorrhea. "Leukorrhea eats holes in the linen," is often quoted as a keynote.

Undescended testes.

CHEST

Violent palpitations, worse from slight exertion, worse heat, better from cold.

Sensation as if heart gripped or squeezed *(Cact)*.

Laryngismus with burning in chest and larynx. Laryngospasm.

Hay asthma.

Dry, painful cough. Croup.

Has been reported in many cures of Pneumonia.

EXTREMITIES

Attacks of rheumatism preceded by diarrhea.

Pulsations felt into the extremities. Tremor.

Bites the nails.

CLINICAL

Adenopathy. Allergy. Anxiety neurosis. Arrhythmia. Asthma. Bronchitis. Cachexia. Compulsive neurosis. Diarrhea. Goitre. Hyperthyroidism. Laryngospasm. Leukorrhea. Pneumonia.

COMPARISONS

Arg-N. Lach. Brom. Spong. Tub. Tarent. Lycop. Iodine salts.

IPECACUANHA

Whenever nausea and vomiting are a prominent element of a case we must think of Ipecac. Virtually any organ system may be affected in this remedy and yet there is nearly always a concomitant action on the stomach. Despite this almost universal tendency for vomiting, there is no amelioration and often a general aggravation from emesis. There are two special areas of usefulness of Ipecac: asthma (or asthmatic bronchitis) and hemorrhage.

Generals

Irritability.

Periodicity (Ipecac is botanically related to China).

Generally worse from vomiting.

Generally warm-blooded.

Hemorrhage.

Head

Migraine headache with severe nausea and vomiting.

Headache extending to face, oral cavity, teeth or root of tongue.

Face flushed and hot on one side *(Acon, Cham)*.

Epistaxis, often clotted.

Stiffness and constriction in the muscles of the face and neck during the cough.

- **Tongue remarkably clean despite constant nausea.**

Gastrointestinal

- **Constant nausea which is incapacitating; stomach seems to hang loose inside; nausea unrelieved by vomiting.**

Nausea and vomiting during the cough.

Nausea and vomiting during the headache *(Meli, Puls, Iris, Sang)*.

Nausea and vomiting during hemorrhage, metrorrhagia, labor.

Loathing food or even the smell of food *(Colch)*.

Abdominal cramping or colic.

Chest

- **Asthmatic bronchitis and coughs especially of children.**

Rattling cough which comes on in warm humid weather.

Pertussis or other severe coughs with retching, vomiting, stiffness, and cyanosis.

Respiration arrested from severity of cough.

- Bronchiolitis. Croup.

Hemoptysis.

UROGENITAL

- **Uterine hemorrhage which starts suddenly with bright red uncoagulated blood, coming in gushes, often with nausea, vomiting and faintness.**

Metrorrhagia, worse motion, worse during labor or postpartum.

Severe dysmenorrhea with nausea.

Threatened abortion.

Hematuria.

EXTREMITIES

Aching in the bones, especially of the thighs and legs.

CLINICAL

Asthma. Bronchitis. Epistaxis. Hemorrhage. Hematuria. Hemoptysis. Metrorrhagia. Migraine. Miscarriage. Pertussis. Recurring fevers.

COMBINED SYMPTOMS

Nausea *and* hemorrhage tendency.

COMPARISONS

Tab. Kali-C. Kali-S. Sang. Ant-T. Puls.

IRIS VERSICOLAR

Iris is preeminently a migraine remedy. Especially to be thought of in classical migraines with visual aura, hemicrania, and marked nausea and vomiting.

HEAD

Classic migraine headache, generally right-sided pain, often centered in temple or below or above the eye.

Headache alternating sides *(Lac-C)*.

Weekend headache *(Sulph)*.

- **Blurred vision before headache;** amaurosis with headache.

GASTROINTESTINAL

Vomiting with the headache which affords no relief.

Internal burning digestive tract from mouth and stomach, through to anus; excoriating diarrhea.

Recurring episodes of cramping and vomiting.

Skin

Shingles, especially the right side of the abdomen.
Psoriasis.

Clinical

Gastroenteritis. Migraine. Neuralgia. Peptic ulcer. Shingles.

Combination

Psoriasis or herpes *with* migraines.

Comparisons

Sang. Kali-Bi. Rob. Ip. Nat-M.

JACARANDA

In cases of **balanitis** with pus under the foreskin, Jacaranda is nearly a specific.

JALAPA

This remedy is mainly for children and infants who are restless and inconsolable. The keynote, "**Cries all night but sleeps all day**," has been confirmed in many cases. Often associated with diarrheal conditions, colic, indigestion, poor appetite and emaciation.

JUGLANS CINEREA

Juglans Cinerea is an important skin remedy, especially in eczema cases, often with marked **cracking of the hands and fingers**.

JUGLANS REGIA

Juglans Regia is an important remedy in hydradenitis producing a severe, scarring form of recurrent **axillary abscesses**. This remedy also has a reputation in occipital headaches.

KALI ARSENICOSUM

The tremendous anxiety found in this remedy is generally related to the health as in Arsenicum Album, and the two remedies may easily be confused. However the anxiety of Kali Arsenicosum is most commonly focused on the heart, often punctuated by true anxiety attacks or hysterical "heart attacks." This is all the more striking because of the typical conservative and reserved character which is true of all the potassium salts. Kali Arsenicosum is also indicated in many cases of asthma, psoriasis, and other skin diseases with or without the typical mental state.

MENTALS

Anxiety about health.
◆ **Fear of heart disease**, or other diseases such as stroke, cancer.
Panic attacks.

GENERALS

Chilly, worse from cold or from entering a cold place.
General aggravation from cold food or drinks after over-heating.
Sleeps on left side with hand on chest as if protecting the heart.
Tendency toward malignancy.

HEAD

Allergy, worse in cold air.
Swelling of the lower lids.

GASTROINTESTINAL

Bruised or hollow sensation in the epigastrium.
Diarrhea, worse at night.

CHEST

Asthma, worse at night, especially from 1 to 3 AM.

SKIN

Burning, itching eruptions, worse undressing, worse cold.
Psoriasis. Eczema. Skin cancer.

CLINICAL

Allergy. Anxiety. Asthma. Eczema. Epithelioma. Leukorrhea. Psoriasis.

COMPARISONS

Ars. Nit-Ac. Aur. Kali-C. Lach.

KALI BICHROMICUM

Kali Bichromicum is always thought of first in connection with the thick, gluey discharges, especially from the nose. However, the personality of the typical Kali Bichromicum patient is also "gluey." The patient is rather a conformist and tends to rigidly adhere to routine (as mucous adheres to the membrane). Often the patient gives a five paragraph answer when a simple sentence would suffice; he seems to cling to your attention. It is unusual for a Kali Bichromicum patient to complain of mental or emotional problems, instead he focuses on his physical pathology. However when the patient feels his material needs are not being met, he may become irritable or gloomy.

Most prominently the mucous membranes are affected, especially in the respiratory tract. Furthermore secretion formation is almost always a problem, with excessive, thick discharges. Arthritic disorders, and alternating physical pathologies are also quite characteristic.

Mentals

Conformists.

Irritability.

Gloominess.

Generals

Chilly and worse from cold.

Alternation of complaints from one spot or organ system to another.

• **Pains felt in one small spot.**

General aggravation from cold damp (except the rheumatism which may be worse from the warm weather).

Periodicity; complaints at the same hour daily.

Obesity.

General aggravation from beer.

General aggravation at 1 AM.

Head

Photophobia then loss of vision with headache.

Headache in one spot - about the size of a dime or a quarter.

Pain, heaviness or burning at the root of the nose *(Kali-I)*.

Headache or trigeminal neuralgia, often associated or resulting from suppressed nasal discharge.

Thick mucous on teeth or in the throat, in strings.

Tongue smooth, red and glossy appearance *(Pyrog)*.

Sensation of a hair on the tongue *(Sil)*.

NOSE

- **Sinusitis** - in both acute and chronic sinusitis. Mainly indicated in maxillary sinusitis but any sinus cavity may be affected.
- **Nasal discharge or post-nasal discharge which is thick, purulent, usually yellow and stringy.**
- **Strong nasal quality to the voice.**

Pressure and fullness at the root of the nose and through the sinuses.

Thick crusts in the nose which adhere and cause bleeding if removed.

Nasal polyps.

Ulceration of the nasal or oropharyngeal mucosa.

THROAT

Thick discharge hawked from throat.

Swelling of uvula.

Hoarseness; laryngitis.

GASTROINTESTINAL

- **Stomach symptoms alternate with rheumatism or asthma.**

Gastritis with burning pains in the stomach.

Peptic ulcers.

Pains felt in a small spot.

Vomiting ropes or strings of mucous.

Aversion to meat.

Craves sweets.

Diarrhea, worse morning on rising, worse beer.

Summer diarrhea. Colitis.

Diarrhea alternating with rheumatism.

UROGENITAL

Kidney stone with stitching pains radiating to the bladder.

Loss of libido can occur, though generally good sex-drive.

Left ovarian cysts.

CHEST

Asthma, worse at night especially 1 to 2 AM.

- **Productive cough with thick or stringy green sputum in asthma or bronchitis.**

Rattling respiration in sleep *(Kali-S in children)*.

Cough worse in morning on waking, worse eating.

Croup.

Tickling sensation as from the bifurcation of the trachea.

Cold sensation in the region of the heart *(Kali-N)*.

Chest pains extending to the back. Pains in the sternum.

BACK

Cold sensation in back or neck.

Sciatica.

Pain in the sacrum or coccyx, worse sitting, worse coition, worse before urination.

EXTREMITIES

Wandering arthritis.

- **Joint pains alternate with respiratory or gastrointestinal symptoms.**

Pains in joints or muscles come and go suddenly.

Arthritic pains worse in warm weather.

SKIN

Skin ulcers, deep and sharp bordered.

CLINICAL

Allergy. Arthritis. Asthma. Bronchitis. Croup. Diarrhea. Gastritis. Headache. Kidney stones. Low back pain. Migraine. Nasal polyp. Neuralgia. Obesity. Ovarian cyst. Peptic ulcer. Pneumonia. Sciatica. Sinusitis. Skin ulcers.

COMPLEMENTARY

Ars.

COMPARISONS

Hydr. Thuj. Sil. Merc. Cinnb. Other Kali salts. Puls.

KALI BROMATUM

Kali Bromatum has strong religious feelings even to the point of delusions. The Bromide adds an element of paranoia, and thus we find the well-known keynote: "Feels he is singled out for divine wrath." Often a history of childhood abuse leads to a sense of isolation, paranoia, and terror. The remedy is useful in patients with disturbances of the nervous system - epilepsy, psychosis, catatonia. Recently Ananda Zaren of Santa Barbara, California presented some excellent cases of agitated, angry patients who responded to Kali Bromatum. In addition to re-emphasizing the well-known symptom, wringing of the hands, Zaren noted a strong tendency for sighing in these cases.

MENTALS

- **Feels singled-out for divine wrath** or forsaken by God.

Excessive religiosity.

Paranoia. Catatonia. Delirium tremons. Autism. Retardation.

Despair of salvation. Feels guilty as of a crime. Suicidal.

Tremendous anxiety states; frantic with anxiety.

Fears: Being poisoned. Injury. To be alone. Insanity.

Anger and rage. Mania.

Somnambulism and night-terrors.

Memory weak. Amnesia.

GENERALS

Right-sided complaints.

Numbness and anesthesia.

Convulsion. Petit mal.

HEAD

Acne, especially of the forehead.

GENITALIA

Fibroid tumors of uterus. Ovarian cysts or tumors.

Hyper-sexual.

MUSCULOSKELETAL

Sudden or electric-like pains in the back.

Low back pain and sciatica.

- **Wring of the hands. Fidgety or restless hands.**

Restlessness.

Fidgety fingers and feet *(Zinc, Tarent, Sulph, Caust, Med, Rhus-T)*.

Numbness of the entire body.

SLEEP

Night-terrors *(Stram)*.

Fear at night, cannot sleep if left alone.

Sleeplessness. Insomnia from grief. Bruxism.

CLINICAL

Acne. Ataxia. Cerebral accidents. Hysteria. Lower back pain. Night-terror. Paranoia. Schizophrenia. Sciatica. Seizures. Uterine fibroids.

COMPARISONS

Ars. Puls. Sulph. Kali-C. Lach. Stram. Hyos.

KALI CARBONICUM

Kali Carbonicum is one of the deepest acting and most fundamental of all our remedies. It is one of our most important remedies in the treatment of arthritis, catarrhs of the respiratory tract, asthma, peptic ulcers, and even malignancies.

The Kali Carbonicum patient can broadly be described as compulsive - rigidly adhering to a code of ethics and rules. It is very difficult for the patient to express feelings and he exercises strong control over his emotions. Duty is one of the most important concepts for the Kali Carbonicum constitutional type. He will not park in a yellow zone. He will always return to a shop to give back change if he was given too much. He sees things in black and white. The patient is often very stoical. He neither complains about (nor notices) the stress he is under until the situation is very severe indeed. Things outside his control are very upsetting. We may find fear of the dark (unseen), of ghosts (the immaterial), the future, but mainly fear of diseases especially that disease is about to appear (impending). Often the patient feels the fear somatically, especially in the solar plexus. It is noteworthy that in Kali Carbonicum the pathology does not progress to either depression or confusion or deeper mental states. Instead the pathology is confined mainly to the physical body.

Mentals

- ◆ **Conservative, loyal, moral, proper people.**
- ◆ **Rigid, unable to break even a trivial rule.**
- **Dogmatic. Dislikes change.**
- Fear: **Impending disease**. Being alone. Dark. Ghosts.
- Anxiety and worry. Anxiety often felt in epigastrium.
- Starting easily, from noises, etc.
- Irritable. Urge to quarrel.
- Aversion to being touched.

Generals

- **Chilly, worse from cold.**
- ◆ **Intolerant of drafts, aggravated by drafts.**
- May have aggravation from heat, especially during the acutes.
- General aggravation from cold drinks when over-heated (Bell-P).
- **Generally worse from coition** (weak, dim vision, depressed).
- ◆ **Generally worse 2 to 4 AM.**
- **Stitching pains** (Bry, Nit-Ac, Hep).
- Chills around 5 to 6 PM.
- Appearance: Stout or obese. Conservative dress - men still combing hair with a "flip" in the front. Sits rigidly during interview.

HEAD

Headaches, especially sinus headaches.

◆ **Swelling of the eyelids**, upper or lower; ptosis.

Bag-like swelling of the upper lid near to the inner corner.

Marked edema of the conjunctiva, especially allergic variety.

Falling of hair from eyebrows.

Chronic, thick nasal catarrh. Sinusitis.

Tinnitus.

THROAT

Pharyngitis with stitching pain in the throat.

Sore throat, worse from cold drafts, worse becoming cold, worse from empty swallowing.

Difficult swallowing.

GASTROINTESTINAL

Desires sweets.

◆ **Anxiety or bruised feeling in the epigastrium.**

Dread or nausea in epigastrium from emotional excitement.

Peptic ulcer. Gastritis.

Stomach pains from cold drinks while over-heated.

Painful hemorrhoids, burning and stitching, worse at night.

Constipation, especially before or during menses.

Vomiting or gagging from the cough.

UROGENITAL

Menses acrid, excoriating. Delayed or absent menses.

Metrorrhagia. Fibroid tumors of uterus.

Delayed labor with intense back pains. Miscarriages.

Kidney stones with stitching pains.

Prostatitis.

Renal failure with swelling, even anasarca, most noted about eyes.

CHEST

◆ **Asthma, worse 2 to 4 AM or at 3 AM.**

Difficult respiration, worse lying flat, ◆better sitting upright, ◆better leaning bent forward with elbows resting on the knees, better lying propped-up.

Stitching, tearing pains which wander about the chest.

Angina pectoris. Congestive heart failure.

Palpitations with flushes of heat and dyspnea.

Cold sensation in the chest.

Swelling of breasts.

COUGH

Spasmodic cough, tickling in the throat.

Cough, worse night especially 2 to 4 AM, worse morning on waking.

Cough with thick, purulent sputum with a cheesy taste.

Whooping-cough. Bronchitis.

Pneumonia, often left-sided, but also right lower lobe.

Pneumonia in children, shriek with sharp, stitching pains on inspiring, can't eat or drink, can't sleep.

BACK

Low back pain. Sciatica especially right-sided.

◆ **Back pain drives him out of bed at night,** must rise in order to turn over, worse menses, sitting, walking, better pressure.

Curvature of spine.

EXTREMITIES

Deforming arthritis. Joint pains, worse cold and cold damp.

Sensitive soles of feet.

SLEEP

◆ **Waking at night, especially 2 to 4 AM.**

Wakes 4 hours after falling asleep.

Sleeplessness without cause, "Simply can't let go."

Jerks or twitches on falling asleep, or in sleep.

Talking in sleep. Starting up in sleep.

CLINICAL

Allergy. Anemia. Angina. Arthritis. Asthma. Cholelithiasis. Congestive heart failure. Connective tissue diseases. Headache. Hypertension. Insomnia. Kidney stones. Low back pain. Migraine. Peptic ulcer. Pertussis. Pneumonia. Prostatic hypertrophy. Psoriasis. Sciatica. Scleroderma. Sinusitis. Uterine fibroid.

COMPLEMENTARY

Phos. Nux-V. Carb-V.

COMPARISONS

Calc - Chilly and worse cold and cold damp, stout, practical people, anxiety, takes on responsibilities and duties, crave sweets, arthritis, cold feet, formation of stones and calcifications.

Ars - Proper and anxious patients, chilly, difficult respiration better sitting upright, insomnia, peptic ulcers, swollen lids.

Sil. Kali-Bi. Dulc. Nat-M.

KALI FERROCYANATUM

This is an important remedy in cases of uterine hemorrhage or heavy menses with **•profuse hemorrhage which is remarkably painless.** Uterine fibroids may cause bleeding even to the point of extreme anemia. The remedy has many similarities to the other Kali salts and is indicated in cases of asthma and allergy where hemorrhage is also prominent.

KALI IODATUM

This remedy was popularly used both by allopaths and homeopaths as an anti-syphilitic, and many of its main symptoms are analogs to syphilitic pathology. Other symptoms of the remedy can be more readily understood from the perspective of thyroid pathology and the effect of the Iodum remedies on the thyroid. The patient often admits to being very difficult to live with due to the harshness of his temper. Kent describes the Kali Iodatum patient as irritable, and even cruel. Vithoulkas has added this remedy in bold type to the rubric, "Fear of evil." Vithoulkas further cautioned that repeating this remedy can bring back old discharges.

Generals

Warm-blooded and worse from heat; flushes of heat.

General aggravation at night, 2 to 5 AM or especially at •5 AM.

Generally worse closed room; craves and ameliorated by open air.

General aggravation from the sea or sea air.

General ameliorated from motion and continued motion.

Bone pains at night (syphilitic).

Swelling, abscess, atrophy of glands (lymphatic, testes, breast, etc.).

Head

Allergic rhinitis with thick yellow or green discharges, burning and inflammation of the nose. The allergy is better in warm rooms, though the patient feels worse.

Recurring sinusitis with pain through the face and especially at the root of the nose.

Sinusitis every time patient catches cold, or with changes of weather.

Burning inside the nose, worse with each inhalation.

Headache, burning or stitching pains, worse 5 AM, worse heat.

Iritis, often syphilitic, worse night; often with greenish discharge.

Boils of the head and face.

THROAT

Goitre, with or without clinical hyperthyroidism.

- ◆ Grave's disease; exophthalmic goitre.

Aphthae and ulcers of the mouth, tip of tongue and throat.

Pharyngitis, worse talking; swelling of the uvula, tonsils, larynx.

Pain at root of tongue on protruding the tongue.

UROGENITAL

Chronic urethritis.

Frequent urination before menses is considered by many a keynote.

Atrophy of the testes.

In our literature considered one of the main remedies for syphilis, both for bubo and chancre.

CHEST

- ◆ **Recurring pneumonia.**

Acute pneumonia, especially right side.

Asthma with aggravation at 5 AM.

Wakes with choking and dyspnea.

Boils of chest and back.

EXTREMITIES

Severe sciatica worse lying on affected side, worse from being still, better from motion and walking.

Arthritis, especially the knee, better motion, better cold, worse heat.

Nocturnal bone pains.

Considered by some authors an important remedy in tumors of the bone and osteomyelitis.

SKIN

Recurring boils.

Urticaria.

Itching worse heat, better cold air or cold bathing.

CLINICAL

Abscess. Allergy. Arthritis. Asthma. Goitre. Headache. Hyperthyroidism. Hypothyroidism. Pneumonia. Iritis. Sciatica. Sinusitis. Syphilis.

COMPARISONS

Kali-S. Lach. Iod. Puls. Ars-I. Ferr-I.

KALI NITRICUM

We often are lead to prescribe Kali Nitricum on the basis of its similarities to other Kali salts. The primary use for the remedy is in respiratory conditions especially asthma and bronchitis and even tuberculosis. Often the patient exhibits symptoms of Nitric Acid, for example holding a grudge, anxiety about health, or craving fat.

MENTALS

Anxiety about health.

Dreams of journeys.

GENERALS

Warm-blooded, and generally worse from heat (except the cough).

General aggravation from eating veal (diarrhea, headache, etc.).

HEAD

Nasal obstruction. Chronic sinusitis. Right-sided nasal polyps.

GASTROINTESTINAL

Craving for fat.

Colitis with acrid diarrhea and severe abdominal cramping.

UROGENITAL

Diabetes insipidus.

Menses with inky black flow.

CHEST

Asthma, worse at 3 AM, must sit up.

Severe dyspnea, unable to drink due to shortness of breath.

Cold sensation around the heart *(Nat-M, Kali-Bi)*.

Cough, worse night, worse cold or open air, painful to chest.

Pneumonia with dyspnea more severe than pathology warrants.

EXTREMITIES

Cold and clammy lower extremities.

Numbness or wooden sensation in the limbs.

CLINICAL

Allergy. Asthma. Bronchitis. Colitis. Diarrhea. Pneumonia. Rhinitis. Sinusitis. Tuberculosis.

COMPARISONS

Kali-S. Nit-Ac. Sang. Samb.

KALI PHOSPHORICUM

We think of Kali Phosphoricum in cases of mental and physical exhaustion, especially after periods of stress or over-exertion. It is needed in students or intellectuals who have made some enormous exertion and have a type of mental breakdown *(Pic-Ac, Con)*. Especially when great exhaustion and mental dullness is associated with nervousness and over-sensitivity we think of Kali Phosphoricum. The patient is often extroverted and easily upset from hearing bad news or hearing of world catastrophes.

MENTALS

Mental fatigue. Irritable, restless, anxious from mental exertion.
Starting from noise; hypersensitivity to all stimuli.
Feeling unable to cope; despondency. Great nervous dread.

GENERALS

Chilly, worse cold.
General aggravation from coition.
Great depletion. Weakness after chemotherapy or cancer surgery.
General aggravation at night.

HEAD

Headache, worse from mental exertion.
Chronic ear discharges.
Swelling and bleeding of gums, especially when digestion disturbed.

GASTROINTESTINAL

Craves: Cold drinks and food. Sweets. Vinegar.
Flatulence, early satiety, food intolerances.
Diarrhea, often very offensive.

UROGENITAL

Offensive menses or leukorrhea.

EXTREMITIES

Arthritis, better motion, better warmth.

CLINICAL

Anxiety. Chronic fatigue syndrome. Diarrhea. Headache. Indigestion. Multiple sclerosis. "Neuresthenia." Vaginitis.

COMPARISONS

Gels. Calc. Sep. Phos. Nux-V.

KALI SULPHURICUM

Kali Sulphuricum is under-prescribed despite the fact that there are many clear indications for its use. It has often been stressed that Potassium Sulphate is found abundantly in the flower of Pulsatilla and that this may explain the great similarity of the two remedies. Kali Sulphuricum is often called "an irritable Pulsatilla" (though Pulsatilla can be irritable enough!). The remedies are similar in their physical pathologies - catarrh of the ears, arthritis, and, most especially, chronic sinus and respiratory symptoms, especially asthma.

The personality of Kali Sulphuricum is soft and rather timid like Pulsatilla but with an unexpected harshness or irritability underneath. The patient may complain about lack of self-confidence, ennui and depression. He is also conservative and anxious to follow rules to the smallest detail, as is true of most of the Kali salts.

MENTALS

Irritability.

Depression and indolence.

Lack of self-confidence.

GENERALS

Warm-blooded, worse from heat or warm wraps.

Generally better from cold and open air.

Hates being over-heated though complaints may be worse cold.

General aggravation from changes of weather, from cold weather.

General aggravation from walking in open air.

General aggravation in a warm room.

HEAD

Chronic otitis with glue ear, sometimes with yellowish otorrhea.

Chronic nasal obstruction, often yellowish post-nasal discharge, worse if much over-heated, worse from cold or cold weather.

Snoring.

Headache, worse from warm room, better walking in the open air.

Yellowish exudate on tongue and in pharynx.

Hay fever.

Yellowish flaking from scalp.

GASTROINTESTINAL

Craves: **Sweets.** Cold food.

Aversions: **Eggs.** Warm drinks.

CHEST

Asthma, worse evening or at night, better from open air.

Wheezing and rattling in chest during sleep, especially in children *(Kali-Bi, Ant-T)*.

Wheezing worse in a warm room, better cool air.

Bronchitis with loose sounding cough, expectoration thick and yellow and must be swallowed, worse winter.

Snoring.

EXTREMITIES

Arthritis, worse heat, worse evening, better cold weather or cold applications *(Led, Guai, Puls, Lac-C, Sulph)*.

Wandering arthritis *(Form, Berb, Puls, Kali-Bi)*.

Cold hands and feet *(opposite Sulph)*.

SLEEP

Terrifying dreams - ghosts, death, robbers, murder.

SKIN

Epithelioma. Psoriasis. Eczema, better open air.

CLINICAL

Allergy. Arthritis. Asthma. Bronchitis. Colds. Eczema. Otitis media. Psoriasis. Sinusitis. Skin cancer. Tuberculosis.

COMPLEMENTARIES

Puls. Carb-V.

COMPARISONS

Puls - Warm-blooded and worse from heat, asthma and allergy, nasal catarrh, wandering arthritis.

Sang. Sulph. Calc-S. Other Kali's.

KALMIA

Kalmia is a remedy to be thought of when we find the combination of neuralgia and rheumatism *(Spig, Cimic, Berb)*. Severe pain is generally described by the patient with his first words to us. Furthermore, when superficial pathology (rheumatism, etc.) is suppressed, we find cardiac disorders, especially rheumatic or other valvular disorders in Kalmia.

Generals

Pains extend from above downward (both as in radiation of the pain and as in involvement of new joints and muscle groups as the disease progresses to lower areas).

Pains increase and decrease during day, with the sun *(Glon, Stann, Sang, etc.)*, though some cases may have an aggravation at night.

Chilly. Cold aggravates.

Head

Facial neuralgia, especially right-sided.

Post-shingles neuralgia.

Face pain, most severe, extending to the teeth or about the eyes.

Stiffness around the eyes and the eyelids *(Ruta)*.

Iritis.

Pains about the eyes, worse during the day, worse moving the eyes.

Headache extending from neck or back to the head *(Gels, Sil, Sang)*.

Chest

Chest pain radiating to left hand and arm (whether from rheumatism, intercostal neuralgia, or cardiac complaints).

Organic heart disease, especially from suppressed arthritis.

Valvular heart disease, cardiac hypertrophy or endocarditis - even resulting in advanced congestive heart failure.

Chest pains or palpitations worse from lying on the left side, better lying on the back.

Palpitations can be very intense; visible lifts and loud murmurs are also well documented with this remedy.

Extremities

Arthritic pains which radiate downward.

Joint pains which move to involve joints progressively from above downward.

Sudden, severe, acute arthritis, worse night, worse motion.

Pain in the shoulder, especially when the pain extends to the elbow, wrist or hand. Bursitis.

Knee pain and inflammation.

Clinical

Angina. Arrhythmia. Arthritis. Bursitis. Fibrositis. Gout. Headache. Neuralgia - facial, intercostal, etc. Valvular disease.

Complementary

Spig.

COMPARISONS

Spig - Combination of neuralgia and heart disease, palpitations and murmur, angina, rheumatism.

Berb - Sharp, neuralgic types of pains in rheumatism.

Lach. Cact. Spong. Phos. Ran-B. Rhus-T. Ruta. Bry. Cimic. Abrot.

KREOSOTUM

Kreosotum is known for its usefulness in cases of vaginal, cervical and uterine excoriation, inflammation and hemorrhage. It is an important remedy in all menstrual and hormonal disturbances. In any inflammation of mucous membranes which gives rise to purulent infections resulting in friability of the tissues and bleeding we must consider Kreosotum.

MENTALS

Irritable and peevish. Irritable children and infants.

Sensitive to music.

Fear and aversion to sex in women.

GENERALS

Excoriation and inflammation of the mucous membranes.

Hemorrhages and abnormal bleeding.

Great offensiveness in the inflamed part.

Pulsations through the whole body.

Left-sided complaints.

General aggravation from 6 PM to 6 AM.

HEAD

Headache, worse before menses or during menses.

Intense headache with radiation to the root of teeth, as from a nerve.

MOUTH

Salivation during pregnancy.

Mouth offensive, especially from inflamed gums or decayed teeth.

• **Decay of deciduous teeth**, "Teeth decay as fast as they rise past the gums."

Difficult dentition; child is irritable and crying *(Cham, Calc-P)*.

Gums inflamed, spongy, and bleed or ulcerate easily.

GASTROINTESTINAL

Craves: Smoked flavored food.

Nausea and vomiting before and during menses; during pregnancy.

Gastritis or sluggishness of the digestion with vomiting of undigested food hours after ingestion.

Nausea and vomiting of pregnancy.

Waterbrash.

Severe constipation, shrieking during stool.

UROGENITAL

- **Leukorrhea with putrid, excoriating discharges and great itching.**

Leukorrhea which causes itching, swelling and excoriation of the vulva, excoriation extending even to the thighs, and causes tremendous burning when urine passes over the area.

Leukorrhea worse during pregnancy, worse before menses.

Severe dyspareunia.

Cervicitis. Cervical dysplasia.

Malignancy of the cervix, uterus or vagina.

Sudden urging to urinate; enuresis with deep sleep.

Menses cease on walking.

Menses excoriating and offensive; heavy flow and clotted.

Metrorrhagia, worse coition.

Premenstrual syndrome with irritability, headache, nausea, etc.

CHEST

Cough and bronchitis with putrid or bloody expectoration.

Cough when changing position in bed.

"Cough provokes yawning," is considered a keynote by many authors.

EXTREMITIES

Pain in thumb, especially the left side.

Itching and excoriation of the skin, especially in skin folds.

CLINICAL

Bronchitis. Cough. Dentition. Dysmenorrhea. Dyspareunia. Gastritis. Gastroenteritis. Headache. Hemorrhage. Malignancy. Metrorrhagia. Premenstrual Syndrome. Pyorrhea. Vaginitis.

COMPARISONS

Sep - Vaginitis, excoriating discharge, painful coition, premenstrual syndrome, nausea of pregnancy, headache.

Murx. Nit-Ac. Merc. Merc-C. Ter. Ars. Carb-An. Calc-P.

LAC CANINUM

The typical Lac Caninum patient is excitable, extroverted (almost like Phosphorous), hysterical, and full of fears. The imagination is over-excited giving rise to many hysterical symptoms and hysterical fears. Of course the chief fear in most Lac Caninum patients is of snakes, but a variety of other intense fears concerning health, insanity, fainting and death may impel the patient to call the prescriber at all hours of the day and night. At times the mental excitement and imagination combine to produce delusions: about snakes, spiders and other vermin, that others look down upon him, that he is floating, etc.

The physical symptoms are characterized by changeability - going from side to side or from site to site. The classical symptom is alternation from right to left and then back again, although it is often not so much alternation as wandering. There is also tremendous sensitivity to noise, light, and to touch.

MENTALS

Fear of snakes *(Lach)*.

Fears: Diseases. Death. **Fainting.** Insanity. Driving. Storms. Earthquakes. Dogs.

Anxiety about health.

Poor concentration. Forgetful.

Low confidence and self-esteem.

Mistakes while speaking or writing.

Floating sensation.

GENERALS

Cold but ameliorated in cold weather.

Complaints alternate sides.

HEAD

Vertigo as if floating, worse walking, worse lying in bed.

Headache alternating sides, either during one attack or from one attack to the next.

Occipital headache radiating to the forehead.

Headache worse from midnight onward, worse morning on waking.

Nasal obstruction or thick, greenish discharge which alternates sides.

Jaws crack while eating.

Cold nose.

Liquids forced out of nose while swallowing.

Photophobia.

THROAT

Pharyngitis with pain alternating sides.

Throat pain extending to ears, better cold drinks.

Has been considered one of the main remedies for diphtheria.

Tonsillitis.

GASTROINTESTINAL

Craves: **Salt. Spicy. Pepper. Warm drinks. Whiskey.**

Milk intolerance.

CHEST

Pain and swelling of breasts, worse before menses, worse jarring; often alternating sides.

Some authors recommend its use to help dry the milk of women who are weaning.

UROGENITAL

High sex drive but worse from coition.

Loss of libido.

Pain in the ovaries alternating sides.

Pain in the uterus extending upwards.

Flatus from vagina.

EXTREMITIES

Heat and sensitivity of the feet.

Uncovers the feet.

Pains in the extremities alternating sides.

Fibrositis. Rheumatism.

Sensitivity in the extremities, must splay the fingers or spread the legs to keep them from touching each other.

Has been recommended in rheumatic fever.

Back pain changing places, sciatica alternating sides.

SLEEP

Sleep on the back with one leg drawn upward so the foot rests on the opposite knee or sleeps curled tightly on the side with the face almost touching the knees.

Dreams of snakes, dogs and vermin.

CLINICAL

Allergy. Anxiety. Arthritis. Diphtheria.. Fibrositis. Hypertension. Migraine. Pharyngitis. Phobic disorders. Rheumatic fever. Sciatica. Sinusitis. Tonsillitis. Vertigo.

COMPARISONS

Phos - Extroverted, suggestible, fears and anxiety, food cravings for salt, spicy, alcohol.

Arg-N - Extroversion, phobias, desires salt, pharyngitis.

Lach - Fears snakes, loquacity, floating, splays fingers, migraine.

LAC DEFLORATUM

Lac Defloratum is thought of mainly in cases of migraine headache preceded by an aura of dim vision. The patient often develops marked nausea and vomiting during the headache. It is also a remedy for diabetes.

GENERAL

General aggravation from milk.

HEAD

Frontal headache with nausea and vomiting and chills.

Headache better cold application, better lying or lying in the dark.

Headache worse noise, worse light, worse menses.

Periodic headache, especially weekly headache.

Blurred vision before headache *(Iris)*.

Photophobia.

Flushes of heat in left face and neck.

GASTROINTESTINAL

Constipation in patients with chronic headache.

Large, hard and painful stool.

Intense aversion to milk; milk intolerance.

UROGENITAL

Copious or frequent urine with the headache.

SKIN

Sensitive to cold touch.

CLINICAL

Constipation. Diabetes. Migraine. Milk or lactose intolerance.

COMPARISONS

Iris. Nat-C.

LACHESIS

Vithoulkas gives the essence of Lachesis as "an over-stimulation seeking an outlet." By this he means that on all levels the Lachesis patient has an inner stimulation or agitation which must be expressed either through the physical symptoms or through behavior or speech. The mind is full of ideas and the patient cannot bear to keep them back (loquacity). The emotions are extremely passionate and the patient will express them with often frightening intensity. Physically there is an inner erethism which is expressed as pulsations, hemorrhage, flushes, and discharges.

Intensity. The Lachesis patient is passionate on all fronts. He works hard, he competes intensely, he loves jealously. The patient is almost always described as "intense" by those around him. Often he is very egotistical and arrogant. The Lachesis patient knows the weakness of others and will not hesitate to strike at these vulnerable points. He has a sarcastic wit and can be cutting even to his friends or physician.

Jealousy. Lachesis has very high sexual energy and passion. The patient needs the outlet of a sexual relationship and he becomes very attached to and possessive of his partner. Lachesis may have an absolutely unreasoning suspicion of his partner. The suspicious attitude does not involve only romantic relationships but also a general view of other's intentions. If carried too far the patient may develop frank paranoia.

Loquacity. Lachesis is the most loquacious of all our patients. He cannot help himself. There is so much inside that needs to be expressed, he cannot contain it all. Many times the patient is so talkative that it is impossible for anyone to get a word in edgewise.

Introverted type. If the outlet for these intense emotions is suppressed in a patient, then the characteristic Lachesis type is not seen. Instead the patient is soft, pleasant and somewhat introverted. He has strong emotions inside but doesn't express them. When this happens, we see feelings of inferiority with a type of hidden envy, a timidity, and a frustrated, critical tendency toward almost everyone around him. In this suppressed state the patient may develop crippling anxieties and phobias.

Children. The Lachesis child is usually unable to effectively control his overly-strong emotions. Often the parent will bring the child for behavioral and emotional problems, typically beginning after the birth of a new baby in the family. The child has tremendous jealousy toward the new sibling *(Hyos, Verat, Stram, Calc-S)*. Often physical pathologies will develop from this strong jealousy, such as asthma. The child will actually say he hates the younger brother or sister. A Lachesis boy may be very jealous of his father. The child may also be very possessive of his friends and demands that they pay attention only to him and no other friends. Also the child seems to have a precocious awareness of the people around him. The child is able to find the most vulnerable spot and verbally strike at you, like a snake. The child cannot bear to be under the authority of another person; he doesn't tolerate restrictions. This pattern may be carried over in adulthood with an extreme aversion to authority, as when a supervisor at work or his wife asks him to do things.

MENTALS

Passionate, intense people.
- ◆ **Jealousy. Envy.**

Suspicion, even paranoia.
- ◆ **Loquacity.**

Anger. Aggressiveness. Hatred and longings for revenge.
- ◆ **Sarcastic.**

Fears: ◆**Snakes.** Poison. Heart disease. Insanity. Vomiting. Someone behind him.

Anxiety of conscience.

Delusions of great guilt; admits to "any crime but murder."

Depressed and anxious, worse morning on waking. Suicidal.

Fantasies of his own funeral.

Great anxiety and deep phobic conditions.

Complaints from grief or disappointed love.

Manic states with pressured speech, aggressiveness, sleeplessness.

Inferiority and inhibition (see "introverted type" above).

Alcoholism or drug addiction.

GENERALS

Hot; aggravation from heat (though some cases will be chilly).
- ◆ **General aggravation during sleep or upon waking; sleeps into the aggravation.**
- ◆ **General aggravation before the menstrual period.**
- ◆ **General amelioration as soon as** (or after) **the flow begins.**
- ◆ **General aggravation at menopause**, or during pregnancy.

General aggravation from suppressed discharges.
- ◆ **Left-sided symptoms.**
- ◆ **Symptoms begin on the left and move to the right.**

General aggravation in the spring and in the fall.

General aggravation from suppressed sexual expression.

Flushes of heat.
- ◆ **General aggravation from lying on left side.**
- ◆ **Purplish discoloration** (the face, skin lesions, boils, hemorrhoids) with a full, plethoric or bursting appearance.

Aversion to touch or pressure.
- ◆ Hypertension.

NEUROLOGICAL

Coma and delirium from stroke, alcohol or fever.

Convulsions. Eclampsia. Paresis. Hemiplegia. Cerebral accidents.

HEAD

Migraine headaches. Pulsating headaches. Bursting headaches.

Head pain on left side or in vertex.

Headache worse heat, worse before menses, better during flow, worse pregnancy and menopause, better pressure.

Flushes of heat to the face.

Left-sided otitis media, severe pain, worse at night.

Retinal hemorrhage.

Hair falling, especially in pregnancy.

Epistaxis.

Trembling of the tongue when protruded.

THROAT

Left-sided pharyngitis, or left going to right. Tonsillitis.

Throat pain, worse swallowing, especially liquids or saliva but better swallowing solid food, worse warm drinks; better cold drinks.

Throat pain pain radiates to ears on swallowing.

Chokes when swallowing.

Lump in the throat sensation, better temporarily by swallowing.

Difficulty swallowing, especially liquids or saliva.

- **Intolerance to tight collars, turtlenecks, necklaces.**
- **Averse to being touched on the throat.**

GASTROINTESTINAL

Craves: **Farinaceous.** Oysters. Pungent food. **Alcohol.**

Intolerance to constricting clothes about the abdomen.

Colitis with relief during the diarrhea.

Hemorrhoids which are congested, strangulated, purplish.

Diarrhea before menses.

Hepatitis. Jaundice.

UROGENITAL

Kidney stones. Nephritis with dark or black urine.

Ovarian tumors or cysts, especially left side.

Severe dysmenorrhea, unable to bear clothing, better with flow.

- **Premenstrual syndrome - irritable, jealous, depressed, headache, flushes of heat.**

Hyper-sexual, nymphomania.

Masturbation, excessive and precocious sexual development.

CHEST

- **Asthma after jealousy** or strong emotions.

  Asthma, worse night, worse during sleep, worse in the morning on waking, worse from hot room.

  Asthma, better open air, better cold, better when sitting bent forward *(Kali-C, Ars, Spong)*.

  Must rip open shirt or nightgown during the crisis of asthma.

- **Wakes with suffocating feeling at night, especially on falling asleep.**

  Angina. Congestive heart failure.

  Myocardial infarction with constriction in chest, pain to left arm.

- **Palpitations, worse lying left side**, worse night, worse sleep.

  Chest oppression, worse lying on left side.

MUSCULOSKELETAL

Splays the fingers; can't bear to have them touch.

Sciatica, right or left side, with hyperesthesia of the legs - even the touch of the sheets is unbearable.

Sciatica during pregnancy.

Varicosities, especially of the legs, usually pinkish or may be black.

Icy cold extremities.

Rarely puts feet out of covers.

Herpes zoster over the left side of the back.

Leg ulcers. Claudication.

Easy bruising. Purpura.

Melanoma. Black or purple skin lesions. Erysipelas.

SLEEP

- **Sleeps on right side, impossible on left.**
- **Starts up in sleep as if suffocating. Sleep apnea.**

  Nightmares.

CLINICAL

Alcoholism. Angina. Arrhythmia. Asthma. Behavior disorders. Cerebral Accident. Claudication. Colitis. Connective tissue disease. Diarrhea. Drug addiction. Emphysema. Endometriosis. Epistaxis. Flushes. Globus hystericus. Hemoptysis. Hemorrhage. Hemorrhoids. Hepatitis. Herpes zoster. Hypertension. Hypertensive crisis. Hyperthyroidism. Kidney stones. Malignancy. Manic-depression. Menopause. Metrorrhagia. Migraine. Myocardial infarction. Nephritis. Nightmares. Otitis. Ovarian cyst. Paranoia. Peptic ulcer. Pharyngitis. Polycythemia. Purpura. Retinal hemorrhages. Scarlet fever. Sciatica. Seizure. Thyroiditis. Toxemia. Uterine hemorrhage. Valvular disorders. Varices.

COMPLEMENTARY

Lyc. Nit-Ac. Hep.

COMPARISONS

Hyos - Loquacity, jealousy, hyper-sexual, paranoia and symptoms of stroke, mania.

Crot-H, Naja, snake venoms - Cardiac and circulatory symptoms, hemorrhage, ecchymosis, sepsis, and left-sided symptoms.

Cimic - Loquacity, migraines and menstrual disorders.

Lac-C - Fear of snakes, sensitivity to touch and cravings for alcohol.

Phos. Sulph. Apis. Med. Plat. Cact. Zinc.

LACTIC ACID

Lactic acid is a specific remedy in nausea of pregnancy. This remedy is also indicated in diabetes, arthritis, and gastritis.

Gastrointestinal

Nausea of pregnancy, worse morning, often accompanied by excess salivation and water brash, better eating.

Eructation, heartburn and nausea.

Urogenital

Copious urine; diabetes.

Extremities

Swelling of joints and rheumatism.

Combined Symptoms

Diabetes *and* rheumatism.

Comparisons

Benz-Ac. Sep. Lac-D. Sym-R. Tab. Nat-S.

LACTUCA

Lactuca is a remedy to be thought of in cases of advanced liver disorders, chronic hepatitis and even cirrhosis.

LATHYRUS

Lathyrus is an important remedy for neurological disorders, especially for neuro-degenerative diseases. Vithoulkas demonstrated that the emotional state of this remedy is characterized by a sense of being trapped by circumstances. The patient is generally very emotional but lacks inner strength. Following a period during which the patient feels unable to overcome this trap or double-bind he notices a weakness usually beginning in the legs, symbolizing his inner inability to escape from the situation. I had unsuccessfully prescribed Staphysagria in the case of a young woman with multiple sclerosis focused mainly in the legs which followed a type of suppression and emotional blackmail by the family. Vithoulkas prescribed Lathyrus with great benefit.

MENTALS

Conditions arising from conflicted situations where the patient feels he has no way to resolve a situation which is intolerable.

GENERALS

- **Yawning** and sleepiness accompanies the complaint.

The reflexes are generally increased even to the point of clonus.

Vertigo on standing with the eyes closed (Rhomberg's sign).

EXTREMITIES

Progressive weakness of the lower limbs.

- **Inability to cross legs without assisting with the hands.**
- **Knocking of the knees on walking.**

CLINICAL

Amyotrophic lateral sclerosis. Multiple sclerosis.
Neurological disorders. Paralysis.

COMPARISONS

Caust. Staph. Con. Alum. Strych.

LATRODECTUS MACTANS

Latrodectus is nearly a specific for the classic symptoms of angina or myocardial infarction. There is great pain in the chest which radiates to the axilla or down the left arm causing numbness and coldness of the hand.

LAUROCERASUS

We think of Laurocerasus mainly in cases of cardiac or respiratory disorders where there is great collapse and coldness *(Carb-V, Ant-T, Camph)*. The characteristic which often leads to the prescription of this remedy is "lack of reaction." That is to say, the patient seems to have no ability to recover from the condition but instead stays the same for days on end showing no sign of improvement. The vitality is very low, even to the point of coma. The remedy may also be used for more minor conditions such as a pneumonia which lingers, or even when a case of bronchitis or influenza fails to recover properly and the patient is very chilly and weak. An unusual characteristic of the remedy is the tremendous somnolence often experienced by the patient after the remedy. In one case treated with Laurocerasus, a patient went on to a good recovery from a severe bronchitis after sleeping 20 hours daily for nearly a week.

GENERALS

Great coldness and intolerance to cold.
Collapse states.
Somnolence. Fainting episodes.
Cyanosis.
◆ **Cyanosis of newborns** *(Ant-T)*.
Sensation of internal coldness.

HEAD

Face pale and cyanotic lips.
Perspiration especially on the nose.

CHEST

Cold sensation in the chest.
Palpitations, rapid and weak pulse.
Congestive heart failure.
Congenital heart diseases - septal defects, transposition.
Dyspnea, oppression of chest from even slight exertion *(Stann)*.
Gurgling in the esophagus on drinking.
Chronic cough.

UROGENITAL

Feeble stream of urine, especially in heart and pulmonary disorders.

CLINICAL

Bronchitis. Coma. Congenital heart disease. Congestive heart failure. Cyanosis. Fainting. Pneumonia.

COMPARISONS

Carb-V - Coldness and collapse states, often with fainting *(Camph)*.

Stann - Pulmonary infections and great weakness.

Ant-T - Cyanosis and collapse states with pulmonary infections.

LECITHIN

Lecithin is a remedy to be thought of in cases of mental weakness. There is great fatigue or weakness from mental exertion *(Pic-Ac)*. Another strong characteristic is that the patient is markedly unrefreshed by sleep.

LEDUM

Ledum is well-known as an acute remedy in bites, stings and wounds. It is also an important remedy in chronic rheumatism. Venous congestion, passive edema and hemorrhage mark the chronic conditions. The patient is unbelievably ameliorated by cold or ice cold bathing in many cases.

MENTALS

Some authors have described the patient as cross and surly.

Cures of alcoholism are recorded with this remedy.

GENERALS

- **Chilly but with local amelioration from cold and aggravation from heat.**
- **Great amelioration from ice cold applications or bathing.**

General aggravation from heat or being heated in bed.

Congestion, purple discolorations and swelling.

Hemorrhage.

HEAD

Kent described the face as "mottled, puffy and bloated."

Congestive headaches, ameliorated by cold air.

Epistaxis.

Periorbital bruises *(Symph, Arn)*.

CHEST

Bronchitis. Hemoptysis.

Kent reported a cure of rheumatic heart disease with this remedy.

EXTREMITIES

Rheumatism, mainly of the lower extremities.

- **Rheumatism ascends during the course of the illness to more proximal joints.**

Rheumatism, worse from being over-heated in bed.

- **Rheumatism with pain and stiffness which is better by cold and cold applications.**
- **Swelling or inflamed foot and ankle (elephantiasis),tremendous desire to put feet in cold or even ice water.**

Gout, affecting especially the knees and feet.

Podagra.

Sprains, especially lower limbs, with marked bruising and effusion.

Pains cross-wise, left shoulder and right hip.

Paronychia.

SKIN

- **Bites and stings of insects, often with much swelling and inflammation.**
- **Puncture wounds** with suppuration. Cat bite. Steps on a nail.

Wounds to areas around nerves *(Hyper)*.

Ecchymosis and bruising *(Arn, Sul-Ac, Bell-P)*. Purpura.

Abscesses which are better with cold bathing or applications.

Cellulitis with swelling and lymphangitis, worse heat, better cold.

Eczema, very inflamed skin, better cold application.

CLINICAL

Abscess. Alcoholism. Bites. Bruises. Ecchymosis. Elephantiasis. Epistaxis. Gout. Headache. Hemorrhage. Paronychia. Purpura. Rheumatism. Sprains. Stings. Wounds.

COMPARISONS

Arn. Ruta. Guai. Puls. Hyper.

LEMNA MINOR

In cases of great nasal obstruction which have not responded to other well indicated remedies, Lemna Minor may do good work. The obstruction is caused by swollen turbinates and generally without much discharge. The condition is markedly aggravated by cold, damp weather.

NOSE

Nasal obstruction without much discharge as in swollen turbinates or polyps.

Obstruction worse cold damp weather.

Sensation of bad odor or bad taste in the mouth.

Loss of sense of smell.

COMPARISON

Teucr. Stict. Sil. Calc.

LILIUM TIGRINUM

Lilium Tigrinum is mainly a woman's remedy, especially suited for hysterical, intense, and rage filled patients. There is often a deep conflict inside the patient between a strongly sexual nature and an equally strong moral side. This conflict or any other strong inner conflict produces a type of frustration which is expressed mainly through anger. We can say that Lilium Tigrinum is the most irritable of all remedies. The patient will take offense no matter how kindly she is treated. At other times the patient alternates between great kindness and sincerity and this angry, nasty state. The Lilium Tigrinum patient can also have great sexual excitement, even to the point of nymphomania. When she crosses a certain barrier she becomes very sexual and cannot restrain these feelings. However when her equally deep moral or religious feelings return she feels great remorse and subsequent depression. Thus from the materia medica we find "religious despair alternates with sexual excitement" or "lasciviousness alternating with anger." Also with the suppression of the sexual energy comes a type of frantic state with a crazy or wild feeling in the head *(Med)*. The patient can be tremendously hurried. Many times this hurriedness is so scattered that the patient is unable to accomplish anything productive at all.

MENTALS

Great irritability or rage; the patient makes everyone feel they must "walk on egg-shells."

Depression and despair of salvation; even suicidal states.

Wild feeling in the head.

Hurried. Feels as if she must do something but cannot focus.

Conflict between religious ideals and sexuality.

Anger after sexual excitement.

Alternation of mental states - lust and guilt, rage and remorse.

Fears: Evil. Insanity. Heart disease. Something bad will happen.

Generals

General aggravation after coition.

General aggravation after anger or excitement.

Head

Vertigo or wild sensation in the head.

Headache from mental excitement, worse in a warm room, better walking in open air.

Visual weakness, worse coition.

Gastrointestinal

Craving: **Meat.**

Ineffectual urge for stool *(Nux-V)*.

Urge for stool but only passes urine.

Diarrhea in morning on waking.

Lump sensation in the rectum, worse standing.

Hemorrhoids.

Urogenital

Hyper-sexual.

Premenstrual syndrome with great irritability.

Bearing-down sensation as if the organs will prolapse through the pelvis *(Sep, Murx, Bell, etc.)*, worse during the menses, worse stool, worse standing.

Must cross the legs to avoid the feeling that the organs will fall out.

Uterine prolapse.

Cystitis with urethral burning.

Chest

Palpitations during pregnancy.

Heart feels constricted as if "grasped by an iron hand."

Extremities

Unable to walk on uneven terrain.

Tendonitis.

Clinical

Arrhythmia. Colitis. Cystitis. Depression. Dysmenorrhea. Headache. Hemorrhoids. Hysteria. Irritable bowel syndrome. Manic-depression. Palpitations. Premenstrual syndrome. Sexual disorders. Tendonitis. Uterine prolapse. Vertigo. Visual disturbance.

Comparisons

Lach - Premenstrual problems, hyper-sexual, irritability, religious despair, and dysmenorrhea.

Nux-V - Irritability, premenstrual syndrome, ineffectual urges.

Sep - Bearing down sensations, dysmenorrhea, irritability.

Murx. Med. Bell.

LITHIUM CARBONICUM

Lithium is indicated especially in arthritic conditions, especially of the hip joint. It also cures arthritis of small joints, often with arthritic nodosities.

Head

Headache ameliorated while eating.

Kent (and Hering) listed right-sided hemianopsia.

Urogenital

Kidney stones.

Frequent urination; nocturia; pain in bladder neck if retaining urine.

Chest

Angina pectoris.

This symptom is quoted by many authors: "Pain in the heart region, worse leaning forward, worse before and during urination but better after urination."

Extremities

Arthritis, especially of the hip.

Arthritic nodosities.

Pains in the small joints.

Clinical

Arthritis. Headache. Cardiac disorders. Cystitis. Kidney stones.

Combined symptoms

Hip pain *and* heart disease.

Rheumatism *and* valvular heart disease.

Comparisons:

Benz-Ac. Calc.

LOBELIA INFLATA

Lobelia is mainly useful in cases of anxiety about health. The patient seems focused on his heart or chest, as if there is an oppression in the chest which creates great anxiety. This may be accompanied by some type of mild pathology of the respiratory tract, such as a mild case of asthma, but the dyspnea and turmoil is exaggerated out of proportion to the disease.

MENTALS

Serious and closed patients.

Anxiety about health; fears death from heart or respiratory disease.

- **Psychogenic dyspnea.** Patient panics, but lungs sound normal.

GENERALS

General aggravation from cold and cold drafts.

General aggravation from change of temperature.

General aggravation from cold bathing.

A tubercular remedy.

HEAD

Sinusitis, especially the right side, better from pressure.

Nasal obstruction; patient feels very distressed as if suffocating.

Trigeminal neuralgia, especially the left side.

Lump in the throat sensation.

GASTROINTESTINAL

Said to be a remedy for nausea with marked sweating.

Mouth dry without thirst *(Puls, Nux-M, Bry)*.

Cravings: Sweets. Fat.

UROGENITAL

Menses suppressed from cold bathing.

Uterine pain, better bending the legs, better from lying on left side.

CHEST

Dyspnea worse from vexation, worse drafts, worse suppressed menses, worse exertion, worse from catching a cold.

- **Hyperventilation.**

Respiratory distress, even cyanosis, but lungs are clear to auscultion and function normally.

Dyspnea in patients with history of pleurisy, pneumonia, etc.

Sensation that the heart may stop *(Gels, Dig, Magnolia)*.

EXTREMITIES

Low back pain from suppressed menses.

CLINICAL

Anxiety. Asthma. Globus hystericus. Hyperventilation. Lower back pain. Neuralgia. Sinusitis.

COMPARISONS

Ars. Kali-Ar. Ign. Lach.

LYCOPODIUM

Lycopodium is one of the most fundamental remedies and is classed with Sulphur and Calcarea as part of the triad *(Lyc - Sulph - Calc)*. The word which Vithoulkas uses to describe the essence of Lycopodium is "cowardice". The patient often has marked feelings of inferiority which he constantly tries to overcome. This liability is faced in two different ways:

1) **Inferiority.** One type of Lycopodium feels this lack in himself and becomes very shy, introverted, soft and often becomes rather a loner. This type has many fears and even phobic states such as agoraphobia or develops anxiety about health, fear to be alone at night, fears about death and survival. Often, however, the main fear is of people.

2) **Egotism.** The other type of Lycopodium takes a sort of counter-phobic response to this inner lack of confidence. Thus the patient becomes bombastic, egotistical, bragging, acting extroverted and assertive. Lycopodium is the main remedy under the rubric, "love of power."

Self-control. Another aspect of Lycopodium is lack of discipline. For example, Lycopodium is the remedy that most craves sweets and eats them to the extent that it is detrimental to his well-being. The same is true in the sexual sphere. The Lycopodium patient will often be promiscuous, making passes at any potentially available woman, even the receptionist. It is not that the patient has a stronger sex drive than the average person but rather that he has a superficial interest which he constantly seeks to satisfy.

Commitment. The Lycopodium patient fears forming long-term relationships. He fears the responsibility of commitment. One aspect of this lack of commitment is a fear of impotence. The patient functions normally with a new partner but later notices he lacks the original excitement and finally develops impotence. Meanwhile he can easily be aroused by other women. Finally he announces to her that he "just doesn't find her attractive." And he may try to convince himself he never really loved her.

Children. Both of the two basic types described above can be seen in Lycopodium children. Many of the children are angry, bossy, and rude to parents who are too "permissive." The parents are often perplexed to find that at school the child gets good conduct scores because this bullying attitude is not tolerated. But the more usual Lycopodium child is extremely shy. He has an inner sense of weakness and in many cases he does in fact lack the normal child's stamina. Rough physical games are frightening and exhausting and in no way attractive to him. The features are usually fine or even delicate. His head may be overly large for his body. The parents describe the child as being "cautious" or fearful of rough games, bikes, slides, or swimming. As the child develops he turns more of his energies to intellectual pursuits such as reading, hobbies, or computers.

Physical. On the physical level, the most affected organ system is the gastrointestinal tract and the liver. Lycopodium covers a wide variety of chronic conditions and is also an important remedy for acute illness. Though often considered an anti-psoric remedy, Lycopodium covers all miasms. It should also be remembered that as in all of our polycrests, many cases which need Lycopodium will show little or none of the personality described above.

MENTALS

- **Problems of self-esteem and low confidence.**
- **Bullying, domineering, arrogant behavior to family and those with less authority, obsequious to superiors.**

Intellectual and withdrawn. Depression.

Anxiety: about health, about conflicts, about career.

- **Weeps from sentimental events or upon being thanked.**

Reverses letters and words while reading and speaking.

- **Stage fright.**

Fears: Ghosts. Cancer. Alone, at night. People. Claustrophobia. Commitment and marriage. Public speaking. Agoraphobia.

Averse to company yet dreads being alone.

GENERALS

- **Right-sided problems or right going to left.**
- **General aggravation from 4 to 8 PM or 3 to 7 PM.**

General aggravation in morning on waking.

General amelioration in the evening or at midnight.

Generally worse from missing a meal or from fasting.

Generally better open air (even though he may be chilly).

Usually chilly patients although many are warm-blooded.

Appearance: Fine features, deep furrows at jowls or brow, anxious appearance, baldness, obese or heavy only in thighs and buttocks.

HEAD

Headache, worse right side, worse 4 to 8 PM, worse heat of the bed.
Cracks in the canthi of the eyes.
Eruptions of the scalp, behind the ears; acne; eczema; psoriasis.
Nasal obstruction, worse at night in bed; snuffles of newborns.
◆ Flaring of the alae nasi in asthma or pneumonia.
Right facial neuralgia.
Right-sided otitis media.
◆ **Deep furrows of the brow or jowls.**
◆ **Grey hair** (head or beard) in streaks or patches, mainly right side.

THROAT

Right-sided pharyngitis or begins on right side and moves to left.
Throat pain better warm drinks, but some cases better cold drinks.

GASTROINTESTINAL

Craving: ◆**Sweets.** Alcohol. Warm drinks.
Aversion: Oysters. ◆**Cold drinks** or food.
Disordered by oysters, onions, cabbage, etc.
Loud rumbling in the abdomen.
◆ **Bloated and distended abdomen, ameliorated by eructation and flatus, worse eating even small amounts of food.**
Early satiety.
Huge appetite; ravenous; appetite increases while eating.
◆ **Wakes at night to eat. Bulimia.**
Stomach pains better by rubbing the abdomen.
Abdomen sensitive to the weight of clothing.
Stool begins hard or constipated and then turns soft or liquid.
Hepatitis, acute or chronic cases.
Cholecystitis with pains worse from eating and deep inhalation.
Inguinal hernia.
Heartburn. Sour eructations *(Rob, Sulph)*.

UROGENITAL

Painful urging for urination.
Right-sided kidney stones. Reddish sediment in the urine.
Enuresis.
Prostatitis. Prostatic hypertrophy.
Right ovarian cysts or tumors.
Sexual promiscuity, adultery. Frigidity is common in women.
◆ **Impotence**, especially with his wife. **Premature ejaculation.**
Herpes, especially right-sided and extending down thigh.

CHEST

Asthma; chronic dry tickling cough.

Pneumonia, especially right-sided.

Palpitations, worse evening in bed, worse indigestion or over-eating.

MUSCULOSKELETAL

Back pain better from urination.

Torticollis *(Lachn, Caust, Nux-V, Strych, Rhus-T)*.

Sciatica, worse lying on the side, better walking.

Hip pain, worse first walking but better from motion.

Podagra, especially right-sided.

Uncovers the feet in bed.

Eczema. Psoriasis. Warts. Tinea.

- **Cracks on heel.**
- **One hand or foot much colder than the other.**

Feet offensive.

SLEEP

Sleeps only on the right side.

Waking from hunger.

Waking as from a fright.

Extremely unrefreshed in the morning.

CLINICAL

Allergy. Anxiety. Arthritis. Asthma. Bronchiolitis. Bronchitis. Bulimia. Cerebral accidents. Cholecystitis. Chronic fatigue syndrome. Cirrhosis. Colic. Colitis. Connective tissue disease. Crohn's disease. Cystitis. Depression. Developmental delay. Diabetes. Eczema. Gout. Headache. Hepatitis. Hernia. Herpes. Hypertension. Impotence. Irritable bowel syndrome. Kidney stones. Malignancy. Migraine. Neuralgia. Otitis media. Ovarian cysts. Peptic ulcer. Pharyngitis. Pneumonia. Premature ejaculation. Pyelonephritis. Sarcoidosis. Scleroderma. Sinusitis. Systemic lupus. Tinea. Tonsillitis. Urethritis. Urinary tract infection. Uterine fibroid. Vaginitis. Warts.

ACUTES

Pharyngitis, often right-sided or begin on the right side and travel to the left, better from either warm or cold drinks. Tonsillitis.

Pneumonia, great dyspnea, prostration, frothy sputum, rattling chest uses accessory muscles, flares nostrils, forehead furrowed.

Cholecystitis.

Kidney stone colic, right side, may note a reddish sand in the urine.

Complementary

Puls. Lach. Nat M. Sulph. Sep. Iod. Chel.

Comparisons

Thuj - Low self-esteem, worse from onions, chilly, eczema, herpes, offensive feet.

Ars - Anxiety, chilly, thirsty in sips, desires warm drinks, needs some company, right-sided complaints, asthma.

Arg-N - Craves sweets, bloated, eructations, anxious, claustrophobia, generally better open air.

Sulph - Anxious and intellectual, desires sweets, extroverted and arrogant, worse fasting, offensive feet, feet uncovered, general worse from fasting, gastrointestinal complaints.

Mag-M - Liver and gastrointestinal problems, worse in morning, unrefreshed sleep.

Med. Carb-V. Graph. Nat-M. Nit-Ac.

LYCOPUS VIRGINICUS

The hall-mark of this remedy is the tumultuous activity of the heart whether from primarily cardiac origin or from hyperthyroidism.

Head

Exophthalmus.

Goitre. Hyperthyroidism.

Gastrointestinal

Suppressed hemorrhoids.

Chest

Dyspnea, oppression of chest, worse exertion, worse lying right side.

Angina.

Valvular disease and loud murmurs. Cardiomegaly.

Violent palpitations with pulsations felt throughout the body.

Cardiac disease associated with kidney disease.

Dyspnea associated with loose stools.

Extremities

Varicosities.

Sleep

Sleep disturbed by palpitations.

CLINICAL

Arrhythmia. Congestive heart failure. Diabetes. Exopthalmus. Goitre. Grave's disease. Hemorrhoids. Valvular disorders. Varicosities.

COMPARISONS

Iod. Lach. Coll. Spong.

LYSSINUM

(See Hydrophobinum)

MAGNESIA CARBONICA

The personality of Magnesia Carbonica is very similar to the more frequently prescribed Magnesia Muriatica. The patient has a long-suffering, sour, tired appearance with an intolerance for quarrels and a need for peace and harmony. The Magnesia Carbonica constitution is, if anything even more broken-down than Magnesia Muriatica with an earthy, sickly appearance. In almost all cases the patient will complain of fatigue and weakness.

The patient has a sense of anxiety and dread of the future. This anxiety lasts all through the day and often is especially bad after eating warm food. However once the patient goes to bed he feels an enormous sense of relief and the anxiety disappears.

Magnesia Carbonica is one of the main remedies in cases of "failure to thrive." The infant does not put on weight, has delay of muscular development and cannot hold up his head. Also we find delayed walking or standing. The complexion is pallid and yellow. The lack of strength is often associated with some pathology of the the liver or digestive tract.

MENTALS

- **Anxiety in the day, ameliorated evening in bed.**

Peacemakers; intolerant of quarrels, confrontations or disharmony.

Fear of aggression or violence.

Tremulous anxiety.

Sensitive to noise.

Indisposed to speak in the morning on waking.

Magnesia Carbonica

Generals

Sour odors from secretions and discharges - perspiration, menses, vomitus, diarrhea, etc. *(Hep, Rheum)*.

General aggravation at 3 AM or 3 to 4 AM.

Generally worse from drafts *(Kali-C, Sil, Psor, Hep)*.

Generally worse from warm food (headache, neuralgia, anxiety).

Obesity or flabbiness in the tissues.

Generally worse in pregnancy (toothache, low back pain, sleepiness, etc.).

Generally worse before or during menses - every month gets a sore throat, coryza, weakness.

Head

Trigeminal neuralgia, especially left sided.

Neuralgia, better heat, worse drafts, better walking, better pressure.

Gastrointestinal

Slow digestion; constipation.

Diarrhea, especially after milk, worse after lunch. Colitis.

Abdominal colic, worse from milk.

Hepatitis. Whitish or pale stool in liver disturbances.

Craving: Meat. **Bread and butter. Vegetables.**

Aversion: •Vegetables. Fruit.

Urogenital

Menses flow during night only; stop during the day *(Bov)*.

Menses early - every 21 days.

Extremities

Feet hot, uncovers them.

Sleep

Waking 3 AM and cannot sleep again; sleeplessness from 3 to 4 AM.

Unrefreshed in morning on waking, lasts an hour or more.

Clinical

Chronic fatigue syndrome. Colic. Constipation. Failure to thrive. Hepatitis. Insomnia. Neuralgia. Pregnancy. Premenstrual syndrome.

Comparisons

Mag-M - Liver weakness, unrefreshed sleep, desire fruit, neuralgia, mental symptoms similar, etc.

Lyc - Averse conflict, unrefreshed sleep, uncovers feet, liver weak.

Calc. Rheum. Hep. Coloc. Chin.

MAGNESIA MURIATICA

It is to Vithoulkas that we owe the deep understanding of the personality of this remedy. The Magnesia Muriatica patient has a look of long suffering and sourness. Along with this sourness is a sense of tiredness, of weakness and of fatigue. The weakness of the liver makes this patient intolerant of aggression. He needs peace and a peaceful surrounding and often describe himself as a pacifist or a peacemaker. The Magnesia Muriatica child will often display great turmoil if his parents argue. If we find a child who develops a liver problem and the parents confess to having many arguments or even one serious argument in front of the child, it is very likely that this child needs Magnesia Muriatica.

The Magnesia Muriatica patient has a strong sense of duty which causes him to take on more and more responsibilities. This gives him a worried and anxious feeling. While the patient is active, the anxiety is less, but at night when he lies down in bed he becomes immediately worse. Then he jumps up and must get up out of bed and pace around. Especially upon closing the eyes he becomes very anxious and must get up. There is great restlessness (*Ars*, *Rhus-T*). The sleep is badly disturbed and horribly unrefreshed and this accentuates the tiredness and mental fatigue.

MENTALS

- **Aversion to quarrels; peacemaker.**

Passivity. Cannot cope with life. Depression.

Anxiety night in bed; anxiety on lying, on closing eyes.

Anxiety, worse reading, worse evening or supper, worse menses.

Restlessness, especially in the evening in bed or on closing the eyes.

Sensitivity to noise.

Convinced he looks old or has suddenly aged.

GENERALS

Chilly and worse from cold.

Desires open air even though chilly (*Lyc*).

General aggravation at 3 AM.

General aggravation from salt (*Phos*) and milk (*Nat-C*, *Aeth*, *etc.*).

Generally worse from lying (anxiety, headache, colic, diarrhea, etc.) or in first hour after lying down.

Generally worse in morning on waking.

Generally worse touch but better from hard pressure.

Generally worse at the sea (*Ars*, *Mur-Ac*, *Tub*, *Nat-M*, *Sep*).

Appearance: Deep furrows (*Lyc*, *Plb*), expression of fatigue and suffering and sourness. Often due to the furrows and dryness of the skin the face has an aged or worn-out appearance.

HEAD

Headache especially in temples, worse menses, better hard pressure, better pressure on eyeballs, better lemon.

Headaches last 2 to 3 days *(Ferr)*.

Coryza, hay fever.

Facial neuralgia, better from heat and pressure *(Mag-P, Mag-C)*.

GASTROINTESTINAL

Hepatitis with pain extending to back.

Liver pains worse lying on left side (although in general prefers left side when acute phase over).

Cholecystitis.

Constipation with hard, knotty stools; the stool crumbles upon leaving the rectum.

Diarrhea or abdominal pains worse milk, worse fruit and fats.

Constipation in newborns when cutting teeth.

Indigestion, eructations, flatulence.

Craves: •**Vegetables. Fruit.** •Light foods. Salad. Sweets.
Aversion: Vegetables (less often than craving). Fats.

UROGENITAL

Retention of urine, better walking, must press long.

Insensible loss of urine *(Arg-N, Caust)*.

Irregular menses.

EXTREMITIES

Feet warm, uncovers them.

Numbness of the extremities.

SLEEP

Restless and disturbed sleep.

Waking as from a fright or an electric jolt; startles on falling asleep.

• **Tremendously unrefreshed on waking; toxic feeling with dullness of mind, needs a full 45 minutes (or much longer) to feel awake.**

Sleeps on the left side *(Nat-M. Bry. Thuj. Calc. Sulph)*.

CLINICAL

Anxiety. Chronic fatigue syndrome. Cirrhosis. Constipation. Diarrhea. Headache. Hepatitis. Neuralgia.

COMPARISONS

Lyc. Mag-C. Nat-M. Chin. Sep.

MAGNESIA PHOSPHORICA

The Magnesia Phosphorica patient is much less affected in the liver and therefore is more dynamic and less sour than the other Magnesias. The patient is on edge, irritable and oversensitive. This is one of the classical remedies for neuralgia. Also when we find the conjunction of neuralgia and colic this remedy covers nearly as many cases as Colocynthis.

MENTALS

Irritability.

May have fears resembling Phosphorous.

GENERALS

- **General amelioration from heat and pressure.**

Generally worse from cold, from cold bathing or cold air and drafts.

Generally right-sided complaints.

Generally better from rubbing the affected part.

HEAD

Headache worse cold, better heat or hot applications, better pressure.

Facial neuralgia, right-sided, better heat and pressure.

Facial neuralgia or odontalgia, worse wind or cold applications.

GASTROINTESTINAL

Abdominal colic, better heat, extremely hot applications, hot drinks.

Abdominal pain, better pressure, bending double, rubbing.

UROGENITAL

Dysmenorrhea, better warmth, better pressure.

EXTREMITIES

- **Writer's cramp**. Carpenter's cramp, etc.

Cramps especially of the hands and fingers.

Sciatica, better heat and pressure, worse motion and cold, right-side.

CLINICAL

Chorea. Colic. Dysmenorrhea. Neuralgia. Migraine. Sciatica. Toothache. Writer's cramps.

COMPARISONS

Coloc - Better warm and pressure, colic, dysmenorrhea, sciatica.

Nux-V - Neuralgia, Colic, better warmth.

Chin. Dros. Cycl.

MANCINELLA

Mancinella is an important remedy in mental disorders associated with great fear, delusions, and hysteria. We may think of this remedy in a child who has been excessively frightened by horror movies and begins to fear he will be possessed, etc. There is an obsession with evil forces, with the devil, or with ideas of demoniac possession. Also sexual ideas may be mingled with obsessions. With these thoughts, the patient becomes convinced he is momentarily about to go insane or is terrified of insanity.

MENTALS

- **Fear of evil, devils and demonic possession.**

Fears: Insanity. Dark. Ghosts. Martians. Sin.
Obsessive disorders. Fixed ideas *(Arg-N)*.
Compulsive thoughts of suicide or of self-mutilation.
Tormented by delusions and fears in the dark.
Complaints after seeing scary movies (psoriasis, anxiety disorder).

GENERALS

Warm, worse from heat.
Mental symptoms coming at the time of puberty or menopause.
General amelioration from motion.

HEAD

Rhinitis.
Head feels as if wrapped in a wire cage.
Intolerant of collars.

GASTROINTESTINAL

Thirst increased before menses.

UROGENITAL

Sexual perversion. Hyper-sexual. Feels sex is evil.

CHEST

Asthma; bronchitis.

CLINICAL

Anxiety. Compulsive disorders. Paranoia. Psoriasis. Schizophrenia.

COMPARISONS

Arg-N. Merc. Puls. Kali-Br. Cann-I.

MANGANUM

Though Manganum is one of our earliest remedies there has been almost no development of a cohesive picture of the remedy or of the mental symptoms. The main guiding symptom is the great amelioration the patient experiences of all his symptoms upon lying down. We cannot be fixed on one way of hearing a problem expressed; many patients may explain this characteristic by saying that they are worse when they stand or sit rather than, "better by lying."

GENERALS

- **General amelioration when lying down.**

  Generally worse from cold and damp weather.

  Anemia.

HEAD

Vertigo.

Chronic otitis media with progressive hearing loss.

Tooth pain extending to ear.

Eye feels strained or dry from exerting vision or looking at light.

UROGENITAL

Anemic women with scanty flow.

CHEST

Cough, better from lying down.

Chronic catarrh and rawness of larynx.

EXTREMITIES

Periosteal soreness, especially over the tibia. (Borland recommends Manganum as a remedy in growing pains especially of the tibia.)

Pain and numbness of the lower extremities.

Heel pain.

Some authors note gait disturbance: Slapping gait. Walks backward.

SKIN

Eczema.

- **Itching on the perspiring parts.**

  Eczema worse from bathing in the sea.

CLINICAL

Anemia. Bone pains. Bronchitis. Cough. Eczema. Hearing loss. Laryngitis. Otitis media. Parkinson's disease. Vertigo.

MEDORRHINUM

This nosode, along with Carcinosin, is perhaps the most under-represented polycrest in the repertory. We will almost never come to prescribe this remedy on the basis of repertorization. Therefore we must have a high index of suspicion when we take the case to find this remedy when it is indicated. Although many cases will not have any hint of the typical mental symptoms of Medorrhinum, it is often the personality of the patient which leads to the prescription of this remedy.

Extremes. The Medorrhinum patient can be described as an extremist. In his physical pathologies, in his mental state, in almost all aspects of his life the patient bounces between extremes: his grades are either "A's" or "F's"; his work is brilliant at one moment and then inept; his relationships are full of passionate love or hate. He is erratic and seems to have a compulsive need to experience more passion until he is driven to extremes of sexual conduct, drug or alcohol use, physical violence, etc.

Aggression. There is often a hardness apparent in the patient. He can be aggressive and violent. He seems to have little connection to those around him; not from withdrawal but from an inner hardness and self-centeredness. The patient may even be cruel to animals or his children. At other times or in other patients we see an opposite state with great sensitivity. In this type of patient, there may be introversion and shyness, even to the point of being unable to speak in the interview.

Anxiety. The patient often complains of his mental processes both as dull and too intense. He may be forgetful of what he is about to say or loses his train of thought mid-sentence. The Medorrhinum patient may look quite a lot like Nux Vomica - a workaholic type. At other times he feels a type of anxious, hurried feeling which not only causes the patient to rush around but also gives him a wild feeling in his head. We also see Medorrhinum patients becoming excessively religious - rather forceful and proselytizing. Some cases present with extreme phobias and anxiety.

Children. The Medorrhinum child often comes with behavioral problems or is found to have excessive aggression in addition to his other physical complaints. He is often pale and looks as though he is poorly nourished, often suffering with eczema, rhinitis, or asthma. He may have violent temper tantrums, kick or strike the parents, and fights with other children. Like the adult patient, the child often has an extremely passionate nature. Other Medorrhinum children are sensitive and may withdraw from the parents and family because of emotional shocks. There is often excessive attachment to animals and also cruel behavior towards animals. Sexual development begins even by the age of two or three and incestuous impulses are strong in this nosode.

MENTALS

Excessively passionate people who are led to problems from strong needs for expression of the passion.

Desire to experience everything. Loves the forbidden.

◆ **Extremists. Erratic performance.**

◆ **Cruel to animals.** Excessive love of pets, especially in children.

Aggressiveness even to the point of cruelty and violence.

Fear or sensation of someone beside or behind him.

Wild sensation in the head *(Lil-T)*.

Fear of dark and monsters in the dark or in the closet.

Claustrophobia. Fear of insanity. Fears about his health.

Begins a sentence and forgets what he was about to say.

Misjudges time - feels a recent event happened long ago.

◆ **Strong tendency to bite fingernails or even the toenails.**

GENERALS

◆ **General amelioration at the sea and from sea bathing.**

General amelioration in the evening; loves the night.

History of gonorrhea in the patient or parents.

History of early heart disease in the parents.

Amelioration from discharges.

General aggravation from damp weather.

HEAD

Chronic rhinitis and sinusitis, often beginning in infancy.

Conjunctivitis. Reiter's syndrome.

Vaguely described but troublesome migraines, often with kaleidoscopic visual aura.

Chronic otitis media, worse left ear.

Chronic post-nasal drip.

◆ **Constant clearing of the throat.**

GASTROINTESTINAL

Peptic ulcers with pain which wakes the patient at 2 AM.

Constipation better by leaning backwards.

Craves: Meat. **Meat fat.** Fish. Salt. Sweets. ◆**Ice.** ◆**Unripe fruit.** ◆**Oranges.** Alcoholic drinks. Tobacco.

Aversion: ◆**Eggplant.** Slimy foods. Beans and peas.

Thirsty for cold drinks.

UROLOGIC

Nonspecific urethritis. Urethral strictures.

Nephritis. Chronic or recurring cystitis.

GENITALIA

Chronic vaginitis, urethritis or cystitis, especially if this occurs after beginning a new sexual relationship.

Genital herpes. Genital warts.

Orchitis. Epididymitis. Prostatitis. Prostatic hypertrophy.

Ovarian pains and tumors; severe dysmenorrhea.

Sex drive extreme; nymphomania; satyriasis.

Masturbation, even in young children.

Extreme sexual behavior or pathology - incest, group sex, etc.

Impotence.

Babies with sharply demarcated, erythematous diaper rash.

CHEST

Chronic bronchitis, bronchiectasis, asthma.

Asthma from childhood; asthma and eczema combined.

Dyspnea better from assuming the knee-chest position.

Angina beginning in early years.

EXTREMITIES

Great swelling of the ankles.

◆ **Great sensitivity of the soles of feet.** Can't walk on rocks.

Hot feet in children - they take off their shoes the moment allowed; they love to walk barefooted on a cold floor.

Uncovers feet at night.

Arthritis with history of gonorrhea.

Restless feet in bed at night.

Coldness of the toes.

SKIN

Eczema from infancy.

Warts or cutaneous tumors. Aggressive urticaria.

SLEEP

Sleeps on the abdomen or in the ◆knee-chest position.

CLINICAL

Allergy. Angina. Anxiety. Arthritis. Asthma. Behavior disorder. Eczema. Herpes. Hypertension. Interstitial cystitis. Leukorrhea. Manic-depression. Migraine. Otitis. Peptic ulcer. Pulmonary fibrosis. Reiter's syndrome. Sinusitis. Urethritis. Vaginitis. Warts.

COMPLEMENTARY

Thuj. Nat-S. Sulph. Cann-I. Puls.

COMPARISONS

Sulph - Egotism, asthma and allergic symptoms, craving fat, sweets and cold drinks, eczema, bites nails, feet out of covers, etc.

Nux-V - Racing mind, asthma and allergy, craving fat, cystitis, extreme sex drive, etc.

Lach - Passionate, jealous, needs an outlet, hyper-sexual, asthma, etc.

Carc. Anac. Tub. Plat. Nat-S.

MELILOTUS

Essentially a headache remedy, Melilotus can be difficult to distinguish from Belladonna or Lachesis due to the congestive nature of the pain. Andre Saine of Toronto presented a case and some reports from the literature which indicate the use of this remedy in mania states.

MENTAL

Loquacious, suspicious, fear of police and poison.

Rage during menses.

HEAD

Throbbing headaches of the greatest severity.

- **Head pain ameliorated by hemorrhage - epistaxis, metrorrhagia, etc.**

Flushing of the face with the headache.

Epistaxis with congested face. Epistaxis relieves the headache.

GASTROINTESTINAL

Vomiting with headaches.

UROGENITAL

Marked dysmenorrhea.

EXTREMITIES

Knee pain. Wants to stretch the knee though it does not relieve.

CLINICAL

Dysmenorrhea. Epistaxis. Hypertension. Mania. Migraine headaches.

COMPARISONS

Lach - Congestive headache with amelioration from hemorrhage.

Glon. Bell. Puls.

MEPHITIS

This remedy is mainly indicated in respiratory troubles - asthma, cough, pertussis, bronchitis.

CHEST

Cough, worse reading or speaking, worse drinking, worse eating, worse lying down, worse exhaling.

Paroxysm of cough, worse after midnight.

Fine during day; extreme paroxysm of cough at night with vomiting.

COMPARISONS

Dros. Ars. Kali-Bi. Rumex.

MERCURIUS

The physical constitution of Mercury has often been likened to the Mercury in a thermometer - that is to say exquisitely reactive to changes in temperature. This metaphor hints that the patient may not only be over-sensitive to heat and cold, but also to many other changes in his environment. In many patients we find this great reactivity is associated with and in fact causes weakness and debility. In fact there are 62 references in the repertory for factors which generally aggravate Mercury but only 8 factors listed which ameliorate, and 5 of these have to do with resting or lying down. Mercury combines weakness and over-reactivity.

Introversion. On the emotional level, the Mercury patient tends to be withdrawn and introverted. The emotions are often strong internally but are rarely given expression. The patient feels different than other people and has a sort of instinctive reserve about expressing himself or even a suspiciousness of others. He puts on a facade of normality and conservatism. The patient will often confirm a noteworthy symptom: It is necessary for him to feel that the person he speaks to is listening carefully, with undivided attention or he will be unable to speak. This need for deep congruency may explain why many Mercury patients feel more comfortable in homosexual relationships.

Impulses. Often in Mercury cases these intense emotions which are withheld take the form of impulses. The patient has a strong impulse to strike or even kill an offending person. But these intense feelings are almost never revealed to others. In fact the Mercury patient often will cultivate a deeply conservative and proper appearance toward the world.

Anxiety. Deeper breakdown states occur in some Mercury patients. The inefficiency of mind often is a cause for concern, and to compensate the patient begins to hurry to try to accomplish all of his responsibilities. Eventually he finds that he is constantly rushing about. The Mercury patient may develop deep phobias and anxieties, especially about his mental health. He comes to the interview looking emotionally weak and broken. This is a remedy we must keep in mind for advanced states of depression, paranoia and even organic brain disease and imbecility.

Children. The Mercury child is often very precocious and seems to have almost adult-like emotions. He can seem flirtatious, intense and sensitive. The child has strong emotions and can be very irritable. More often the child is shy or withdrawn. In almost all cases the child suffers with poor resistance to infections - chronic otitis media, pharyngitis and stomatitis. The child usually exhibits the typical confirmatory keynotes.

MENTALS

Introverted, closed, emotionally intense and suspicious.

Internal impulses, often violent, destructive ideas (stabbing, etc.).

Impulse to scream.

Hurriedness. Irritability.

Precocity.

Fears: Disease. Death. Insanity. Darkness. Cemeteries. High places. Ghosts. People. Agoraphobia. Fear of poverty (great stinginess).

Slow to answer. Stammering.

Anxiety and panic attacks with great fear of insanity.

Compulsive disorders.

Withdrawn and depressed. Suicidal.

GENERALS

Syphilitic remedy.

General aggravation at night.

◆ **General aggravation from both heat and cold** (*Nat-C, Ip*).

General aggravation from becoming heated in bed.

General aggravation from damp weather.

Generally worse from open air.

Offensiveness of discharges.

Suppressed discharge aggravates.

Great debility and weakness.

General aggravation from perspiring.

Night sweats.

Appearance: Serious, pale face and skin with blotchiness and a translucent quality, like marble.

HEAD

Acne which is chronic, discharges pus easily, and leaves scars.

Rhinitis which is chronic and smouldering with greenish discharge.

Aphthae in mouth and on tongue. Ulceration in mouth or pharynx.

Otitis media both in acute and chronic cases.

- **Tongue imprinted with the teeth.**
- **Metallic taste in the mouth.**
- **Offensive breath.**
- **Excessive saliva, especially at night in bed.**

Gingivitis. Toothache.

THROAT

Acute or chronic pharyngitis, with dirty tongue and salivation.

Cervical adenopathy.

Flushes of the throat and upper chest with strong emotions *(Nat-M)*.

GASTROINTESTINAL

Craving: •Bread and butter. Sweet. Salt.

Aversion: Sweets. Salt. Artichokes.

Acute gastroenteritis with strong urging for diarrhea and the famous "Never get done" sensation.

Stool offensive.

Ulcerative colitis.

UROGENITAL

Intense and sometimes perverted sexual inclinations.

Premature ejaculation.

EXTREMITIES

Tremor, especially of the hands, worse writing or eating.

SKIN

Eczema. Itching, worse heat and heat of the bed, worse perspiration.

Ulceration of the skin, usually superficial and tending to spread.

Offensive eruptions. Psoriasis. Boils. Erysipelas.

CLINICAL

Abscess. Acne. Anxiety. Balanitis. Bruxism. Colds. Colitis. Conjunctivitis. Connective tissue disease. Eczema. Gastroenteritis. Glossitis. Iritis. Malignancy. Orchitis. Otitis Media. Paranoia. Parkinson's disease. Pharyngitis. Phobic disorder. Premature ejaculation. Rhinitis. Sexual disorders. Sinusitis. Stomatitis. Syphilis. Tonsillitis. Ulcerative colitis. Upper respiratory infections. Vaginitis.

COMPLEMENTARIES

Ars. Bad. Puls. Aur.

INIMICAL

Sil.

COMPARISONS

Ars - Anxiety, miserliness, impulses, offensiveness, diarrhea, ulceration, general syphilitic tendency.

Puls - Chronic otitis media of children, catarrhs with greenish mucous, craving for butter.

Plb - Slowed speech, weakness of memory, tremor of hands, Parkinson's disease.

Kali-br - Paranoia, anxiety disorder, fear of insanity, aggressive impulses, compulsive disorders, sleep disturbance.

Nat-M. Alum. Sil. Syph. Nux-V.

MERCURIUS CORROSIVUS

Although many of the characteristics of Mercurius Solubulis are also found in Mercurius Corrosivus, we can distinguish the latter by its intensity of tenesmus and excoriation.

GENERALS

Burning, excoriating discharges.

Generally worse at night.

◆ **Tenesmus.**

HEAD

Iritis with intense burning, lacrimation and photophobia.

Conjunctival ulceration.

Pharyngitis or ulcerations with intense burning pains and constant disposition to swallow despite fierce pain on swallowing.

Throat pain and pressure, worse from external touch.

Spasms of the throat or esophagus on swallowing.

Salivation.

Pyorrhea.

Gastrointestinal

- **Colitis or dysentery with constant tenesmus, straining which is undiminished upon passing stool.**

Bloody, mucus filled, burning diarrhea.

Diarrhea with the sensation that the stool is hot.

Urogenital

- **Cystitis with strong urging for urine, often unrelieved by voiding; tenesmus.** Constant urging for urination.

Dysuria, burning from the urethra.

Urethritis with purulent discharge, intense burning and excoriation.

Phimosis. Balanitis.

Clinical

Balanitis. Colitis. Crohn's disease. Cystitis. Iritis. Pharyngitis. Phimosis. Urethritis.

Comparisons

Canth - Urging and tenesmus from bowel and bladder, hemorrhagic diarrhea and urine, burning sensations and excoriation.

Merc. Nux-V. Ars.

MERCURIUS IODATUS FLAVUS
MERCURIUS IODATUS RUBER

When we have acute (or even in some chronic cases) illness with general indications for Mercurius Solubulis but in which the case is strongly localized to the right or the left side of the body, we must think of Mercurius Iodatus Ruber *(Biniodatus)* or Mercurius Iodatus Flavus *(Protoiodatus)*.

Mercurius Iodatus Flavus is for right-sided complaints, especially pharyngitis but also otitis, tonsillitis, etc. It may even be thought of for right-sided neuralgia.

Mercurius Iodatus Ruber is for left-sided complaints and is in fact the main remedy for left-sided tonsillitis or pharyngitis - even before Lachesis.

MEZEREUM

Mezereum is used mainly for skin diseases or complaints which originate on the skin. The skin symptoms are intense and varied but are often associated with suppuration, cracking and crusting of the lesions. The Mezereum patient is often anxious and serious. There can be a horrible anguished or anxious sensation felt in the epigastrium.

Mezereum has often been called a "vegetable Mercury" because of the symptoms of bone pains, ear disorders, neuralgia and skin diseases which mimic the syphilitic symptoms of Mercury (although Phytolacca has also been called "vegetable Mercury" with perhaps better justification).

MENTALS

Anxiety, felt in stomach *(Ars, Calc, Kali-C, Kali-Ar)*.

Anxiety when alone.

GENERALS

Chilly, aggravated by cold. "Cold to the bone" or "Frozen."

Coldness felt in single spots or limbs.

Generally worse from suppressed skin eruption (neuralgia, deafness, sciatica, asthma, anxiety, etc.).

Sensitive to touch.

HEAD

• **Eczema, psoriasis or other skin disorders of the scalp; thick crusts on scalp which crack and ooze a purulent discharge (which causes hair to mat).**

Sensitive scalp; can't tolerate touch of the scalp.

Headaches or neuralgias of the face from suppressed eruption.

Loss of hearing following suppressed eruption.

Ears sensitive to cold air or wind; feel as if air is blowing in them.

Eruptions on face, at the margin of the hair, or in the eyebrows, which are often crusted, oozing, intensely itchy.

Herpes zoster of the face.

Cracked lips.

GASTROINTESTINAL

Anxious, anguished, empty feeling in stomach as if dying.

Cravings: Fat. •Ham fat. Ham.

Gastritis. Peptic ulcer.

CHEST

Asthma from suppressed eruptions.

EXTREMITIES

Pain in the bones, especially the tibia, worse at night.

Inflammation of the periosteum.

Typical eczema in the antecubital and popliteal fossae.

Eruptions in a "stocking-glove" distribution on hands and feet.

SKIN

Eruptions, eczema, which generally begin with intensely itching and burning vesicles which crust or thicken on scratching.

Itching is worse from heat, from heat of the bed; may be better from cold application.

Cracking skin; geometrically patterned cracks.

Itch without eruption. Dermatographia.

Shingles. Herpes.

CLINICAL

Anxiety disorders. Asthma. Eczema. Headache and neuralgia. Hearing loss. Herpes Zoster. Peptic ulcer. Psoriasis.

COMPARISONS

Sulph - Eruptions with craving for fat, itch worse heat, suppressed eruptions, asthma.

Hep - Eruptions, chilly, craving fat.

Nit-Ac. Merc. Graph. Psor. Kali-C.

MOSCHUS

The hysterical nature of the personality and the complaints of Moschus are well known. The patient complains intensely but the symptoms are erratic and follow no expected course. The patient is anxious, fears his condition and feels he could die. There is also great anger and fits of rage. Spasms of muscles and smooth muscle characterizes the physical complaints. Michael Carlston of Santa Rosa, California presented two cases of asthma cured by Moschus. The characteristics were sudden, severe, even life-threatening asthmatic crisis, especially coming during cold or after bathing and both cases were associated with anxiety and abdominal pain. Nancy Herrick of the Hahnemann Clinic has confirmed these observations in a case of life-threatening asthma, worse smoke, with sudden crisis. This patient had both violent temper and sexual excitement..

Mentals

Hysteria.
Fits of anger; "Scolds until blue in the face."
Anxiety; feels he will die.
Fraudulent or hysterical disease.

Generals

Hysterical fainting, fainting from emotions, fainting from eating.
Hysterical convulsions.
Spasms of muscles.
Chilliness in general and cold in parts.
Generally worse before or during menses (faintness, dyspnea, etc.).

Head

Globus hystericus.
One cheek pale, one cheek red; one cheek cold, one cheek hot.

Gastrointestinal

Nausea and vomiting at the sight of food.
Flatus.
Craving: **Cheese.**
Abdominal pain associated with asthma.

Urogenital

Copious urination. Strong odor from urine.
Reported as curative in cases of diabetes
Intense sexual excitement.
Promiscuity.
Masturbation.

Chest

Hysterical asthma and stridor.
Spasms of the chest which are frightening.
Sudden, severe asthma *(Cupr)*.
Palpitations in hysterical patients.

Clinical

Asthma. Arrhythmia. Fainting. Globus hystericus. Hysteria. Hysterical convulsions. Palpitations. Sexual disorder. Vertigo.

Comparisons

Ign. Lil-T. Plb. Cupr. Tarent.

MUREX

Often described as a "highly-sexed Sepia," this remedy has its main focus on the urogenital tract. The patient often has a thin, wiry appearance which is also similar to Sepia.

UROGENITAL

Leukorrhea, excoriation and hypersensitivity of the genitalia.

Great sensitivity of the genitalia. Even slight touch is painful or alternatively may provoke strong sexual arousal.

Bearing down sensation in the pelvis, must cross the legs.

Uterine prolapse.

Pains in the uterus, bladder, or ovaries extending upward to the chest or to the opposite-sided breast.

Pains shooting upwards from the uterus.

Sexual instinct excessive. Promiscuity.

CLINICAL

Cervicitis. Cystitis. Uterine prolapse. Vaginitis.

COMPARISONS

Sep. Lil-T. Kreos. Plat.

MURIATICUM ACIDUM

The Acids are often remedies of collapse, and Muriatic Acid is especially indicated when the collapse comes on the physical level rather than in the emotional or mental sphere. Muriatic Acid is especially to be considered when there is profound weakness during or as a consequence of prolonged febrile illness. The patient may be completely weakened, unable to raise up in the bed; he sleeps 18 or 20 hours in a day or wakes long enough only to eat or drink.

Of course we will not always see this advanced state and may find the remedy in cases where the weakness is in isolated locations - most notably in the urinary and rectal sphincter muscles.

GENERALS

Weakness and collapse states.

General aggravation from sea bathing.

Extremely peevish and weak.

General aggravation from lying on the right side.

"Sliding down in the bed or chair" from weakness.

GASTROINTESTINAL

Tongue dry, shrunken and weak.

Rectum protrudes during stool or even during urination.

Hemorrhoids protruding.

Hering gave the symptom, "Hemorrhoids in emaciated children."

Involuntary stool when passing urine.

Has been considered one of our best remedies in typhoid fever.

CLINICAL

Chronic fatigue and collapsed states. Fever of unknown origin. Hemorrhoids. Incontinence. Mononucleosis. Rectal prolapse. Sepsis. Typhoid fever.

COMPARISONS

Gels. Laur. Stann. Ph-Ac. Carb-V. Carb-An. Sel.

NAJA

The similarities in Naja to the symptoms of other snake venoms may make this remedy hard to differentiate, especially from Lachesis. In Naja, the left-sided complaints, the intolerance to collars, the suffocation, the night time aggravation and especially the cardiac symptomatology all closely correspond to Lachesis and the other venoms. However in this remedy the hemorrhagic and septic tendencies are notably absent and especially valvular and cardiac symptoms are prominent. The marked tendency for valvular lesions is so strong that Kent was led to recommend its use almost as a specific in valvular lesions of children. The Naja patient is like a mild tempered Lachesis, without the forceful loquacity and without the jealousy and aggressiveness. The patient seems to dwell on unimportant or minor problems, making his troubles exaggerated.

Mental

Exaggerates problems; dwells on imaginary troubles.

Generals

Left-sided complaints.

Faintness and collapse, associated with palpitation or heart disease.

Head

Left frontal and temporal headache.

Hay fever.

Constriction of the throat; intolerant to collars.

Chest

- **Valvular lesions**, even in advanced cases may palliate.

Loud cardiac murmurs.

Angina with radiation of pain to the throat, neck, to the left arm and hand. Sharp, stitching pains in heart.

Violent palpitations, worse from even slight exertion, worse from lying on left side, worse from talking.

Pulse rapid or markedly slowed *(Dig)*.

Asthma, worse at night. Cardiac asthma.

Cardiomegaly. Endocarditis.

Suffocating feeling at night; wakes up gasping, worse lying left side.

Urogenital

Left ovarian cyst and pains.

Extremities

Edema of extremities.

Sleep

Unable to sleep on the left side.

Clinical

Allergy. Angina. Arrhythmia. Asthma. Congestive heart failure. Endocarditis. Headaches. Hypertension. Migraines. Ovarian cyst. Valvular disorders.

Comparisons

Lach - Cardiac disorders, constriction of throat and intolerance to collars, left-sided complaints, asthma, aggravation at night, aggravation from lying on left side, suffocation sensation, etc.

Spig. Kalm. Spong. Phos. Crot-H. Elaps. Cact.

NATRUM ARSENICUM

At the present stage our knowledge of Natrum Arsenicum is quite limited but we may be led to its use when there are symptoms of both Arsenicum (such as anxiety) and of the Natrum family (such as grief, aphthae, etc.). In the 1990 International Foundation for Homeopathy case conference, Sheryl Kipnis of Seattle presented a case of pulmonary sarcoidosis cured with this remedy.

MENTALS

Anxiety about health.

Grief. Emotions suppressed.

Ambitious; super-achievers; practical; perfectionistic; fastidious.

GENERALS

Chilly.

Great sensitivity to exposure to smoke *(Spig)*.

Weakness.

HEAD

Headache, especially mid-forehead or at the root of the nose, worse from reading.

• **Headache from smoke or in smokers.**

Dry, tired eyes.

Aphthae.

Allergy and nasal catarrh.

GASTROINTESTINAL

Intolerant to milk.

CHEST

Asthma. Rattling chest and productive cough.

• **Respiratory illness due to smoke or soot** (miner's lung).

Pulmonary sarcoidosis.

SKIN

Psoriasis *(Sep, Ars, etc.)*.

CLINICAL

Allergy. Asthma. Headache. Leukemia. Psoriasis. Sarcoidosis.

COMPARISONS

Nat-M. Nat-S. Spig.

NATRUM CARBONICUM

It was Vithoulkas who pointed out the gentle, self-sacrificing nature of the typical Natrum Carbonicum patient (Silica, Staphysagria). He also has emphasized the inability of the Natrum Carbonicum patient to "assimilate" whether on the physical level (food is poorly assimilated), or the emotional level (intolerant to certain people). Natrum Carbonicum may also be difficult to distinguish from the other Natrum remedies.

In the early stages of pathology the patient will complain of physical problems, especially digestive troubles and food allergies or intolerances. Later there is more emphasis on emotional difficulties and depressions (which may be difficult to distinguish from Natrum Muriaticum) caused by grief and loss. It has been often noted that the Natrum Carbonicum patient seems cheerful and jocular, even when he feels sad inside. It is therefore all the more surprising to find that this sweet-natured patient has strong aversions to specific people - even family members - for no particular reason. This aversion amounts to a type of bias or prejudice. The aversion can even take the form of racial or ethnic prejudice which is out of character for this type of person all together and which may take even the patient by surprise ("I can hardly believe I am having these feelings but I have developed a prejudice towards...."). Finally from emotional exhaustion or from poor assimilation the patient may develop mental weakness, poor mental stamina, and inability to concentrate.

MENTALS

Gentle, refined, selfless people.

- **Aversion to certain people**; aversion to family members.

Sensitive to music; weeping and bittersweet melancholy from hearing music; purposely plays sad music.

Sadness and grief.

Cheerful demeanor, excessively cheerful.

Mental dullness and exhaustion.

Complaints from mental exertion or from reading.

Averse to company, ameliorated when alone.

Timid.

GENERALS

- **General aggravation from the sun**. Sunstroke (*Glon*, *Carb-V*).
- **Food allergy, especially sensitive to milk.**

Sensitive to both heat and cold (*Merc*); narrow comfort range.

Generally worse during a storm or from change of weather.

Neurological weakness (multiple sclerosis, paresis).

Defective metabolism (skeletal troubles, kyphosis, stoop-shouldered).

HEAD

Headache from the sun and from over-heating.
Headache from mental exertion.
Headache alternating with digestive troubles.
Aphthae in mouth and nose.
Herpes of lips or face.
Peeling skin on the nose.
Itching in the whiskers. Tinea.
Hay fever and chronic nasal obstruction.

GASTROINTESTINAL

Dyspepsia; indigestion; weak digestion, worse dietary indiscretions.
Food allergies. Gastritis. Peptic ulcers.
◆ **Milk intolerance** - diarrhea, flatus, etc.
Stomach pains, worse touch, worse milk. Emptiness in stomach.
Eructation, heartburn, flatus.
Sputtering diarrhea with flatus.
Craves: Potatoes. Sweets. Milk.
Aversion: **Milk.**

UROGENITAL

Chronic cystitis; pain at the end of urination.
Urethral irritation or fissures causing stinging and burning.
Herpes of the genitalia, buttocks and the thigh or back.
Sterility; semen said to slide immediately from the vagina.

EXTREMITIES

Eczema of the fingertips or in the antecubital region.
Herpes of the buttocks or thighs.
Weakness of the ankles.
Stoop-shoulders.

CLINICAL

Allergy. Cystitis. Eczema. Food allergies and intolerance. Gastritis. Headache. Herpes. Infertility. Irritable bowel syndrome. Multiple sclerosis. Peptic ulcer. Urethritis.

COMPARISONS

Sil - Gentle, refined, poor metabolism, milk intolerance, headache.
Nat-M - Grief, averse company, sensitive to music, worse sun, worse milk, herpes.
Staph. Lyc. Mag-M.

NATRUM MURIATICUM

Natrum Muriaticum is one of the most psychologically complex and poignant remedies in our materia medica. Because deep grief and sorrow are hallmarks of the character of Natrum Muriaticum, and because these emotions have (or will have someday) touched and shaped each human life, almost everyone will deeply identify with this remedy description.

Sensitivity. The Natrum Muriaticum personality is highly sensitive and refined. It is easy to see how such an individual could come to be wounded by life - whether by criticisms, insults, intentional rejections, or inevitable losses. In Natrum Muriaticum, these wounds are deeply felt and result in the patient placing a psychological wall around himself to avoid further pain. Thus the patient may appear closed or even hard.

Introversion. The Natrum Muriaticum patient is introverted and overly serious. He is responsible and perfectionistic. Often the patient is overly mentalized. In the interview he often offers very little information, and hesitates before his answers. During the course of the interview a significant grief is often discovered. The patient will discuss this grief only with reluctance or may show hostility that he is being asked such personal questions which result in bitter, involuntary, or hysterical tears.

Hysteria. There is an opposite presentation in which the patient seems abnormally open and can discuss even intimate aspects of his life, apparently not at all embarrassed. This is especially true of patients who have undergone psychotherapy and have "learned to be open." Yet this behavior is unnatural to him and comes across as forced or almost hysterical. Of course a great number of Natrum Muriaticum patients will not present in either of these extreme forms.

Reserve. The Natrum Muriaticum patient has extremely easily hurt feelings. The patient dwells on insults or criticisms and finds it very difficult to forgive. Anything which implies criticism, humiliation or rejection is intolerable. He is unable to ask for help because of the humiliation. For this same reason he is unable to accept, or is even aggravated by consolation. Despite this inhibition, the patient may be very sympathetic to the problems of others and finds that many people confide in him. These confidences are given because others feel that the Natrum Muriaticum patient is kind, but also so closed as to never divulge secrets.

Grief. When a loss (for example, through death), or a serious rejection ("Unrequited love") occurs the patient experiences abnormally prolonged grief and depression. Many times physical conditions - either functional or pathological - may occur from such griefs. Natrum Muriaticum is our most prominent remedy in patients whose problems begin from grief or insufficiently processed grief.

Romantic. The Natrum Muriaticum patient is often highly romantic but after a disappointment closes himself to further relationships for many years. This patient is rarely the cause of a separation, being loyal and dedicated to his loved ones. Often we will discover that the patient has been existing in an unhappy relationship for many years - too closed to his partner to fix the problem yet too loyal to leave.

Perfectionism. The typical patient is controlled and perfectionistic. Often the patient can be compulsively fastidious, trying to control the environment. As regards health matters, the patient may develop a type of hypochondria which is expressed as an anxious desire to find the cause of every blemish or pimple. This tendency goes along with the fastidious control of the environment and perfectionism. Excessive control can cover an inner hysteria in Natrum Muriaticum patients. When the inhibitions are broken the patient may cry hysterically, express long denied anger, or even exhibitionistic tendencies.

Children. The Natrum Muriaticum child is well-behaved and often mature beyond his years; "like a little adult." The child has a strong need for affection and is overly vulnerable. Like the adult, the child prefers to be alone with his griefs and will shrug off his parents consoling hug. Even as adolescents this same sensitivity and inability to accept help is problematic. The child is also extremely responsible about his homework or his family's needs. It should be recalled that a Natrum Muriaticum type may resort to drug use to help numb his emotional pain.

MENTALS

Closed, responsible, dignified and much affected by grief.

◆ **Ailments from grief and disappointed love. Silent grief.**

Depression, even suicidal feelings.

Too serious and overly proper and responsible.

Easily offended or wounded; complaints from humiliation.

◆ **Sad yet unable to weep.**

Involuntary and hysterical weeping.

Aversion to company. Desires and ameliorated by being alone.

Dwells on past griefs and humiliations.

Fastidious. Perfectionistic. Always on time. Compulsive.

Averse to consolation.

Fears: **Robbers** or people breaking in to the house. Dark. Storms. **Claustrophobia**. Insects. Germs. Heights.

Hypochondria. Anxious about tiny blemishes.

Sensitive to noise and music.

Uses alcohol to loosen inhibition; "When I drink I love everyone."

Premenstrual syndrome with irritability and sadness.

Bites fingernails.

GENERALS

Warm-blooded and generally aggravated from heat although some patients are chilly.

◆ **General aggravation from the sun.**

General aggravation at 10 AM.

General aggravation from the sea; sometimes better at the sea.

Periodic complaints.

Recurring fevers; periodic fever.

General amelioration from perspiration.

Malaria or even a family history of malaria.

Anemia.

Neurologic disease: main remedy in multiple sclerosis.

Twitches or tremor, especially of the face and head.

Appearance: The patient often has a serious appearance. The hairstyle is practical and unflattering. He wears thick, awkward glasses. The face and lips are thin or pinched. The neck is long and thin but often the patient is heavy in the thighs and buttocks. The skin is pale and fine with blue veins showing.

Vertigo, worse pregnancy, worse tea, worse looking to distance; vertigo causes marked nausea.

Vertigo with tendency to fall, especially to the left.

HEAD

◆ **Headache; Migraine.**

Headache, worse light, worse sun, worse reading, worse before or after the period, worse noise, worse head injury.

◆ **Headache worse 10 AM or from 10 AM to 3 PM.**

◆ **Headache "like hammers beating the head."**

Headache from grief.

Headache in schoolgirls.

Headache, better from lying in dark, quiet room, better by perspiration, better cold application.

Headache felt in any location, more often right-sided hemicrania, but also occipital, etc.

Numbness in face or lips (or even extremities) before headache.

Facial neuralgia, worse from suppressed malaria or use of quinine, especially on the left side.

Whitish crusts on the scalp; eruptions at hair margin *(Sulph)*.

◆ **Hay fever**, especially in over-mentalized patients.

◆ **Coryza albuminous or "egg-white."** Colds begin with sneezing.

◆ **Herpetic eruption - lips**, face, corners of nose and mouth, chin.

Cracks of the lips, especially of the corners of the mouth.

Aphthae of mouth, gums, tongue; glossitis.

EYES

- ◆ **Lacrimation of the eyes, worse open air or wind**, worse cough, worse reading.
- ◆ **Eyelid with transverse line through the middle of the upper lid, especially in children.**

A fine line under the margin of the lower lid.

Pains of the eyes, worse looking, worse reading.

Visual disturbance before headache.

Allergic "shiners."

THROAT

Emaciated appearance of throat, neck and face.

Goitre and thyroid conditions.

Pharyngitis with stitching pains.

Sensation of a lump in the throat.

GASTROINTESTINAL

Peptic ulcers, often beginning from grief or conflict.

Craves: ◆**Salt. Sour**. Lemon. Bitter. Beer. Chocolate. Fish. Burned food or burned toast. Bread. Milk.

Averse: **Fat. Rich foods. Slimy foods** and egg-white. **Chicken.** Bread. Salt. Milk.

Thirsty for ice cold drinks *(Phos, Sulph)*.

Colitis with sudden urging for diarrheic stool, hemorrhage from rectum after stool.

Bleeding hemorrhoids, worse after hard stool. Constipation.

UROGENITAL

- ◆ **"Bashful kidneys." Unable to urinate in front of others.**

Stress incontinence.

Chronic nephritis.

Falling out of the pubic hair.

Uterine prolapse. Chronic leukorrhea.

During sex, the desire to use dirty words.

Painful coition. Vaginal dryness. Vaginitis.

Aversion to sex in women, especially after the emotions are closed down due to grief.

CHEST

- ◆ **Asthma in the evening**, worse 5 to 7 PM.

Palpitations at night, worse lying left side, worse noise.

Sighing.

EXTREMITIES:

- **Back pain and low back pain, better lying on something hard or pressing against the fist or an object such as a book.**

Cracked skin of fingers.

Peeling of the fingertips.

Cracked nails.

Eczema. Urticaria. Psoriasis. Ringworm.

Hangnails.

Tremor of hands (and whole head).

Bites the fingernails.

SLEEP

- **Insomnia; cannot fall asleep from thoughts of griefs of the day and disagreeable things from long past.**

Sleeps on the left side.

Dreams of robbers.

CLINICAL

Allergy. Anemia. Aphthae. Arrhythmia. Asthma. Chemical sensitivity. Chronic fatigue syndrome. Colitis. Connective tissue diseases. Depression. Diabetes. Dyspareunia. Eczema. Fever. Fever of unknown origin. Gastritis. Globus hystericus. Goitre. Grave's disease. Headache. Hemorrhoids. Herpes. Hypertension. Inflammatory bowel disease. Irritable bowel syndrome. Insomnia. Lower back pain. Malaria. Malignancy. Migraines. Multiple Sclerosis. Nephritis. Obesity. Peptic ulcer. Premenstrual syndrome. Psoriasis. Sciatica. Sexual dysfunction. Stomatitis. Suicidal states. Thyroiditis. Tinea. Urticaria. Vaginitis. Vertigo.

COMPLEMENTARIES

Apis. Bry. Ign. Lyc. Sep.

COMPARISONS

Nat-C - Headache, worse sun, worse milk, grief, sensitive noise and music, aphthae, herpes.

Nat-S - Headache, gastrointestinal disorders, grief and severe depression, sensitive to music, asthma, head injury.

Ign - Grief, globus hystericus, aversion to consolation, sighing, etc.

Sep - Emotionally withdrawn, aversion to sex, amelioration while alone, aversion salt, amelioration from exertion, etc.

Aur - Serious, proud, grief and disappointed love, sensitive music, heart symptoms, severe depression.

Staph. Phos. Kali-C. Chin. Bor. Caust. Cocc.

NATRUM PHOSPHORICUM

The Natrum Phosphoricum patient has both the tendency for grief and depression of Natrum Muriaticum and the sympathy and fears of Phosphorous. He seems open in the interview but is also very self-contained and refined. He is balanced between extroversion and reservedness. The keynote tendency for nocturnal seminal discharges may also be reflected in complaints which linger for years after a period of seminal discharges.

MENTALS

Extremely refined patients.
Fears: Dark. Storms. Insects. Death and illness.
Mental dullness after seminal emissions.
Clairvoyance; clairvoyant dreams.

GENERALS

General aggravation from thunderstorms - palpitations, headache.
Symptoms develop during a period of seminal discharges.

HEAD

Headache during a storm.
• **Yellow coating of tongue, base of tongue, or the throat.**
Hay fever.

GASTROINTESTINAL

Craving: Eggs. •**Fried eggs. Salt**. Spicy. Fish. Ice Cream. Beer.
Hyperacidity; sour eructations.

UROGENITAL

• **Nocturnal seminal emissions.**

CHEST

Asthma, worse in the evening, worse exertion.

EXTREMITIES

Weak or trembling in extremities or back after seminal emissions.
Recorded as a remedy for rheumatism of children.
Contractures of tendons; Dupuytren's contracture.
Podagra; gout.
Eczema on the ankles.

SLEEP

Sexual dreams.

CLINICAL

Allergy. Asthma. Contracture. Gout. Rheumatism. Sexual disorders.

COMPARISONS

Nat-M. Phos. Sel. Cob. Staph. Kali-P. Pic-Ac.

NATRUM SULPHURICUM

Natrum Sulphuricum is a deep-acting remedy useful in a wide variety of pathological conditions, from asthma, to ulcerative colitis to leukemia and rectal cancer. It is significant how often Natrum Sulphuricum is prescribed as a "specific" remedy for physical conditions (i.e. head injury) or combinations of symptoms (i.e. asthma and history of severe depression, or asthma and history of diabetes, etc.). These physical conditions may often lead to the prescription of this remedy without the typical mental symptoms.

The usual Natrum Sulphuricum patient is serious, responsible, closed and melancholic. The patient tends to be slightly less refined than the other Natrum remedies; more focused on business matters than on interpersonal relationships. Yet he may have great sensitivity, for example the patient may mention that he weeps from hearing music, all the more striking in such a practical patient. Alternatively, some Natrum Sulphuricum patients are more wild, need excitement, sexual stimulation and drugs and are more artistically inclined. Grief plays an important role in most Natrum Sulphuricum cases as in other Natrums. Great depression can be indicative of this remedy. Natrum Sulphuricum is one of our most important remedies in suicidal patients, whether from grief or head injury or other organic causes. The patient may say that he constantly must restrain himself from the impulse to take his own life.

MENTALS

Closed, serious and overly responsible patients.

- **Suicidal longings but restrains himself because of his duties to his family. Wishes to hang or shoot himself.**

Weeping from music.

- **Confusion or mental dullness after a head injury.**
- **Cheerful after stool.**

Strong attachments. Incapacitated by divorce or death of spouse.

Fastidious.

Wild patients with drug use and excessive sexual behavior.

GENERALS

Generally warm-blooded.

General aggravation from damp weather - rainy, foggy, etc.

General aggravation from warm humid weather.

◆ **General aggravation from injury to head or spine.**

◆ **General amelioration after stool.**

Convulsions which begin after head injury.

Green colored discharges or discolorations.

Sycosis. History of gonorrhea.

◆ **Diabetes mellitus.**

HEAD

Gastric or bilious headaches - bitter taste in the mouth, vomiting bile, indigestion with headache.

Headache after head injury.

◆ **Photophobia**, often during the headache.

Chronic nasal catarrh, post-nasal discharge; greenish discharge.

Greenish discoloration of the tongue (or sometimes grayish).

Tinnitus, especially right ear.

GASTROINTESTINAL

Craves: ◆**Yogurt**. Fish. Ice.

Aversion: Yogurt.

Gastritis and peptic ulceration.

◆ **Diarrhea in the morning after rising.**

Sudden urging to stool.

Diarrhea with flatus mixed in causing a sputtering stool.

Diarrhea from vegetables, farinaceous or acid foods.

Diarrhea of nursing infants with asthmatic mothers.

Ulcerative colitis or proctitis.

Acute and chronic hepatitis; cholecystitis; in liver and gallbladder disease often has the desire to lie on right side with legs curled up.

Loud rumbling in the abdomen.

Urging for stool but passes only flatus or bloody mucous.

◆ Rectal cancer or malignant colorectal polyps.

UROGENITAL

Condylomata of the genitalia or perianal region.

Gonorrhea, suppressed gonorrhea; greenish urethral discharge.

CHEST

Asthma, ◆worse 4 AM, worse damp, worse exertion.

◆ **Asthma of children. Asthma after grief.**

Asthma may stop at puberty and recur in the thirties or later.

Chronic bronchitis; rattling, mucus filled cough.

Weak feeling in the chest; must hold the chest when coughing.

Pneumonia, especially the left lower lobe; productive cough with greenish sputum.

Considered by many authors an important remedy for tuberculosis.

MUSCULOSKELETAL

Arthritis of the spine; sciatica.

Back pain worse rising from a seat.

Arthritis of the left hip.

Warts of the hands; plantar's warts.

Itching after undressing, especially lower limbs.

SLEEP

Sleeps on the left side.

CLINICAL

Allergy. Arthritis. Asthma. Cholecystitis. Colitis. Concussion. Connective tissue disease. Diabetes. Diarrhea. Gastritis. Head injury. Headache. Hepatitis. Leukemia. Malignancy. Meningitis. Peptic ulcer. Pneumonia. Rheumatism. Sinusitis. Suicidal states. Tinnitus. Ulcerative colitis. Warts.

COMPLEMENTARY

Ars. Thuj. Med.

COMBINED SYMPTOMS

Asthma *and* diabetes.

Asthma *and* depression.

Asthma *and* colitis or colorectal polyps or malignancies.

COMPARISONS

Nat-M - Serious, closed people, depression, colitis, head injury, sleeps on left, fastidious, sensitive to music, etc.

Aur - Depression and suicidal feelings in serious, business types, sensitivity to music, grief.

Med - Asthma, warts, catarrh, worse damp weather, history of gonorrhea.

Chin. Chel. Dulc. Kali-C. Kali-Bi. Sulph.

NITRICUM ACIDUM

The Nitric acid patient can be difficult to manage due to a typically negative attitude about life and health. And while it is true that some Nitric Acid patients are unpleasant, we must avoid stereotyping patients ("He can't be Nitric Acid, he's too nice!"). In the early stages the patient may be quite kind and sympathetic towards his loved ones though plagued by periods of irritability. Especially upon waking in the morning, the patient is so irritable that he cannot be spoken to, and the family learns to avoid him during these hours. The irritability eventually worsens and he develops a peevish and nasty character. The patient is often involved in long-standing quarrels with people in his neighborhood or work place. This is described in our texts as "unmoved by apologies", and may reach the stage where family members refuse to speak to each other for years. The patient is deeply selfish and feels others are motivated in the same way as himself. This gives him a nihilistic, pessimistic attitude towards life. Yet at other moments he may exhibit great tenderness and sympathy especially for others' helpless suffering.

One of the other prominent characteristics of Nitric Acid patients is the tremendous anxiety about health. Nitric Acid is the most hypochondriacal remedy in all our materia medica. The patient especially fears fatal diseases like cancer or AIDS, often greatly out of proportion to his state of health, age or family history. When a case involves the combination of hypochondria and a strong fear of death, we should always consider this remedy. Even when told by the physician that a particular lesion is nothing to worry about, the patient remains unconvinced. He has an unshakable belief that he has a serious condition and that the physician has misdiagnosed the problem. This fatalistic attitude may even give rise to suicidal ideas.

When we reflect about this patient, who is both vindictive by nature and has great anxiety about health, it is easy to understand that he will make his physician's life miserable. The Nitric Acid patient will report at follow-up that not only is his problem unimproved but that the remedy given has made him feel infinitely worse. No patient will accuse his homeopath with such vehemence. Even having been given the correct remedy, a Nitric Acid patient is very reluctant to admit to any positive results and therefore the homeopath must be very cautious about changing his prescription. Then once the remedy has had some effect, the patient will be obsessed with worries about antidoting, and may call the prescriber constantly to inquire about potential antidotes from hair sprays, perfumes, electric watches, etc. Remember, as always, that we can prescribe Nitric Acid on physical indications alone with none of these mental characteristics.

MENTALS

Anxiety about health.

Fears: **Cancer. Death**. AIDS. Poverty. Antidoting his remedy.

• **Irritable and peevish, worse in morning.** Desire to kill.

• **Holds grudges, "unmoved by apology."**

Hard person, his suffering is etched on his face.

Nihilistic attitude. Pessimism. Depression.

Cursing. Angry at life. Blames everyone for his problems.

Selfish and preoccupied with his own needs.

Sympathy for the suffering of helpless people.

Accuses the doctor of causing him harm.

GENERALS

Chilly and aggravated cold, though at times neutral temperature.

Stitching or splinter-like pains.

Offensive odor of perspiration or discharges.

General amelioration while riding.

Ulceration, especially of the mucous membranes.

HEAD

Headache like external pressure or worse pressure or wearing hats.

Iritis.

Offensive otorrhea. Stitching in ears; extending to ears from throat.

Acrid coryza.

Epistaxis, worse at night.

Cracking of the temporomandibular joint.

Severe, often cystic acne.

Fissures, ulcers of tongue.

Halitosis.

Eruptions, herpes, warts, fissures about the lips, especially at the corners of the mouth.

THROAT:

Pharyngitis with stitching or splinter sensation.

Ulcers of pharynx and tonsils with stitching pains.

GASTROINTESTINAL

Peptic ulcer.

Craving: •**Fat** (takes the fat from another's plate). **Salty.** Herring. Cheese. Bread. Inedibles (dirt, chalk).

Aversion: Eggs. Bread. Cheese.

Indigestion and nausea from milk.

Thirst in the morning.

RECTUM

Hemorrhoids with great pain after stool lasting for hours.

Stitching or splinter-like pains of the rectum.

Rectal warts. Anal fissure or fistula. Anal abscess.

Colitis with acrid, offensive diarrhea.

Constipation; ineffectual urging.

Rectal malignancy.

UROGENITAL

Genital warts, may be hypersensitive and bleed easily.

Genital herpes. Gonorrhea. Syphilis.

Chronic urethral discharge, may be bloody. Nonspecific urethritis.

Ulcers of genitals. Ulcers or stricture in urethra with stitching pains.

Prostatitis. Balanitis.

Vaginitis, itching before or after menses, worse coition.

Acrid leukorrhea.

Sex drive excessive.

• **Urine foul odor or strong, "like a horse's urine**." *(Benz-Ac)*.

EXTREMITIES

Back pain after coition.

Back injury; cold, clammy hands and feet after back injury.

Pains under the nails like splinters. Paronychia.

Perspiration offensive. Perspiration smells "like a horse's urine."

Cracks at the bends of the joints; cracks on the fingers.

Warts. Psoriasis. Eczema.

SLEEP

Waking at 2 AM.

CLINICAL

Acne. Anxiety. Balanitis. Colitis. Fissure. Gonorrhea. Headache. Hemorrhoids. Herpes. Low back pain. Malignancy. Panic disorder. Peptic ulcers. Pharyngitis. Rectal cancer. Skin ulcers. Syphilis. Ulcerative colitis. Ulcers and aphthae. Urethritis. Vaginitis. Warts.

COMPLEMENTARIES

Ars. Calc. Lach.

COMPARISONS

Ars - Anxiety about health, irritability, chilly, craves fat, colitis, etc.

Nux-V - Irritable, chilly, craves fat, rectal problems.

Sulph. Rat. Lyc. Agar. Med. Aur. Anac.

NUX MOSCHATA

Confusion and drowsiness are the central features of the Nux Moschata patient. This mental picture can occur acutely following infection, allergy, shock, etc. or as part of a constitutional condition. The patient may complain only of a mild "spacey" feeling or may come to the interview markedly obtunded. It may be difficult to differentiate the Nux Moschata patient from other remedies such as Opium, Cannibis Indica, or even Alumina. There can be a hilarity and giddiness as we see in Cannibis, or alternatively, a marked mental dullness or stupefaction as we find in Alumina or Helleborous. Often the patient has a weak memory and confusion which results in an absentmindedness; he enters the kitchen but forgets what he came there to find. Especially when mental confusion or haziness is associated with sleepiness we must consider the remedy Nux Moschata. (Nux Moschata is not botanically related to Nux Vomica.)

MENTALS

- ◆ **Sleepiness. Over-powering sleepiness.**
- **Feels as if in a dream; "Spaced-out."**
- **Giddiness.** A cheerful, hazy feeling.
- **Forgetful**; thoughts wander or vanish.
- ◆ **Forgets why he has come into the room.**
- Seems intoxicated, as if on drugs.
- Confusion - makes mistakes in directions, in speech.
- Hesitates in speech. Chatters.
- Dizzy and absent-minded.
- Stupefaction, worse menses; comes to his senses with a start.
- Moods changeable.
- Fear of the sight of blood.

GENERALS

- Chilly and worse cold damp.
- General aggravation from windy and stormy weather.
- General aggravation during menses.
- **Fainting spells**, worse with palpitations, worse from the sight of blood, hysterical fainting.
- ◆ **Sleepiness,** worse during chills and fever or between the chills, worse from eating particular foods (food allergy).

HEAD

- Headache, worse motion of the head, worse over-eating.
- Coryza and nasal obstruction; hay fever with marked sneezing.
- **Dry eyes,** making it difficult to open or close them.

MOUTH

- **Dry mouth and tongue; "cotton mouth" sensation.**
- **Tongue so dry that it adheres to the roof of the mouth.**

Dry mouth with unquenchable thirst.

Dry mouth but no thirst; desires to hold water in the mouth to moisten it then spits it out.

Thick, slimy mucous or saliva in the mouth.

Tongue numb and thick.

Smacks the lips.

GASTROINTESTINAL

Stubborn constipation; must mechanically remove the stool with his finger *(Alum)*.

Colic of newborns with marked constipation.

Umbilical hernia, especially in newborns.

Fullness and distention of the abdomen.

Food allergy.

Thirstless.

CHEST

Heaviness and oppression of the chest.

EXTREMITIES

Arthritis. Wandering joint or muscle pains.

Numbness of the extremities.

SLEEP

- **Overwhelming sleepiness**. Narcolepsy.

CLINICAL

Allergy.Alzheimer's disease. Colic. Constipation. Food allergy. Narcolepsy. Organic Brain Syndrome. Petit mal. Sjogren's syndrome. Syncope. Vertigo.

COMPARISONS

Cann-I - Confused, hazy state, laughing immoderately, loses direction.

Op - Sleepiness, narcolepsy, constipation, mental dullness.

Alum - Constipation, requires mechanical aid to defecate, and mental dullness, slow speech.

Hell. Cocc. Puls. Gels. Carb-S.

NUX VOMICA

The typical Nux Vomica patient is readily recognized by almost all homeopaths and is in fact one of the most commonly prescribed remedies.

Work. The popular concept of "type A personality" describes the typical Nux Vomica patient very well. The Nux Vomica patient is impatient, competitive and ambitious. The major focus of his life is on his work and achievement. He is confident and even arrogant. The patient is compulsive with his work and in all aspects of his life, even to the point of fastidious cleanliness and ordering of his house or office.

Anger. People of such a focused nature often have strongly aggressive personalities, and this is very characteristic of the Nux Vomica patient. The patient can be irritable, first only sporadically but as he becomes more pathological the irritability becomes anger, then rage, then frank violence. In the usual case, however, the patient is irritable mainly from impediments to his ambitions. He becomes infuriated at the slowness and inefficiency of his co-workers, of waitresses, cashiers, etc. Even an inanimate object can anger the patient: he may tear his shirt if the buttons don't come out easily; he breaks the phone if he gets a busy signal on an important call. He may have long standing, unresolved anger towards his parents or others. In advanced states, the patient develops increasingly violent behavior patterns which may even end in criminal behavior.

Competition. In almost all aspects of his life the Nux Vomica patient is competitive. When he plays cards he must win; when he jogs, he must jog faster than the others on the track; when he drives, he cannot bear the idea that the person in the next lane may get ahead of him, so he switches lanes to always be in the fast lane even if that requires forcing himself into the path of another car. He wants to try everything and is not overly cautious about things he may explore. Any type of stimulant - coffee, alcohol, amphetamines, even cocaine will attract this patient. He may also be hedonistic in sexual matters. The Nux Vomica patient fears and avoids marriage, not out of fear of responsibility as in Lycopodium but from fear of the loss of freedom or fear of being humiliated in marriage.

Collapse. It is easy to understand that the patient described could be subject to collapse states from over-work or abuse of substances or from indulgence and excess. Nux Vomica is one of the best remedies for patients in collapsed states, not only for the collapse itself but to help him to be more moderate in his behavior in the future.

Physical. On the physical plane, Nux Vomica pathology centers largely on the gastrointestinal tract. Since so many of the symptoms of Nux Vomica are related to its heavy strychnine content, it should come as no surprise that spasm and cramping are very prominent. Additionally the nervous system is often disturbed.

Children. The Nux Vomica child is irritable and often affected with gastrointestinal problems such as colic or colitis. At school age, the child is extremely competitive about his grades and sports. He is a terrible loser. The parents may say that the child can under no circumstances admit that he is at fault or that he has made a mistake. Jealousy of his other siblings or toward other gifted children at school is often a problem. In adolescence the child may develop strongly bitter feelings towards his parents, especially the same-sex parent. It can be astonishing to find how rudely this child can speak towards his parent in such cases. These children are very concerned about fair-play both towards themselves and others and can seem very idealistic. Many Nux Vomica children exhibit strong fears, especially fear of the dark.

MENTALS

- **Irritable, impatient, ambitious and driven patients.**
- **Easily offended.**
  Anger from contradiction *(Aur)*.
  Tendency to break things from anger and frustration.
  Premenstrual irritability.
- **Impatient - hates waiting in lines or in traffic.**
- **Competitive.**
- **Workaholic. Compulsive.**
  Fastidious, especially angry if objects not in their proper place.
  Fear: Marriage. Humiliation. Dark (especially in children). Failure.
  Substance abuse. Alcoholism. Delirium tremens.
  Weeping from anger. Weeping before menses.
  Aversion to tight clothing - in a hurry to take off watches, ring, tie.
  Great sensitivity to stimulation - light, noise, odors, etc.

GENERALS

  Chilly and worse from cold and from cold, dry wind.
- **Chills, rigor from moving under his blanket** (during fever).
  Generally better from warmth and warm applications.
  Collapse and fatigue states from overwork.
  General aggravation from eating.
  Convulsions, worse anger, worse touch.
  Faintness, worse odors, worse labor.
  Cerebral accidents with paresis, expressive aphasia, convulsion.
  General aggravation from dry weather.
  General aggravation from suppressed hemorrhoids (peptic ulcer, etc.).
  General aggravation from alcoholic drinks or from abuse of alcohol.
  Breakdown from substance abuse.
  Simple "hangover."

HEAD

Headache and migraine, worse noise, worse light, worse mental activity or vexation, worse before menses.

Photophobia.

Allergy and hay fever, even hay asthma.

◆ **Sneezing and coryza in morning on waking or on rising.**

Fluent coryza in the morning but obstructed at night.

Coryza worse in open air.

Bruxism.

GASTROINTESTINAL

Craving: **Spicy. Fat. Alcohol. Coffee**. Tobacco. Any stimulant.

Peptic ulcers in workaholic patients. Gastritis from alcohol abuse.

Hepatitis, either infectious or alcoholic.

Hernia, inguinal or umbilical.

Nausea and vomiting, worse anger, worse alcohol, worse menstrual colic or other abdominal pains, worse smoke.

Stomach pains, worse anger, worse tight clothes, better warmth, warm applications or warm drinks.

Cramping or sharp pains in abdomen, worse after eating, worse cold, better warmth or warm drinks, better stool.

Infants with colic and angry arching of the back.

RECTUM

◆ **Constipation with constant, ineffectual urging for stool**; small amounts are passed which temporarily relieves the urging only to return moments later.

Constipation in children with hard, painful stool; the child fears going for stool.

Diarrhea alternating with constipation; constant urging for stool but passes small amounts. Diarrhea, worse cold, worse alcohol.

Urging for stool during urination.

Hemorrhoids; pains better warmth, better after stool.

UROGENITAL

◆ **Cystitis with constant urging for small amounts, better from heat or warm bathing.**

Painful urinary retention.

Sex drive increased; promiscuity.

Kidney stones; renal colic.

Pyelonephritis.

Dysmenorrhea with urge for stool before or during the flow.

Uterine or rectal spasm during sexual orgasm.

CHEST

Cough, worse morning, or morning in bed.

Asthma, often worse exertion, worse night, worse 3 or 4 AM, worse cold, worse in the morning.

Angina pectoris.

Palpitations from coffee, from excitement.

MUSCULOSKELETAL

Back pain, worse night in bed, worse turning in bed, must rise to turn, worse during fever, worse during urge for stool.

Fibrositis, worse cold, better warmth.

Cramps and contractures of muscles.

Twitching, tics, tremor and muscle spasms anywhere in the body.

SLEEP

- **Insomnia, wakes especially 3 or 4 AM and cannot sleep due to thoughts about work** or how to accomplish tasks.

Sleepiness during day, worse eating, worse when sitting, worse watching TV.

ACUTES

- Influenza or other febrile conditions with high fever and violent chills and rigors which are worse from every movement which stirs the air under the covers.

Cystitis with nearly constant urging, relieved for moments only on passing small quantities of urine and relieved by warm applications or warm bathing.

Gastritis with pains from alcohol abuse or from over-eating. Acute colic - kidney stones, cholecystitis - with cramping pains better from heat, worse touch.

CLINICAL

Alcoholism. Allergy. Angina. Arrhythmia. Arthritis. Asthma. Behavior disorder. Cerebral accidents. Chemical sensitivities. Chronic fatigue syndrome. Colds. Colic. Constipation. Crohn's disease. Cystitis. Endometriosis. Fibrositis. Headaches. Hemorrhoid. Hypertension. Inflammatory bowel disease. Influenza. Insomnia. Irritable bowel syndrome. Kidney stones. Lower back pain. Lupus. Migraines. Multiple Sclerosis. Neuralgia. Peptic ulcer. Premenstrual syndrome. Prostatitis. Pyelonephritis. Rectal fissure. Sciatica. Ulcerative colitis.

COMPLIMENTARY

Sulph. Kali-C. Phos. Sep. Staph.

INIMICAL

Ign.

COMPARISONS

Med - Extremes of behavior, workaholic, irritable, allergy, peptic ulcer, craves fat, alcohol and spicy, urinary symptoms, etc.

Lil-T - Intense irritability, dysmenorrhea, ineffectual urging.

Cham - Anger, over-sensitive to stimulation, colic.

Sep - Irritable, thin, sensitive to noise, premenstrual syndrome, constipation, abuse of drugs, cystitis, etc.

Sulph - Ambitious, arrogant, craving fat and alcohol, hemorrhoids, colitis, insomnia, etc.

Aur - Workaholic, haughty, irritable, insomnia, craving alcohol.

Calc - Workaholic, breakdown from over-work, chilly, constipation.

Ign - Easily offended, ambitious, cramps and spasms, rectal pathology, back pains.

Anac. Carc. Asar. Strych. Lyc. Stram.

OCIMUM CANUM

Ocimum is an excellent remedy in renal or ureteral colic. The pains are often quite violent and mainly, but not exclusively, on the right side. **When the kidney stone colic is accompanied by marked nausea and vomiting,** Ocimum is the first remedy to be considered.

COMPARISONS

Berb. Nux-V. Coloc. Lyc. Lach. Bell. Sars.

OENANTHE

Oenanthe is a specific remedy for convulsive disorders, often associated with the menstrual period or with menarche. The seizures are often violent, generalized, tonic-clonic convulsions. Many cases in our literature show the power of Oenanthe to cure convulsions originating from head injury while also correcting mental deterioration or mania symptoms which accompanied the disorder.

NEUROLOGICAL

- **Convulsions during or before menses.**

Convulsions worse during the sleep, worse during pregnancy or suppressed menses, worse after head injuries.

Generalized tonic-clonic seizures (Grand mal). Petit mal.

Falling during convulsions.

Deep post-ictal stupor.

Incontinence during convulsions.

HEAD

Convulsions of the face.

Face blue during convulsions *(Cupr)*.

Biting of tongue with convulsions.

Froth develops at mouth during convulsions.

Risus sardonicus; clenching of the jaw.

GASTROINTESTINAL

Constipation.

Incontinence during seizure.

EXTREMITIES

Clenching of the hand *(Cupr)*.

CLINICAL

Constipation. Head injury. Seizure disorders.

COMPARISONS

Caust. Hyos. Bufo. Cic. Cupr.

OLEANDER

A broad range of skin conditions, especially of the scalp, respond to Oleander. Hahnemann confirmed its use in deeper disorders, even paralysis. Many gastrointestinal conditions are covered by the remedy.

GENERALS

- **Marked aggravation from eating oranges or other acid or citrus fruits** (tomatoes, lemons).

General aggravation from change of weather.

HEAD

- **Dandruff and other scaling eruptions of the scalp with giant flakes (up to 1 cm) falling from the head.**
- **Scalp eruptions worse eating oranges.**

Psoriasis of scalp with white flakes. Seborrhea. "Cradle cap."

Dry, itching scalp.

Cracks on the face.

Eruptions about the eyes.

Eruptions behind the ears. Vesicles in the ears.

In the provings, many headaches occurred which were ameliorated by looking sideways or crossing the eyes.

GASTROINTESTINAL

Diarrhea, worse hot weather, worse eating fruit, especially oranges.

Ravenous appetite, especially with diarrhea *(Petr, Sulph)*.

Empty sensation in stomach, not relieved by eating *(Sep)*.

Stool watery, lienteric, offensive.

EXTREMITIES

Painless paralysis primarily of the upper extremities.

SKIN

Psoriasis.

Eczema.

Herpes.

CLINICAL

Colitis. Dandruff. Diarrhea. Eczema. Food allergy. Headache. Herpes. Paralysis. Psoriasis. Seborrhea.

COMPARISONS

Sulph - Itching scalp, diarrhea, increased appetite.

Graph. Petr. Cit-V.

OLEUM ANIMALE

The main keynote indicating Oleum Animale is the **sensation of water in the stomach which sloshes back and forth**. Jonathan Shore reported an interesting cure of delayed development in a child based upon strong cravings for eggs and potatoes.

ONOSMODIUM

Onosmodium has been well-known as a remedy for difficulty in focusing the vision and in headaches from straining the eyes. In general we can say that the patient has trouble focusing in his life in a broader sense. The patient cannot find himself or his life's work. Onosmodium is also an important remedy in what our texts describe as sexual neurasthenia, a broken-down state. The patient has a strong preoccupation with sex and a desperation to regain his lost sexual performance.

MENTALS

Sexual neurasthenia.
Directionless. Listless.
Inability to focus or concentrate.
Irritable and complaining.

HEAD

Headache or migraine with eye-strain *(Ruta, Nat-M)*.
Vision blurry, eyes feel strained.
Dryness of nose and throat.

UROGENITAL

Impotence with much sexual preoccupation.
Masturbation excessive.
Nocturnal seminal emissions.
Loss of libido.

EXTREMITIES

Weakness of lower extremities.
Numbness and tingling in the legs and feet.
Tendency to lift the legs too high when walking.

CLINICAL

Chronic fatigue syndrome. Eye-strain. Headache. Impotence.

COMPARISONS

Cann-I - Lost and directionless, sexual pathology, fatigue.
Ruta. Agn. Sel. Phos.

OPIUM

Traditionally, all homeopathic discussions of Opium begin with warnings against its allopathic use because it masks the true homeopathic symptoms of the case. Hahnemann points out that Opium in its provings was the only remedy which did not produce a single painful reaction. In the 1960's, a popular phrase was coined which describes very well the Opium state: "Blissed-out." This phrase indicates a dream-like, peaceful and euphoric state which mimics the effect of all opiates. However in the "secondary action" of Opium, the prover experiences just the opposite of this painlessness - many pains and hyperesthesias both physical and mental. Both sides of these proved reactions are exhibited in clinical practice.

Opium cases are not always "blissed-out." In one state the patient is hurried and intense - almost like Nux Vomica. The patient has great desire for work and carries out tasks rapidly and with an extremely clear mind. If the patient exhausts his resources, an opposite state of confusion, somnolence and dullness occurs. These two states may also alternate within the same patient. While dreaminess and euphoria are the typical mental characteristics, fear is the opposing state to which Opium patients are subject. In acute conditions, Opium may rouse from the stupor with marked fright. Likewise, Opium is one of our main remedies in ailments brought on by fright.

Many homeopathic authors comment on the lack of conscience in opium or heroin addicts who will lie or steal for the drug. Opium has been recommended therefore in patients who are amoral and in children who develop morals rather late.

Physically, Opium is commonly used in neurological conditions such as narcolepsy, convulsions, delirium, and strokes.

MENTALS

- **Blissful, peaceful, drowsy, sensuous, dream-like states.**
- **Stupor and coma.**

Speech thick and obtunded.

Somnambulism.

Workaholic. Great mental acuity.

Hurried and impatient.

Excitement, nervousness and insomnia during withdrawal from narcotics or sedatives.

All senses very acute.

Delusions: Animals. Faces. Beautiful things.

Complaints from fright (convulsions, tremor, insomnia, chorea).

Aggravation or renewed fright on every recollection of the frightening event which triggered the symptoms.

GENERALS

Warm-blooded and aggravated by heat.

General aggravation from fright *(Acon)*, also from excitement or even joy *(Coff)*.

◆ **Anesthesia. Painlessness of normally painful complaints.**

Alternation between stupor and restlessness.

Hot perspiration.

Sometimes recommended as a remedy to clear the case.

Appearance: Face often bloated, flushed and red, thick lips and dull, sensuous or dreamy expression.

NEUROLOGICAL

◆ **Narcolepsy.**

Convulsion, worse fright, worse heat; eclampsia.

Tremor; chorea.

Cerebral accident.

Paralysis; hemiparesis.

HEAD

Injury to head *(Nat-S, Arn, Hell, Cic, etc.)*. Concussion.

Face flushed deep red or mottled purple.

Basilar headache.

Eyes heavy and half closed.

Pupils constricted or dilated.

MOUTH

Drooping jaw.

Paralysis of tongue.

GASTROINTESTINAL

Constipation with no urge; fecal impaction.

Constipation of newborns.

Diarrhea from excitement or fright.

Abdominal cramps and colic.

Bowel obstruction; intussusception.

Post-surgical ileus *(Carb-V, Raph)* often with marked vomiting.

UROGENITAL

Urinary retention, worse fright, often with spasms of the sphincter.

Urinary retention in nursing children after mother receives a fright.

Enuresis in toilet-trained children after a fright.

Arrested labor. Eclampsia.

CHEST

- **Respiration slow, noisy, obstructed.**
- Cheyne-Stokes respiration in coma.
- **Snoring.**

Makes a puffing sound with each respiration.

MUSCULOSKELETAL

Tremor, worse fright.

Paralysis; cerebral accident with hemiparesis.

SLEEP

- **Sleep heavy, stuporous and difficult to disturb.**

Sleep apnea *(Lach, Grind, Sulph)*.

- **Narcolepsy**; over-powering sleepiness when concentrating.

Sleeplessness, worse from slight noise, worse drug withdrawal.

Wakes suddenly with a sensation of suffocation.

Vivid, pleasant dreams.

ACUTES

Head injury, concussion with somnolence and confusion.

Cerebral accident with stupor, bloated and mottled face, great heat and perspiration, stertorous respiration, constricted pupils.

Coma or delirium with high fever, flushed face, hot perspiration.

Meningitis. Encephalitis.

CLINICAL

Bowel obstruction. Cerebral accident. Chronic fatigue syndrome. Concussion. Constipation. Diarrhea. Fecal impaction. Fever. Insomnia. Meningitis. Narcolepsy. Seizure disorder. Sepsis. Sleep apnea.

COMPARISONS

Nux-M - Narcolepsy and sleepiness, constipation, confusion or mental dullness.

Bapt - Delirium and sleepiness or stupor, hot, flushed face.

Nux-V - Hyper-active, workaholic, constipation, sleep disturbance.

Bell - Red, flushed face with high fever, hallucination, talking in the sleep, constipated, pupil dilated (Opium more often constricted).

Alum - Mental confusion and dullness, extreme constipation and retention of urine, warm-blooded.

Calc. Coff. Lach. Arn. Acon.

ORIGANUM

Origanum is an important remedy in patients with over-excitement of the sexual sphere. It has been found especially useful in precocious sexual development, especially of girls from two to five years of age.

MENTALS

History of romantic disappointment or sexual abuse.

GENERALS

Desire for intense exercise such as running or dancing.

UROGENITAL

- **Masturbation in young girls**, often by rubbing thighs together.

Marked sexual thoughts but prefers masturbation to intercourse.

Promiscuity.

Comparisons

Plat. Grat. Hyos. Med. Staph.

OXALICUM ACIDUM

Oxalic acid has its greatest use in cardiovascular disease, both in arrhythmia and angina symptoms. There is marked aggravation of all symptoms as soon as the patient thinks of the problem. This important keynote is not absolutely necessary in the prescription.

MENTALS

Symptoms aggravated upon thinking of them.

GENERALS

Pain in spots *(Kali-Bi)*.

General aggravation from eating fruit, especially strawberries.

Left-sided symptoms.

HEAD

Headache in specific spots. Sore spots on the scalp.

Headache, worse thinking of the pains, worse wine.

THROAT

Hoarseness associated or alternating with cardiac complaints.

GASTROINTESTINAL

Diarrhea

Urging for stool on thinking of bowels.

UROGENITAL

Tearing or neuralgic pains in the epididymis or spermatic cord.

CHEST

Angina pains, sharp and stitching, which may extend to shoulder, arm or abdomen, better from rest, worse thinking of the pain.

Sudden stitching pain in the left lower lung.

Congestive heart failure with dyspnea, cyanosis, fibrillation.

Palpitation, worse thinking of it, worse lying.

MUSCULOSKELETAL

Numbness of arm with cardiac disease *(Naja, Acon, Cact, Rhus-T)*.

Cold, cyanotic fingers.

Cases of spinal meningitis have been reported cured with low back pain and weakness, numbness and coldness in the legs.

CLINICAL

Angina pectoris. Arrhythmia.Congestive heart failure. Diarrhea. Headache. Hoarseness.Neuralgia. Pleurisy. Spinal meningitis.

COMPARISONS

Cact - Angina pectoris, left arm numbness, arrhythmia, neuralgia, headache, cyanosis.

Lach. Helon. Spig.

PAEONIA

It may be very difficult to distinguish Paeonia from other remedies for hemorrhoids or rectal fissures. The rectal conditions of Paeonia are associated with extreme pain after stool which characteristically causes the patient to lie for minutes to hours with the buttocks held spread apart.

RECTUM

Hemorrhoids. Congested or thrombosed hemorrhoids.

Rectal fissure.

Ulcerations about the anus.

Severely painful bowel movements. Pain wiping after stool.

Pain lasting for a long time, even for hours, after the stool.

Touch of the rectum is unbearable.

Must lie with buttocks held apart to relieve rectal pains and spasms.

EXTREMITIES

Ulceration and bedsores.

SLEEP

Terrifying nightmares.

CLINICAL

Hemorrhoids. Nightmares. Proctitis. Rectal fissure.

COMPARISONS

Aesc. Rat. Nit-Ac. Sulph.

PALLADIUM

Although Palladium is often compared to Platinum (with which metal it is found in nature), the personality of the patients is quite different. Palladium is often described as being egotistical but the actual characteristic is the need for approval and praise with a type of subtle self-centeredness. In fact, the patient may be very pleasant and eager to please the prescriber, giving good follow-up reports to gain his approval. This explains why the patient, "keeps up brightly in company and is afterwards exhausted." The patient has a strong need for other people to express appreciation and to show that they value her. Especially she is very vexed and hurt if she feels that she is ignored by others. Often the patient will say she feels "snubbed" or offended where no insult is intended. It is often considered a remedy for wounded pride and mortification. Palladium is more often a woman's remedy. It is often a specific remedy in the treatment of ovarian cysts.

MENTALS

- **Easily offended and feeling of being ignored or insulted.**
  Strong desire for approval
  Complaints from mortification.
  Cheerful and up-beat in company though exhausted by the effort.

HEAD

- **Headache which travels in a band across the top of the head from ear to ear.**

UROGENITAL

Right-sided ovarian cysts and pains.

Ovarian pains worse from a jar, worse after menses, worse from excitement, better bending the legs, better lying left side.

Uterine prolapse.

CLINICAL

Headache. Ovarian pains and cysts. Uterine complaints.

COMPARISONS

Apis-Irritable and easily offended, right ovarian cysts or pains.

Nux-V. Sep. Bell. Lyc. Plat. Puls.

PAREIRA

Pareira is a remedy of the urinary tract and especially focuses on the prostate gland. The main guiding symptom is the retention of urine, especially from an enlarged prostate.

UROGENITAL

- **Urinary retention with enlarged prostate.**
  Painful urging to urinate.
  Dribbling, involuntary urination, especially in prostatic complaints.
  Pains in bladder extending down the legs and thighs when pressing at urination.
  Calculi in bladder or kidneys.
  Urethritis.

Extremities

Cramps in the legs during urination.

Clinical

Prostatic hypertrophy. Prostatitis. Renal or bladder calculi. Urinary tract infection.

Comparisons

Chim. Caust. Berb.

PARIS QUADRIFOLIA

Vithoulkas has described the personality of Paris in some detail which I will only mention briefly. The patient has intense irritability. Furthermore there is a type of hardness, negativity and sarcasm. Generally the case will present for treatment of headache or migraine.

Generals

Swollen sensation.

Heat and coldness or freezing in opposite sides or locations.

Head

- **Headache as if the head were enlarged** or pressured from inside.

Sensation of both burning heat and cold in the head.

Constricted sensation of the head or scalp.

- **Sensation of a string pulling backwards or a drawing sensation in the eyeballs.**

Eyes feel enlarged or protruding.

Feels as if the lids would not close.

Comparisons

Nux-V. Plb. Ruta. Crot-T. Lil-T. Lach. Sep.

PETROLEUM

Petroleum has a wide range of action on skin conditions and to a lesser extent on the mucous membranes. The conditions which respond to Petroleum are almost always very dry and it is the first remedy which we consider when the patient complains about tremendous dryness of the skin, so dry that no cream or salve is of any benefit. While eczema and fissured skin are the most common reasons for prescribing this remedy, the combination of eczema and herpetic eruptions is also common.

Mentals

Delusion or imagination of a person lying next to him or of being double has long been considered a keynote.

Fear or delusion that death is near.

Loses his way in well known streets (*Glon, Nux-M, Cann-I*).

Generals

Chilly and worse from cold.

General aggravation during the winter.

Internal sensation of coldness (chest, heart, abdomen, etc.).

General amelioration in summer.

Weakness or mental symptoms from inhaling petrochemical fumes (*Sul-Ac, Nux-V, Phos, Sep, etc.*).

General aggravation from suppressed skin eruptions.

Seasickness. Motion sickness. Airplane sickness.

Head

Vertigo; motion sickness.

Eczema of scalp or head. Eruptions and cracks behind the ears.

Occipital headache or heaviness spreading to vertex and forehead.

Chronic obstruction of ear and hearing loss.

Cracks of the nostrils or canthi of the eyes.

Infections of the lacrimal duct.

Gastrointestinal

- **Ravenous appetite during diarrheal conditions or after stool** (*Olnd, Sulph*).
- **Diarrhea in the daytime only.**

Diarrhea from cabbage or sauerkraut.

Colitis with cramping pain before stool.

Empty sensation in the stomach, better eating (*opposite Sepia*).

Cold sensation in abdomen.

Aversion: **Meat. Fat.**

UROGENITAL

- **Genital herpes. Herpes spreading to anus and thighs.**

Eruptions and moisture of genitalia, scrotum, inner thighs.

Perineal herpes and excoriation.

CHEST

Cough worse at night.

Asthma associated with severe eczema.

EXTREMITIES

- **Cracking of the hands and the tips of the fingers. Deep cracks in the palms.**

Dry eczema of hands in laborers, carpenters, or hair-dressers who work with tar or petroleum chemicals.

Dry, parched look to hands, or a dirty look to the skin of the hands.

Splinter-like pains in the heel, worse walking or standing.

Chilblains.

SKIN

Dry, cracking skin disease. Cracks often deep and bloody.

Skin conditions worse winter, better summer.

Itching less intense than Sulphur yet may be quite strong.

Scratches the skin until raw.

Itching generally worse night and from heat of the bed.

Cold sensation of the skin after scratching.

Skin unhealthy and suppurates from wounds.

Psoriasis. Eczema. Herpes simplex and zoster. Boils.

COMBINED SYMPTOMS

Eczema *and* herpes.

Motion sickness *and* eczema.

CLINICAL

Asthma. Diarrhea. Eczema. Environmental illness. Headache. Hearing loss. Herpes. Motion sickness. Otitis media. Psoriasis. Shingles. Vertigo.

COMPARISONS

Graph - Fissures, unhealthy skin, colitis, averse meat, catarrh of ear.

Sulph. Calc. Mez. Jug-C. Psor. Rhus-T. Sars.

Main remedies for genital herpes include: Apis. Ars. Bor. Caust. Crot-T. Dulc. Fl-Ac. Graph. Lyc. Med. Merc. Nat-C. Nat-M. Nit-Ac. Petr. Plat. Rhus-T. Rhus-V. Sars. Sep. Sulph. Thuj.

PETROSELINUM

Petroselinum is a remedy for the urinary tract, and especially the urethra. Urethritis and cystitis which produce intense pains, tickling and itching. At times the patient may say that the tingling and itching is so intense that he wants to take an object and run it into the urethra to relieve himself. There can also be a sudden desire to urinate. There is a classical description: The child has a sudden, painful urge to urinate which causes him to dance about or jump up and down.

UROGENITAL

Urethritis; gonorrhea.

Sudden, intense urging for urination.

Intense itching in the urethra or bladder.

COMPARISONS

Canth. Cann-S. Sars. Puls.

PHELLANDRIUM

The main use of Phellandrium in clinical practice has been in mastitis. Many authors have recommended this remedy in cough and even tuberculosis.

MENTALS

Vithoulkas has added this remedy under the rubrics, "Anxiety about health" and "Fear of someone behind him."

CHEST

Right breast pain, stitching pain through to the back *(Aster)*.

Pain in nipples when child nurses.

COMPARISONS

Bell. Sil. Phyt.

PHOSPHORICUM ACIDUM

Phosphoric Acid is a remedy for grief, especially when the patient becomes overwhelmed by his loss and is unable to respond. He becomes weak, apathetic, slow to answer, fatigued and drained. The patient is flat, indifferent or even lifeless. Characteristically, he appears more collapsed than grieving. The Phosphoric Acid state can be reached through other stresses beside grief, such as debilitating illness like mononucleosis, or chronic diarrhea. Drug abuse and alcoholism may lead to a similar picture.

Mentals

Depressed, apathetic patients - almost dead inside.
Slow to answer. Forgetful. Mental weakness after grief.
Indifferent to all external events - wants to lie and watch TV.
Ailments from grief or disappointed love.

Generals

Collapse states from grief, illness, drug or alcohol abuse.
Collapse after long diarrhea or any fluid loss *(Chin)*.
General aggravation after coition.
General amelioration from sleep, even a short nap.

Head

Headache with heaviness "as if a weight pressed down on the head."
Hair loss or grayness after grief.
Hair loss, even from the eyebrows and chest, or other areas *(Sel)*.

Gastrointestinal

Craving for fruit and fruit juices, refreshing things.
Diarrhea which is painless and odorless. Diarrhea after grief.
Involuntary diarrhea. Diarrhea from slight dietary indiscretions.
Profuse diarrhea not producing the expected prostration.

Urogenital

Milky urine or with whitish curds at the end of urination.
Impotence. Seminal emissions without erection.

Clinical

Alopecia. Chronic fatigue syndrome. Colitis. Depression. Diabetes. Diarrhea. Headache. Impotence. Mononucleosis. Sepsis.

Comparisons

Mur-Ac. Pic-Ac. Phos. Sep. Carb-V. Ign. Aur.

PHOSPHORUS

As one of our most important polycrest remedies, Phosphorus must be clearly understood in a variety of stages of pathology. It is interesting that none of our past homeopathic masters recognized the true center of this remedy until Vithoulkas. The essence as described by Vithoulkas is "diffusion" - like the bubbles from a carbonated drink. It is often seen that the Phosphorus patient is bubbly and out-going or extroverted. The patient seems to "sparkle" with intelligence, creativity, and enthusiasm. However he seems to have no strong boundaries between himself and others; he is not grounded or centered. He is extremely sympathetic and can become involved with even strangers. Once he turns his attention to another project he may forget all about this stranger he befriended, thus he may appear "flighty." He loves company. He can be gullible and suggestible. He may even be clairvoyant.

There are prices to be paid for these poor boundaries. In the first stages of pathology in Phosphorus, we find great anxiety. Any idea may enter his mind and be a cause for anxiety. However, he is also easily reassured. Generally the anxiety takes the form of concern about health. But as the pathology worsens the patient has more and more "free-floating anxiety" and the fear that something bad will happen. The patient has many fears, especially of things which are symbolic of his lack of boundaries such as darkness, deep water, death, etc. These fears may develop into a debilitating phobic state. Especially, these fears come when the patient is alone, and are better in company.

In later stages the patient is so sensitive to others and to outside stimulation that the well-known desire for company is lost. The patient prefers to be alone and is intolerant of strangers or of hearing of other's problems. As more and more of the inner vitality is lost, so also is lost the "bubbly" and sparkling nature. Eventually the patient becomes slow and indifferent and apathetic, much like Phosphoric acid or Sepia.

Children. The Phosphorus child is sensitive, precocious and open. He can make contact with anyone, child or adult. The parents say that they fear the child could be kidnapped because of this open, trusting nature. The child is both curious and sympathetic for others. There are often strong fears and great desire for company. The child often has great anxiety that something bad will happen to his parents and becomes very concerned about the least illness in the family. Often the Phosphorus child experiences fast growth and suffers from this growth with fatigue and poor resistance to illness. A large percentage of Phosphorus children suffer with epistaxis, bleeding gums, bruising or other bleeding problems.

MENTALS

- ◆ **Open, bright, excitable, suggestible, anxious patients.**
- **Anxiety when alone; ameliorated in company.** Even the radio provides company.
- Fears: **Alone. Death. Dark. ◆Thunderstorms. ◆Something bad will happen.** Diseases. Future. For others. Ghosts. Insanity. Robbers. Insects. Water. Earthquakes. Any fear.
- ◆ **Sympathetic.**
- **Dependent on the physician. Easily reassured.**
- **Gullible.**
- **Clairvoyant.** Out of the body experiences.
- Startles easily.
- Mentally distractible and "spacey."
- Slow, apathetic, dull-minded state (late stage).
- Unable to exert the mind.
- Answers slowly.

GENERALS

- Appearance: thin and often tall, fine featured and long fingered.
- Generally chilly or even freezing but may be very warm-blooded. (But while the general temperature is variable, the reaction to the temperature in certain organ systems is quite fixed: the head and stomach symptoms are better by cold and worse from heat or hot applications; the chest symptoms are worse from cold and better from heat.)
- General aggravation from changes in the weather.
- Flushes of heat. Menopausal flushes from any emotion.
- **Generally worse from fasting.**
- **Generally worse from lying on the left side.**
- **General amelioration from eating.**
- **General amelioration from cold drinks.**
- **Generally worse from spicy foods, warm foods, and salt.**
- **General amelioration from sleep.**
- **General amelioration from rubbing the affected part.**
- **General aggravation at twilight.**
- **Hemorrhagic tendency from any wound - even hemophilia.**
- **Easily dehydrated.**
- **Debility and collapse states.**
- Left sided symptoms.
- Great sensitivity to odors. Chemical sensitivity.
- Cerebral accidents; hemiparesis.
- Tumor formation. Fibrous and fibrocystic growths. Malignancy.
- Diabetes mellitus.

HEAD

Vertigo, worse exerting the vision, especially looking upward, worse rising, better lying.

Meniere's disease.

Headache, often migraine headaches, worse fasting, worse cough, worse heat, better sleep, better cold and open air.

Detached retina. Retinal hemorrhage. Retinitis. Optic neuritis.

Glaucoma (*Eser, Phys, Osm, Calc*).

Flashes in the vision, worse falling asleep.

Pyorrhea, easily bleeding gums, periosteal inflammation from root canal procedure.

Dry lips and tongue with dehydration.

Smell very acute, worse headache. Intolerant of perfumes, flowers.

Hay fever.

• **Epistaxis**. Children frequently, less often continuing to adulthood. Bright-red, fluid blood. Bleeding from blowing the nose.

Excessive bleeding after dental extraction.

THROAT

Hoarseness, usually without pain though at times may be quite painful. Voice lost entirely. Laryngitis.

Pain and sensitivity of larynx, worse touch, worse cough.

GASTROINTESTINAL

Peptic ulcer. Hematemesis: bright red blood or coffee grounds.

Gastritis with nausea and vomiting, better by cold drinks but returning as soon as the liquids become warmed in the stomach.

Appetite ravenous, even gets up at night to eat.

Appetite increased with headache, during fever; returns soon after eating.

Craves: •**Chocolate.** •**Ice cream or cold foods. Salty. Spicy. Rice. Milk. Alcoholic drinks, especially wine.** Fish. Fat. Hamburger. Eggs. Chicken. Cheese. Carbonated drinks. Sweets.

Aversion: **Sweets**. Warm foods. Eggs. Oysters. Meat (except hamburger). Fruit. Tea. Carbonated drinks. Fish. Fish soup.

• **Tremendous thirst for cold drinks.**

Indigestion, eructations, regurgitation.

Infectious or inflammatory diarrhea and even involuntary stool.

Rectal hemorrhage, worse stool. Hemorrhoids.

Colitis. Proctitis.

Anus relaxed and partially open or sensation of looseness.

Hepatitis. Liver congestion. Cirrhosis.

UROGENITAL

Involuntary urination with cough.

Sex drive increased, even pathological.

Uterine fibroids. Uterine prolapse.

Metrorrhagia with bright red blood, almost never clotted.

Ovarian cysts and tumors, especially left-sided.

CHEST

Recurring respiratory infections; every cold goes to chest.

Lingering, tickling coughs, worse cold air, worse exertion, worse talking and laughing, worse change of temperature and weather, worse lying flat or on left side, better sitting or lying on right.

Pneumonia, especially left-sided, with oppression of the chest and a painful, burning cough, often hemoptysis.

Pulmonary tuberculosis or history of tuberculosis in past or even in the family.

Chronic bronchitis. Asthma. Emphysema.

Fibrocystic breast disease.

Palpitations, worse lying on the left side, worse excitement, worse exertion or even slight motion, worse rising.

Heart murmurs, congestive heart failure.

Angina pectoris, pains worse from stress, worse lying of the left side, better from cold drinks.

MUSCULOSKELETAL

Numbness of fingers, especially in the morning on waking.

Multiple sclerosis with numbness and weakness in the legs. Ataxia.

Back pains, better motion, better heat, better massage.

Fibrositis.

Twitching. Tremor.

SKIN

Dry skin. Psoriasis. Eczema. Ichthyosis.

Itching worse heat and at night.

Ecchymosis. Purpura.

SLEEP

Generally sleeps well and greatly refreshed by sleep.

Sleeps on right side, unable to sleep on left in most cases.

Somnambulism.

Talking in the sleep.

Unrefreshed sleep in later stages.

Child wakes at night and comes to parents bed *(Puls, Stram)*.

COMPLEMENTARY

Ars. Nux-V. Kali-C. Tub.

INIMICAL

Caust.

CLINICAL

Alcoholism. Angina. Anxiety. Arrhythmia. Arthritis. Asthma. Ataxia. Bronchitis. Chemical hypersensitivity. Chronic fatigue syndrome. Cirrhosis. Coagulopathy. Colds. Congestive heart failure. Connective tissue disease. Croup. Detached retina. Diabetes. Eczema. Emphysema. Environmental illness. Epistaxis. Fibrocystic breast disease. Gastritis. Headaches. Hemophilia. Hepatitis. Hypertension. Ichthyosis. Influenza. Malignancy. Manic-depression. Meniere's syndrome. Migraines. Multiple sclerosis. Peptic ulcer. Petit mal. Pharyngitis. Phobic disorders. Pneumonia. Psoriasis. Purpura. Respiratory infection. Retinal hemorrhage. Schizophrenia. Scoliosis. Senility. Skin ulcer. Tinnitus. Tuberculosis. Uterine fibroids. Uterine hemorrhage. Uterine prolapse. Valvular heart disorders. Vertigo.

COMPARISONS

Puls - Open patients who desire reassurance, crave ice cream and cold foods and averse to warm foods, worse from lying on the left side, worse at twilight, chest and menstrual troubles.

Caust - Sympathetic, many fears similar, especially that something bad will happen, chest conditions and hoarseness, craves salt and is averse to sweets, numbness of fingers, multiple sclerosis.

Ars - Many fears and anxiety for others, dependency on the physician, gastrointestinal symptoms, asthma, craves fats, thirsty, burning pains.

Arg-N - Open and suggestible, anxieties and fears, dependent on the physician, desires salt and fat, neurological problems and vertigo.

Sep - Burned-out patients, averse to company, apathetic and dull-minded. Also, Sepia children resemble Phosphorus with openess, excitability and fears.

Rhus-T. Sulph. Med. Tub. Sep. Coff. Thuj.

PHYSOSTIGMA

Physostigma is a remedy for eye troubles, especially if the ocular pathology coincides with smooth muscle or neurological problems.

EYES

Myopia. Eye strain.
Blurred vision and unable to accommodate. Astigmatism.
Photophobia.
Twitching lids.
Glaucoma *(also Eserine, a derivative of Physostigma)*.

UROGENITAL

Paresis or irritability of bladder.

EXTREMITIES

Muscle spasms and cramps. Rigid muscles.
Spinal cord inflammation.
Numbness of distal extremities.

CLINICAL

Ataxia. Glaucoma. Myopia. Mydriasis. Twitching of the lids. Urinary infections or retention.

COMPARE

Ruta. Onos. Agar.

PHYTOLACCA

Kent described Phytolacca as a "vegetable Mercury" because of the many corresponding symptoms: the syphilitic relationship, the effects on bone, glands, and the throat. Phytolacca was an important remedy for diphtheria in the past. Most of the symptoms in the remedy are in the glands themselves - especially breast, parotids and tonsils.

GENERALS

Generally worse from cold and cold damp.
General aggravation at night.
Syphilitic history.

HEAD

- **Painful dentition or dental pain with relief from clenching the gums or teeth.**

Glossitis. Coated tongue. Tip of tongue red.

Pain at root of tongue, worse on protruding tongue.

Iritis.

THROAT

Marked pain, dark red discoloration and inflammation of tonsils, pharynx, or root of the tongue, worse on the right side.

Throat pain better cold drinks and worse warm drinks.

Throat pain extends to the ears on swallowing.

Pain in throat as from a "burning hot ball."

Parotitis. Mumps.

Our literature is full of cures of diphtheria with this remedy but the opportunity and wisdom of trying to treat such a condition in these times may be questionable.

Hard, painful swelling of the cervical glands.

Neck pain and stiffness, worse night, worse right side, worse from slight motion.

CHEST

- **Mastitis: Great pains with nursing, worse in the left breast, the pain radiates to the whole body.**

Breast abscess.

Cracks in nipples.

Fibrocystic breast disease, tenderness of breasts, worse before and during menses.

Painful tumors of breast, even palliates in malignancy.

UROGENITAL

Painful orchitis.

EXTREMITIES

- **Pains at the insertions of tendons. Tendonitis or bursitis.**

Rheumatism in cold weather. Pains worse from heat.

Pains in the bones, especially tibia, worse at night.

Sciatica.

"Plantar fasciitis with lameness" (Steven Subotnick, DPM).

SKIN

Psoriasis with a purplish hue.

CLINICAL

Arthritis. Breast abscess. Bursitis. Fibrocystic breast disease. Iritis. Mastitis. Mumps. Orchitis. Pharyngitis. Plantar fasciitis. Psoriasis. Sciatica. Sprains. Tendonitis. Tonsillitis.

COMBINATION

Psoriasis *and* bone pains.

Rheumatism *and* cervical or parotid adenopathy.

COMPARISONS

Merc - Pharyngitis, cervical adenopathy, general aggravation at night, syphilitic troubles, etc.

Sil. Bell. Calc. Con.

PICRICUM ACIDUM

For the most part, the acid remedies are indicated in cases going towards collapse. In Picric Acid, the collapse is mainly in the area of the intellectual functioning. Often the causation of Picric Acid is mental exertion, such as in students who are pushing themselves at the time of examinations, or professionals who are over-exerting, for instance a lawyer preparing for an unusually important case. In almost all cases, this collapse is caused by exertion. Great dullness and tiredness which comes on after exerting the mind in any way. The patient may say that he feels well and can concentrate when he first sits to study but after only a few minutes he is unable to think. Our texts refer to this state as "brain-fag".

MENTALS

- **Mind dull and unable to concentrate or read more than a few minutes at a time. "Brain-fag."**

Mental weakness and confusion, unable to take on projects.

GENERALS

- **General aggravation or exhaustion from reading or mental exertion** (weakness, diarrhea, headache, back pain).

Weakness, worse exertion, worse heat, worse stool, worse concentrating mind.

General amelioration by lying down, by rest or a good sleep.

Head

Dull, heavy, full feeling in forehead which prevents concentration.
Headache from mental exertion.
Headache in occiput and neck.
Boils inside the ears.

Urogenital

Increased sexual desires; lascivious thoughts.
Constant or troublesome erections.
Priapism.

Musculoskeletal

Weakness and heaviness in the back.
Burning pains in the spine, worse mental exertion.
Heaviness, numbness and weakness of the lower extremities.

Clinical

Abscess. Back pain. Chronic fatigue syndrome. Headache. Priapism.

Combined Symptoms

Spinal disorders *and* priapism.
Dull headache *and* mental exhaustion.

Comparisons

Ph-Ac - Mental weakness and collapse states.
Kali-P - Exhaustion from mental strain.
Gels. Lec. Nat-C. Nux-V. Phos. Sep. Con.

PIPER METHYSTICUM

Kava is used as an intoxicant in its raw form. Therefore it should come as no surprise that homeopathically it is used in patients who have a peculiar syndrome of **feeling constantly intoxicated**. In some cases the patient will describe a type of headache which makes him feel as if he were "drunk."

PLATINUM

Platinum is a fascinating remedy type with elevation of passion in one of two ways: the ego or the sexual sphere. Platinum is the haughtiest of all our remedies. In Platinum, the patient seems to feel that her very soul is superior or even exalted. The Platinum patient does not take pride so much in her achievements (Aurum) or her intellect (Sulphur), but rather in her person. From the repertory we find the rubric, "Delusion she is of royal blood." In today's society this is often expressed more as a delusion of coming from the best social or educational background, or even of being spiritually more advanced than others. It is more often a woman's remedy.

If the egotism is less marked, then we find the appearance of sexual pathology. Every type of sexual excess or "perversion" may be explored by this patient. She may become promiscuous but in the beginning there is a highly developed sense of romance. The extreme degree of passion makes any lasting relationship very difficult and thus we often find a history of extremely stormy relationships. When there is frustration of the passions or outlets, we find the development of more anger, violent impulses and deep phobias. The patient may have violent urges or impulses to kill. Naturally such a patient will also project these impulses on to others, giving rise to delusions and fears that she would be subjected to violence.

MENTALS

- **Haughty, affected, self-absorbed, narcissistic patients.**

Excessively passionate, needs excitement or drama.

- **Impression or delusion that she is taller than others or that she is looking down from a high place.**
- **Delusion that she is "of royal birth."**

Rude and insolent. Contemptuous.

Aversion to children; feels children will interfere.

Violence impulse. Impulse to kill, to kill spouse who she loves, fears husband will die or be kidnapped whenever he goes out.

Fears: Death. Violence. Health. Ghosts. Animals. Strokes.

Fears being abandoned by spouse or death of spouse. Anxiety attacks.

Weeps from anger.

Jealousy.

Dress flamboyantly, sensually. "Hollywood" types; dark sunglasses.

GENERALS

Constrictions, as if bandaged, as if a band about the part.

Mental symptoms alternate with physical problems.

Painlessness of affected parts *(Op)*. Numbness.

Syphilitic miasm.

HEAD

Numbness (or coldness) about head and face, especially about the cheek-bones and lips.

Bell's palsy; painless paralysis of the face.

Facial neuralgia. Pain may alternate with numbness.

Constricting headache, slow onset and fading.

Thick, fleshy, sensual lips.

Numb sensation, especially in the teeth during sexual arousal.

GASTROINTESTINAL

Bulimia.

Constipation, worse traveling, worse menses, worse pregnancy.

Drawing sensation about the umbilicus *(Plb)*.

UROGENITAL

Increased sex-drive; promiscuity; sexual excesses; sexual perversion. Sexually aroused by slightest touch.

May describe her problem as frigidity which indicates a feeling of being unfulfilled rather than loss of libido.

History of sexual abuse.

Numbness of the genitalia.

Voluptuous itching of the genitalia. Herpes.

Hypersensitivity of vagina; unable to tolerate penetration.

Ovarian cysts, especially left-sided.

Malignancy of the uterus, ovaries, testes, external genitalia.

Menses may be early, profuse, dark, stringy.

Dysmenorrhea, intense, often with bearing-down sensation.

EXTREMITIES

Band sensation about the part.

CLINICAL

Bell's palsy. Bulimia. Constipation. Dysmenorrhea. Headache. Herpes. Malignancy. Metrorrhagia. Narcissism. Neuralgia. Obesity. Ovarian cysts. Phobic disorder. Sexual disorder.

COMPARISONS

Nux-V - High sex-drive, anger, egotism, constipation, neuralgia, weeps with anger.

Med - High sex-drive, egotism, erratic moods, genital pathology.

Aur - Arrogance, syphilitic miasm, violent impulses, pathology of the testes or ovaries, may also be promiscuous.

Sulph. Pall. Lach. Lil-T. Grat. Lyc. Hyos.

PLUMBUM

The diseases of Plumbum are slowly progressive and often do not reach the homeopath until much of the condition is irreversible. Especially the neurological and circulatory systems are affected in this remedy. Plumbum is an important remedy in arteriosclerotic diseases. Often the arteriosclerosis involves the cerebral vasculature, thus producing neurological symptoms such as progressive paralysis from repeated small vascular accidents. The patient is often materialistic in orientation and may give the impression of having indulged himself extensively. Eventually, however, ennui and apathy become prominent. In the advanced cases depression and mental dullness are the rule.

MENTALS

Selfish and self-indulgent patients.

Memory poor for words, for expressing himself. Slow perceptions.

Feigning of illness.

GENERALS

Appearance: Described as yellow or sallow complexion in our literature, often Plumbum cases are dark, and earthy. There are often deep furrows to the face despite the fact that the patient is thin or even emaciated. Especially there are often deep jowl lines.

Drawing, contracting pains.

Contractures.

Emaciation of the affected parts.

Hyperesthesia of skin, especially in association with paralysis.

Advanced atherosclerosis (cerebral accidents, claudication, etc.).

Anesthesia of the affected part.

HEAD

Oily face.

Paresis in face. Twitches of face.

The famous blue or purplish discoloration in the gums is a poisoning symptom which I have not confirmed in practice to date.

ABDOMEN

Drawing sensation in abdomen, most characteristically at the umbilicus. "Scaphoid" abdomen.

Colic; painter's colic; pain better from leaning backwards *(Dios)*.

Abdominal pains extending to groin or limbs.

Bowel obstruction. Intussusception.

Constipation very marked; stool knotty or in small, dark balls.

STOMACH

Esophageal inflammation.

Craves: Salty foods. Allergy to eggs and fish.

UROGENITAL

Sex desire increased. Impotence.

Retraction of testes. Vaginismus.

Retention or urine from paralysis of the bladder.

Miscarriage.

CHEST

Angina pectoris.

Palpitations, worse lying on the left side.

Drawing pains in the chest.

EXTREMITIES

Contractures of tendons.

Thickened and contracted tendons in the palms.

Emaciation of paralyzed limbs.

Progressive paralysis, often more noted in upper extremities.

Wrist-drop. Ankle-drop. Paralysis of mainly extensor muscles.

Tremor, spasm, twitching of muscles.

Tremor of arm and hand, worse writing or trying to eat.

Tearing, shooting pains in extremities, better from rubbing.

Offensive foot sweat.

Sciatica pains with numbness in leg.

Arthritis.

COMBINED SYMPTOMS

Weak memory *and* atherosclerotic disease.

CLINICAL

Amyotropic lateral sclerosis. Angina. Cerebral accident. Claudication. Constipation. Contractures. Dementia. Diabetes. Hypertension. Multiple sclerosis. Neuralgia. Neuro-degenerative disorders. Parkinson's disease. Tremor.

COMPARISONS

Alum - Slow reactions, forgetful, constipation, paralysis.

Lyc - Deep furrows, difficult speech, constipation, self-indulgent, cerebral accidents.

Merc - Slow perception and reaction, tremor, impulses.

Med. Sulph. Cocc. Plat. Op.

PODOPHYLLUM

The efficacy of Podophyllum in acute diarrhea is so marked that our thoughts turn automatically to this remedy in such a condition, and must be forced by the symptoms to look elsewhere. This remedy may be used palliatively in chronic colitis or inflammatory bowel disease, and is also a constitutional remedy in intestinal, liver, uterine and ovarian disorders.

MENTALS

Is reported to have delirious loquacity during or following chills in febrile conditions.

Depression.

GENERALS

- **Weakness or faintness from diarrhea, or after stool.**

General aggravation at 4 or 5 AM.

Generally warm-blooded.

HEAD

Headache alternating with diarrhea.

GASTROINTESTINAL

- **Profuse diarrhea, often mixed with gas, sputtering.**
- **Explosive diarrhea, soils the whole toilet bowl.**

Diarrhea, worse 4 AM, worse morning, worse evening, worse drinking or eating, worse heat, sudden urge for stool.

Periodic diarrhea or diarrhea alternating with constipation.

Stool is watery and profuse and sometimes horribly offensive.

Stool may be yellow, pasty, mucus filled or even bloody.

Abdominal pain and cramps, worse before or during stool, better after stool, better holding abdomen and bending forward.

Also may have painless diarrhea.

Uneasy sensation such that he cannot tell whether he is about to vomit or pass stool.

- **Empty, anxious, sinking sensation after stool.**

Gurgling in the abdomen before stool.

Involuntary stool.

Rectal prolapse, worse stool, worse straining, worse pregnancy.

Prolapsed rectum in children.

Liver pains ameliorated by rubbing the liver is considered a keynote by some authors.

Gallbladder colic. Hepatitis.

UROGENITAL

Pain and inflammation of ovary, especially the right ovary.

Ovarian tumors or cysts.

Uterine prolapse, worse during stool.

Bearing-down pains during stool.

EXTREMITIES

Back or joint pains during the chill.

Back pain from stool.

CLINICAL

Arthritis. Colitis. Diarrhea. Dysentery. Gastroenteritis. Hepatitis. Inflammatory bowel disease. Ovarian cysts. Proctitis. Rectal prolapse. Uterine prolapse.

COMBINED SYMPTOMS

Colitis *and* rheumatism.

COMPARISONS

Aloe - Diarrhea mixed with gas, involuntary stool, profuse stool, rumbling abdomen before stool, etc.

Ars - Diarrhea, weak, faint, and empty after stool, offensive stools, right ovarian pains.

Sep - Bearing down sensation, empty feeling in the stomach, prolapse.

Crot-T. Gamb. Lyc. Murx. Sulph.

PRUNUS SPINOSA

Although an unusual remedy, Prunus is of great value in certain cases of headaches or migraines. The headaches are generally right-sided and may extend to the occiput. Another characteristic is headache in the right forehead which feels as if a tumor were pushing outward or as if the head was swollen and about to burst. Neuralgic pains are also felt about the eyes or extending to the eyes from the head.

COMPARISONS

Sang. Bell. Par.

PSORINUM

The first nosode, Psorinum, is useful not only when the force of the disease is on the skin, but also when the pathology is suppressed to deeper layers of illness, lack of vitality and mental disorders. In fact the inherent weakness of the Psorinum constitution allows easy suppression to deeper layers not only of skin eruptions but also of perspiration, of discharges, etc. The poor defense mechanism is also reflected in the great tendency for acute illness we find in Psorinum patients; they catch every cold and are slow to recover. Our texts describe a tendency to be dirty and offensive, but in today's society with the ease of showers, topical steroids, etc., this description is less often accurate.

The essence of Psorinum is poverty. There is a California term which describes the personality quite well: "Poverty consciousness." The patient seems to expect poverty and disappointment or is unable to think in more expansive terms. He accepts a limited job and humble living conditions. There is fear and anxiety concerning the health, prosperity and the future in general. This leads to a marked depression and a despairing outlook. Eventually suicidal feelings and thoughts predominate.

MENTALS

Anxiety and hopelessness about the future. Pessimism.

Fears: Poverty. Health. Cancer. Future. Failure.

Suicidal thoughts and feelings.

Deep anxiety states with restlessness and anguish.

Anxious restlessness at night *(Ars)*.

Despair. Despair of recovery. Feels forsaken or isolated.

Anguished and despairing from skin diseases.

GENERALS

Appearance: Skin has a dingy look, as if dirty, even if recently washed.

- **Chilly and aggravated from cold.** The coldest remedy although less chilly in cases where Sulphur will follow. Lacks vital heat.

General aggravation from open air or from drafts.

General aggravation before a storm.

General aggravation from changes in the weather.

Generally worse in the winter, better in summer.

Perspires profusely from slight exertion.

Aggravation from suppressed eruption, sweat, discharges.

General aggravation from fasting.

Frequent acute illness *(Calc, Tub, Merc, Sulph, Bar-C)*.

Offensiveness. Offensive, purulent discharges any location.

- **Feels inexplicably well the day before is about to get ill.**

HEAD

- **Must wear a warm or fur hat all year, even in summer.**

Headaches, worse from fasting, worse from suppressed eruptions, worse drafts and open air.

Chronic infection of eyes, sinuses, ears.

Chronic discharges from ears, offensive discharges.

Acne. Rosacea. Oily skin.

Eruptions behind ears, on neck, face, scalp and head, very itchy.

Crusty or scaly eruptions on head and face.

Styes. Blepharitis.

Aphthae.

Hay fever.

- **Face has a dirty look even when well washed.**

GASTROINTESTINAL

Tremendous appetite and yet often thin.

Appetite increase before or during headache.

Appetite increased at night or in pregnancy. Must get up to eat.

UROGENITAL

Eruptions about the genitalia.

Aversion to sex.

CHEST

- **Cough, bronchitis or asthma with dyspnea and fatigue better from lying down, especially from lying on the back with arms spread out "as if crucified."**

Cough worse open air, worse cold, worse cold drinks.

Palpitations, worse lying on the left side.

EXTREMITIES

- **Eruptions in the folds of the joints.**

Eruptions between the fingers or about the nails.

Sciatica and low back pain.

SKIN

Eczema, tremendous itching.

Itching worse night, worse from being over-heated, worse from the heat of the bed, must scratch until she bleeds.

Sleepless from the intense itching.

Recurring or suppressed scabies.

Yellow, offensive discharges from skin.

Boils. Warts. Skin dry or excessively oily.

COMBINED SYMPTOMS

Depression with suicidal thoughts *and* offensive odors.

Great chilliness *with* frequent acute illness.

CLINICAL

Abscess. Acne. Allergy. Anxiety. Aphthae. Asthma. Boil. Bronchitis. Colds. Connective tissue disease. Depression. Dermatitis. Eczema. Headaches. Insomnia. Otitis media. Pharyngitis. Phobic disorders. Psoriasis. Scabies. Sciatica. Skin ulcers. Upper respiratory infection.

COMPLEMENTARY

Sulph.

COMPARISONS

Ars - Anxiety, fear about health, poverty, and future, suicidal thoughts, very chilly, offensiveness, eczema, etc.

Sulph - Skin diseases with tremendous itching, increased appetite, sleeplessness, anxiety.

Nit-Ac - Anxiety and despair, chilly, skin diseases, warts.

Calc - Despair recovery, anxiety about the future, fear of poverty, chilly, frequent illness.

Mez. Petr. Phos. Hep. Carb-An.

PTELEA

Ptelea is a remedy of digestive and especially liver disorders.

GASTROINTESTINAL

Intolerance of rich, fat food, especially meat fat or cheese.

Abdominal pain lying on left side, better lying right side.

Abdominal pain, often right sided or right upper quadrant.

Eructations, rumbling in intestines, flatulence.

Digestive symptoms ameliorated by drinking lemon.

CLINICAL

Cholecystitis. Colitis. Hepatitis.

COMPARISONS

Mag-M. Card-M. Chel.

PULSATILLA

Though Pulsatilla is well-known to all homeopaths, we often have some difficulty in recognizing a Pulsatilla case, especially if we expect always to see the typical blond, blue-eyed, mild and tearful patient. This is true because greater psychological "sophistication" teaches people to compensate or hide their natural tendencies. Also, the descriptions below may not apply to a case which is ill mainly on the physical level who has not developed the typical personality of the remedy.

Softness. The central essence of Pulsatilla is "changeability with softness." It is primarily a feminine remedy. When a man needs Pulsatilla, he is generally a soft, gentle type of man. The Pulsatilla patient requires strong support from those around her. The patient is easily dominated or influenced. There is often a strong family figure or a strong religious figure or teacher in the patient's life. She needs support and reassurance. The patient is also deeply emotional, sentimental and sympathetic.

Shyness. Although the typical Pulsatilla type makes excellent contact with others, there is often an initial shyness or bashfulness. The patient blushes easily and feels embarrassed from slight causes. Yet there is something flirtatious about this timidity which telegraphs the strong desire for affection and reassurance.

Weeping. One of the main characteristics of the Pulsatilla patient is the ease with which she weeps. She frequently weeps in the office when telling about her problems. She also weeps during any confrontation. The weeping often is soft and tender. The patient is unselfconscious in her desire for and acceptance of comforting and consolation.

Consolation. There is often a strong desire for tenderness and reassurance in the typical Pulsatilla patient. The family may note that the patient often asks, "Do you love me?" or "Tell me that you love me." This dependency will also be projected on to the prescriber.

Changeability. The patient is very emotional yet the moods are very changeable. She is soft and weepy one moment and irritable the next. Many prescribers early in their career are surprised to find how irritable the Pulsatilla patient can become. This occurs generally if the patient needs attention and feels she is deprived. There can also be a stubbornness in Pulsatilla, especially regarding her security.

Dogmatism. If the patient is dependent upon a particular religious system, she may rigidly defend this as the only correct system and appears anything but yielding. In fact she may be a fanatic toward this security system, yet internally this fanaticism is based upon the need for support. The tendency for rigid thinking is also reflected in fixed ideas that she has sinned, that sex is sinful - "puritanical" ideas. In the end stage Pulsatilla can go into deeply apathetic states, senility or even catatonia.

Children. The typical Pulsatilla child is shy and clings to the mother. She makes good contact with the prescriber from the safety of her mother's lap. She is vulnerable to other children, easily bullied. She craves attention and affection. Often the mother will reveal that the child comes to sit on her lap at any opportunity and often asks the mother, "Mommy, do you love me?" Yet she can be pouting and irritable at other times. Often the parents complain that the child comes in to their bedroom at night to sleep.

Physical. The physical complaints are characterized by changeability of the condition. The patient himself may state that, "no two stools" or "no two periods" are the same. However, as Nancy Herrick of the Hahnemann Clinic has taught, often the prescriber finds this characteristic after a frustrating interview during which the patient finds difficulty describing her symptoms because, "I just can't seem to find a pattern!" This lack of a pattern often indicates a changeability.

There are two main spheres of action of Pulsatilla on the physical plane: the hormonal system and the circulation. The hormonal disturbances are particularly strong in the female cycle. Pulsatilla is one of the main remedies for almost all forms of menstrual problems, from premenstrual syndrome to amenorrhea to menopausal hot flashes. It is also one of the most important remedies in pregnancy related disorders.

In the circulatory sphere, Pulsatilla patients are often plethoric and congested. Varicosities, flushing and typically rosy cheeks, congestive type headaches, engorged conjunctiva, etc., point to the sluggish and overfilled vasculature. Thus, anything which cools the body core will ameliorate and anything which raises the body heat will aggravate the patient.

MENTALS

- **Soft, timid, easily influenced and dependent patients.**
- **Open and malleable. Easily influenced.**
- **Weeps easily.**
- **Weeps in interview telling her problems** *(Sep, Med, Staph)*.

Sadness, worse in warm room, worse before the menses, worse evening, better open air.

Changeable moods.

Feels forsaken.

- **Asks mother or spouse, "Do you love me?"**
- **Desires and ameliorated by consolation.**

Fears: Heights. Claustrophobia. Insanity. Dark. Robbers. Mirrors.

Fanatic or rigid religious ideas; puritanical; excessive praying.

Irritability, worse before menses.

Jealousy.

Disgust; has a visceral response to events or objects.

Generals

Appearance: Often, but by no means exclusively blond, red-cheeked, red lips, plump, phlegmatic individuals.

Warm-blooded and aggravated by heat.

General aggravation from the sun.

- ◆ **Craves and ameliorated by open air or in breezes.**
- ◆ **General amelioration walking slowly in the open air.**
- ◆ **General aggravation at twilight or in the evening.** Also worse at 2 PM or 4 PM.

General amelioration from cool, crisp weather.

General amelioration from cold bathing.

General aggravation from getting the feet wet.

- ◆ **General aggravation from fatty or rich foods**, from pork, from bread.

Fainting from warm or stuffy rooms, from emotions, from menses.

General aggravation during pregnancy, at menopause, before or during menses, from suppressed menses.

Generally worse after measles.

Obesity in some cases.

One-sided perspiration.

Chills before or during menses.

Head

Vertigo, worse looking upward, worse menses, better lying down.

Headaches, often migraines, which occur at the last hour of the menstrual flow.

Headaches, worse menopause, worse heat, worse sun, worse exertion, worse after emotional stresses.

Headaches better open air, cold or cold applications, better pressure.

Headaches are often pulsating or pressing outwards.

Red cheeks, blushes easily. Flushes of heat to the face.

Mumps; parotitis.

Hirsutism.

Facial neuralgia.

Tooth pain, better from cold, worse heat or warm food.

- ◆ **Dry mouth but no thirst.**

Nose

Hay fever, coryza, sneezing often worse in open air, worse evening, worse warm room.

Bland and often greenish nasal discharge.

Chronic nasal obstruction.

EYES

Conjunctivitis, allergic or infective.

Blocked lacrimal ducts of infants *(Sil)*.

Greenish discharge from the eyes.

Itching, lacrimation, and pain in eye, better cold application.

EARS

◆ **Acute and chronic otitis media.**

Ear pain, often worse at night, worse heat; pulsating pain.

Discharges from the ears. "Glue ear."

Hearing diminished from otitis media.

GASTROINTESTINAL

Craves: ◆**Butter.** ◆**Cream and whipped-cream. Cheese**. Sweets. **Ice cream. Cold food. Peanut butter**. Hard-boiled eggs.

Aversion: ◆**Fat. Butter**. Warm food. ◆**Pork.**

Indigestion from fats and rich foods, ice cream, pork.

Bloating and abdominal distension.

Nausea and vomiting from headache.

Nausea of pregnancy.

◆ **Thirstless.**

Diarrhea in children.

Hemorrhoids.

UROGENITAL

Bladder pain, worse at the end of urination, worse if trying to retain urine.

Involuntary urination, worse in pregnancy, worse with coughing.

Prostatitis. Prostatic hypertrophy.

Orchitis, epididymitis, worse left side, worse suppressed gonorrhea, worse mumps.

Sexual energy is generally high, even excessive in some cases. In women there is more often an emphasis on emotional connection rather than sex. There may be an aversion to sex based on strongly held moral or religious beliefs. Because of the need for deep connection, preferences may be toward homosexuality.

Labor delayed and ineffectual.

Malpresentation; may help to turn fetus even in last days of gestation.

Menses easily suppressed. Amenorrhea. Also metrorrhagia.

Menses short duration.

◆ **Menses irregular. Menstrual flow changeable.**

Marked dysmenorrhea beginning at puberty. Endometriosis.

Uterine prolapse.

Chest

Asthma, often allergic asthma.

Dyspnea or oppression in the chest, worse lying, worse evening and night, worse from taking a cold, worse suppressed eruptions, worse emotions, worse heavy exertion, worse warm room, better sitting, better open air.

Cough at night in bed, preventing or interrupting sleep, ⧫especially in children. Bronchitis.

Palpitations, worse night in bed, worse lying on the left side.

Galactorrhea. Mastitis. Fibrocystic breast disease.

Back

⧫ **Sensation of cold water poured on the back.**

Back pain before menses, in labor, or from suppressed menses.

Extremities

Wandering arthritis.

Pains worse first motion but better from moving.

Pains worse heat and better cold.

Pains in the heels.

Arthritic pains especially hips and knees.

Chilblains.

Eczema with itching worse at night and worse from heat.

Skin ulcers. Eczema. Psoriasis.

Varices, worse pregnancy, better cold.

Heat in the feet and must put them out of the covers.

Sleep

⧫ **Sleeps on the abdomen or on the back with the arms raised over the head.**

⧫ **Sleep disturbed by a particular song or phrase of a song running through her head.**

Acutes

Otitis media with pains which wake the child, she cries and needs comfort but without the anger of Chamomilla.

Upper respiratory infection or influenza with bland coryza, sneezing, and conjunctivitis.

Night-time coughs of children.

Cystitis. Pyelonephritis.

Hay fever, marked sneezing and red and itchy eyes.

Measles. Mumps. Chicken pox.

Mastitis.

CLINICAL

Allergy. Amenorrhea. Anxiety. Arthritis. Asthma. Bronchitis. Conjunctivitis. Connective tissue disease. Cough. Cystitis. Dementia. Depression. Dysmenorrhea. Eczema. Endometriosis. Food allergy. Gastritis. Headaches. Labor. Menstrual disorders. Menopause. Metrorrhagia. Migraine. Mumps. Obstructed lacrimal duct. Orchitis. Otitis Media. Pregnancy. Premenstrual syndrome. Prostatitis. Psoriasis. Rhinitis. Sarcoidosis. Sinusitis. Systemic lupus. Urethral stricture. Urethritis. Urticaria. Uterine prolapse. Varices. Vertigo.

COMPLEMENTARIES

Sil. Lyc. Kali-S. Fl-Ac. Tub. Calc.

COMPARISONS

Phos - Open, better consolation, dependent, craves ice cream and cold foods, high sexual interest, respiratory troubles.

Sulph - Warm, better cold, red lips and cheeks, puts feet out of covers, worse evening in bed.

Arg-N - Open and emotional, warm and better cold, desires ice cream, averse to pork, indigestion.

Merc - Otitis, craves bread and butter, worse at night, disgust.

Kali-S - Asthma and allergy, worse when over-heated, night-time cough, irritable.

Sep. Staph. Bar-C. Lyc. Med. Caps.

PYROGENIUM

The suppurative quality of Pyrogenium should be no surprise considering the fact that it originates from putrescent meat. Certain forms of infection, suppuration, and even sepsis will respond to this remedy. Thus far it has been used almost exclusively in acute conditions or in conditions which began from acute infections.

MENTALS

Reportedly curative in delirium with symptoms similar to Baptisia such as feeling as if another person were in the bed, or as if he covered the bed or as if he was crowded by too many limbs.

Great restlessness during fever.

GENERALS

- ◆ **Disparity between the pulse rate and the temperature. For example, the pulse is 140 though there is only a moderate fever or vice-versa.**

Restless and better from motion *(Rhus-T)*.

Offensiveness.

Never well since serious infection.

HEAD

Throbbing headache, better from pressure.

Tongue is red and shiny or coated.

GASTROINTESTINAL

Vomiting of liquids once warmed in stomach *(Phos)*.

Offensive stool.

CHEST

- ◆ **Consciousness of the heart.**

Palpitations.

Bronchitis. Pneumonia.

Extremities

Aching through the whole body, better from constant motion.

Sore, bruised feeling; bed feels too hard *(Rhus-T, Arn, Bapt)*.

Lymphangitis.

Chills beginning between the shoulder-blades.

Abscess. Cellulitis.

ACUTES

Influenza: high fever, aching and restlessness *(Rhus-T, Ars, Eup-Per)*.

- ◆ **Puerperal fever** with aching, offensive discharge and lochia. It is almost a specific for the condition.

Typhoid fever was said to respond dramatically to this remedy though such a condition is rarely seen in Western countries.

CLINICAL

Abscess. Cellulitis. Influenza. Lymphangitis. Puerperal fever or endometritis. Sepsis. Skin ulcers.

COMPARISONS

Bapt - Sepsis, delirium, offensive discharges, sore, bruised feeling.

Rhus-T - Fever, soreness, restlessness, red tongue.

Ars. Sulph. Ail.

RADIUM BROMATUM

Radium Bromatum has been shown to be a deep-acting remedy. However our knowledge of this remedy is very incomplete. When we find a combination of skin problems and arthritic complaints, we must consider this remedy. In any rheumatic condition which has followed radiation treatment we can consider Radium Bromatum.

GENERALS

Warm-blooded.

General aggravation from becoming heated in bed.

General aggravation at night.

Complaints after exposure to radiation or radiation treatment of malignancy.

Complaints go from right to left or left to right.

EXTREMITIES

Arthritic complaints; gout; sciatica.

Joint pains similar modalities to Rhus Toxicodendron, especially worse at night and better motion.

Pains better in cool air, worse heat of the bed.

Pains focused in the knees and lower extremities.

SKIN

Eczema. Psoriasis.

Ringworm with lesions which are perfectly circular.

Dry, burning skin eruptions.

Eruptions over thighs and genitalia.

ACUTES

Influenza with strong occipital headache.

Acute rheumatism.

CLINICAL

Arthritis. Connective tissue disease. Eczema. Influenza. Radiation poisoning. Rheumatism. Tinea.

COMBINED SYMPTOMS

Skin problems *and* arthritic complaints.

COMPARISONS

Rhus-T. Sulph. Puls. Ars.

RANUNCULUS BULBOSUS

Ranunculus Bulbosus is a remedy primarily for arthritic conditions and rheumatism, although it has strong effects on the skin, the respiratory tract, and the nerves as well. This remedy has one of the most marked reactions to cold and damp of all our materia medica. In our literature there is much written concerning the use of Ranunculus Bulbosus in alcoholics. However in practice, while it is quite common for alcohol to aggravate or poison the Ranunculus Bulbosus patient, generally the patient has an aversion to alcohol. Therefore it more often acts on acute alcoholic symptoms than as a constitutional remedy for alcoholics.

MENTALS

Irritable and touchy.

Great dejection about his condition which is out of proportion to the severity of the illness.

GENERALS

Generally worse in cold and cold wet weather, or from changes in the weather.

General aggravation in open air or from drafts; also worse walking in open air.

General aggravation from alcohol.

Generally worse in the evening.

Generally worse from getting wet.

General aggravation from and aversion to touch.

Painful, cold spots on the body.

HEAD

Right frontal headaches.

Headache from alcoholic drinks.

Rheumatic headaches, worse wet weather or changes of weather.

Hay fever.

CHEST

◆ **Intercostal neuralgia, especially of the lower left chest.**

Chest pains worse motion, worse inspiration, worse lying on the painful side, worse on turning, worse walking, worse touch, worse cold, better by splinting the respiration.

Pleurisy. Painful bronchitis or pneumonia. Painful respiration.

Cold sensation in the chest and lungs, worse breathing cold air.

Herpes zoster of chest, especially left side. Post-herpetic neuralgia.

GASTROINTESTINAL

Indigestion and hiccoughing from alcoholic drinks.

Right upper quadrant or liver pains on inspiration.

BACK

Rheumatism and stiffness of the neck.

Pain around the inner angle of the left scapula.

Fibrositis.

Back muscles sore to the touch.

Stabbing pain between scapula and spine.

Back pains worse cold, worse damp, worse walking.

Burning or cold spots in chest or back.

Sciatica, worse cold, damp weather.

Herpes zoster of the back.

EXTREMITIES

Arthritic pains worse cold, damp weather or changes of weather.

Chronic stiff joints.

Ulcers on fingers.

Fibrositis.

SKIN

Herpes zoster.

Vesicular eruptions which form hard crusts.

Hard, horny callosities.

CLINICAL

Allergy. Arthritis. Back pain. Bronchitis. Callosities. Eczema. Fibrositis. Gastritis. Headache. Herpes zoster. Migraine. Neuralgia. Pleurisy. Pneumonia. Rheumatism. Sciatica. Shingles.

COMPARISONS

Bry - Left-sided intercostal neuralgia and pleurisy, worse from motion and inspiration, rheumatism, irritable. Bryonia is better lying on the painful side *(opposite Ran-B)*.

Rhus-T - Rheumatism and worse from cold, damp weather, vesicular eruptions and herpes zoster.

Dulc. Kali-C. Rhod. Calc.

RAPHANUS

Raphanus is mainly used acutely and especially after surgery when ileus remains long after the expected time. The main keynote of Raphanus is the incarceration of flatus, especially at the splenic flexure.

Gastrointestinal

- **Sensation of incarcerated flatus, especially in the left upper quadrant othe abdomen.**

Urogenital

Hyper-sexual.

Clinical

Bowel obstruction. Post-surgical ileus.

RATANHIA

Ratanhia has been used almost exclusively in cases of rectal pathology or cases which result from the suppression of rectal symptoms. It was by careful observation of such typical pathology that Vithoulkas discovered the compulsive neurosis to which Ratanhia patients are prone. He has described a type of superstition with compulsions of a religious nature. The patients may be quite compulsive in general and in specific concerning their rectal hygiene. Ratanhia has a general tendency for fissure formation - at the rectum, nipples, and other locations.

Mentals

Obsessive and compulsive thinking and behavior.

Gastrointestinal

Rectal fissures and hemorrhoids.

- **Pain in rectum after stool lasting for minutes to hours.**

Severe burning, cutting, splinter or "broken glass" pain in rectum.

Pains worse from touch and from passing a hard stool.

Pains better warm bathing, by lying, or from slowly walking.

Hemorrhoids protrude with stool.

Rectal excoriation and oozing.

Craving: Chicken. Salt. Sweet. Fat.

Clinical

Rectal fissure. Hemorrhoids. Proctalgia. Constipation. Anxiety and compulsive neurosis. Fissure.

Comparisons

Paeon. Aesc. Coll. Nit-Ac. Ars.

RHEUM

Rheum has been used mainly in children and infants with subacute or chronic diarrheas and also during dentition.

Mentals

Whiny and irritable, crying, shrieking.

More upset and restless at night *(Jalap)*.

Capricious.

Does not want to play normally.

Generals

Sour odor of perspiration and discharges.

General aggravation during dentition.

Tired and easily perspires.

Excessive perspiration from slight motion.

Head

Dentition.

Excessive saliva.

Head and face sweat, especially in the sleep.

Gastrointestinal

Diarrhea; especially diarrheas of children, especially with dentition.

Sour odor from stool.

Colic.

Comparisons

Mag-C. Calc. Calc-P. Hep. Cham. Jalap. Cina.

RHODODENDRON

Rhododendron is another rheumatic remedy and most of the symptoms are of the joints. The symptoms may be very difficult to distinguish from those of Rhus Toxicodendron, with morning aggravation, improvement from motion and heat, and strong effects from the weather. All of the symptoms of Rhododendron are strongly aggravated before a storm, or from large barometric changes.

MENTALS

Nervous and over-sensitive.

Faintness, confusion, excitement before a storm. Fear of storms.

GENERALS

- **General aggravation before storms and thunderstorms.**

General aggravation from exposure to wind, and especially to prevailing winds, such as the Fohn, or the Santa Ana.

General aggravation from cold, wet weather.

General amelioration from motion.

HEAD

Neuralgia or headaches, worse before a storm, in bad weather or change of weather, better from motion.

Toothache, worse from storm.

UROGENITAL

Orchitis. Epididymitis.

Pain in testicle, more often the right side, may be described as if crushed.

Pain in testicle, amelioration from motion.

Pain in testicles extending up to the abdomen.

Swelling of testes and chronic inflammation.

Testicular (or ovarian) pain worse before storm or weather changes.

Hydroceles have been reportedly cured with this remedy.

MUSCULOSKELETAL

Joint pains, worse morning, worse changes of weather or in wet weather, better motion or by walking, better heat.

Pains in upper extremities, in tendons, in fingers and toes.

Wandering arthritis.

Arthritic nodosities.

Neck or low back pain, worse changes of weather, better motion.

Pain in the heel.

Sleep

Sleeps with legs crossed at the ankles.

Clinical

Arthritis. Bursitis. Epididymitis. Gout. Headache. Injury to tendons. Neuralgia. Orchitis. Rheumatism. Toothache.

Comparisons

Rhus-T - Arthritis worse wet weather and before a storm, better warmth and motion and stretching.

Ran-B. Phos. Dulc. Ruta.

RHUS TOXICODENDRON

Rhus Toxicodendron is one of our most important polycrests. Though it is often thought of as a remedy for arthritis, it cures mental disorders as well as deep pathology of the nervous system, the heart and almost all other organ systems. It is a general rule that patients suffering on the level of the joints and muscles tend to be relatively unaffected on the psychological planes. Therefore it is not surprising that we do not have great insight into the personality of the Rhus Toxicodendron patient.

There are several stages to the psychological state of Rhus Toxicodendron. The early stage finds a patient who is cheerful, joking and very lively; he is quick-witted and friendly yet peculiarly timid. This animated stage is replaced by an inner restlessness and agitation. Often, in this stage, the patient becomes irritable and easily frustrated. In fact, Rhus Toxicodendron can be a very useful remedy in behavior disorders of children with restlessness and great irritability or even maliciousness. In adults the patient is often very serious, hard working, impatient and somewhat driven, like Nux Vomica.

As the pathology deepens, the patient becomes as stiff and rigid on the emotional plane as he is on the physical plane. At this stage we find depression and moroseness. In the later stages the patient becomes stiff and fixed mentally as well. Here we find a stage of compulsiveness and ritualistic behavior. Rhus Toxicodendron is one of the most superstitious of all remedies. The patient has fixed ideas and even ritualistic behavior.

Rhus Toxicodendron has a strong effect on the nerves, mucous and serous membranes, and skin. The hallmark of the remedy is progressive stiffness, often coming after a period of restlessness or overuse.

Mentals

Joking, restless, cheerful patients.

Mind restless; jumps from subject to subject.

Irritability. Impatience. Hurried.

Anxiety for his own children.

Fears: Killing someone. Poison.

Timid. Self-conscious.

Depression; moroseness.

Superstitious; ritualistic; fixed ideas. Compulsive disorder.

Generals

- **General aggravation from cold and cold wet weather.**

General amelioration warm weather, from warm bathing.

General aggravation from drafts.

Generally worse in cloudy, overcast, or foggy weather.

General aggravation from getting wet.

General aggravation from uncovering or getting one extremity cold.

General aggravation before and during a storm.

Generally left-sided complaints.

Periodic complaints, especially chills and fevers.

Sudden periodic chills, worse at night.

General aggravation in the autumn.

General aggravation from over-exertion.

General aggravation in the evening after the exertions of the day.

General amelioration from motion; cannot sit still.

Generally worse in the morning on rising.

Neurological

Parkinson's disease, great stiffness, better motion, the patient is stiff in his emotions and facial expressions, tremor.

Chorea. Twitches. Tics.

Hemiplegia, especially on the left side.

Vertigo, worse rising, tendency to fall backwards.

Head

Headaches, worse from damp weather, worse from storms, worse from changes of weather, better motion.

Acne rosacea. Erysipelas of the face.

Eruptions at the tip of the nose *(Caust, Aeth, Nat-C)*.

Fever blisters about the lips. Cracks at the corners of mouth.

Swelling and inflammation of the eyelids *(Apis, Kali-C, Ars)*.

Iritis.

OROPHARYNX

- ◆ **Red tip of tongue or a triangle of redness on the tongue.**
- Cracking jaw. Temporomandibular joint syndrome.
- Pharyngitis, better warm drinks.
- Laryngitis and hoarseness, worse from over-use of the voice but may be better from speaking (motion).

GASTROINTESTINAL

- Craving: ◆**Cold milk**. Cheese. Sweets.
- Aversion: Meat.
- Thirsty for sips.
- Desires cold drinks.

UROGENITAL

- **Herpes of the genitals.**
- **Eruptions on the genitals or on the inner thigh.**
- Frequent urination.
- Enuresis, especially in boys.

CHEST

- Asthma, especially in association with or from suppression of eczema.
- Cough, worse cold or damp weather, worse before or during chill.
- Bronchitis; Pneumonia, often producing rusty sputum.
- Palpitations.
- Cardiac hypertrophy. Valvular disorders.
- **Angina, worse from exertion, extending to the left arm.**

BACK

- **Low back pain and sciatica.**
- **Back pain, worse after muscle strains as in car accidents or over-lifting.**
- **Back pain, worse sitting still which causes him to stiffen.**
- **Back pain, better heat or hot baths or showers.**
- **Back pain, better motion and forces him to get up and move about.**
- **Back pain better from hard pressure and massage.**
- Cracking of the neck and back. Torticollis.
- Stiffness and pains in the trapezius muscles into the neck.
- **Cervical stiffness which causes the patient to stretch and move the head, worse from being irritated, worse cold damp, better heat. The stiffness may go to the occiput and cause headache.**

Extremities

- **Arthritis, acute or chronic rheumatism.**
- **Arthritis worse in the night in bed, worse in the morning on waking, worse in damp and cold weather or before storms, worse exertion.**
- **Arthritis better heat or hot bathing, better dry weather, better motion.**

Pain in the left shoulder.

- **Pain in the inner, upper left scapula.**

Restless extremities, even to the point of chorea.

Restless legs in bed.

Bursitis. Tendonitis. Sprains.

Numbness from lying on the arm or leg.

Numbness of left arm in heart conditions.

Cracking joints.

Arthritic nodosities.

Skin

Eczema with small vesicles which are intensely itchy.

- **Itching better from scalding hot water** *(Rhus-V)*.

Herpes. Shingles. Poison oak or ivy.

Urticaria. Psoriasis.

Thickened skin in long-standing skin disorders.

Erythema nodosum.

Erysipelas with dark reddish splotches.

Sleep

Restless sleep, must constantly shift in his sleep and can not find a comfortable position.

Dreams of work or long walks or exertions.

Acutes

Influenza with much aching which forces the patient to shift around constantly. The fever may come rapidly especially at 10 AM.

Chicken pox. Impetigo. Scarlet fever.

Pharyngitis, better warm drinks with restless uncomfortable feeling in the body. Upper respiratory infection.

Pneumonia, cough producing a rusty colored sputum.

Sprains with a stiff, sore sensation but the patient feels the need to be flexing and moving the joint.

Back injuries.

Injuries to the tendons or muscles, worse from over exerting.

CLINICAL

Angina. Arthritis. Asthma. Behavior disorder. Bronchitis. Cervical strain - "Whip-lash." Chicken pox. Chorea. Compulsive disorders. Connective tissue disease. Contusion. Eczema. Enuresis. Erysipelas. Erythema Nodosum. Fibrositis. Headache. Hemiplegia. Herpes. Impetigo. Influenza. Laryngitis. Low back pain. Parkinson's Disease. Pemphigus. Pharyngitis. Pneumonia. Rheumatic fever. Rheumatism. Sciatica. Shingles. Sprains. Tendonitis. Urticaria.

COMPLEMENTARIES

Bry. Calc.

INIMICAL

Apis.

COMPARISONS

Phos - Arthritis with pains better motion and heat, worse before a storm, chilly, craves cold milk, angina, coughs and hoarseness.

Tub - Arthritis with similar modalities, worse night, worse from cold damp and from storms, restless, ritualistic, craves cold milk, eczema, respiratory troubles.

Ruta - Arthritis and injuries with similar modalities, stiffness, neck pains and stiffness.

Calc - Chilly and worse from cold damp, worse from over-exertion, arthritis, crave sweets, cracking skin and eczema.

Ars - Especially in acutes may be confused with fever, chilliness, restlessness, thirst for sips, irritable, skin symptoms, respiratory troubles, may crave milk.

Apis - Acute rheumatisms, fevers, skin symptoms, erysipelas.

Ran-B. Rhod. Cimic. Dulc. Calc-P. Rad-Br. Stel.

RHUS VENENATA

For the most part, Rhus Venenata is similar to Rhus Toxicodendron with more focus on the skin and less on the joints. Especially the skin has prominent cracking. It also has eczema with similar characteristics as Rhus Toxicodendron: marked itching ameliorated by scalding water. When eczema of this sort is not accompanied by the characteristic milk craving or joint symptoms, we prefer Rhus Venenata. It is also an important remedy in the treatment of scleroderma.

ROBINIA

Robinia is a specific remedy, to be thought of mainly in cases of severe hyperacidity. The intensity of the burning in the digestive tract is the main keynote to its use.

Head

Cured cases of neuralgia and migraine are recorded.

Gastrointestinal

Severe burning and acidity of the whole digestive tract.

Heartburn, worse at night and in bed.

Sour, acrid eructations and waterbrash.

Clinical

Reflux esophagitis. Hiatus hernia. Peptic ulcer.

Comparisons

Sulph. Lyc. Ars. Phos. Iris.

RUMEX CRISPUS

Rumex is primarily a cough remedy, though the keynote symptom - aggravation from uncovering or undressing - has led to its prescription in skin and digestive complaints as well.

Generals

General aggravation from cold or open air.

General aggravation from change of temperature either direction.

◆ **General aggravation from uncovering or undressing.**

Gastrointestinal

Fullness in the stomach which rises to throat and triggers coughing.

Diarrhea, especially morning diarrhea.

Larynx

Rawness in the larynx or trachea, worse open air.

Copious mucous production, especially in the upper airways which must be coughed out. Kent mentions it for tubercular laryngitis.

Catarrh, irritation, and thick mucous in the larynx.

COUGH

Worse cold or open air. Worse uncovering.

Worse inspiring, irregularity of breath, talking, laughing.

Worse especially in the morning on waking or at 11 PM.

- **Worse touch or pressure on the throat or larynx.**
- **Worse change of temperature** (warm to cold or cold to warm).

Cold air causes a tickle in the throat, triggering a cough.

Better by sucking on candy, better by drinking.

Dry, tickling cough. Croup. Pertussis.

SKIN

- **Marked itching immediately on uncovering or undressing.**

COMPARISONS

Coc-C. Spong. Dros. Phos.

RUTA

Ruta is useful mainly in rheumatic and connective tissue problems. The most prominent fact in cases where Ruta is indicated is the horrible stiffness the patient feels in the muscles and tendons. Ruta is also one of our most important remedies for trauma and injury. Vithoulkas produced some remarkable cures of anxiety disorder with Ruta.

MENTALS

Anxious, irritable, rigid patients.

Mental dullness and aversion to thinking.

Suspicious. Remorseful. Quarrelsome.

Anxiety and panic disorders with fear of death which comes on especially during fever or if over-heated.

GENERALS

Generally stiff through the body.

Easily fatigued, worse from exertion.

General aggravation from cold, damp weather.

General amelioration lying (some pains may be worse from lying).

Soreness of part lain upon.

Injuries to connective tissue, tendons and periosteum.

Restlessness.

HEAD

Vertigo, worse evening, worse long sitting.

- **Eye strain**; general stiffness about the eyes which is caused by and worse from exerting the vision, especially doing fine work, such as needlepoint or watch-repair, or reading fine print.

Burning and redness of the eyes.

Facial neuralgia, worse cold, worse lying.

GASTROINTESTINAL

Constipation, ineffectual urging.

Rectal prolapse.

BACK

Back pain, low back pain and sciatica, ameliorated by lying.

Cervical stiffness

Thoracic pains in the back which restrict respiration.

Lame feeling in the back.

EXTREMITIES

Arthritic pains, worse cold damp weather, worse exertion, worse from strains.

Bruised or sore pains with stiffness.

- **Injuries to tendons, from strains or twisting of joints which results in a stiff, bruised pain.**
- **Acute bursitis and tendonitis, often with effusion.**
- **Injuries to the periosteum; bruises of the periosteum.**
- **Chronic overuse or injury to tendons cause fibrosis, and nodular growths, especially common in the wrists.**

Weakness and stiffness prevent raising from a chair.

Ganglion cysts. Neuroma.

CLINICAL

Arthritis. Bursitis. Eye strain. Fibrositis. Headache. Low back pain. Muscle strains. Headaches. Injury to periosteum and tendons. Neuralgia. Neuroma. Panic disorder. Rectal prolapse. Sciatica. Sprains. Tendonitis.

COMPARISONS

Rhus-T - Stiffness, worse in the morning, better motion, worse cold, damp weather, injuries to tendons, neck stiffness.

Kalm. Ran-B. Plb. Caust.

SABADILLA

Sabadilla is primarily a remedy for hay fever and coryza. The main keynote symptom is the tremendous sneezing and paroxysmal nature of the sneezing.

MENTALS

"Delusions as to the state of his body," is considered by many a keynote, but in practice is rarely found in cases of Sabadilla.

Irritable and easily startled.

GENERALS

Chilly and worse from cold.

Sore or burning spots.

Some authors assert that symptoms go from left to right.

HEAD

- **Hay fever with tremendous sneezing; where sneezing is the primary complaint.** Paroxysms of sneezing of ten or more sneezes, worse cold, worse odors and perfumes.

Itching and tingling in the nose.

Generally thin and copious nasal discharge, often acrid.

Coryza symptoms better by warmth and warm drinks.

Pharyngitis, may begin left side, better warm drinks, worse cold air.

Sensation of something in the throat which causes swallowing.

GASTROINTESTINAL

Craves: Warm drinks. Lemon. Onion.

Aversion: Onion.

Has a reputation for the treatment of worms of all varieties.

CHEST

Asthma which comes during general allergic and hay fever periods.

Cough, dry and irritated.

CLINICAL

Allergy. Asthma. Colds. Cough. Pharyngitis. Worms.

COMPLEMENTARY

Sep.

COMPARISONS

All-C. Euphr. Ars. Sang.

SABINA

Sabina is especially useful in uterine complaints: hemorrhage and the excruciating pelvic pains from menses, during or after labor and miscarriage, or from cysts and tumors. The great guiding symptom of the pains in Sabina is "pain from the low back radiating into the pubis." However, many cases will not have this specific symptom but a more general pain felt in the back and pelvic bones, or more internally.

HEAD

Epistaxis.

GASTROINTESTINAL

Craves: Lemon. Salt. Refreshing things.

UROGENITAL

Severe dysmenorrhea or uterine pains of other origin, beginning in low back and sacrum and extend to pubis.

Pains "as if the bones are breaking open."

Metrorrhagia with active gushing flow, the blood is often bright red or red mixed with clots.

Metrorrhagia, worse motion, worse at menopause, worse from fibroids, worse from retained placenta, paradoxically may be better by walking.

Miscarriage; both to try to prevent a specific episode or to take away a chronic tendency toward miscarriage.

Menses delayed or too early.

Condylomata. Leukorrhea.

Sexual desires increased; desires increased during the metrorrhagia.

EXTREMITIES

Back pains in menses, labor, uterine complaints.

Heel pains; thigh pains.

CLINICAL

Dysmenorrhea. Metrorrhagia. Miscarriage. Retained placenta. Leukorrhea. Condylomata. Epistaxis.

COMBINED SYMPTOMS

Uterine disorders *and* epistaxis.

COMPARISONS

Sec. Bell. Phos. Ip. Erig.

SAMBUCUS NIGRA

The main action of Sambucus is in respiratory problems, both of the upper respiratory tract and nose as well as in pulmonary disorders.

GENERALS

"Dry heat during sleep, marked perspiration during the day or upon waking," is the keynote, but often the perspiration is heavy during the whole attack, even before the patient awakens.

Perspiration over whole body except head.

Body very hot but feet icy cold *(Bell)*.

Weakness with excessive perspiration.

Head

Nasal obstruction; snuffles, especially in newborns.

Nasal obstruction so pronounced the child is unable to nurse.

Cyanosis. The face turns blue during asthma or cough.

THROAT

Laryngospasm.

Hoarseness with much mucous in the larynx.

CHEST

Asthma, worse at night and after midnight.

Respiration difficult at night and the patient jumps up with a feeling of suffocation.

Asthma associated with heavy perspiration.

Respiration difficult, worse lying.

Asthma of children.

Croup. Pertussis. Bronchitis.

EXTREMITIES

Cold feet or cold hands and feet with warm body.

CLINICAL

Allergy. Asthma. Bronchitis. Croup. Laryngospasm. Pertussis. Rhinitis.

COMBINED SYMPTOMS

Asthma *and* heavy perspiration.

COMPARISONS

Lyc. Kali-C. Kali-S. Kali-N. Lach. Nux-V.

SANGUINARIA

Sanguinaria is generally not considered a "deep acting" remedy yet it treats a wide range of serious clinical conditions. This is a strongly right-sided remedy. It is especially useful in allergy and allergic asthma, in migraine headaches and in bursitis.

GENERALS

- ◆ **General amelioration from eructation, flatus, vomiting.**
  Right-sided complaints.

HEAD

- ◆ **Migraine headache on the right side, typically begins in the neck or even the trapezius muscles on the right side and extends to the forehead and eye.**
- ◆ **Headache better from vomiting**, better by sleep, better by passing flatus or eructation.

Headache worse light, worse noise, worse jar, worse fasting.

Headache with flushing of the face, with bounding pulse in carotids.

Gastric headache.

Periodic headaches, often every 7 days.

Pain and bursting sensation in the right eye.

FACE

Facial neuralgia.

Flushes of the face in menopause.

Circumscribed red circles on the cheeks.

NOSE

- ◆ **Hay fever, "rose colds,"** the patient is very sensitive to odors, flowers and airborne pollen.

Watery coryza; frequent sneezing.

Right-sided coryza *(Ars)*.

Burning in nose, mouth, throat.

Summer colds.

Nasal polyps.

GASTROINTESTINAL

Vomiting with headaches.

Esophagitis, marked heartburn and reflux. Acrid belching.

Craves: Spicy foods.

Eructations caused by coughing.

CHEST

Allergic asthma; "hay asthma." Asthma worse odors, worse flowers.

Asthma associated with heartburn and acrid eructations.

Reflux esophagitis and aspiration pneumonitis.

Pneumonia, especially right-sided, with painful cough, hemoptysis, dyspnea and burning extremities.

◆ **Cough better from eructation or flatus, better vomiting.**

Cough, worse from lying, worse from irritation in larynx or throat pit *(Rumex)*.

Pertussis. Bronchitis. "Colds go to the chest."

Offensive sputum.

Kent and others recommend its use in late stage tuberculosis.

EXTREMITIES

◆ **Bursitis, especially of the right shoulder.**

◆ **Shoulder pain worse turning in bed, worse at night in bed, worse lying on it, worse trying to raise the arm.**

Pain in the right deltoid.

Shoulder pain extends to the neck and head or downward to hand.

Burning palms and soles.

Feet hot at night and puts them out of the covers.

CLINICAL

Allergy. Arthritis. Asthma. Bronchitis. Bursitis. Colds. Cough. Esophagitis. Flushes. Hypertension. Menopause. Migraine. Nasal polyps. Neuralgia. Pertussis. Pneumonia. Tuberculosis.

COMBINED SYMPTOMS

Asthma *and* heartburn.

COMPARISONS

Bell - Migraine headache, on right side from occiput, right eye pain, flushes, pulsing carotids, hypertension.

Lyc - Right-sided, pneumonia, eructation and gastric problems, asthma with gastric problems, feet out of covers.

Ferr - Shoulder pains, worse from raising arm, migraines, flushes, metrorrhagia *(Ferr-M)*.

Chel - Right shoulder pain, right sided pneumonia, gastric headache, liver disorders.

Puls - Migraine with vomiting, allergy, asthma, uncovers feet.

Sabad. All-C. Kali-S. Sulph.

SANICULA

Sanicula is not well described in our literature but it is so useful, especially in children, that we must think of it almost as a polycrest. The water of this spring contains trace amounts of many important remedies including Natrum Muriaticum, Calcarea, Borax, and Silica. Therefore it is not surprising that the remedy holds features of these better known remedies. In children who are stubborn, irritable and restless, this remedy can easily be confused with Calcarea Phosphorica or even Chamomilla. The children can be demanding or even aggressive and are averse to being touched. Older patients complain of weakness of concentration and inability to finish tasks.

The physical disorders are of metabolic origin, centering around absorption and assimilation of minerals.

MENTALS

Irritable, peevish, stubborn children *(Sil, Calc-P).*

Mental weakness, poor concentration and unable to complete tasks.

Fears: Something bad will happen. Dark. Robbers. Descending.

GENERALS

Chilly, worse cold, and better from heat.

◆ **Offensive discharges, especially with a fishy odor** or like rotten cheese *(Hep).*

General aggravation from 9 PM to midnight.

Offensive perspiration, especially on parts on which he lays.

Weakness and exhaustion.

HEAD

Perspiration of scalp, especially the occiput, especially during sleep.

Blepharitis. Photophobia.

Lacrimation, worse wind *(Calc, Euphr, Puls, Nat-M).*

Offensive ear discharges.

Burning tongue; must allow it to hang outside the mouth to cool.

Acne, especially around the chin.

STOMACH

Craves: **Ham. Bacon.** Sweets. Salt. Fat. Cold milk. Soft eggs.

Thirsty for small quantities.

Vomiting immediately after eating.

Projectile vomiting.

Frequent vomiting, spitting-up, and milk intolerance in newborns.

ABDOMEN

Constipation; stool may recede *(Sil)*.

Large, hard stool. Stool too large to pass or sometimes must be manually extracted.

Involuntary stool.

Diarrhea which is offensive.

Abdomen enlarged and flabby.

UROGENITAL

Vaginitis with odor like fish-brine or like old cheese.

Enuresis. Involuntary urine.

Offensive condyloma.

EXTREMITIES

Low back pain, worse as the day progresses.

Cold sensation of the sacrum and low back.

Rheumatism of shoulder, worse right side, worse on putting the arm behind his back.

Cracks on the dorsum of the hands and at joints.

Feet burning, especially soles, puts them out of the covers.

Offensive foot-sweat.

CLINICAL

Acne. Allergy. Blepharitis. Condyloma. Constipation. Diarrhea. Eczema. Enuresis. Lower back pain. Marasmus. Otitis media. Rheumatism. Vaginitis.

COMBINED SYMPTOMS

Calcarea but with hot feet.

COMPLEMENTARY

Chamomilla is the acute of Sanicula.

COMPARISONS

Sil - Stubborn and irritable children, head sweat in sleep, constipation and receding stool, offensive foot-sweat, acne.

Calc - Stubborn children, fears of dark and of the future, constipation though stool does not recede, offensive foot-sweat, craves sweets, salt (but not fat), cracks on hands, flabby, enlarged abdomen.

Calc-P - Head perspires in sleep, complaining and irritable, craves sweets, salt, bacon, low back pain.

Sulph. Cham. Rheum. Tub.

SARSAPARILLA

Sarsaparilla is one of our great specifics for the urinary tract. It is, across the board, our best remedy for uncomplicated cystitis and will also serve in more advanced disorders of the urinary system.

GENERALS

Kent describes a weakened and sluggish vitality, although this is not seen in the usual acute or subacute cases.

UROGENITAL

- **Cystitis with pain at the end of urination.**

Burning urination and frequent urging.

Unable to urinate without standing.

Urine filled with sediment, often red, which settles in the container.

Hematuria. Pyelonephritis.

Calculi of kidneys or bladder with burning and hematuria..

Enuresis.

Eruptions and excoriations about the genitalia or buttocks.

Herpes.

CHEST

Retraction of the nipples.

EXTREMITIES

Cracks of the hands and soles of the feet. The cracks may be transverse to the skin lines.

Dry palms.

SKIN

Dry, thick skin.

Itching which changes location, especially after scratching.

Thick folds of skin, especially after weight loss.

CLINICAL

Urinary tract infection - cystitis, pyelonephritis, prostatitis, urethritis. Ureteral colic. Kidney stones. Eczema with cracking skin. Herpes.

COMBINED SYMPTOMS

Skin *and* urinary symptoms.

COMPARISONS

Canth. Equis. Lyc. Petr.

SCUTELLARIA

Louis Klein of Vancouver, Canada reported several cured cases of chronic fatigue syndrome at the International Foundation for Homeopathy case conference in 1990. The major points of prescription were fatigue, anxiety, cloudy thinking and dizziness. The condition generally follows a flu-like illness or a sinusitis suppressed by antibiotics.

SECALE

Secale acts mainly on the circulation. Allopathically, ergotamines are used for their (primary) vasoconstrictive properties; homeopathically Secale is useful for circulatory imbalances of whatever type. Of special importance is the use of Secale in hemorrhagic complaints, and most specifically, on uterine hemorrhage. The main guiding symptom for the remedy is the tremendous aggravation from heat and amelioration from cold. It is perhaps the hottest remedy in the materia medica and it is difficult to prescribe Secale without this characteristic.

MENTALS

Discouragement, indifference and mental dullness.

Senility. Confusion of mind. Secretly feels he may lose his sanity.

GENERALS

◆ **Burning and heat. Worse heat, both generally and locally.**

General amelioration from cold and from uncovering.

General amelioration from open air or being fanned.

Skin feels cold to the touch but the patient feels burning hot and cannot tolerate covers.

Hemorrhagic tendency - uterine, epistaxis, purpura, etc.

Passive hemorrhages, often dark, unclotted blood, though may have active bleeding.

Paralysis. Convulsion.

Appearance: generally thin or even emaciated patients with wrinkled, old-looking, exhausted face - "like a dead man."

HEAD

Epistaxis.

Face looks old; Hippocratic; wrinkled.

GASTROINTESTINAL

Diarrhea. Involuntary stool.

Secale was considered one of our main remedies for cholera with bloody, involuntary stools and icy cold skin.

Gastritis with strong burning sensation and hemorrhage.

UROGENITAL

- **Uterine hemorrhage, continuous yet passive, often with dark, thin blood.**

Bright red and clotted blood.

Labor weak or ceasing.

Endometritis.

Threatened or incomplete abortion, especially at the third month.

EXTREMITIES

- **Claudication; cramping in legs on walking or exerting.**

Gangrene or incipient gangrene of the distal parts with numbness.

Formication of the extremities; crawling or numb sensations, especially in the calves.

Burning, constricting pains of the legs, better from cold.

Convulsions of the hands.

Clenches or must splay the fingers *(Lac-C, Lach)*.

Intolerance of constriction about the extremities; marked sensitiveness to the blood-pressure cuff.

Raynaud's syndrome.

Varicosities, often with burning pains, worse heat, better cold air.

Feet hot and must be uncovered.

SKIN

Ulcers which are black and burning *(Anthr)*.

Formication.

Blue spots in areas of poor circulation; ecchymosis.

CLINICAL

Claudication. Cholera. Diarrhea. Ecchymosis. Epistaxis. Gangrene. Miscarriage. Raynaud's syndrome. Seizure disorder. Skin ulcers. Uterine hemorrhage. Varices.

COMPARISONS

Sulph - Burning pains and aversion to covering, worse heat and better cold, emaciation, etc.

Ars - Burning pains, weak and debilitated, gangrene, etc.

Sabin. Lach. Chin. Plb. Ham. Crot-H.

SELENIUM

Selenium is a remedy of weakness and collapse, events which are becoming all too common with today's stresses. The weakness of Selenium is often associated with sexual excesses *(Agn, Ph-Ac, Onos)* or long febrile illness. Sexual dysfunction is a common concomitant (impotence, prostatic dribbling, seminal emissions). Although Selenium is the only remedy in bold type in our repertory for the symptom, "Weakness from heat," this is a common symptom of chronic fatigue syndrome and multiple sclerosis which often requires other remedies.

Mentals

Theorizing.

Morose. Irritable.

Said to be useful in alcoholics or after drug abuse. Kent mentions the symptom, "Dipsomania before menses."

Generals

Weakness after sexual excesses, loss of fluids, or fevers.

General aggravation from heat, sun, fever and over-heating.

General aggravation from mental exertion *(Pic-Ac)*.

General aggravation from alcohol, from tea, from foods.

Weakness after coition.

General aggravation after sleep.

General aggravation from exertion.

Loses hair from whole body (axilla, genitalia, eyebrows, etc.).

Head

Headaches over the left eye. Headache worse tea, salt, sun, heat.

Hair painful to the touch.

Alopecia.

Gastrointestinal

Craves: Alcohol, especially brandy.

Aversion: Salt.

Constipation; impaction.

Urogenital

Prostatitis. Prostatic hypertrophy.

Dribbling of semen during stool.

Premature ejaculation.

Impotence. Impotence with prostatic dribbling.

Urination dribbling.

LARYNX

Laryngitis with much mucous and scraping of throat.

Hoarseness, worse singing.

BACK

Weakness of back associated with coition or seminal discharge.

SLEEP

Catnaps all through the night.

CLINICAL

Alopecia. Chronic fatigue syndrome. Constipation. Impotence. Laryngitis. Prostatitis. Prostatic hypertrophy.

COMPARISONS

Onos. Calad. Sulph. Agn. Ph-Ac. Pic-Ac. Cann-I.

SENEGA

Senega is a remedy for chronic bronchitis or catarrh of the respiratory tract. The prescription is difficult because there is no definite guiding symptom but rather a "gestalt" of symptoms leading to the remedy.

HEAD

Eye-strain.

Inflammation of the eye and eyelids.

CHEST

Chronic bronchitis with much thick, viscid mucous.

Chronic respiratory troubles in elderly patients.

Rattling in the chest *(Kali-S, Kali-Bi, Ant-T, Hippoz)*.

Difficult expectoration.

Cough, worse cold air or change of temperature, worse from lying, worse from irritation in larynx.

Oppression, marked soreness and weakness of the chest.

Respiration difficult, worse lying, better sitting upright, better taking a deep breath.

Kent and others describe its use in advanced tuberculosis.

LARYNX

Mucous and scraping from larynx.
Irritation of larynx and hoarseness.

CLINICAL

Asthma. Bronchitis. Emphysema. Eye-strain. Pneumonia.

COMPARISONS

Phos - Rattling chest, worse lying left side, better sitting, eye- strain.
Ant-T - Rattling chest, viscid mucous, oppressed chest in old people.
Kali-Bi. Kali-C. Kali-S. Samb.

SEPIA

Sepia certainly ranks within our top 10 polycrests and much higher in women where it is in the top 3 remedies prescribed. It is more difficult to identify cases of Sepia in men and children and therefore it is under-prescribed in these groups. Vithoulkas has given as the central theme of the remedy "stasis" or a state brought about by neutralization of the dynamic tensions which animate all organisms. This is reflected physically by laxness in the tissues and in the smooth musculature, and especially in the hormonal and sexual dysfunctions. Prolapse, constipation, varicosities, and sagging tissues all reflect the physical stasis. Emotionally we see a similar neutralizing effect which produces indifference and disconnectedness. Mentally there is also stasis, sluggishness, and mental dullness.

Children. In the early stages of Sepia - that is in children and teenagers - we do not see any sign of the typical stasis. The child is alive, excitable and affectionate. She is often the center of attention. The complaints in this stage include fears and over-sensitivity and over-excitability. The next stage of pathology occurs from stress, grief and disappointment. The child becomes more self-contained, introverted and closed. The patient will complain mainly of physical disorders such as headache, menstrual disorders and skin troubles, such as psoriasis or ringworm.

Irritability. The patient becomes progressively more detached from his family and community. Here we see the development of marked irritability, depression, and indifference. Any demand by the family is viewed as a further burden and met with anger. She finds herself shrieking at her children and cannot control her temper.

Guilt and isolation. Often the patient feels guilty and afraid of these internal changes and presents with tearfulness and desperation. Eventually she loses her connection to others to the extent that she no longer feels remorse for her behavior. Because of the detachment, the patient can see clearly into the weaknesses of those around her and will lash out with cutting, accurate, sarcastic, hurtful words.

Men. Male Sepias can be somewhat difficult to identify. The best word to describe the patient is "wimpy," that is to say weak in spirit and confidence and masculinity. It can be difficult to differentiate this patient from Staphysagria, Pulsatilla or Gelsemium. The patient appears worn-out and pitifully inadequate. He often has a great deal of difficulty motivating himself to work, often longing to give up his job and responsibilities.

Physical. The physical ailments of Sepia are frequently centered in the hormonal sphere, especially in female patients. The menstrual function, libido and maternal functions are imbalanced and show signs of weakness, stasis and insufficiency. Another main area of difficulty is in the smooth muscles which are weakened and lax causing constipation, pelvic weakness and prolapse, urinary incontinence, Raynaud's phenomena, etc. When the case is in an early stage, physical exertion rouses the patient, dramatically easing the sluggishness and stasis. However in latter stages Sepia patients are too exhausted to exercise or even aggravated by exertion.

MENTALS

Hard and indifferent patients.

Tearful, care-worn and pathetic patients.

- **Weeping. Involuntary weeping, knows not why she weeps.**
- **Sarcastic, cutting remarks often followed by remorse; the patient has great intuition concerning other's weakness.**

Disconnected and indifferent to the family.

Irritability.

- **Mother angry and at least disturbance yells at children.**
- **Housewives irritable and overwhelmed. Especially while making supper becomes irritated with her children.**

Premenstrual irritability, depression and weeping.

- **Aversion to company.**
- **Ameliorated when alone.**

Aversion to company yet dreads being completely alone.

Mental dullness, sluggishness and confusion.

Fear: Ghosts. Poverty.

Despair of recovery.

Depression, even suicidal states.

Complaints brought on by spiritual pursuits emphasizing celibacy.

Loves dancing and thunderstorms.

GENERALS

Chilly and worse from cold.

- ◆ **General amelioration from vigorous exercise and from any occupation** (though many cases are exhausted by exertion).

General amelioration in the evening.

- ◆ **General aggravation from 2 to 4 PM or 3 to 5 PM.**

General aggravation before or during the menses.

General aggravation from pregnancy, miscarriage or abortion.

- ◆ **Menopause.** Flushes of heat with perspiration, worse at night.

General aggravation from coition or from frequent sex.

General aggravation from loss of fluids as in nursing or diarrhea *(Chin, Ph-Ac)*.

Periodicity every 28 days even in men or non-menstruating women.

Left-sided symptoms.

Fainting tendency.

General aggravation at the sea.

General collapse state from abuse of drugs, alcohol, sexual energy.

Side-effects from chemotherapy - both nausea and debility.

A remedy to be thought of when the case is disordered or unclear.

Appearance

1) Tall, thin, flat breasted and narrow hips, angular, hard face.
2) Round, plump, "washer-woman," care-worn face.

Head

Left-sided headaches, especially over the left eye.

Headache worse fasting, worse menopause or before or during menses.

Rhinitis. Sinusitis with nauseating post-nasal discharge.

Chloasma.

Yellow or brownish "saddle" across the bridge of the nose.

Herpes simplex.

Cracking of lips, either at corners or middle of lower lip.

GASTROINTESTINAL

- ◆ **Empty feeling in stomach, not ameliorated from eating.**

Nausea and vomiting of pregnancy.

Craves: Sweets. Vinegar or sour things. Bread. Salt.

Aversion: Fat. Salt.

Constipation, usually without urging.

Lump sensation in the rectum or prostate.

Itching of the rectum.

Rectal tumor or malignancy.

GENITALIA

- **Vaginitis with white, offensive or excoriating discharge.**
- **Itching of the genitalia brought about from leukorrhea.**

Menses: Scanty and too early. Amenorrhea. Dysmenorrhea.

Premenstrual Syndrome.

- **Uterine prolapse**, bearing down sensation or as if the pelvic contents will prolapse and she must sit with her legs crossed.

Pregnancy: Vaginitis or vaginal itch, lump sensation in rectum and ineffectual urge for stool, nausea and aversion to odors of food or even husband's odor, aversion to sex.

Infertility. Miscarriage, especially first trimester. Weak labor.

Herpes of the genitalia or perineal and perianal region.

Genital warts.

- **Aversion to sex, to being touched sexually.**

Dyspareunia.

Homosexuality (as a characteristic, not a disease).

Impotence or premature ejaculation.

Prostatitis.

URINARY

Stress incontinence, worse cough, worse laugh, worse sneezing.

Enuresis.

Urinary frequency and sudden urging.

CHEST

Cough worse night, worse lying, better sitting.

Scanty lactation.

Breasts lose mass and fullness and become flat.

BACK

Low back pain, better hard pressure or lying on hard floor or objects *(Nat-M, Rhus-T)*.

Back pain before or during menses.

EXTREMITIES

Raynaud's Syndrome.

Hands and feet always cold, often more pronounced in hands.

Cracks on hands.

SKIN

Thickened and parchment-like skin. Dry skin.

- **Psoriasis.** Ringworm. Impetigo. Vitiligo.

Hirsutism.

CLINICAL

Anemia. Bronchitis. Chronic fatigue syndrome. Condyloma. Connective tissue disease. Constipation. Cough. Cystitis. Depression. Dyspareunia. Endometriosis. Enuresis. Flushes. Gastritis. Headache. Herpes. Hirsutism. Leukorrhea. Low back pain. Menopause. Migraine. Miscarriage. Nausea of pregnancy. Pelvic inflammatory disease. Peptic ulcer. Premenstrual syndrome. Prostatitis. Pruritis ani. Psoriasis. Rectal fissure. Raynauld's syndrome. Rhinitis. Sciatica. Scleroderma. Sexual dysfunction. Sinusitis. Stress incontinence. Tinea. Uterine prolapse. Vaginitis. Varices. Warts.

COMPLEMENTARIES

Nat-M. Nux-V. Sabad. Lyc. Ign.

COMPARISONS

Nat-M - Introverted, averse company, herpes, averse coition, better exercise, back pain better hard pressure, averse to fat, worse sea.

Puls - Hormonal problems, weeping, irritability, cough better sitting and worse night, stress incontinence, headaches, etc.

Nux-V - Irritable, aggressive, premenstrual syndrome, constipation, low back pain, rhinitis, migraine, etc.

Ph-Ac - Deadness and apathy, headache, loss of libido.

Carb-V - Indifferent, irritable, sharp-tongued, chilly, exhausted.

Carc - Dancing, loves thunderstorms, sensitive, constipation, etc.

Ign. Petr. Lil-T. Murx. Thuj. Gels. Nit-Ac.

SILICA

In our texts the summations of Silica often start by likening the need for this remedy with the need for internal "grit." The patient is often refined, delicate, sensitive and yielding. Generally speaking the emotional level is fairly well-balanced in Silica patients except for problems with self-esteem. The self-confidence of the patient is often very poor.

The patient may complain of some mental dullness and a feeling of inefficiency. He feels uncertain of his abilities and doubts all of his work. This feeling causes him to dwell compulsively on small details, trying to compensate for his weakness ("Conscientious about trifles"). This conscientiousness results for some patients in a severe anxiety state. The patient is almost paralyzed by irresolution and insecurity about his perceptions or performance and may wish to give up his work altogether.

Children. Silica children can be over-sensitive and actually irritable and obstinate. The child is demanding at these early ages but as he grows older he takes on the more typical refinement and yielding nature. By the age of 6 or 7 years, the child is quite proper, well-behaved and serious. He may be very shy in the office, refusing to answer any questions. Instead, he whispers his responses to the mother who must then relay the information to the prescriber. The Silica child often suffers repeated infections, such as colds, otitis media, or pharyngitis. Often the stamina is very poor. The features are fine and delicate, the hair is often quite thin, the skin is pale, and the head may be overly large.

Physical. Physically Silica patients suffer from low stamina quite commonly. The defensive resistance is low which allows for frequent infections, especially of the upper respiratory tract, the sinuses, or the ears. Even the skin and mucous membranes can have poor resistance which allows for abscess formation and low-grade smouldering infections of the skin, the gums, the rectum and other areas.

The other central aspect of the physical conditions of Silica revolve around the metabolism. The bones, nails, and teeth are often weak and defective. In any condition of defective growth or maintenance of these hardened tissues, Silica can be considered.

MENTALS

Yielding, refined, delicate patients. Quiet and self-contained.

Lack of self confidence.

◆ **The patient will admit to having convictions which he does not argue**, even seeming to acquiesce to another's viewpoint though internally keeping his own view.

Anxious conscientiousness over small details.

Anxiety from noise. Anxious and depressed.

Stage-fright.

Paralyzed by anxiety and indecision.

Performance anxiety. Test phobia.

Mental dullness. Dreads or is aggravated by mental exertion.

Weak memory. Mental deterioration. Dementia.

Fear of pointed objects or pins.

Obstinate children who "weep when reprimanded."

Shy children who will not answer the prescriber directly but instead whisper to the mother who must relay the information.

Psychic capacity; clairvoyant.

Fixed ideas.

GENERALS

Chilly and aggravation from cold weather.

General aggravation from warm, stuffy rooms during acutes.

General aggravation from drafts or from uncovering, even one limb.

- **General aggravation from suppressed sweat, most often of the feet.**

Weakness and fatigue. Collapse.

Delayed development in children.

Failure to thrive in infants, cannot assimilate nutrition, do not tolerate breast milk and lose weight.

Frequent colds and flus.

Glands become enlarged and hard and may suppurate.

Defects of bone, spine, hair, nails, teeth, from poor metabolism of minerals.

Sour perspiration.

General aggravation from the new or full moon.

General aggravation after vaccination (convulsion, otitis media, etc.).

Chills before menses.

Hard fibrous tumors or growths anywhere in body.

General aggravation from coition.

Appearance

1) Infants may show signs of emaciation with enlarged bellies. Often the head is enlarged out of proportion to the body.
2) Adults are often thin, small-boned, and delicate-featured. The skin tends to be pale and the hair coloring light or blonde.

HEAD

Sweats on the scalp, especially during sleep.

Acne which leaves small pits in the face.

Headaches and migraines, often begin in the occiput and radiate to the forehead or right side of the head.

Headaches worse from cold and drafts, worse from mental exertion, worse menses, worse uncovering head.

Headache better lying with eyes closed and in the dark, better from warming or wrapping the head.

Sinus headaches.

Hair loss and premature balding.

Wears a hat even in moderate weather *(Psor)*.

EYES

- **Infection of tear duct or blocked tear duct of newborns.**

Styes.

OROPHARYNX

- **Dental abscesses, fistulas and infections of the gum.**

Difficult or slow dentition, teeth decay or break easily. Toothache.

Sensation of a hair on the tongue *(Kali-Bi)*.

Pharyngitis with pain like a splinter.

Acute or chronic pharyngitis; recurring pharyngitis and tonsillitis.

Enlarged cervical glands which may be hard and painful.

EAR

Meniere's syndrome with marked vertigo associated with chronic sinus problems.

- **Acute and chronic otitis media and serous otitis**; long smouldering cases of otitis and otorrhea, often with hearing loss.

NOSE

Sinusitis, frontal or maxillary, with thick post-nasal discharge.

Nasal polyps.

- **Chronic, dry nasal obstruction.**

GASTROINTESTINAL

- **Constipation with no urging; "bashful stool" which seems to recede after nearly extruding.**

Hard stool with straining.

Constipation with the sensation that more stool is still in the rectum.

Constipation in children.

Constipation before or during menses.

Craves: Sweets. Eggs. Rarely milk.

Averse: **Fat**. Meat. Salt. **Milk**. Warm food.

- **Infants unable to tolerate even mother's milk and will frequently vomit the milk** *(Aeth)*.

Cramps and diarrhea from milk.

Rectal abscess. Rectal fissure and fistula.

UROGENITAL

- **Bartholin's cysts.**

Vaginitis with foul-smelling discharge.

Eruptions about the genitalia.

- After pains, worse while nursing.

Prostatitis.

Enlarged inguinal glands.

Sexual desire low to normal.

Menses delayed or suppressed. Amenorrhea.

CHEST

Mastitis of nursing women

Breast abscess. Breast nodules.

Fibrocystic breast disease.

Cough, worse cold drinks, better warm drinks.

Bronchitis lasts all winter.

Asthma, especially in children, worse exertion and cold.

Has a reputation as both an effective and potentially dangerous remedy in tuberculosis and empyema.

BACK

Scoliosis.

Spinal curvatures, calcification and defects.

Coccygodynia.

EXTREMITIES

- **Foot-sweat, often offensive and profuse, more prominent in children than adults. The sweat can be corrosive, causing excoriation of feet and holes in the socks.**

Arthritis, may be deformative, worse cold and cold, damp weather.

- **Bunions.**
- **Ingrown toenails** *(Calc, Mag-Aust)*.

Crippled nails, fragile nails, white spots on nails.

Fungal infections of nails and between toes. Paronychia.

Cracks of the skin, especially hands and feet.

SKIN

- **Abscess** formation anywhere on the body.

May help to promote expulsion of foreign bodies through the skin.

Ringworm. Impetigo.

Vitiligo *(Sep, Ars-S-F)*.

Skin unhealthy, every wound becomes infected.

Skin tumors, cysts, keloids, warts.

CLINICAL

Abscess. Acne. Anxiety. Arthritis. Asthma. Bartholin cysts. Blocked tearduct. Bronchitis. Bunions. Chronic Fatigue Syndrome. Colds. Connective tissue disease. Constipation. Fissures. Fibrocystic breast disease. Fistula. Headache. Ingrown nails. Keloid. Meniere's syndrome. Night sweats. Otitis media. Pharyngitis. Psoriasis. Scoliosis. Serous otitis. Sinusitis. Styes. Tinea. Tonsillitis. Upper respiratory infection. Uterine fibroids. Vertigo. Vitiligo.

COMPLEMENTARY

Puls. Fl-Ac. Calc. Thuj. Sanic.

INIMICAL

Merc.

COMPARISONS

Staph - Refined, yielding, self-contained patients, can be averse to milk, abscesses and styes.

Calc - Chilly, worse cold, damp, mental fatigue and generalized weakness, nail problems, abscess, chronic or frequently recurring infections, head-sweat at night in sleep, worse from full moon, craves eggs, problems of metabolism, spinal curvature, arthritis, cold feet, foot-sweat, bunions, constipation, etc.

Hep - Chilly, worse from uncovering, frequent infections and unhealthy skin, abscess formation, splinter pains in throat, fatigue.

Sanic. Merc. Puls. Nat-C. Kali-C. Nit-Ac. Carb-An.

SINAPIS NIGRA

Mainly a remedy of allergy and hay fever, Sinapis Nigra has only a few characterizing symptoms.

HEAD

Left-sided coryza, may be accompanied by left-sided lacrimation.

Dry, hot nasal coryza, worse on left side.

Coryza alternating with nasal obstruction.

Coryza alternates sides.

Intense sneezing, often worse at night.

Aphthae. Halitosis.

GASTROINTESTINAL

Averse: Sweets.

COMPARISONS

All-C. Arund. Sabad. Euphr. Wyeth.

SPIGELIA

Spigelia is recognized by its nearly exclusively left-sided focus (left-sided headache and neuralgia, cardiac disorders, left colon infestations, etc.). Most frequently used for headaches of either sinus or migraine types, the remedy is also useful for neuralgia, cardiac disorders and parasitic infections. The pains of Spigelia are of the most severe character - piercing and sharp.

MENTALS

Fear of pointed objects.

GENERALS

- **General aggravation from smoke** and tobacco.

General aggravation from walking in open air.

General aggravation from touch.

HEAD

- **Left-sided (or rarely right-sided) excruciating headaches, generally above or through the left eye or orbit.**

Stitching headaches, may radiate from the occiput or extend inward from the forehead or eye.

Headache, facial neuralgia and ocular pains, worse motion, touch and jar, worse stooping, worse noise, worse open air, worse smoke.

Sinusitis with great pains in the frontal sinuses.

Left-sided otitis media.

- **Left facial neuralgia or ciliary neuralgia;** the patient can point to the spot.

Glaucoma. Iritis.

GASTROINTESTINAL

Worms: pinworms or others.

Constipation associated with heart disease.

Craves warm drinks.

CHEST

Angina pectoris.

Chest pain, worse motion or inspiration, worse lying on the left side, •better from warm drinks.

Palpitations, tumultuous and said to be visible through chest wall.

Palpitations, worse deep inspiration, worse stooping forward, worse lying on left side, worse motion.

Cardiac murmurs. Valvular disorders.

EXTREMITIES

Rheumatism.

CLINICAL

Angina. Arrhythmia. Glaucoma. Headache. Hyperthyroidism. Iritis. Migraine. Neuralgia. Otitis media. Pericarditis. Rheumatic heart disease. Sinusitis. Toothache. Valvular disorder. Worms.

COMPARISONS

Kalm - Neuralgia, cardiac troubles, rheumatism.

Lach - Left-sided complaints, cardiac conditions, worse from lying on the left side.

Naja. Spong. Cact.

SPONGIA TOSTA

Though by far the most common use for Spongia is in acute respiratory infections and coughs, there are a number of important chronic conditions which require this remedy. No remedy covers more types of acute coughs (especially of the dry and croupy variety) than Spongia. However it is also an important remedy in asthma, cardiac disorders, testicular diseases, and goitre or thyroid disease. Since the sponge is a salt-water animal, it is not surprising that it is closely related in its action to other halogens such as Iodum, Bromium, Chlorum and the Muriatic remedies. This is most clearly seen in its broad range of action on the larynx and respiratory tract, and in its effect on glands and endocrine organs (also common in Iodum and its salts, Bromium, etc.).

GENERALS

General aggravation from heat.

General aggravation from exertion and motion.

Inflammation and enlargement of glands.

THROAT AND LARYNX

Constriction, tickling, and dryness in throat.

Pain from cough, talking, swallowing, touch.

Must clear throat frequently.

Hoarseness.

Goitre or thyroid conditions.

CHEST

- **Cough, usually dry, usually worse before midnight, often of a harsh or barking or croupy character.**
- **Dry cough resembling, "a saw going through wood," or a "seal's bark."**
- **Croup, worse before midnight.**

Cough from tickling or irritation in throat or chest.

- **Cough better eating and drinking**, especially warm drinks.

Cough worse from cold drinks.

Cough, better eating sweets.

Asthma, worse at night or during sleep, worse from respiratory infection or colds, worse menses.

Asthma better from leaning forward, better bending head backward, better warm food or drinks.

Suffocating sensation, worse during sleep at night and wakes him from sleep *(Lach, Grind, Sulph, Op)*.

Angina pectoris.

Cardiac valvular disorders.

Palpitations, worse night, worse before menses, worse lying.

In our literature, cases of tuberculosis have responded to Spongia.

UROGENITAL

Swelling, inflammation and pain in testes or epididymis.

EXTREMITIES

Gout.

CLINICAL

Angina. Arrhythmia. Asthma. Bronchitis. Cough. Croup. Epididymitis. Goitre. Gout. Hyperthyroidism. Orchitis. Valvular disease.

COMBINED SYMPTOMS

Asthma *and* thyroid conditions.

Respiratory conditions *and* testicular pains.

COMPARISONS

Phos - Hoarseness, cough and respiratory infections, worse lying on left side, angina, palpitations, etc.

Lach - Asthma, worse lying on the left side, cardiac disorders, suffocating sensations at night.

Rumex. Coc-c. Hep. Spig. Kali-S. Lycop.

SQUILLA MARITIMA

Also listed in some texts as Scilla, this is primarily a remedy of respiratory conditions - cough, asthma, bronchitis.

CHEST

Hard or violent coughs either dry or loose.
Asthma.
Respiratory infections - bronchitis, pneumonia.
Sharp pains, especially in the left lower chest.

UROGENITAL

Involuntary loss of urine during cough.
Profuse, clear urine.

GASTROINTESTINAL

◆ **Involuntary stool from coughing.**
Reputation for pains or disorder of spleen.

COMPARISONS

Puls. Caust.

STANNUM

Stannum is of tremendous value in cases of weakness and depletion, especially when associated with respiratory disorders. Especially when the weakness is felt primarily in the chest itself, Stannum is likely to act. The most common occurrence for this pattern of illness is found during or at the end of serious respiratory infections such as pneumonia or bronchitis. Stannum is also an important remedy for tuberculosis (which is almost never treated homeopathically in Western countries due to legal considerations) or in patients with persistent fatigue following standard treatment for tuberculosis.

MENTALS

Sadness and weeping, especially before the menses.
Great tiredness from talking or conversing.

GENERALS

- **Weakness, worse slight exertion, worse talking, better lying.** Too feeble to talk; can scarcely cross the room.

General aggravation during day or coming and going with the sun.

General aggravation at 4 to 6 PM.

Pains gradually increase and decrease.

Great weakness and lassitude; tremulous weakness.

Night sweats.

HEAD

Headache or neuralgia with gradual onset and fading.

Neuralgia alternates with leukorrhea.

Speech difficult from weakness in the throat or chest.

UROGENITAL

Uterine prolapse, worse from stool.

CHEST

Soreness, irritation and mucous of the upper airways and trachea.

- **Respiration difficult or weak; dyspnea on slight exertion, even crossing the room or talking briefly.**
- **Empty, hollow feeling in the chest.**
- **Cannot speak or exert from weak, hollow feeling in chest.**

Weakness of chest following cough and expectoration.

Cough, hard, painful and deep, productive of thick, green mucous.

Must hold his chest when he coughs.

- **Expectoration copious, sweet or salty taste**, or offensive.

EXTREMITIES

Trembling of hands.

Cramping on writing.

Deltoid pains and weakness.

CLINICAL

Asthma. Bronchitis. Chronic Fatigue Syndrome. Headache. Neuralgia. Pneumocystis. Pneumonia. Recurring fever. Respiratory infection. Tuberculosis. Uterine prolapse. Vaginitis.

COMPARISONS

Gels - Weakness, tiredness, tremulousness, neuralgia and headache.

Laur - Chest troubles and fatigue, poor recovery from respiratory infections, general depletion.

Mur-Ac - Weakness with fever, prolapse symptoms.

STAPHYSAGRIA

Staphysagria is one of our most commonly used polycrests, and yet the majority of cases are found not through detailed information about physical symptoms or generalities or keynotes. Rather in this remedy, the prescription is often based entirely on the basis of the "essence" or causation.

Sweetness. The Staphysagria patient is extremely sweet and gentle in the office. She gives the impression of making every effort to be a good patient and will draw out the sympathy of the prescriber. This is especially true because the story the patient tells is often one of sorrow.

Suppression. The underlying cause of illness in the Staphysagria patient is suppression. Generally the patient is so sweet, that she is unable to stand up for herself. Especially it is a remedy for wives of abusive husbands, children of abusive or aggressive parents, etc. It is important to know that after taking this remedy, the patient will find inner strength to end a bad marriage or relationship. This is an extra burden of responsibility that we as prescribers must take seriously.

Expression of anger. Staphysagria is most noted in our literature for suppression of anger. It is an important remedy in patients whose complaints originated from anger or insults which have been swallowed. In many of the chronic cases, however, the patient will say that she never gets angry or even feels any anger. Rather the anger is so deeply suppressed that the patient feels guilty or ashamed where a normal person would feel anger. Confrontation is very difficult for the patient. It is only in the late stages when the anger is finally too great to be suppressed, that the Staphysagria patient has really overt expression of anger. There can be outbursts of anger generally demonstrated by the marked, instinctive tendency to throw things - often in the direction of the offending party!

Sexuality. In almost direct proportion to the degree of suppression, we find in Staphysagria an excitement of the sexual sphere. The romantic and erotic inner life of the patient is truly excessive. This is often expressed through frequent masturbation, especially because the patient is shy and unable to actively seek out sexual partners. Staphysagria is one of the main remedies to consider in cases with a history of sexual abuse.

Children. The Staphysagria child resembles Natrum Muriaticum greatly. The child is usually quiet, serious and composed. She has a sensitivity, an inhibition and vulnerability which is very apparent. There may be infrequent periods of emotional, angry outbursts. In most cases there is a history of an abusive parent or older sibling who suppresses or humiliates the patient. We must consider carefully whether Staphysagria should be given to a child living in an abusive household. If we stir the child's reactivity against a superior force, unproductive turmoil can result.

MENTALS

Sweet, suppressed patients who draw our sympathy.

Ailments from grief.

Patients who have histories involving multiple griefs over many years *(Caust)*.

Ailments from suppressed anger.

Ailments after insults or humiliation.

Talking to himself out loud.

◆ **Tendency to throw things when very angry.**

Weeps during the interview.

Low self-esteem.

Depression.

Sentimental and romantic, writes poetry.

Rage in very late stages.

Fear: heights, anger, doctors.

Patient hangs on to terrible marriages with spiritual justifications.

Constant and often distressingly frequent sexual fantasies.

In patients with history of incest or sexual abuse or alcoholic parents.

GENERALS

◆ **General aggravation after taking a nap in the daytime, especially from an afternoon nap.**

General aggravation from sleep (irritable, unrefreshed, etc.).

General aggravation after surgery.

General aggravation from masturbation.

Mainly a sycotic remedy.

HEAD

Headache often described as "a block or ball of wood" in the forehead or occiput.

Headache worse from anger or suppressed anger, worse from grief and emotions, worse masturbation.

◆ **Styes or tumors on the eyelids.**

Iritis.

Psoriasis or other eruptions on the scalp, especially in the occiput.

Alopecia areata after grief or suppression.

Lacerations or incisions to the eyes.

Crumbling teeth in children - premature decay of teeth.

Tooth pain, worse cold, worse after eating, worse menses.

Facial neuralgia.

Twitches of the face or eyelids.

GASTROINTESTINAL

Craves: Sweets. Milk.

Aversion: Fat. Milk.

Abdominal colic which dates from surgery.

Abdominal pain after anger.

Peptic ulcer.

Encopresis, especially in children.

UROGENITAL

- **Cystitis which begins from the first intercourse or may happen after every intercourse.**

Urethritis.

Frequent urging for urine.

Enuresis.

Painful condyloma of the genitals.

- **Masturbation. Many sexual fantasies.**

High sexual desire, weak resistance, sometimes promiscuous.

Nocturnal seminal emissions.

Prostatitis.

Benign prostatic hypertrophy; retained urine.

Orchitis, especially left-sided.

Tumors of testes.

Atrophy of testes.

Impotence.

CHEST

Chronic cough, continues long and maddeningly frequent but soft.

Nervous or emotional cough.

EXTREMITIES

- **Trembling from anger or emotions.**

Twitches. Chorea. Paresis.

Paresis after cerebral accidents.

SKIN

- **Psoriasis after grief or suppression of anger or other emotions, especially in children.**

Scars or skin tumors are often sensitive and painful.

Skin tumors, warts.

Skin unhealthy and easily infected.

Skin wounds. Surgical incisions.

SLEEP

◆**"Sleepy all day but sleepless at night."**

Insomnia often accompanied by sexual thoughts or with frequent masturbation to help himself sleep.

CLINICAL

Cerebral accidents. Chorea. Condyloma. Connective tissue disease. Cystitis. Dentition. Depression. Enuresis. Headache. Hemorrhoids. Insomnia. Multiple sclerosis. Orchitis. Peptic ulcer. Post-surgical pain. Prostatitis. Psoriasis. Strabismus. Styes. Tics.

COMPLEMENTARY

Caust. Coloc. Nux-V.

COMPARISONS

Puls - Sweet, tearful, sexually aroused, easily bullied, headache, urinary symptoms, fear heights, desire sweets and averse fats.

Sil - Sweet, yielding, headache in occiput, styes, unhealthy skin, averse milk and fat.

Nat-C - Sweet, helpful patients, peptic ulcer, averse to milk and fat.

Caust. Anac. Nat-M. Nux-V.

STELLARIA MEDIA

Stellaria is a remedy used mainly in rheumatic conditions, even in quite advanced cases. We have few indications for its use, but the modalities of the remedy fall in between those of Rhus Toxicodendron and Bryonia. Stellaria has marked pain from slight motion like Bryonia and yet may be better from continued motion. The patient is averse to being touched or examined. When Bryonia fails in a rheumatic case we can consider Stellaria. The pains may migrate as in Berberis or Pulsatilla.

COMPARISONS

Rhus-T. Bry. Berb.

STICTA

Sticta is used primarily for nasal conditions and it has a broader usefulness in allergic conditions and the respiratory tract in general. It is also a rheumatic remedy. Sticta has cured a peculiar floating sensation.

HEAD

- **Nasal catarrh. Tremendous stuffiness in the nose. Constant urging to blow the nose but produces nothing.**

Nasal secretions dry quickly and form crusts in the nose.

Chronic nasal obstruction.

Pain and fullness at the root of the nose and forehead from catarrh with crusts and mucous plugs.

Frontal sinusitis. Post-nasal mucous.

Hay fever.

Tingling sensation in the nose.

Great sneezing.

Dryness of the throat and palate.

CHEST

Allergic asthma and cough.

Dryness and tickling in the throat and larynx provokes cough.

Night-time cough which disturbs the sleep.

MUSCULOSKELETAL

Nash recommends Sticta in acute inflammations of the knee joint and it is considered by others as a specific in "housemaid's knee".

Floating sensation in the legs.

Rheumatism and stiffness of the neck and shoulders.

Arthritis with bright red spot in the skin over affected joint.

Stiffness and heat of joints.

ACUTES

Acute rheumatism or bursitis with hot joint and redness of skin.

Influenza.

CLINICAL

Allergy and rhinitis. Asthma. Arthritis. Influenza. Sinusitis.

COMPARISONS

Kali-Bi - Nasal catarrh with pressure in the frontal sinuses, crusts in the nose, arthritis.

Teucr. Sil. Calc. Kali-S. Lem-M.

STRAMONIUM

The degree of violence in our culture has made Stramonium an ever more common remedy, especially in children. We often expect to see very advanced mental conditions or mania states in Stramonium cases but there are a great number of patients who can benefit from this remedy who are perfectly normal mentally. In these early stage cases we will see only hints of the violence and fear which are common in the later stages. However all through the pathology we will find tremendous intensity and energy. Stramonium is also an important remedy in acute illness with delirium and febrile convulsions.

Violence in action, in thought, in the physical symptoms is the central fact of Stramonium: violence or the fear of violence. Stramonium is mainly a remedy of the nervous system. The violence often seems to be of a neurological type, coming almost as a convulsion. Epilepsy, strabismus, sleep disturbance, attention deficit disorders, and even schizophrenia are common manifestations of Stramonium, pointing towards an underlying fragility and imbalance in the nervous system and helping to explain the violence of the remedy. It is in this type of excitement and upheaval of the nervous system that we find the sphere of action of this remedy. Any neurological insult may provoke a Stramonium state: fever, alcohol, injury.

In adults, Stramonium patients often present without any aggressive behavior at all, but rather with intense fears. The fears almost always have to do with violence or death or with things which symbolize death (darkness, cemeteries) or violence (animals).

Often we will find true mania cases in Stramonium, these patients can be frighteningly violent. Stramonium mania can even lead to homicidal rages. This remedy is able to cure patients with tremendously advanced mental conditions.

Children. The Stramonium child is often placid in the office showing little or none of the violence described by the parent. Sometimes the child becomes dreamy or drowsy as the parent describes the problems. The troubles often begin after a strong fright such as a car accident, a sexual abuse, the witnessing of an act of violence in the environment, or after a neurological insult such as meningitis or encephalitis. The precipitating event is often followed by nightmares or terrible night-terrors and eventually the development of rages. The rage in Stramonium is uncontrolled and impulsive - that is, without malicious forethought. It comes in an outburst, almost as a convulsion or neurological discharge. It would be unusual for a Stramonium case to develop such a violence without equally strong fears. Remember that the parents may for various reasons be reticent about explaining the full degree of pathology in such a child.

MENTALS

Rage and violence. Has the capacity to commit murder.

Violent behavior of any type - biting, striking, strangling, etc.

Mania with red face, dilated pupils, superhuman strength.

Fear of death - especially violent death or murder.

Fear of dark - sleep with a light, goes into the parents bed.

Fear of water - especially getting the head in water, even a shower, and of running water.

Fear to be alone - especially at night or in the dark.

Fear: Animals. Dogs. Mirrors, reflecting objects. Disease. Ghost. Injury. Insanity. Suffocation. Claustrophobia. Agoraphobia.

Complaints after fright - especially violent things or where death may have been narrowly averted.

Night-terrors: the child shrieks out and sits up, he is filled with terror but not really awakened, makes no contact with the parents or may think his parents are trying to hurt him not comfort him, recognizes no one, has no memory of the event when truly awake.

Jealousy.

Loquacity.

Cursing.

Laughter, loud and cruel or wild.

Hyperactive children. Behavior disorders.

Stammering; the patient may show the most excruciating effort in order to speak and the word finally comes explosively.

GENERALS

Convulsions often violent. **Convulsion of children.**

Febrile convulsion. Violent delirium.

Sunstroke.

Neurological disorder from head injury, vaccination, fright, meningitis.

Chorea, athetosis, jerks of muscles or whole limb, tics, gestures.

Unrefreshed sleep.

HEAD

Violent jerking of the head.

Head injury.

Severe headaches, worse sun. Head jerks during headache.

Grimacing. Tics. Twitches. Bruxism.

Meningitis, encephalitis, or complaints arising from these disorders.

Fearful expression in eyes or face.

Strabismus. Diplopia. Pupils dilated.

Tongue dry and cracked.

Hirsutism.

GASTROINTESTINAL

Craving for sweets.

Offensive diarrhea.

Violent hiccoughing.

Thirst increased.

UROGENITAL

Violent sexual desires, aggressive, vulgar language, promiscuous.

Masturbation.

Patients with history of incest or any type of frightening sexual abuse.

Constant touching of the genitals.

Enuresis, especially after a fright.

Metrorrhagia.

CHEST

Angina. Arrhythmia.

Chronic cough and bronchitis. Spasmodic asthma.

EXTREMITIES

Left hip pain or abscess.

SKIN

Abscess.

CLINICAL

Abscess. Angina. Arrhythmia. Asthma. Behavior disorder. Cerebral accidents. Chorea. Delirium. Diarrhea. Enuresis. Febrile convulsion. Head injury. Headache. Hirsutism. Hyperactive children. Mania. Manic-depression. Meningitis. Metrorrhagia. Night-terrors. Phobic disorder. Strabismus. Schizophrenia. Seizure disorder. Sexual disorders. Stammering.

COMBINED SYMPTOMS

Any two of these fears: Dark. Death. Being alone. Animals. Water.

- **Temper problems *and* fears or nightmares.**
- **Convulsions *and* fears.**

COMPARISONS

Hyos - Mania, sexual expression, loquacity, violence and anger, cursing, convulsion.

Bell - Febrile convulsions. Anger and mania, fear dogs, dilated pupils, increased strength in mania or delirium.

Verat. Cupr. Lach. Anac. Med. Kali-Br.

STRONTIUM

The main use for Strontium has been in post-surgical cases with a picture like Carbo Vegetabilis: coldness, collapse, and prostration. In such a case in the post-surgical setting, Strontium is to be preferred. Vithoulkas has mentioned that constitutional cases are relatively healthy on the mental and emotional planes, appearing quite vital and socially active.

GENERALS

Post-surgical weakness, collapse, coldness.
Chilly and worse from cold and cold, damp weather.
Generally better warm wrapping; aggravation from uncovering.
Hypertension.
Injuries, extravasation, hemorrhage. History of severe trauma.

HEAD

Coldness of head; headache on uncovering the head.
Flushes of heat in the face.

GASTROINTESTINAL

Abdominal pains after eating.

UROGENITAL

Sex drive surprisingly absent in one so vital.
Nephritis; suppressed urine.

EXTREMITIES

Sprained wrists or ankles, or chronic tendency to such sprains.
Varicosities. Veins dilated.

CLINICAL

Post-operative faintness. Sprains. Nephritis. Headache. Hypertension.

STRYCHNINUM

Much of the information collected about Strychninum comes from poisonings, and therefore the convulsive symptoms are especially well described. It is also helpful to remember that Strychnine is the main ingredient of Ignatia and Nux Vomica. The mental symptoms involve great sadness similar to Ignatia as well as the irritability of Nux Vomica. Also several cases have demonstrated a marked anxiety over supernatural forces.

MENTALS

Grief.

Feels trapped or resentful of life circumstances (J. Shore).

Awareness and fear of evil forces (J. Shore).

GENERALS

Twitches, jerking, spasms.

Convulsions, worse from touch, worse draft, worse motion.

Tetany.

Spasms, especially if stimulated by slight touch.

HEAD

Lockjaw. Tension, spasm or pain of the temporomandibular joint.

Convulsions of face; distortion of features.

Choking, constricted sensation in the throat.

GASTROINTESTINAL

Cramping of the abdomen.

Constipation.

BACK

Tension, stiffness and spasms of the back, especially in the cervical region.

Opisthotonos. Torticollis.

Twitching in the back.

EXTREMITIES

Convulsions of limbs.

Stiffness.

Cramps of feet.

Twitches anywhere.

CLINICAL

Convulsion - epilepsy, twitches, cramps, spasms.
Temporomandibular joint syndrome. Torticollis.

COMPARISONS

Cupr. Zinc. Nux-V. Ign. Cic. Crot-C.

SULPHUR

It is almost impossible to make brief the essential points about Sulphur, for the scope of the remedy is so vast that almost any characteristic which can be mentioned, may seem to be contradicted by equally characteristic but opposite symptoms. Sulphur is certainly our most frequently prescribed remedy, and as Kent once said, one cannot tell the difference between an experienced prescriber and a novice on the basis of how often he uses Sulphur - only on how successfully he uses it. Sulphur is more predominantly a man's remedy. There are two main types of personalities for this remedy:

1) **The philosophical type** who has great intellectual interest but poor connection with friends and family. He is a truly deep thinker, looking long at profound questions in a detached manner. His intelligence tends to set him apart from others and he becomes egotistical concerning his mind and accomplishments. His greatest desire would be to discover some truth or knowledge which will make him famous. He is ambitious, intellectual, detached. This gives him a cynical and condescending attitude. He may even feel disgust for others. His self-confidence is unshakable.

2) **The "practical idealist"** whose main focus is on service and social interaction. This type of patient tends to be extroverted, friendly, charming, and to some extent innocent. People depend upon him; he is vital and enthusiastic. This type needs approval and affection from other people, though he seems to have a lot of confidence, he searches for acknowledgement. Though he may seem to bluster egotistically, he does so in a naive way which is not offensive. He can be very generous. This patient can have a lot of anxiety, often about the health and about his family. He may go into periods of moroseness and anxiety or depression.

Women. The female Sulphur patient may not show the same personality as seen in the male. Though she may be egotistical and intellectual, often she seems to have a greater focus on business and practical matters. She is highly competent, enjoys keeping busy, is alert and quick-witted. There is another type of Sulphur woman who, though intelligent and accomplished, appears very scattered and disorganized. Also there is often a somewhat masculine or domineering quality to the typical Sulphur woman. She enjoys positions of authority, control and responsibility. Emotional symptoms will be brought out by the family rather than the patient herself. The family complains mainly about the patient's obstinacy and irritability. There can also be a great deal of anxiety and hypochondria. The patient is often stout but very solid in build.

Laziness is one of the grand characteristics of the Sulphur patient. He constantly procrastinates in his tasks. He thinks of many projects but rarely undertakes them. He may prefer to sit and discuss philosophy to actually working on practical matters. One Sulphur patient expressed this trait by reading many magazine reviews of books because, although he wished to be well-versed on current literature, he just couldn't find the effort needed to read the book itself.

Slovenliness is another characteristic of Sulphur. In the past this was even more evident before the advent of easy hygienic facilities, hot showers, and advanced techniques for suppressing the typical "dirty looking" skin lesions. Despite this Sulphur patients are often disheveled, clothes stained with last week's lunch, hair greasy and uncombed, shirts buttoned wrongly or untucked. The patient may have a great laziness or aversion to bathing or bathes only in a limited way. His house and office may look a like disaster zone with piles of books and papers and dirty dishes. Alternatively Sulphur patients can be abnormally fastidious.

Criticism is another Sulphur trait. The patient can find fault with anyone. He seems to feel that he could have written any book slightly better than its author, etc. There may even be a type of disgust for other people, for example for people who are obese or aged.

Anxiety is also quite common in Sulphur, this can often be about the health or the family. The Sulphur patient can be a true hypochondriac. He can also have irrational anxiety about the family's well-being; if someone is late, his mind turns immediately to car accidents, etc.

Egotism is another characteristic, though some Sulphur patients describe a low-self esteem and strong need for reassurance. Generally the patient takes great pride in his mental acuity and intelligence. The patient has great self-confidence and finds most people boring, especially if they do not find him fascinating.

Children. Sulphur children are curious, robust, strong-willed and extroverted. They need to be the center of attention and may react in a jealous, angry way if others take center stage. The arrogance that we see in adults can often be found in the children as well. Sulphur boys are very mechanical and astute at figuring out how things work. The boys are often large, heavy and pugnacious. If the temperament is good, they will be popular at school and become leaders. If the temperament is bad, they will become bullies or behavior problems. Also Sulphur children can be very open and innocent. They enjoy contact with adults and resent not being treated as adults, finding it unfair when they are sent to bed early while the adults continue the conversation.

Physical. Any physical pathology can be covered by Sulphur. Common areas of problems include the skin (abscess, acne, eczema, psoriasis, etc.) and the digestive tract (diarrhea, ulcers, hemorrhoids, etc.).

MENTALS

- ◆ **Egotism. Bragging.**
- ◆ **Laziness.**
- ◆ **Dirty or messy. Indifferent to appearance.** Averse bathing.
- ◆ **Intellectual, philosophical, theorizing.**
- **Extroverted, boisterous and friendly.**
- **Extroverted, mechanically inclined, bossy children.**
- **Anxiety about health.**
- **Anxiety about the family or children - accidents, diseases.**
- **Ambitious.**
- **Critical.**
- ◆ **Disgust** - a visceral sense from odors, objects or even people.
- **Fear of heights, even when others are in a high place.**
- Fears: Disease. Claustrophobia. Infection. Cancer. Rejection. Failure.
- Fastidious. Compulsive. Bites nails.
- Stubborn.
- Low self-confidence; need to be praised.
- Collects things. Delusion or impression that "rags are like riches."
- Impulse to hurt the family which frightens him.
- Weeping at menopause.
- Repeats the question before answering.

GENERALS

- **Warm and aggravated from heat**, though some patients are chilly.
- **General and local aggravation from the heat of the bed.**
- **General aggravation in the winter.**
- ◆ **General aggravation at 11 AM** with hunger, headache, etc.
- General aggravation at night, or at night in bed.
- ◆ **General aggravation from standing** (low back pain, diarrhea, faint).
- General amelioration on lying.
- ◆ **General aversion to and aggravation from bathing.**
- **Offensive** discharges, feces, sweat, etc.
- **Sweats excessively.**
- **General aggravation from suppressed eruption or discharge.**
- **Burning pains.**
- General aggravation on the weekend.
- General aggravation cloudy days, when sun peeks through the clouds.
- Appearance:
  1) Thin, stooped-shouldered, gaunt.
  2) Plump, ruddy-checked, plethoric, red lips. Unkempt, greasy or uncombed hair, etc.

HEAD

- **Headaches on the weekend.**

Headaches, often as if a band about the head.

Headache or burning on the vertex, better cold applications.

Headache, worse winter, worse odors.

Eruptions of the scalp, or at the scalp margin.

Dandruff, seborrhea of scalp, scalp margin, eyebrows.

Recurring dental infections.

Ruddy-faced, sometimes an alcoholic flush or enlarged veins in nose or cheeks.

Menopausal hot flashes.

Otitis media, otorrhea, especially left side.

Acne. Rosacea. Acne on nose.

Red lips.

EYES

- **Thick, bushy eyebrows.**
- **Conjunctivitis with the sensation of sand or grit in eyes.**

Blepharitis; redness, burning and irritation of the margin of the lids.

Iritis.

Retinitis. Retinal hemorrhage.

NOSE

Great sensitivity to odors.

- **Aversion to body odors of others (but loves his own).**

Sinusitis. Chronic, purulent nasal discharge.

Hay fever.

Nasal polyps.

STOMACH

Craves: **Sweets. Chocolate. Ice Cream. Fats. Spicy food. Alcohol especially Beer or Whiskey**. Meat. Pungent things. Apples.

Craves sweets and chocolate before the menses.

Aversion: •**Eggs**, especially soft egg yolk. Fish. Sour Foods. Olives. Squash. Liver. Rarely sweets.

Big appetite, loves eating.

- **Empty hungry feeling every day at 11 AM.**

Great thirst for ice cold drinks.

Gastritis; Peptic ulcers.

Heartburn, especially from dietary indiscretions.

Indigestion during menses.

RECTUM

- **Diarrhea or soft stool every morning, often driving him out of bed in the morning, especially at 5 or 6 AM. May have several stools every morning.**

Diarrhea from beer.

Sudden, strong urging for stool.

- **Stool highly offensive**; whole family knows when he defecates.

Flatus, offensive.

- **Itching or burning at the rectum, worse heat, better cold.**

Hemorrhoids. Rectal fistula.

Oozing around the rectum which is very irritating.

UROGENITAL

Eruptions around the genitalia. Herpes.

High sex drive is common in the plethoric type. In the lean, philosophical type, sex can be a low priority or even distasteful.

Impotence or loss of erections.

Enuresis.

Phimosis. Balanitis.

Prostatitis, burning in the urethra or prostate. Prostatic hypertrophy.

Urethral discharge.

Offensive urination.

Leukorrhea, yellow and offensive. Vaginal itching.

Offensive perspiration of the groin.

CARDIAC

Angina.

Palpitations, worse night in bed, worse sleep.

Advanced cardiac disease.

CHEST

Asthma, worse from catching colds.

Respiration worse evening.

Sleep apnea, jumps up from sleep with a suffocating sensation.

Cough, worse at night in bed.

Pneumonia. Bronchitis. Emphysema. Tuberculosis.

BACK

Weak back, slumps in his chair.

Low back pain and sciatica.

Back pain worse long standing, worse stooping.

Unable to stand erect.

Acne on the back.

EXTREMITIES

Left shoulder pains.

Arthritis, worse over-heating and better from cold applications.

Rheumatoid arthritis. Gout. Psoriatic arthritis.

Cellulitis, lymphangitis, especially forearms. Paronychia.

Varices.

Nails thick and distorted, especially toenails.

Feet sweat and offensive odor.

◆ **Feet burning and must be put out of the covers or restlessly searches for cold spots on the sheets.**

SLEEP

Insomnia. ◆Sleeps well for 3 or 4 hours then wakes and dozes on and off the rest of the night.

Sleep apnea, rises up with a suffocating sensation.

Laughing in sleep *(Lyc)*.

Nightmares, ◆especially when sleeping on the back.

Prefer to sleep on the left side.

SKIN

Eruptions usually moist and itching tremendously.

Itching worse heat, worse heat of bed, worse night, worse bathing, worse wool.

◆ **Eczema**. Psoriasis. Seborrhea. Poison oak. Scabies.

Boils, painful, often a recurrent tendency.

Herpes. Impetigo. Tinea. Chicken pox. Erysipelas. Cellulitis.

CLINICAL

Abscess. Acne. Alcoholism. Allergy. Angina. Amyotropic lateral sclerosis. Anxiety. Arrhythmia. Arthritis. Asthma. Blepharitis. Bronchitis. Bursitis. Chronic Fatigue Syndrome. Cirrhosis. Colitis. Congestive heart failure. Conjunctivitis. Connective tissue disease. Constipation. Dandruff. Dementia. Depression. Diabetes. Diarrhea. Eczema. Gout. Headache. Hemorrhoids. Hepatitis. Herpes. Hiatus hernia. Hypertension. Impetigo. Inflammatory bowel disease. Iritis. Lower back pains. Malignancy. Menopausal flushes. Migraine. Multiple sclerosis. Nasal polyps. Otitis media. Peptic ulcer. Pharyngitis. Pneumonia. Proctitis. Prostatitis. Psoriasis. Rectal fissure, abscess, fistula. Reflux esophagitis. Rheumatoid arthritis. Rhinitis. Sciatica. Seborrhea. Sinusitis. Tinea. Tonsillitis.

COMPLEMENTARY

Ars. Nux-V. Psor. Acon. Puls. Cycle: Sulph - Calc - Lyc - Sulph.

ACUTES

In lingering, "neglected" colds, flus, tonsillitis, bronchitis, pneumonia, the patient is warm, sweaty, wears old clothes and forgets to change for days, the hair becomes greasy and plastered to the head.
Measles *(Apis, Bell, Bry, Euphr, Gels, Puls, Rhus-T)*.

COMPARISONS

Nux-V - Ambitious, egotistical, impatient, craves fat, spicy, gastrointestinal disorders.

Puls - Warm-blooded, worse heat, fears heights, irritable, disgust, craves sweets, headaches, hot feet, skin problems.

Arg-N - Warm-blooded, extroverted, fear heights, gastrointestinal disorders, diarrhea, craving sweets.

Psor. Aloe. Med. Lyc. Plat. Ant-C. Graph. Mez.

SULPHURICUM ACIDUM

Sulphuric Acid is one of the main constituents of exhaust fumes from combustion engines of all sorts. Hurriedness is the chief characteristic of this remedy. By metaphor, it is thus both a by-product of our culture's frantic pace (cars, airplanes, etc.) and a cause of that same hurriedness.

The frantic hurriedness of Sulphuric Acid is expressed in all facets of the patient's life - he eats fast, walks fast, and does things in such a hurry that he gets confused and out of order. Or he may be preoccupied internally with plans for ten different projects or tasks that he must perform. The other great characteristic of this remedy is tremendous sensitivity to fumes and smoke. Chemical hypersensitivity syndrome and environmental illness can be cured with this remedy.

On the physical plane, mucous membrane symptoms are prominent as is the tendency for hemorrhage and ecchymosis.

MENTALS

Hurriedness. Wants others to hurry.

So hurried he does things out of order.

Mind scattered but full of plans for what he must do.

Talks to himself.

Dissatisfied and peevish.

GENERALS

- **General aggravation from fumes and car exhaust.**

General aggravation from smoke, dust, and aromatics.

Chilly and worse from cold.

Fatigue and exhaustion, trembling from weakness.

Pains appear gradually and disappear suddenly.

Right-sided complaints (except for the head).

General aggravation at the menopause.

Sour odors (as in febrile or septic conditions).

Perspiration from slight exertion or from warm food.

Restless sleep, frequent waking. Sleeps two hours then begins to wake again and again.

Nightmares before the menstrual period.

Tendency to bruising and hemorrhage.

HEAD

Headache and neuralgia, often left-sided, increase slowly and disappear gradually, better at the sea.

Brain feels loose inside the head.

Neuralgia coming after influenza.

Left-sided submaxillary and parotid gland swelling.

Coryza and hay fever with burning and itching in palate and nose.

Egg-white sensation on the face.

Aphthae which are painful on the tongue, inner cheeks and whole gastrointestinal tract, often coming periodically.

GASTROINTESTINAL

Gastritis.

Eructations and indigestion, worse from alcohol use.

Water causes a cold feeling in the stomach.

Craving brandy and alcohol in general.

Aversion to water unless liquor or brandy is added to it.

UROGENITAL

Premature ejaculation.

CHEST

Asthma, worse from smoke, fumes and dust.

EXTREMITIES

Bruising and ecchymosis, follows Arnica in acute injuries.

Injuries to soft tissue. Gangrene after injury.

Itching of the fingertips.

Clinical

Allergy. Aphthae. Asthma. Ecchymosis. Environmental illness and chemical hypersensitivity. Gastritis. Headache. Purpura. Sprains.

Combined Symptoms

Hurriedness *and* complaints of exhaustion.

Complementaries

Puls. Arn.

Comparisons

Tarent. Med. Nux-V. Iod.

SYMPHYTUM

Symphytum is a remedy for injury. It has mainly been used for fractures, both acutely and in cases with non-union of fractures. It is also a useful remedy in injuries to periosteum and bone with persisting pains long after the injury. In blunt trauma to the eye, Symphytum is the specific remedy, though Arnica is more useful in injuries to the orbit.

Injury

Trauma to the eye and orbit *(Arn)*.

Fractures - both for pain and improved reunion of bone.

Phantom limb pain after amputation.

Periosteal pains after wounds heal.

SYPHILINUM

In the syphilitic miasm we see a destructiveness on all levels but not a violent destruction - more like an erosion. On the physical level we see erosions of the bone (i.e. the nasal bones, etc.); on the emotional level the patient may have a type of nihilism or a feeling to let everything crash down around him; and on the mental level we see a breakdown into insanity. There is a tendency for lack of strong connection with others in the syphilitic patient. Families with strong hereditary tendency to alcoholism are generally syphilitic.

On the physical level the syphilitic patient is often pale skinned and has the fine texture of skin which allows you to see into the deeper tissue of the skin. They tend to be slender and rather graceful in their movements. There are several characteristics of syphilitic health problems: 1) General aggravation at night, or from sundown to sunup. 2) Bone pains or destruction, especially bone pains at night. 3) Ulceration of the skin or mucous membranes. 4) Distortions of anatomy, often congenital (facial features, cleft palates, strabismus, etc.). 5) Neuralgia.

Now let us turn specifically to Syphilinum the remedy rather than the miasm. The mental state of Syphilinum is characterized by fear and anxiety. The fear often concerns matters of health or disease. Especially there is a strong fear of infectious disease or germs. Especially there is a fear of deep infections such as tuberculosis, etc. When we hear people who are irrationally afraid of AIDS or Lyme's disease we must consider Syphilinum (*Ars, Bor, Calc, Sulph*). This fear will often lead them to a profound aversion to dirt or to touching dirty things.

There is also a strong tendency to check things: "Did I remember to turn off the stove?" This uncertainty will lead to compulsive neurosis. Syphilinum is one of the main remedies for compulsive neurosis. If we combine these two tendencies - compulsive neurosis and fear of infection- we arrive at the great keynote of Syphilinum: desire to wash the hands. The Syphlinum patient may wash his hands literally a hundred times a day. Every time he touches a public doorknob, every time he handles money, every time he shakes somebody's hand, he is taken by an irresistible desire to wash. The desire for cleanliness is also centered around his clothing. Naturally the patient recognizes that his feelings are not normal. He feels that there is something seriously wrong and he may develop a strong fear of insanity. In fact the patient may be right on the border of serious mental breakdown.

MENTALS

Compulsive checking. Compulsive hand washing.

Fear of infection, disease, insanity.

Alcoholism.

Great irritability during the headache.

Megalomania.

GENERALS

General aggravation at night, dreads the night because he knows he will feel miserable.

General aggravation 2 to 4 AM.

Bone pains - especially the skull and the long bones, worse at night. This may include growing pains in children.

Head

Headache, may be felt in bones of the head, worse night.

Strabismus.

Distorted facial features; may have only mild asymmetry of face.

Nasal or oral cancer.

"Saddle" nose.

Chronic post-nasal discharge.

Salivation profuse, especially at night in bed.

Hair loss; alopecia.

Teeth deformed, decay below gum line. The teeth break from chronic clenching of the jaw.

Mouth ulcers.

Cleft palate.

Facial neuralgia, worse night.

Gastrointestinal

Desires alcohol.

Constipation.

Chest

Aneurysm.

Genitourinary

Profuse leukorrhea, may be greenish, soaks through a tampon.

Induration of spermatic cords.

Extremities

Bone pains, worse heat of the bed, better cold applications.

Back pain at night.

Osteomyelitis.

Curvature of spine.

Skin ulcers, especially of the legs. Psoriasis.

Sleep

Insomnia, often waking 2 to 4 AM.

Clinical

Abscess. Acne. Alcoholism. Alopecia. Aneurysm. Anxiety. Bone pains. Compulsive disorder. Headache. Insomnia. Leukorrhea. Malignancy. Mouth ulcer. Neuralgia. Psoriasis. Scoliosis. Skin ulcer.

Complementary

Ars. Aur. Kali-I. Merc. Nit-Ac. Phyt. Plat. Sulph.

TABACUM

Tabacum produces (as any child who has once snuck a cigarette can attest) a state of tremendous nausea. The patient feels as if he must die from it, becomes cold, clammy and pale. This may be in seasickness, motion sickness, acute gastritis, from chemotherapy or any cause whatever. Tabacum is a remedy to consider in conditions brought on by tobacco abuse - either by chewing or smoking.

HEAD

Headache with deathly nausea.

Face pale and drawn

Vertigo worse from opening the eyes, better in open air.

GASTROINTESTINAL

- **Deathly nausea; sinking of stomach.**

Nausea with or without vomiting which incapacitates.

Nausea of pregnancy, with spitting.

Nausea, better from cool air and uncovering the abdomen, worse upon opening the eyes.

Craving for tobacco

Constipation, especially in tobacco users.

Straining and sweating during stool.

Rectal spasm.

CHEST

Reputedly effective in cases of atherosclerotic heart disease in tobacco users.

EXTREMITIES

Spasms of muscles or jerking of limbs.

CLINICAL

Constipation. Gastritis. Headache. Motion-sickness. Nausea. Rectal spasm. Seasickness. Vertigo. Vomiting.

COMPARISONS

Ipec. Sep. Cocc.

TARAXICUM

Taraxicum is useful in digestive disorders and cholecystitis. The main keynote for this remedy is the discoloration and mapping of the tongue.

HEAD

Headache, occipital, worse lying.

• **Mapped**, excoriated tongue. Raw patches on tongue.

ABDOMEN

Cholecystitis. Gastritis.

Indigestion worse fatty foods.

CLINICAL

Cholecystitis. Gastritis. Glossitis. Headache.

COMPARISONS

Ptel. Chel. Chin.

TARENTULA CUBENSIS

Ignoring discussions of the original source of the remedy (a spoiled specimen of the spider), Tarentula Cubensis produces and cures skin symptoms, with intensely burning lesions, similar to Anthracinum. The lesions include infection, abscesses, ulcers and eczema. The skin is often dark, purplish or mottled blue. Awful burning of the whole body localizing to one vulnerable spot characterizes a pregangrenous condition.

HEAD

Mouth ulcers with marked burning, may spread to include the whole gastrointestinal tract *(Ars)*.

SKIN

Burning, aggressive paronychia.

Pustule. Carbuncle. Abscess.

Abscess with burning, stabbing pains and mottled blue discoloration.

Kent cured a syphilitic case with abscess in an inguinal bubo.

Burning skin ulcers.

Agonizing, burning spots with incipient gangrene (Kent).

COMPARISONS

Anthr. Hep. Lach.

TARENTULA HISPANICA

Tarentula is a remedy for over-stimulation of the nervous system. This is reflected first as an over-activity and marked industriousness: workaholism. This rather normal phase is followed by intense hurriedness and impatience. It is perhaps the most hurried of all our remedies. The patient is hyperactive and can hardly bear even to see anyone else moving slowly. There is a marked love of music and dancing, even wild dancing.

If the activity and physical movement is not sufficient to relieve the inner stimulation, destructiveness develops. Tarentula is a mania remedy with violence and rages similar to Stramonium, Belladonna, etc. There is also an aspect of Tarentula which may be subtle and cunning and very deceitful. The patient can manipulate conversations and situations to bring about his ends by cunning or even lying rather than by persuasion.

On the physical plane, Tarentula affects first the nervous system with restlessness, twitches, and even chorea. Also the heart, skin and genitalia are prominent sites of pathology.

MENTALS

- **Tremendously hurried, intense, excited, and restless.**

Industrious. Works at an unbelievable pace.

Impatient - intolerant if others are moving slowly.

- **Loves music and dancing.** Music excites or calms him.

Aversion to being touched.

- **Aversion to strong colors** or specific colors.
- **Cunning,** manipulative and dishonest.

Destructive - breaks, tears, throws things.

Mania and rages with tremendous passions or even extreme violence and desire to kill.

Increased strength during the manic episode *(Stram, Bell, Hyos)*.

Sudden destructive behavior.

Feigns illness *(Plb, Mosch, Verat)*.

Obstinate and disobedient. Hyper-active children.

Laughing and wildness.

GENERALS

Tremendous restlessness and better from exertion.

Great amelioration from music (especially loud, wild music) and dancing.

Chilly and worse from cold.

Periodicity.

Emaciation *(Iod)*.

Neurological

Twitches and jerks.

Chorea.

Hyperesthesia. Formication. "Pins and needles" sensation.

Gastrointestinal

Craves: Salty foods. Spicy foods. Raw things. Sand.

Aversion to meat.

Kent cured a case of severe constipation and anxiety with Tarentula.

Urogenital

Hyper-sexual patients; promiscuous.

Uterine fibroids.

Burning in the uterus.

Tumors and diseases of the ovaries and testes.

Metrorrhagia.

Marked itching of the vulva and vagina, worse after menses.

Urine sediment; tenesmus.

Chest

Angina pectoris.

Mitral valve disease.

Sudden, violent palpitations.

Extremities

Restlessness.

Legs restless in bed.

Chorea.

Twitches and jerking.

Hypersensitivity of the fingertips, ameliorated by rubbing them.

Numbness in legs.

Sleep

Restless sleep, the bed is in complete disarray by morning.

Skin

Abscess.

Skin ulcers.

Formication *(Coca, Sec)*.

Combined Symptoms

Heart *and* ovarian disease.

Hurriedness *and* genital itching.

CLINICAL

Abscess. Angina. Arrhythmia. Behavior disorder. Chorea. Diabetes. Eczema. Hyperactivity. Mania. Metrorrhagia. Mitral valve disease. Restless leg syndrome. Sexual disorders. Skin ulcers. Uterine fibroid. Tumors of testes. Vaginitis. Valvular disease.

COMPARISONS

Nux-V - Hurried, industrious, anger, chilly, craves spicy food.

Sul-Ac - Extreme hurriedness, anger, chilly, ecchymosis.

Ars - Restlessness, irritability, periodicity, burning pains, right-sided complaints, vaginitis, cardiac disease.

Lil-T - Hurriedness, hyper-sexual, rages and anger, uterine disorders.

Med. Bell. Stram. Hyos. Tub.

TELLURIUM

Although most commonly used in acute low back pain and sciatica, Tellurium is also useful in some skin disorders. The back pains resemble very closely the clinical picture of acutely ruptured discs: pain from motion, from touch, from straining at stool and from cough.

HEAD

Chronic otorrhea with acrid, excoriating and offensive discharge, often with a fishy odor.

Eruption at the margin of the hair.

BACK

- **Pain worse touch, cough, sneeze, and straining at stool.**

Severe pain in the back, often with radiation down the sciatic nerve.

Right-sided sciatica.

Pain in the back extending to head upon touch or pressure (Clarke).

CLINICAL

Back pain (even metastasis to spine). Eczema. Otorrhea. Psoriasis.

COMPLEMENTARY

Sulphur follows and completes the case.

COMPARISONS

Rhus-T. Coloc. Bry. Kali-I. Lach. Dios. Graph. Sanic.

TEREBINTHINA

Similar to Kreosotum in its tendency to produce corrosiveness and burning in the affected organ, as well as a hemorrhagic tendency. Terebinthina is especially useful in nephritis and urinary tract disorders producing the keynote characteristic of smokey colored urine.

GENERALS

Burning pains through all of the mucous membranes.

Edema.

HEAD

Glistening tongue *(Kali-Bi, Pyrog)*.

Itching eyelids. Purple swelling under the eyes.

GASTROINTESTINAL

Distention of abdomen.

Diarrhea and rectal hemorrhage.

Peritonitis. Ascites.

UROGENITAL

Urine bloody or ♦smokey colored.

Urine smells of violets.

Nephritis.

Severe urinary tract infections, even pyelonephritis, with burning pains over the kidneys and prostration.

Hemorrhagic cystitis. Marked burning with urination.

Uterine tumors or infection.

Urethritis with marked burning; chronic discharges.

EXTREMITIES

Edema of the extremities.

Purpura.

Perspiration or cold perspiration mainly on the lower extremities has been considered a keynote by some authors.

CLINICAL

Bronchitis. Cystitis. Nephritis. Peritonitis. Purpura. Urethritis.

COMPARISONS

Kreos - Burning, inflammation and hemorrhage affecting the urogenital tract, though Kreosotum is more of the genitals.

Canth. Merc-C. Apis.

TEUCRIUM

Mainly indicated in cases of polyps. Teucrium is a main remedy in nasal polyps but is also indicated in uterine, urological, or colorectal polyps. This remedy also has a reputation for curing pinworms.

THEA

Mainly indicated in deep psychiatric states with strong, violent impulses *(Merc, Plat, Ars, Iod, Hep, Nux V, Sulph)*. There are urges to kill a close family member or loved one and especially one's own child *(Merc, Nux-V, Sulph, Arg-N)*. The patient may complain of tremendous fear that he will kill his child and may even send the child to a neighbor to protect it. The entire nervous system is excited.

THERIDION

When we find a combination of vertigo, insomnia, and tremendous over-sensitivity to noises Theridion is the remedy. The patient is often anxious, depleted, exhausted, over-excited and hysterical. Theridion is most often a remedy for women.

MENTALS

Marked over-sensitivity to noise (causes pains, toothache, etc.).

Hysteria and anxiety. Panic disorder.

HEAD

Vertigo, worse closing eyes, worse motion or riding in a car, feels the car is still moving, nausea with vertigo.

Hysterical vertigo.

Vertigo with headache.

Headache, worse about the left eye, worse motion, worse talking.

Tooth pain from noises.

Nasal obstruction, greenish discharge, sneezing.

GASTROINTESTINAL

◆ **Craves bananas.**

UROGENITAL

Nocturnal emissions.

Amenorrhea.

CHEST

Hysterical palpitations.

SLEEP

◆ **Horrible insomnia though exhausted.**

CLINICAL

Allergy. Anxiety. Arrhythmia. Headache. Insomnia. Neuralgia. Nocturnal emissions. Panic disorder. Toothache. Vertigo.

COMBINED SYMPTOMS

Sensitivity to noise *and* vertigo.

Insomnia *and* vertigo.

COMPARISONS

Asar - Sensitivity to noise, vertigo, hysteria.

Nux-V. Sep. Coff. Con. Cocc. Ars. Iod.

THLASPI

Thlaspi is primarily to be thought of in hemorrhagic conditions related to or during pregnancy.

HEAD

Epistaxis during pregnancy.

GENITALIA

Bleeding during pregnancy. Hemorrhage during labor.

Miscarriage or threatened abortion.

COMPARISONS

Sabin. Erig. Ip. Phos. Mill. Ust.

THUJA

Bill Gray, M.D. of Concord, California has contributed enormously to the understanding of the remedy Thuja, building upon the observations of Vithoulkas. Though Vithoulkas mentions an early phase of Thuja with confidence and arrogance, the usual patient suffers with marked lack of self-esteem and feelings of worthlessness. This inner doubt causes the patient first to spend great energy to portray a pleasing and expected image to the world. The focus on image and hiding the unpleasant leads later to a secretiveness or even deceptiveness and lying. Depression and low self-esteem are often the primary reasons that the patient seeks treatment. There is also a frequent history of abuse or neglect in childhood.

There exist three main precursors to the chronic conditions of Thuja: 1) Suppressed gonorrhea. 2) Suppressed warts. 3) Vaccination. The use of Thuja where there is a history of vaccination was pioneered by Burnett. Specifically this remedy has marked relationship to the smallpox vaccine though a lesser capacity to remove the untoward effects of other immunizations. The pathology corresponds to the sycotic miasm - growths and tumors, chronic sinus and respiratory pathology, genital disorders.

MENTALS

Low self-esteem and feelings of worthlessness.

Feels unattractive or spends much time perfecting the appearance.

Depression. Loneliness and sadness from sense of being separate.

Desperate to "fit in."

• **Feels others "wouldn't like me if they really knew me."**

Fixed ideas or delusions: •Something is alive in abdomen. Pregnant. •That he is fragile or glass and could break.

Secretive, even lying about life circumstances.

• **When talking the last words of the sentence are mumbled.**

Over-bearing and dictatorial in earlier stages.

Fears: Others will not like him. To reveal himself. Loosing control.

GENERALS

Chilly and worse from cold.

Chills on exposure to warm air.

General aggravation from damp weather.

Left-sided complaints.

Perspires on uncovered parts.

• **Perspiration is oily and sweet-smelling or offensive.**

• **General amelioration of chronic complaint during a cold.**

• **History of repeated smallpox vaccine** or vaccine reactions or failure to respond to the vaccine. Also bad effects other vaccines.

Head

Left frontal or temporal headache.
Headache like "a nail driven inward."
Face greasy or oily.
Severe or even scarring acne.
Fever blisters about the lips.
Teeth decay at gum line.
Hair dry and sticks out; hair cannot be combed.
◆ **Eyebrows are thin or become absent on the lateral half.**
Warts or tumors on face or eyelids. Styes.

Nose

Chronic sinusitis and thick post-nasal drip.
Thick scabs or crusts on the septum. Ulcers on septum.
Coryza, hay fever.
◆ **Coryza during stool.**

Gastrointestinal

◆ **Intolerance to onions.**
Craving or aversion to onions and garlic.
Craves sweets.
Bulimia.
Sensation of something alive in the abdomen.
Rectal fissure.
Condylomata of the anus.
Diarrhea in the morning.

Urogenital

Condylomata of the genitals.
Herpes.
◆ **Forked stream of urine.**
Urethritis, recurring urethral discharge.
Prostatitis. Prostatic hypertrophy.
Uterine tumors or polyps.
Ovarian cysts, especially left-sided.
Profuse, greenish leukorrhea.
Sex drive is generally high.

Chest

Asthma, worse cold, damp weather.

BACK

Scoliosis.

EXTREMITIES

Warts on the hands and fingers.

Plantar warts which are often painful.

Paronychia.

Nails brittle or distorted.

Eruptions between the toes.

Cracks on the feet.

Feet perspire excessively and are offensive.

Rheumatic troubles with history of gonorrhea.

SLEEP

Sleeps on the left side.

Falling dreams which may rouse the patient from sleep.

Waking at 3 or 4 AM.

SKIN

- **Warts and skin tags and any tumors of the skin.**

Eczema. Psoriasis. Tinea.

CLINICAL

Abscess. Acne. Allergy. Arthritis. Asthma. Bulimia. Chronic fatigue syndrome. Condylomata. Connective tissue disease. Depression. Eczema. Gonorrhea. Headache. Herpes. Insomnia. Malignancy. Neuralgia. Ovarian cyst. Paronychia. Proctitis. Prostatic hypertrophy. Prostatitis. Psoriasis. Rectal fissures. Rheumatism. Scoliosis. Seizure disorder. Sinusitis. Sycosis. Tinea. Urethral strictures. Urethritis. Uterine polyps and fibroids. Warts.

COMPLEMENTARY

Ars. Nat-S. Med. Sil. Sabin.

COMPARISONS

Lyc - Poor self-confidence and projects an image to compensate, chilly, intolerant to onions, offensive feet, diarrhea in the morning, cracks on the soles of the feet.

Sil - Low confidence, chilly, feet sweat, sinusitis, bad effects from vaccination, scoliosis, nails distorted or brittle.

Staph - Low esteem, hides feelings, condyloma and fibroids, headache, premature tooth decay, high sex drive.

Phos. Nit-Ac. Nat-S. Ars. Med. Anac.

TUBERCULINUM

The Tuberculinum patient is known for his inner discontentment, romantic and longing nature, and constant need for change and travel. The dress and style often exhibit a romantic and poetic sensitivity. However, though the romanticism is very appealing, it leads to a sense of ennui and boredom with the mundane routine of life. The patient is unable to explain the cause of this dissatisfaction at all and may feel that it is a normal part of life. Often this frustration is expressed in maliciousness, especially common in children. Adults often seek every possible outlet for excitement - dangerous sports, drugs, nightlife, etc. Frequent changes in the job, in relationships, in homes and the desire to travel are part of this same tendency.

Another aspect of Tuberculinum to keep in mind is compulsive behavior and ritualism. The patient may return knocking at the office door 3 or 4 times after the interview has ended with some slight detail he wishes to impart. This reflects an inner compulsion which can also be expressed in ritualistic behavior.

Children. Tuberculinum is an important childhood remedy in simple recurring infectious illness of childhood such as otitis media and recurring bronchitis. It is also an important remedy in more advanced pathology such as failure to thrive, developmental defects, mental retardation and attention deficit disorders.

In classic hyperactivity, Tuberculinum is a mainstay of practice. The child is unable to remain long in one place, is loud and very demanding and capricious. We especially think of Tuberculinum when the parents tell us that the child is coldly and deliberately destructive and malicious. He breaks his mother's favorite vase right in front of her if contradicted. The child may have great anger, even violence and tendency to strike others. He seems completely indifferent to punishment or reprimand. Tuberculinum is also one of our best remedies in cases of mental retardation and even autism. In these cases, ritualistic behavior and head-banging are common expressions of the pathology.

Physical. Many patients who need Tuberculinum do not exhibit these psychological tendencies and must be diagnosed on the basis of previous tubercular history or family history and upon the keynotes or physical symptoms. Especially we think of Tuberculinum when there is strong allergic tendencies and respiratory disorders. Recurring, even unexplained fevers, connective tissue diseases and rheumatic conditions are also among the more common disorders found in tubercular cases.

MENTALS

- **Romantic, unfulfilled, "cosmopolitan" patients.**
- **Needs change and excitement. Frequent changing of jobs.**
- **Desire for travel. Passionate about travel.**

Irritability and even violence.
Malicious behavior; breaks things; breaks other's valuables.
Hyperactivity. Behavior disorders of children.
Obstinate and disobedient children.
Fears: •**Cats**. Dogs. Animals. Disgust with cats and furred animals.
Substance abuse.
Compulsive and ritualistic behavior.
Constant feeling that he has forgotten something.
Returns repeatedly to office door to give insignificant information.
Shrieking in sleep, especially before menses.
Mental dullness and difficult concentration.

GENERALS

Generally worse before storms or from any change of weather.
Generally better in mountains, especially in pine forests.
General aggravation from cold and damp weather.
General aggravation from getting wet or from cold bathing.
General amelioration in warm and dry weather.
Weak, depleted constitutions.
General aggravation in the evening.
General aggravation by the sea.
General amelioration in open air or driving with the windows open.
Menopausal flushes with perspiration.
Recurring fever; fevers come regularly in the afternoon or at night.
Frequent colds and flus.
Night sweats.
Emaciation despite eating heavily.

- **Allergy to milk.**
- **Allergy to cats** *(Kali-C, Ars, Dulc, Puls, Sulph).*

HEAD

Bruxism.
Compulsive or angry head banging.
Headache or migraine, may be "like an iron band." Periodic headache.
Recurring otitis media.
Many cured cases of meningitis exist in our literature.
Adenopathy and hard glands of head and neck.

FACE

Alopecia. Alopecia of the beard region. Tinea capitis.

Tubercular, circumscribed red areas on cheeks.

EYES

• **Long, fine eyelashes especially in children.**

• Astigmatism.

Blue sclera *(Carc)*.

GASTROINTESTINAL

Craving: •**Smoked meats and bacon. Pork. Ham. Salami. Milk,** especially cold milk. Fat. Salty. Ice cream.

Constipation. Diarrhea. Recurring diarrhea.

• **Milk allergy.**

UROGENITAL

Hyper-sexual; promiscuity. Early or excessive masturbation.

Amenorrhea.

Recurring cystitis. Enuresis.

CHEST

Recurring chest colds, bronchitis or pneumonia.

Acute respiratory infections even pneumonia in cases with family history of tuberculosis.

Hard, short, dry, constant cough. Chronic shallow cough.

Thin, narrow chest. Weak chest.

Asthma, better open air, better driving with window open.

Swelling and tenderness of breasts, especially before menses.

BACK

Dark or long, fine hair on back of children, along the spine.

Scoliosis.

EXTREMITIES

Arthritis with joint pains worse from cold, wet weather, worse on rising, worse at night with restlessness, better from heat and from motion *(Rhus-T, Rhod, Ruta, Phos)*.

Wandering arthritis.

Athlete's foot.

Perspiration of the feet.

SKIN

Tinea. Eczema, often starting at birth. Psoriasis. Discoid lupus.

Itching of skin better from heat, especially radiant heat.

SLEEP

Sleeps in knee-chest position.

Nightmares.

COMBINED SYMPTOMS

Respiratory troubles *and* rheumatism.

CLINICAL

Adenopathy. Alcoholism. Allergy. Alopecia. Amenorrhea. Arthritis. Asthma. Astigmatism. Autism. Behavior disorder. Bronchitis. Bruxism. Colds. Compulsive disorders. Connective tissue disease. Croup. Enuresis. Flushes. Headaches. Hodgkin's disease. Hyperactivity. Lymphoma. Malignancy. Meningitis. Menopause. Mental retardation. Osteomyelitis. Pneumonia. Respiratory infection. Rheumatoid arthritis. Scoliosis. Sexual disorders. Systemic or discoid lupus. Tinea. Upper respiratory infection.

COMPLEMENTARY

Puls. Phos. Calc. Con. Sulph. Stann.

COMPARISONS

Calc-P - Desires to travel, discontented, worse from cold, damp, craves smoked meat and bacon, salty, ice cream, joint pains.

Med - Asthma, craves fat and salt, behavior disorders, sexual excesses, needs excitement.

Bac - Tubercular symptoms, frequent colds, craves sour, alopecia.

Carc. Sanic. Rhus-T. Verat. Plat.

URTICA URENS

Urtica Urens has been used primarily for its beneficial effects on conditions of the skin, in urticaria, burns and eczema. Burnett promoted its use in gout and rheumatism, malaria and recurring fevers, and for agalactorrhea. In these conditions he used the remedy mainly in material doses.

GENERALS

Allergic reactions to shellfish.

Complaints from suppressed eruptions.

CHEST

Absent, deficient or inappropriate lactation.

UROGENITAL

Eruptions and itching or swelling of the genitalia.

EXTREMITIES

In provings and cured cases, rheumatism of the right deltoid *(Caust)*.

Gout, many cases of acute gouty arthritis have been reported cured, generally in material doses.

SKIN

Burns, especially first and second degree burns *(Canth)*, may also be used in tincture topically.

Urticaria with sensitivity and burning, stinging pains.

Urticaria from over-heating and exertion.

Insect bites and stings *(Led, Apis)*. Chicken pox.

CLINICAL

Agalactorrhea. Burns. Fever. Gout. Malaria. Rheumatism. Urticaria.

USTILAGO

Ustilago is a remedy mainly for uterine hemorrhage and miscarriage. At the International Foundation for Homeopathy case conference in 1991, Laurie Dack of Vancouver, Canada presented three beautiful cases of uterine fibroids cured with Ustilago.

UROGENITAL

Left ovarian or pelvic pains, may radiate into legs.

Uterine fibroids with hemorrhage.

Metrorrhagia, often with dark clots.

Excessive menses, especially when approaching menopause.

Third month miscarriages or threatened abortion.

Postpartum hemorrhage.

Masturbation and sex drive excessive.

CLINICAL

Miscarriage. Uterine fibroids. Uterine hemorrhage.

COMPARISONS

Sabin. Sec. Kali-Fer. Erig. Xanth.

VALERIANA

Valeriana is an hysterical remedy with a predominance of rheumatic and neurological symptoms. The herbal use of Valerian for insomnia carries over to its homeopathic use. Valeriana is indicated to calm excited, restless, and nervous patients.

Mentals

Excitable, animated, anxious, irritable, restless, and distracted patients with marked mood swings.

Floating sensation.

Generals

General aggravation at rest and amelioration from moving about.

Pains or cramps coming in different locations.

Flushes of heat.

Head

Headache and stitching pains about the head, face and eyes.

Sensation of a thread hanging down the throat.

Gastrointestinal

Intolerance to milk.

Back

Low back pain and sciatica, worse sitting, worse standing, worse during pregnancy, ameliorated walking about.

Nash mentions a case of sciatica with pain ameliorated by standing with the leg raised on a chair.

Extremities

Rheumatic pains, worse while sitting, better by moving about.

Pains in the lower limbs, the ankles, the Achilles tendon, the heels.

Twitches.

Sleep

Insomnia.

Clinical

Anxiety. Arthritic pains. Headache. Neuralgia. Sciatica.

Comparisons

Cimic. Lac-C. Rhus-T. Zinc.

VERATRUM ALBUM

Veratrum has its greatest use in the mental sphere where it produces marked over-stimulation, and eventually mania. The patient is over-mentalized and not connected to those around him. He may seem hardened and is often harshly critical. Eventually this trait leads to the well-known haughtiness and self-righteousness of Veratrum. As the patient goes toward manic states, this self-righteousness becomes delusional. He believes he is a messenger from God or that he has become "enlightened." He may have delusions of being Christ or some other religious figure. The classic image is of the religious psychotic preaching from the street-corner. There is also a depressive state of moroseness and despair of salvation.

Children. The pathology begins with excessive mental development and precocity. The child is curious and almost adult level in conceptual ability. But this over-stimulation of the mind is eventually also reflected in a great restlessness. There is an inner frustration which leads to disobedience and behavior problems. The child has a tremendous restless feeling which is typically expressed by senseless, repetitive behavior such as stacking things or cutting papers into ever smaller bits. In some cases, he is so restless he cannot sit down to eat but instead must be moving constantly. The child may be extremely disconnected, or also hard and tough. He shows no emotion even when reprimanded or punished. This child may be difficult to distinguish from other remedies for behavior disorders such as Tarentula, Anacardium, Stramonium, Sulphur or Hyoscyamus.

MENTALS

Hyperactive and disobedient children.

- **Meaningless, repetitive actions: cutting or tearing things.**
- **Precocity**. Asks many questions; philosophical.

Haughty.

- **Religiosity. Excessive praying.**
- **Delusions of religion and identity** - believes he is Christ or a savior or prophet or that he has a divine mission.

Mania; acute or chronic psychosis (violence, spending, etc.).

Critical or censorious. Rude.

Anger and violence. Cursing.

Jealousy.

Feigns illness *(Mosch, Tarent, Plb)*.

Despair of salvation.

Amorous. Hugs and kisses inappropriately.

Lying and hardly seems to know himself that he does so.

Runs away from home at early age.

GENERALS

Cold and worse from cold.

Internal coldness or feels as if ice-water in the veins not blood.

Weakness and collapse states, especially with vomiting or diarrhea.

Perspiration during menses.

Chills and perspiration with stool.

Convulsions.

HEAD

Vertigo with vomiting and cold sweat.

Severe headache, often with vomiting.

Headache with icy coldness, especially on the vertex.

Cold face.

Sensation that water he drinks slides down the outside of his throat.

- **Profuse cold sweat, especially on the forehead.**
- **Cold breath** and tongue in the acute or collapsed states.

GASTROINTESTINAL

- **Gastroenteritis with simultaneous vomiting and diarrhea** *(Ars)*. Considered a main remedy in cholera.
- **Vomiting and diarrhea during menses** with dysmenorrhea.
- **Projectile vomiting.**

Cravings: **Sour. Sour fruit. Lemon. Salt. Ice**. Fruit. Sardines.

Intense thirst.

Cramping pains in the abdomen. Distention.

Diarrhea profuse and debilitating. Colitis.

Diarrhea, worse during chills, worse during menses.

Vomiting with cough.

UROGENITAL

- **Severe dysmenorrhea with coldness, vomiting, diarrhea, and weakness or prostation.**

Hyper-sexual.

CHEST

Asthma.

Pneumonia.

Frothy sputum.

EXTREMITIES

Cold hands; Raynaud's syndrome.

Cold feet.

Cramps and twitches.

CLINICAL

Behavior disorder. Chemical sensitivity. Cholera. Dysmenorrhea. Gastroenteritis. Headache. Hyperactivity. Mania. Manic-depression. Neuralgia. Pneumonia. Raynaud's disease. Schizophrenia. Seizures.

COMPARISONS

Hyos - Hyperactivity, cursing, exhibitionism, mania, convulsions, delusions, jealousy.

Ars - Restless, religious, censorious, despair of salvation, vomiting and diarrhea concurrently, great coldness and prostration, Raynaud's syndrome, craves sour.

Tub. Med. Stram. Tarent. Camph. Plat.

VERATRUM VIRIDE

Veratrum Viride is less frequently used than Veratrum Album yet the mental characteristics may be similar. It has achieved its best results in cases of pneumonia, especially in early phases of pneumonia.

MENTALS

Restlessness and disordered states similar to Veratrum Album.

Strikes himself.

HEAD

- **Red streak down the center of the tongue.**

Tongue variously discolored or coated, especially the center.

Congested head and flushing of face.

Cold perspiration on forehead.

CHEST

Pneumonia with rapid onset, anxiety, rapid pulse, vomiting and high fever.

- **Rapid pulse during pneumonia.**

Rapid, bounding pulse.

EXTREMITIES

Twitches.

COMPARISONS

Bell. Verat. Ars.

VERBASCUM

Verbascum is an important remedy for trigeminal neuralgia. Perhaps its effect in the treatment of painful neuralgia explains its usefulness in acute otitis as a topical infusion (Mullein oil).

HEAD

Face pains, generally on the left side. Trigeminal neuralgia.

Pain worse talking or chewing, worse motion, worse change of temperature and from air, coming in severe attacks of pain.

Topical infusion of the warm oil of mullien in the ears often gives prompt relief of pain in acute otitis media.

CHEST

Deep, "trumpet-like" coughs.

Cough worse night, better breathing deep.

CLINICAL

Facial neuralgia. Cough and bronchitis.

COMPARISONS

Mag-P. Coloc. Caust.

VIBURNUM

Viburnum is a specific uterine remedy useful in dysmenorrhea, false labor, after-pains, and threatened abortions. The main keynote is that the pains radiate from the sacrum to the pelvis and into the upper, inner thighs.

GENITALIA

Dysmenorrhea with pains extending into the thighs.

Uterine hemorrhage.

Miscarriage.

COMPARISONS

Sabin - Dysmenorrhea, pains extending down the legs, miscarriage.

Cimic. Xanth. Caul.

VIOLA ODORATA

Viola Odorata has a specific local affect on the wrists and mainly the **right wrist**. There may be marked pain and numbness even into the hand and fingers as in carpal tunnel syndrome.

COMPARISONS

Caust. Guai. Act-S.

VIOLA TRICOLORATA

Viola tricolorata has an unusual but confirmed keynote: **the urine smells like the urine of a cat**.

WYETHIA

Wyethia is a specific remedy for hay fever.

HEAD

Tremendous itching in the nose, throat and palate and sometimes extending to the ears.

Must forcibly rub the tongue back and forth over the palate to sooth the itching.

Throat swollen and irritated.

Constant clearing of the throat.

COMPARISONS

Arund. Arum-T. Nux-V. Agar.

XANTHOXYLUM

Xanthoxylum is mainly a remedy of uterine disorders.

GENERALS

Sharp, shooting, neuralgic pains.
Disturbing numbness.

HEAD

Headaches before or during menses.
Flushes or redness of the face during the dysmenorrhea.

UROGENITAL

Pains in uterus or ovary extending into thighs *(Vib, Cimic)*.
After-pains.
Uterine hemorrhage.

BACK

Low back pain and sciatica.
Back pain during menses.

COMPARISONS

Vib. Sabin. Cimic.

ZINCUM

The hallmark of Zincum is the tremendous excitation of the nervous system which results in restlessness, abnormal or involuntary movements, twitches, and even convulsions. Likewise in the mental sphere the patient initially has a phase of great stimulation and mental activity. This over-stimulated state is often followed by a collapse which results in mental dullness, dissatisfaction, great depression and even suicidal thoughts.

Throughout, Zincum is prone to irritability and even rages. The tremendous complaining of this remedy is similar but even more intense than that of Calcarea Phosphorica. Nothing in the patient's life seems satisfactory. There can even be suicidal feelings. In the later stages, Zincum shows a picture of mental deterioration with slow speech, inability to focus the mind, scattered ideas, use of incorrect words, and confusion.

MENTALS

Hyper, over-stimulated and over-sensitive patients.

Complaining and dissatisfied, "drives others to distraction with his constant complaining."

Racing thoughts and abundant ideas. Loquacious.

Irritability and rage.

Mental confusion and dullness.

Confusion markedly worse from wine.

Repeats the question before answering *(Sulph, Caust)*.

Mistakes in speech and writing.

Depression and suicidal thoughts.

Thinks of death calmly, thoughts of death relieve him.

Aversion to noise and especially conversation.

Superstitious.

Shrieking.

Delirium with anger, violence and desire to escape.

Behavior problems in children.

GENERALS

General aggravation from suppressed eruptions.

General aggravation from suppressed menses and better with the flow. Only feels well during menses.

◆ **General aggravation from wine** and alcoholic drinks.

General amelioration in the evening.

General aggravation from vaccination.

General aggravation from cold or cold bathing.

Weakness after anger.

Appearance is "withered, wrinkled, old-looking and unhealthy."

NEUROLOGICAL

Restlessness. Chorea, especially of the feet and lower extremities.

Twitches, jerks, fasciculations. Convulsions.

Parkinson's disease with marked tremor, paresis and mental dullness.

Meningitis, encephalitis with rolling head, shrieking, delirium, convulsion and finally stupor.

HEAD

Headache, especially occipital headache.

Headache from drinking wine.

Head cold in front or forehead and warm in occiput.

Teeth loose and falling.

Concussion or history of head injury.

Face

Facial tics and grimaces.

Cracking of the lips, especially at the corners.

Wrinkled, old-looking face.

Thick lips.

EYES

Photophobia.

Strabismus.

Stitching pains in the inner canthi.

STOMACH

Gastritis.

Indigestion or vomiting after eating.

Indigestion worse wine, bread, milk, veal.

Empty, hungry feeling in stomach at 11 AM.

Aversion: Fish. Sweets.

ABDOMEN

Colic, worse eating, worse noise, worse conversation.

Constipation or diarrhea from drinking wine.

Diarrhea during headache.

UROGENITAL

Urinary retention from prostatic problems or paralysis.

Unable to void when standing; urinates better when sitting or when leaning backwards.

Urinary incontinence during convulsion.

Stress incontinence with cough and sneeze.

Enuresis.

Prostate enlarged.

Seminal discharge on passing stool *(Sel)*.

Sexual passion excessive; promiscuity.

Premature ejaculation.

CHEST

Asthma from suppressed menses.

Cough worse sweets.

BACK

Burning pains in the spine, worse sitting.

EXTREMITIES

- **Restless legs; constantly moves the legs and feet.**

Restless legs or extremities in bed at night, often preventing sleep.

Twitches and jerks in any muscle group.

Nocturnal myoclonus.

Heel pains, especially from wine.

Peripheral neuropathy; numbness or burning.

SLEEP

Insomnia from restlessness or jerking. Bruxism.

Strong jerks which wake the patient almost constantly.

Wakes at night with shrieking, recognizes no one.

SKIN

Eczema. Exanthems.

Eruptions easily suppressed.

ACUTES

Meningitis or encephalitis with piercing shriek, convulsion, tremor, boring or rolling the head, stupor or coma, tremendous headache.

Chronic complaints from suppressed exanthem.

CLINICAL

Asthma. Bruxism. Chorea. Colitis. Constipation. Cough. Dementia. Depression. Diarrhea. Eczema. Encephalitis. Enuresis. Gastritis. Head injury. Headaches. Incontinence. Low back pain. Meningitis. Neuralgia. Nocturnal myoclonus. Parkinson's disease. Prostatic hypertrophy. Prostatitis. Restless leg syndrome. Seizure disorder. Strabismus. Tics. Tremor. Twitches. Urinary incontinence. Urinary retention.

COMPARISONS

Nux-V - Over-stimulation, irritability, spasms and neurological problems, gastritis, constipation, aggravated by alcohol.

Cupr - Convulsions and jerking, neurological problems from suppressed eruption, shrieks, grimaces, asthma, cough, irritable.

Stram - Spasms and convulsions, night-terrors, irritability and behavior disorders.

Rhus-T - Restless legs, chorea, skin eruptions, grimacing, behavior problems, urinary problems, Parkinson's disease, superstition, chilly and worse from cold bathing.

Agar. Cic. Caust. Lach.

Index

A

B

C

D

E

F

G

H

I

J

K

L

M

N

K

P

R

S

T

U

V

W

XYZ

NOTES

Notes

NOTES

NOTES